Disability, Sexuality, and Abuse

Disability, Sexuality, and Abuse

An Annotated Bibliography

by

Dick Sobsey, R.N., Ed.D.
Sharmaine Gray
Don Wells
Diane Pyper

and

Beth Reimer-Heck, LL.B.

University of Alberta
Edmonton, Canada

·P A U L ·H·
BROOKES
PUBLISHING C°

Baltimore • London • Toronto • Sydney

Paul H. Brookes Publishing Co.
Post Office Box 10624
Baltimore, Maryland 21285-0624

Manufactured in the United States of America by
The Maple Press Company, York, Pennsylvania.

This annotated bibliography was prepared as part of a project funded by Health and Welfare Canada under project number 6609-1465-CSA. Additional work was completed with assistance from the University of Alberta Central Research Fund. Findings and opinions expressed are those of the investigators and not necessarily those of Health and Welfare Canada or the University of Alberta.

Library of Congress Cataloging-in-Publication Data
Disability, sexuality, and abuse: annotated bibliography / by Dick Sobsey . . . [et al.].
    p.   cm.
"Prepared as part of a project funded by Health and Welfare Canada under project number
6609–1465–CSA."
   Includes bibliographical references and index.
   ISBN 1-55766-068-9
   1. Handicapped—Abuse of–Abstracts. 2. Sex crimes—Abstracts. 3. Handicapped—Sexual
behavior—Abstracts. I. Sobsey, Richard. II. Canada. Health and Welfare Canada.
[DNLM: 1. Child Abuse, Sexual—abstracts. 2. Handicapped—abstracts. 3. Sex Behavior—abstracts.
4. Sex Offenses—abstracts.   Z5703.4.S4 D611]
HV6626.7.D57   1991
364.1'53–dc20
DNLM/DLC
for Library of Congress   90-15042
                                                                           CIP

Contents

Foreword *Sandra S. Cole* vii

Introduction ix

Abbott to Ayrault 1

Badgley to "Bus driver charged with sex assault." 7

Caffey to Cullen 18

Dale to Dykes 29

Edmonson to Evans 38

Fantuzzo to Fujii 43

Gabinet to Gunner 50

Haavik to Hurley 60

"Immunity found in parental termination action." to "Is there a difference?" 70

Jacobson to Joseph 72

Kaeser to Kusinitz 74

LaBarre to Lutzer 81

MacDonald to Myre 85

Nanaimo to Nunno 100

Oates to Oswin 103

Page to Purnick 105

Qualey to Quinn 111

Rabb to Ryerson 111

Sanders to Szymanski 120

Taitz to Turner 142

Ufford Dickerson to U.S. Senate Subcommittee on the Handicapped 145

Vadasy to von Hentig 147

Wagner to Wright 150

Yates to Yuille 155

Zadnik to Zwerner 156

Name Index 159

Subject Index 169

Foreword

With the publication of *Disability, Sexuality, and Abuse: An Annotated Bibliography*, Dick Sobsey and his colleagues have attempted to document all of the critical work accomplished to date in the challenging and disconcerting area of sexual exploitation, abuse, neglect, and vulnerability among persons with disabilities. This remarkable effort has crossed international boundaries and, in addition, has created a very special network among those of us who work in various aspects of health care, rehabilitation, and developmental disabilities.

The occurrence of sexual exploitation has a lifelong impact on the individual, and as a result, it should command our fullest attention. However, programs, resources, and information are scarce, and training opportunities for professionals are rarely available. In many cases, professionals find it difficult to recognize the subtle symptoms of sexual exploitation, perhaps because they lack fundamental training in sexual health education and sexual exploitation or perhaps because the subject is emotionally too difficult to perceive.

It has long been recognized that society has regarded individuals with disabilities as asexual and, therefore, not even candidates to be sexually abused. Consequently, it has been an invisible problem, easily avoided by focusing attention on the more medical, intellectual, or physical aspects of a disability.

Since the early stages of research in the late 1970s, study after study has indicated that the statistics are higher for sexual abuse among persons with disabilities than they are for the general public. In addition, caregivers, acquaintances of persons with disabilities, and family members are generally the offenders. Society prefers not to acknowledge the specifics of such situations. Since the late 1980s, I have titled many of my own presentations to professionals as "Don't Tell Me What I Don't Want to Know," in an effort to attract the attention of caregivers and other professionals who could make a significant difference in addressing problems of this nature.

Frequently, the burden of risk involved in disclosure is on the person who is experiencing the abuse. Societal neglect helps to shape the victims and yet does not attend to the survivors. We frequently question the competency and reliability of the person with the disability when he or she identifies an incidence of sexual exploitation. In general, society simply does not know how to address the problem. These offenses are sexual violations that create social, moral, ethical, and legal responsibilities. Institutions, agencies, and organizations, as well as administrators and other professionals, are cautious about becoming involved. Information is difficult to document, and informational and service resources are extremely difficult to obtain.

The publication of this annotated bibliography introduces a whole arena of topics that fall under the broad description of sexual exploitation of persons with disabilities. It contains citations of articles and publications that focus on families, agencies, institutions, facilities, hospitals, and those who care for persons with disabilities. Quality of life and the living conditions of people with disabilities are identified. Reviews and commentaries regarding professionals and their skills, competencies, and training are available. Information about existing instructional materials for professionals and educational materials for families and persons with disabilities will not only provide valuable teaching information, but will also encourage others to create new materials and programs. Without a doubt, this collection of resources will generate an increased awareness and stimulate fresh ideas.

I have had the pleasure of working with Dick Sobsey since 1988, and we have begun to develop a resource network to access these scarce and special materials. Through our work, we have learned that in many cases funding is difficult to obtain and training is difficult to achieve because these issues are not perceived to be as important as others in the societal scheme of life. In some cases, funding for training is withheld because of the perception that further training will increase the frequency of detection, which, in turn, will increase the need to provide services to respond, services for which funds are not available. We must continue these cooperative ventures toward improving such societal dilemmas.

It is hoped that this annotated bibliography will encourage helping professionals in both public and private sectors to speak up, to intervene, and to be active in developing and exchanging new information regarding material, ideas, and methods for teaching and prevention. The results of continuing this difficult work will yield decreased vulnerability and prevalence of sexual exploitation of persons with disabilities and increased prevention, personal safety, human services, and self-esteem for persons with disabilities and for professionals who work with them.

Profound thanks and acknowledgment are to be expressed to all the individual men and women who have come forward with their own stories and to all the professionals who have cared enough to have taken the lonely risks involved in understanding and identifying these truths. We must now continue for we have just begun to be aware.

Sandra S. Cole, Ph.D.
University of Michigan Medical Center
Ann Arbor, Michigan

Toward a Scientific Understanding
An Introduction

When Gary Heidnik, self-anointed minister of the "United Church of the Ministers of God," was found guilty of kidnapping, raping, mutilating, and murdering a number of women in Philadelphia in 1987, little attention was given to the fact that he recruited his victims from a center serving people with mental handicaps. Other related facts of the case, such as Heidnik's previous conviction for kidnapping another resident of this same center less than 10 years earlier; the center's earlier decision to cancel social events to prevent Heidnik from harassing clients; and the fact that Hednik's accomplice, who lured the victims to him, was employed by this center (Gruson, 1987), also received little coverage. Regardless of the horror of this particular case, one might wish to assume that it represents a rare and isolated exception to society's generally benign treatment of people with disabilities. In some of its aspects this case probably is unique, but other aspects follow patterns typical of sexual abuse and assault of people with disabilities.

Sexual abuse of children with disabilities and sexual assault of adults with disabilities are widespread but infrequently discussed problems in contemporary society. These problems are invisible to most casual observers and even to many people working with individuals with disabilities. Rarely do accounts of the worst atrocities receive public attention, and these atrocities are often viewed as isolated anomalies without recognition of the frequency or underlying contextual patterns. Research suggests that most people with disabilities will experience some form of sexual assault or abuse; some of these victims will suffer significant physical harm, but all will suffer social, emotional, or behavioral consequences of the abuse (Sobsey & Varnhagen, 1989). Analysis of this research also suggests that services that have been established to provide care and protection to people with disabilities are sources of the greatest risk for sexual abuse (Sobsey, 1988).

The existence of a relationship between the presence of any of a variety of disabilities and the likelihood of an individual being physically or sexually abused has been recognized for more than a decade (e.g., Buchanan & Oliver, 1977; Diamond & Jaudes, 1983; Friedrich & Boriskin, 1976; National Center on Child Abuse and Neglect, 1980). However, until recently, little had been done to explore the extent or precise nature of this relationship.

Although the contribution of physical abuse and neglect as a cause of physical and mental disability was well known (Buchanan & Oliver, 1977), the use of improved detection methods that are now available suggest that the extent of this contribution was underestimated (Dykes, 1986; McCelland, Rekate, Kaufman, & Persse, 1980). Nevertheless, understanding that disabilities result from abuse or neglect does not help to explain the high rates of abuse among children and adults with disabilities of other known, pre-existing etiologies. Family stress has often been suggested as a factor increasing risk of abuse of people with disabilities; however, this explanation has also been criticized for lacking research support and failing to explain the results of empirical studies. For example, some studies suggest that dependency and stress are poor predictors of abuse within families (Pillemer, 1985; Pillemer & Finkelhor, 1989), and others suggest that much of the increased risk of abuse of people with disabilities comes from outside families (Sobsey, 1990).

Cases of sexual abuse of children with disabilities and sexual assault of adults with disabilities share many of the characteristics and concerns that are common in other forms of abuse, but they also differ in some important ways. Although sexual abuse and assault do cause serious social, emotional, behavioral, and, sometimes, physical harm, these rarely appear to be causal factors in the initial disability. Although these crimes may be associated with stress experienced by the offender, sexual abuse and assault are particularly difficult to explain in the context of the traditional dependency, stress, frustration, and abuse model.

Sexual abuse of people with disabilities also remains complicated by the wide array of issues that exist relating to other aspects of the sexual adjustment of people with disabilities. For example, although the United States Military Government made it a crime to sterilize people with mental retardation in Germany in 1947, declaring involuntary sterilization to be a crime against humanity (Sengstock, Magerhans-Hurley & Sprotte, 1990), the United States and other allied countries continued the practice for several decades. Since people with disabilities often depend on caregivers for intimate care that is not required by other members of society, appropriate sex education and opportunities for sexual expression are often denied to people with disabilities. No explanation of sexual abuse of people with disabilities can be complete without inclusion of these interacting factors, along with a basic understanding of how physical and sexual abuse and assault affect all members of society. Any attempt to explain abuse and assault as a unique phenomena for people with disabilities must be considered inherently incomplete. Researchers, advocates, and service providers concerned with abuse of people with disabilities must carefully consider and incorporate relevant findings of other abuse research. The unique findings related to sexual abuse of people with disabilities may help us to refine our understanding of this phenomenon and, in turn, may contribute to our broader understanding of abuse.

The purpose of this annotated bibliography is to bring together literature from a wide range of disciplines and perspectives that is relevant to the sexual assault and abuse of people with disabilities. When this research on sexual abuse of people with disabilities began, we quickly discovered that information on this topic was difficult to locate. We have determined three reasons for this difficulty. First and most obvious, publications on the topic were genuinely rare and often in sources that have limited circulation. For example, some excellent studies and position papers have been prepared by consumer groups and advocacy agencies, but these are rarely available through libraries. Second, most work in this area is relatively recent, which makes it more difficult to trace through the usual search techniques. For example, many of the newly issued publications do not cite previously relevant work because it is often too difficult to locate, and this, in turn, makes it more difficult to find earlier works through the references in new publications. Third, since abuse of people with disabilities has not been identified as an area of scholarly interest by most database organizers, available descriptors often fail to identify relevant publications. For example, there are many publications linking the presence of disability to risk for abuse, but few of these are identified through electronic searches using descriptors related to disability. As a result of these obstacles, the development of this annotated bibliography took several years, but we believe that it is the most comprehensive, single source of information available. Nevertheless, we continue to search for new sources of information, and in spite of these efforts, there will always be omissions. It is hoped that readers will find that enough information has been provided to facilitate their own work in this area. We would be pleased to hear about other relevant items and would be especially happy to receive copies of them.

In addition to research studies, this annotated bibliography includes position papers, program descriptions, clinical reports, and media accounts. Along with the manual search methods used to compile this annotated bibliography, references have also been located using electronic searches of eight major databases and by requesting information from international organizations and individuals concerned with this topic. All of the entries presented here are abstracted in English, although some are only available in other languages.

The authors hope that this annotated bibliography will help other researchers attain a better understanding of sexual assault and abuse of people with disabilities. We also hope that this bibliography will serve as a resource for service providers and advocates in their efforts to develop more appropriate programs of prevention, detection, and treatment of this problem. We have attempted to provide information on treatment and counseling for therapists, diagnosis and forensic examination for physicians, cases and legislation for lawyers, sex education for teachers, and other related topics.

This annotated bibliography was developed as part of the activities conducted by the University of Alberta Sexual Abuse and Disabilities Project. Since its inception in 1987, the mission of this project has been to seek information, identify resources, carry on independent research, disseminate information, and advocate for social changes that might reduce the risk of sexual abuse and assault for people with disabilities and ensure accessible and appropriate services for victims with disabilities. Work on this project is expected to continue for several years, and readers are invited to contact the authors. We would be particularly interested in hearing from agencies that might provide assistance in distributing the "Victim's Report" forms that help us to gather information to analyze patterns of abuse. Funding for various activities of our project has come from a number of sources, including the National Health Research and Development Program of Health and Welfare Canada, the Alberta Premier's Council on the Status of Persons with Disabilities, Alberta Manpower, and the University of Alberta Central Research Fund. All royalties generated by sales of this annotated bibliography will be split between Victims of Violence and The Association for Persons with

Severe Handicaps, two organizations that have actively worked for the rights of people with disabilities.

Literature that is relevant to sexual abuse of children with disabilities is included along with sexual assault of adults with disabilities because authors often combine the discussion of these topics and sometimes they fail to clearly identify which group is being discussed. While some issues relevant to sexual abuse of children and sexual assault of adults with disabilities do generalize across the life span (e.g., many people with disabilities continue to require intimate contact with caregivers throughout their lives), it is important to recognize that the concerns for and needs of children and adults with disabilities are distinct.

Objectivity is a fundamental canon of academic research. Investigators with prior knowledge of their subjects or who care about the direction of their findings are considered to bias research (Best & Kahn, 1986). The American botanist, Luther Burbank, is cited in *The Great Quotations* (Seldes, 1967) expounding this position, "The scientist is a lover of truth for the very love of truth itself, wherever that may lead" (p. 918). While we agree that the truth is important for its own sake, we also feel that the illusion of total objectivity may be the most dangerous bias a researcher can hold. As researchers studying fellow humans who are abused, we naturally respond emotionally to their suffering. We are aware of strongly held beliefs that shape many aspects of this work, and we hope that this work will contribute to social change that will empower people with disabilities and all vulnerable individuals to resist abuse and hope that it will ensure better treatment for those who have experienced abuse. Considering the emotional aspects of studying abuse, it is important to guard against personal judgments and ill-conceived remedies that might only further complicate the issue. We have tried to maintain some degree of objectivity because we believe that accurate understanding is a powerful instrument for social reform. As Malcolm X (1964) suggests, "Truth is on the side of the oppressed," and as Eugene Victor Debs suggests, "The truth has always been dangerous to the rule of the rogue, the exploiter, the robber" (Seldes, 1967, pp. 919-920). Therefore, we believe that enhanced knowledge regarding abuse will ultimately help to combat abuse. Exposure of the vulnerability of people with disabilities to abuse is not without risks, but failure to expose the full extent of this problem can only result in perpetuation of abuse and exploitation. With this belief in mind, we have attempted to include all relevant research and related theoretical and practical information, even when we disagree with the findings or perspectives of the original authors. The attempt has been made to abstract material objectively according to relevance, without evaluating merit or perspective. Please note that the views and opinions expressed are not necessarily those of the authors of this annotated bibliography.

The first attempts at presenting the information contained in this annotated bibliography categorized entries under several headings (e.g., physical abuse, sexual abuse, sex education, sexual alternatives). These categories were never quite satisfactory since most entries could be legitimately included in several of them. As the number of entries grew, it became clear that categories only served to complicate access to the information sought. Therefore, all entries in this annotated bibliography have been alphabetized in a single sequence and a comprehensive index has been compiled by both subject and name.

The authors wish to thank Sheila White, who provided useful advice along with expert electronic database searches, and Tanis Doe, who provided powerful insights at several stages during this project. Sandra Cole provided valuable support and suggestions for this annotated bibliography. We are appreciative of Connie Varnhagen's excellent work on early stages of our research project and we are also grateful to Beverly Harnaha and Alice Huang for their assistance in the final stages of preparation of this document. Sarah Cheney, Melissa Behm, and Roslyn Udris of Paul H. Brookes Publishing Company provided encouragement, support, guidance, and tactful feedback in getting this annotated bibliography into its published form. We also wish to acknowledge the assistance of many others who suggested sources and ideas and provided encouragement. We thank all of the authors whose work we have abstracted here and all of the survivors of abuse and advocates who have spoken out against abuse. Together, these people made our work possible.

Dick Sobsey
Sexual Abuse & Disabilities Project
6-102 Education North
University of Alberta
Edmonton, AB T6G 2G5

REFERENCES

Best, J. W., & Kahn, J.V. (1986). *Research in education* (5th ed.). Englewood Cliffs, NJ: Prentice-Hall.

Buchanan, A., & Oliver, J. E. (1977). Abuse and neglect as a cause of mental retardation: A study of 140 children admitted to subnormality hospitals in Wiltshire. *British Journal of Psychiatry, 131,* 458-467.

Diamond, L. J., & Jaudes, P. K. (1983). Child abuse in a cerebral-palsied population. *Developmental Medicine and Child Neurology, 25,* 169-174.

Dykes, L. J. (1986). The Whiplash shaken infant syndrome: What has been learned? *Child Abuse & Neglect, 10*(2), 211-221.

Friedrich, W. N., & Boriskin, J. A. (1976). The role of the child in abuse: A review of the literature. *American Journal of Orthopsychiatry, 46*(4), 580-590.

Gruson, L. (1987, March 27). Prosecutors ask death penalty in torture case. *New York Times,* p. A12.

Malcolm X (1964, May 29) Address, Militant Labor Forum Symposium, New York.

McCelland, C. O., Rekate, H., Kaufman, B., & Persse, L. (1980). Cerebral injury in child abuse: A changing profile. *Child's Brain, 7*(5), 225-235.

National Center on Child Abuse and Neglect. (1980). *Child abuse and developmental disabilities: Essays.* Washington, DC: Author.

Pillemer K. A. (1985). The dangers of dependency: New findings on the domestic violence against the elderly. *Social Problems, 33,* 146-158.

Pillemer, K., & Finkelhor, D. (1989). Causes of elder abuse: Caregiver stress versus problem relatives. *American Journal of Orthopsychiatry, 59,* 179-187.

Seldes, G. (Ed.). (1967). *The great quotations.* New York: Pocket Books.

Sengstock, W. L., Magerhans-Hurley, H., & Sprotte, A. (1990). The role of special education in the Third Reich. *Education and Training in Mental Retardation, 25* (3), 225.

Sobsey, D. (1988). Sexual offenses and disabled victims: Research and implications. *Vis-a-Vis: A National Newsletter on Family Violence, 6*(4), 2-3.

Sobsey, D. (1990). Too much stress on stress? Abuse & the family stress factor. *News and Notes: Quarterly Newsletter of the American Association on Mental Retardation, 3*(1), 2, 8.

Sobsey, D., & Varnhagen, C. (1989). Sexual abuse of people with disabilities. In M. Csapo, & L. Gougen (Ed.), *Special education across Canada: Challenges for the 90's* (pp. 199-218). Vancouver: Centre for Human Development & Research.

Disability, Sexuality, and Abuse

•A•

1. Abbott, D. A., & Meredith, W. H. (1986). **Strengths of parents with retarded children.** *Family Relations Journal of Applied Family and Child Studies, 35*(3), 371-375.

In this study, two groups of 60 parents were compared on marital and family strengths and on parental family strengths. One group was made up of the parents caring for children with mental retardation, while the other group cared for children with average intelligence. Findings indicate that the parents of children with special needs were less critical of family members and had fewer persistent family problems. Coping resources for these parents were evaluated and included participation in a parents' group, religious beliefs, and spousal support.

2. Abel, G. G., Becker, J. V., & Cunningham-Rathner, J. (1984). **Complications, consent, and cognitions in sex between children and adults.** *International Journal of Law and Psychiatry, 7*, 89-103.

Child-adult sexual interactions are discussed in light of three areas of concern to people working within the context of the criminal justice system. In an extensive review in the first section of this article, Abel, Becker, and Cunningham-Rathner identify 25 factors that aid in the clear evaluation of the consequences for the child. The second portion of the article addresses the designation of criteria necessary in establishing a child's capacity to give informed consent. The third section deals with the cognitions of adults who are sexually involved with children and is of direct relevance to those working with these adults. Seven cognitive distortions are discussed (e.g., the offender's belief that "some time in the future our society will realize that sex between a child and an adult is alright..." [p. 99]).

3. Abrams, H. A., Nuehring, E., & Zuckerman, M. (1984). *Preventing abuse and neglect: A staff training curriculum for facilities serving developmentally disabled persons* (Vol. 1). Miami Shores, FL: Barry University, Abuse and Neglect Prevention Project.

This 4-part training program for direct care staff who work with persons with developmental disabilities presents instructions for abuse and neglect identification and reporting. It explains normalization and presents a bill of rights for persons with developmental disabilities. It also discusses behavior management and aggression control techniques (ACT). Trainer tips include advice on preparation, delivery techniques, and learning theory. The first three modules provide instructions for delivery of training and include planning notes, objectives, preparation checklists, outlines, lesson plans, handouts, visual aids, post-tests, and evaluation forms. The last module, on ACT, contains an implementation plan, including the following: a system of certification, retraining, and monitoring; seven references; four appendixes concerning the ACT test; and approximately 50 illustrations.

4. Abramson, P. R., Parker, T., & Weisberg, S. R. (1988). **Sexual expression of mentally retarded people: Educational and legal implications.** *American Journal on Mental Retardation, 93*(3), 328-334.

This article examines legal consent, competency, and the relevant psychological literature in relation to an institution's policy for sexual management of individuals with mental retardation. It discusses the significance of comprehensive sex education and offers suggestions for minimizing the prejudicial treatment of people with mental retardation without restricting their sexual expression.

5. Ad Hoc Committee on Adults in Need of Protection. (1987, November 5). *A review of proposed legislation: Adult Protection Act.* A paper presented to special legislative committee on Bill 77, Adult Protection Act, Charlottetown, Prince Edward Island.

This paper is a presentation by the Ad Hoc Committee on Adults in Need of Protection on the proposed law, Adult Protection Act, to the special legislative committee holding hearings on the act. The paper states that there are a large number of dependent adults (including elderly persons and individuals with physical and mental disabilities) who are abused and neglected. The definition of abuse includes physical, mental, and financial aspects. The committee recommends the following: a) the justice system must accommodate the act by sentencing which reflects the seriousness of the crime and by reducing delays prior to the trial; b) reporting abuse should be mandatory; c) accountability and the possibility of being charged need to be made clear in the legislation; d) the definition of "in need of protection" owing to physical or mental infirmity should be reworded to mean physical or mental disability (or mentally handicapped); e) the act looks at short-term intervention that could lead to further abuse should the adult return to his or her former situation; f) the act could penalize individuals financially by having them bear the costs of medical attention and legal action arranged for them by the Court/Minister; g) the act takes all responsibility away from health professionals and institutions for treatment by removing all liability; h) intervention has to be in the best interests of individuals, allowing them to make their own choices; i) a major campaign must be directed to raise public consciousness, resulting in increased awareness and affecting change in the attitudes of caregivers who abuse or neglect; j) a method of reporting adult abuse or neglect must be designed to deal with increased public involvement; k) education and support of caregivers is essential; and l) the Department of Health and Social Services must provide the necessary staffing levels to accommodate this act.

6. **Adam, H., & Gudalefsky, A. B. (1986, August).** *Sexuality and mental retardation.* **Paper presented at the World Congress of the International League of Societies for Persons with Mental Handicap, Rio de Janeiro, Brazil. (ERIC Document Reproduction Service No. ED 288 334)**

This paper contains two presentations made during a precongress course of the Ninth World Congress of the International League of Societies for Persons with Mental Handicaps. The first presentation is divided into two parts: Part I discusses theoretical aspects such as the moral perceptions of sexuality, normalization, and the prejudices and misjudgments concerning a mentally impaired individual's sexuality; Part II describes the development of relationships between institutionalized West German men and women when coed living was introduced. This presentation offers suggestions for sex education programs for persons with mental handicaps that focus on body image, appropriate behavior, puberty, pregnancy, and childbirth and includes sample instructional materials. The second presentation, "Ethical Issues Concerning Mentally Handicapped Persons," deals with ethics and the nature of human society, cites United Nations documents dealing with the rights of persons with handicaps, and discusses issues such as the person's with handicaps right to life and education.

7. **Adams, G. L., Tallon, R. J., & Alcorn, D. A. (1982). Attitudes toward the sexuality of mentally retarded and nonretarded persons.** *Education and Training of the Mentally Retarded, 17*(4), 307-312.

This article describes a survey of 40 institution-based facility staff members (SMs) and 36 community-based SMs and 39 college students (CSs). The survey was conducted to discover attitudes toward actual and potential sexual behaviors of persons with mental retardation and nonretarded persons in locations such as the bedroom, the bathroom, and the living room. The results of this survey reveal that community-based SMs were no more liberal in their sexual attitudes than institution-based SMs. Findings include the following: 1) institution-based SMs believed the percentage of homosexual behavior was higher than the percentage of heterosexual behavior among persons with mental impairments, 2) institution-based SMs tolerated heterosexual behavior in the living room less than the other two groups, 3) institution-based SMs tolerated masturbation by individuals with mental impairments more than the other two groups, 4) all three groups had a greater acceptance of sexual intercourse with contraception than sexual intercourse without any type of birth control, and 5) CSs believed that sexual activity between consenting adults conducted in private is socially acceptable.

8. **Adams, K. (1986). The disciplinary experiences of mentally disordered inmates.** *Criminal Justice and Behavior, 13*(3), 297-316.

This study compares the disciplinary experiences of inmates referred to mental health units at two maximum-security prisons to the experiences of inmates who were not referred. Referred inmates were found to have higher infraction rates, and they were more likely to engage in rule violations that reflect symptomatic behavior. Furthermore, although disciplinary committees make a limited effort to deal with the serious emotional problems of inmates in deciding case dispositions, they are not very willing to dispense with punitive measures. In roughly half of the cases in which inmates were referred to the mental health unit for prison rules violations, punishment was imposed as well. The data also suggest that under some conditions punitive responses to infractions by inmates with emotional distress may result in an escalation of disruptive behavior. As a result of the data, the author suggests that within prison settings, pathology and disruptiveness are interrelated. Although they do incorporate some elements of a flexible rules approach, disciplinary committees operate according to a legalistic model instead of a treatment model.

9. **Adelson, L. (1972). The battering child.** *Journal of the American Medical Association, 222*(2), 159-161.

This article addresses the infant's vulnerability to violence from older children. Five case histories are described in which death resulted from head trauma. There were no indications that these infants had been previously abused. One of the five assailants was a girl with mental retardation and violent aggressive tendencies, and one boy had an IQ below normal. The role of childhood hostility, jealousy, and playfulness are discussed.

10. **Adler, R. (1986). Physical maltreatment of children.** *Australian and New Zealand Journal of Psychiatry, 20,* 404-412.

The author of this article discusses abuse in regard to parent factors, infant factors, and parent-child interaction. In relation to infant factors, two studies are cited that deal with handicaps and abuse. The author states that the evidence is difficult to interpret since it is not clear whether the abuse is caused by or due to the handicap. As well, the author finds little to suggest that infants with difficult temperaments are more likely to be abused but believes further study is warranted. In the area of prevention, the author maintains the following: Before prevention programs can be implemented, it is necessary to predict vulnerable families. Prediction instruments have been used, but there are many problems with them. These problems include uncertain sensitivity or specificity, the risk of labeling and creating self-fulfilling prophecies, and the risk of overpredicting in disorders of low incidence.

11. **Adult Protection Act. S.P.E.I. c. A-5 (1988).**
The purpose of this act is to recognize responsibility for the provision of assistance and protective services to dependent adults who are incapable of providing

necessary care for themselves or who are the victims of abuse or neglect by those responsible for their care. Abuse includes offensive mistreatment, whether physical, sexual, mental, emotional, material, or any combination thereof, that causes or is reasonably likely to cause the victim severe physical or psychological harm or significant material loss to his or her estate. Neglect means a lack of or failure to provide necessary care, aid, guidance, or attention that causes or is reasonably likely to cause the victim severe physical or psychological harm or significant material loss to his or her estate. A dependent adult includes adults with mental and physical handicaps, including the elderly.

The act is to be applied with respect to the following principles: a) persons with disabilities deserve quality of treatment, care, and attention; b) persons with disabilities have a need for self-determination and to have their person, estate, and civil rights protected; c) an adult is entitled to live in the manner in which he or she wishes provided that it is his or her conscious choice; and d) any intervention should be designed for specific needs of the adult, limited in scope, and subject to review and revision. Section 4 of the act provides for reporting of cases of persons in need of assistance or protection. Reporting is not mandatory. Persons in need of assistance include an adult who is a victim of abuse by someone having recognized supervisory responsibility for the person's well-being. Once a report is made, the Minister may direct his officials to conduct an investigation, and if that reveals cause for concern, a full assessment of the social, economic, and medical circumstances may be undertaken. If the person is determined to be in need of protection or assistance, under section 8, the Minister may prepare a case plan to remedy the problem. It is intended that the case plan be developed on a cooperative basis, taking into account the wishes of the person and the observations of the person having supervisory responsibility.

The assistance given (section 10) may include provision of, arrangement of payment for, or referral to counseling, speech and hearing therapy, occupational therapy and physiotherapy, legal counsel and financial management, application for trustee or guardianship functions, residential accommodation and personal nursing care, and any other health, social, or other type of service that may be determined necessary for the person's welfare. Section 12 authorizes the court to make a protective intervention order, which may include directions concerning the conduct of a person found to be a source of harm or danger to the person in need of protection. Sections 15 to 19 provide for guardianship of the person or estate of the person requiring assistance or protection. It is incumbent on the Minister to show that protective intervention is in the best interests of the person and that the least intrusive option is being sought. An order for protective intervention must be reviewed within six months from the date it is made. Sections 23 and 24 relate to emergency intervention, without a court order, to protect the person or estate. The Minister is obliged to explain in simple terms to the person affected and the person providing care what assistance or other interven-

tion is proposed. The act also relieves the health care professional or institution or its staff of liability in rendering treatment to a person who is in need of assistance or protection.

12. **Agathonos, H. (1983). Institutional child abuse in Greece: Some preliminary findings.** *Child Abuse & Neglect, 7*(1), 71-74.

This article discusses a long-term study on child abuse and neglect being conducted in Greece at the Institute of Child Health. It describes a multidisciplinary team that is testing a system of therapeutic intervention to families, evaluating the adequacy of child protection in cases of child abuse and neglect, and examining the efficacy of the law. The author concludes that there are many similarities between child abuse in institutions and child abuse in the family.

13. **Aiello, D. (1984-86). Issues and concerns confronting disabled assault victims: Strategies for treatment and prevention.** *Sexuality and Disability, 7*(3/4), 96-101.

Problems confronting persons with disabilities who have been sexually assaulted include lack of information, lack of transportation, and communication difficulties. This article addresses what aspects should be included in counseling the victim with disabilities. It is noted that special accommodations need to be made in both medical and legal services to help victims with disabilities. Education is also needed for these individuals in areas of sexuality, empowerment, safety, and self-defense.

14. **Aiello, D., Capkin, L., & Catania, H. (1983). Strategies and techniques for serving the disabled assault victim: A pilot training program for providers and consumers.** *Sexuality and Disability, 6*(3/4), 135-144.

This article describes a training program on sexual assault and disability that was conducted by Moss Rehabilitation Hospital of Philadelphia. The purpose of the program was to provide information on medical, psychological, social, and criminal justice concerns in the area of assault of persons with disabilities. Four areas were addressed, including myths and attitudes concerning rape victims with disabilities, emergency crisis services to assault victims, the criminal justice process in relation to assault, and strategies for prevention.

15. **Akuffo, E. 0., & Sylvester, P. E. (1983). Head injury and mental handicap.** *Journal of the Royal Society of Medicine, 76*, 545-549.

In this article, mental handicaps as a result of head injury are discussed. The case histories, accident report forms, and post-mortem records of 1400 residents of a long-term stay British hospital are reviewed. The authors find that injury resulting from shaking or battering contributes significantly to mental handicaps but that this type of nonaccidental injury may be missed during a hasty physical examination. The authors suggest that careful histories be taken and that information be collected from health visitors, social workers, close relatives, other doctors, and hospital records. The incidence of this type of abuse may be reduced if this information is coupled with support for and appropriate management of abusers.

16. **Amary, I. B. (1980).** *Social awareness, hygiene, and sex education for the mentally retarded-developmentally disabled.* **Springfield, IL: Charles C Thomas.**

This book deals with the topic of sex instruction for people who are mentally handicapped. The author emphasizes the need for comprehensive and appropriate education programs for persons with developmental disabilities. The sex education curriculum should include the gradual teaching of basic anatomy and body functions of both genders. The author also discusses the principles of good grooming, health, and hygiene. Furthermore, the topic of social awareness and sexual behavior is discussed. The author deals with the role of the family in sex education of persons with mental handicaps.

17. **American Foundation for the Blind. (1975).** *Sex education for the visually handicapped in schools and agencies: Selected papers.* **New York: Author.**

This book includes articles on program development and implementation, the need for such programs, and ideas for curriculum development. The opening paper is especially eloquent in discussing the need for normal sexual development for persons with visual deficits.

18. **American Nurses' Association. (1979).** *A report on the hearings on the unmet health needs of children and youth.* **Kansas City, MO: Author.**

This report describes findings from hearings held in five metropolitan American cities in 1978. Findings reveal the following: For every suspected case of child abuse reported to authorities, three go unreported, and having a special child in the family increases the likelihood of abuse. Health issues are discussed as well as the characteristics of abusive parents. Possible solutions involving government, medical professionals, social workers, schools, the media, the public, and the family are examined.

19. **Ames, T. R. H., & Boyle, P. S. (1980). The rehabilitation counselor's role in the sexual adjustment of the handicapped client: The need for trained professionals.** *Journal of Applied Rehabilitation Counseling, 11*(4), 173-178.

This article discusses the preparation of rehabilitation counselors for dealing with clients' sexual questions, concerns, and needs. As an example of one of a number of counseling techniques available, the PLISSIT model is examined. The authors use case histories to illustrate three of the four levels in the PLISSIT model: Level 1 (permission), Level 2 (limited information), and Level 3 (specific suggestion). The authors suggest referring clients requiring Level 4 (intensive therapy).

20. **Ammerman, R. T., Cassisi, J. E., Hersen, M., & Van Hasselt, V. B. (1986). Consequences of physical abuse and neglect in children.** *Clinical Psychology Review, 6*(4), 291-310.

This article reviews research in four areas of functioning in children who have been physically abused or neglected: medical and neurological status; cognitive and intellectual functioning; emotional adjustment and psychopathology; and social development. Regarding cognitive and intellectual functioning, these children were often found to display deficits. Methodological shortcomings of the papers reviewed are discussed and include the use of heterogeneous samples, failure to match participants on relevant variables, and the use of psychometrically weak assessment instruments. Recommendations for future research are made and include gathering descriptive information about abused and neglected populations and using assessment instruments that delineate specific deficits in child functioning.

21. **Ammerman, R. T., Hersen, M., & Lubetsky, M. J. (1988). Assessment and treatment of abuse and neglect in multihandicapped children and adolescents.** *International Journal of Rehabilitation, 11*(3), 313-314.

This article briefly describes the objectives of a study aimed at investigating factors associated with the abuse and neglect of children with handicaps who are living at home. Objectives include the development of an assessment strategy for examining incidence and characteristics of abuse and neglect in psychiatrically referred children with multihandicaps and their families and the implementation and evaluation of a comprehensive behavioral treatment plan for remediation in these families. The proposed methodology is described. Expected outcomes also include measures of the incidence of abuse and neglect in psychiatrically hospitalized children and adolescents with handicaps and multihandicaps, the description of the psychosocial characteristics of the abusing parent(s), and the description of the behavioral and psychiatric characteristics of the abused children and adolescents as compared to unabused counterparts. The remedial program is a 12-week skills-based intervention that emphasizes child management skills, stress reduction, anger control training, and problem-solving training.

22. **Ammerman, R. T., Hersen, M., & Lubetsky, M. J. (1990). Assessment of child maltreatment in special education settings.** *International Journal of Special Education, 5*(1), 51-65.

This article reviews the literature linking disability with maltreatment risk and describes an assessment strategy to assist in the recognition and delineation of abuse and neglect in children with disabilities and their families. The assessment strategy uses three approaches:

gathering clinical information, psychometric evaluation, and behavioral observation. Together, these approaches yield data on stress, psychopathology, parenting practices, social networks, and child behavior problems. The section on psychometric evaluation lists more than 17 measures. Proposed factors contributing to the etiology of child abuse and neglect include societal risk factors, parental risk factors, child risk factors (including the presence of a handicapping condition), and buffers promoting resilience in the child. The authors emphasize the need for research regarding the heightened risk for abuse and neglect of children with disabilities.

23. **Ammerman, R. T., Van Hasselt, V. B., & Hersen, M. (1987). The handicapped adolescent. In V. B. Van Hasselt & M. Hersen (Eds.), *Handbook of adolescent psychology* (pp. 413-423). Toronto: Pergamon Press.**
This article addresses the psychological adjustment of adolescents with handicaps. A variety of studies have found that many children and adolescents with disabilities are at increased risk for increased psychological maladjustment. The authors discuss the nature and characteristics of problems encountered by these adolescents and discuss methodological problems that have made studies in this area difficult to interpret. Topics include personality characteristics, psychopathology and behavioral disorders, social adjustment, and a short discussion on treatment. Abuse is not discussed in the article.

24. **Ammerman, R. T., Van Hasselt, V. B., & Hersen, M. (1988). Maltreatment of handicapped children: A critical review. *Journal of Family Violence, 3*(1), 53-72.**
This review focuses on risk factors for abuse. Investigations of abuse and neglect with specific populations of children with handicaps are addressed. Methodology and research recommendations are discussed.

25. **Ammerman, R. T., Van Hasselt, V. B., Hersen, M., McGonigle, J. J., & Lubetsky, M. J. (1989). Abuse and neglect in psychiatrically hospitalized multihandicapped children. *Child Abuse & Neglect, 13*, 335-343.**
Medical histories of 150 consecutive admissions of children with multihandicaps to an American psychiatric hospital were examined, and they reveal that 39% had experienced abuse or neglect or showed signs of likely abuse or neglect. Physical abuse was most common (69%), followed by neglect (45%), and then sexual abuse (36%). The data indicated that clients with less severe impairments were more likely to have a history of abuse. The child's maltreatment was rarely a focus of treatment during hospitalization. A high percentage of sexually abused children also experienced other forms of abuse.

26. **Anderson, C. (1982). *Teaching people with mental retardation about sex abuse prevention: An illusion theatre guide.* Santa Cruz, CA: Network Publications.**
This document describes how puppets may be used to teach children with mental retardation about sexual abuse. (Note: Puppets may offer a viable alternative to role-playing.)

27. **Anderson, J. (1987, November). Educating deaf children about sexual abuse and their safety. *Child Sexual Abuse Newsletter,* pp. 5, 8.**
The principal of a Vancouver school for children with hearing impairments outlines the learning needs of these children in regard to sexual abuse. Three main needs are identified: 1) children with hearing impairments need a standardized vocabulary to talk about sexual abuse and prevention, 2) a variety of media should be employed to make up for a lack of social experience (teaching children to distinguish between good and bad feelings and to judge appropriate and inappropriate behavior are of the utmost importance), and 3) children with hearing impairments need more time to integrate the concepts. Notably, the use of puppets was found to be an effective teaching tool for working with children who have impaired hearing.

28. **Anderson, S. (Speaker). (1985). *Sexual abuse of the developmentally disabled* (Cassette Recording No. L-172-14). Seattle: Seattle Rape Relief Crisis Center.**
This 104-minute cassette is a workshop presentation given by Shirley Anderson, a pediatrician working with the Seattle Rape Relief Crisis Center. Much of the information presented is an account of the experience of the Seattle Center in serving clients with a wide range of disabilities. Incidence and prevalence figures are cited, service delivery issues are discussed, and principles for accommodating special populations are presented. Figures reported suggest that problems of sexual abuse are as common or more common in this population than with the nondisabled population. Also, there is a tendency for underreporting cases in this population that exceeds underreporting with other populations and that generic services require some specialization to meet the needs of this group.

29. **Andre, C. E. (1985). Child maltreatment and handicapped children: An examination of family characteristics and service provision. *Dissertation Abstracts International, 46*(3), 792A.**
The purpose of this study was threefold: 1) to estimate the prevalence of children with handicaps in the population of children served by public social service agencies; 2) to identify differences between groups of children who are handicapped and nonhandicapped with respect to family characteristics that differentiate maltreated children from nonmaltreated children in each group; and 3) to examine the nature of services provided to maltreated children with and without

handicaps. A sample comprised of 308 maltreated children with handicaps, 301 nonmaltreated children with handicaps, 295 maltreated children without handicaps, and 319 nonmaltreated children without handicaps was drawn from a nationally representative stratified random sample of children receiving public social services in 1977 and was surveyed by WESTAT, Inc. under contract to the U. S. Children's Bureau. Data were analyzed using bivariate correlation analysis, two-way analysis of variance, discriminant analysis of variance, and discriminant analysis. Findings reveal a higher prevalence of children with handicaps among maltreated children (23%) than among all children served by public social service agencies (16%). Maltreated children with handicaps were distinguished by a higher incidence of substance abuse and emotional problems among their caregivers and by their greater likelihood of not being under parental custody. These children were also the children most likely to be in out-of-home placements. With the exception of the provision of protective services, there was little discrimination in the service response to maltreated children, with or without handicaps, and nonmaltreated children. A lack of child-oriented services to maltreated children with or without handicaps, such as counseling or mental health services, was notable. Findings suggest that maltreated children with or without handicaps may be subject to professional neglect. The relative lack of child-oriented services to these children must be addressed by service planners. Also, the large proportion of maltreated children with handicaps in long-term placement indicates a need for services designed to facilitate a child's return to the natural family or for arrangements for permanent placement through adoption.

30. **Andron, L., & Ventura, J. (1987). Sexual dysfunction in couples with learning handicaps.** *Sexuality and Disability, 8*(1), 25-35.

This article describes sexual dysfunctions and their treatment in couples in which both partners have developmental disabilities or learning disabilities. Factors that contribute to sexual dysfunction, such as sexual abuse, are discussed. Emphasis is placed on raising clinicians' awareness of and sensitivity toward sexual dysfunction in these populations.

31. **Applicable standards and required evidence. (1986).** *Mental and Physical Disability Law Reporter, 10*(2), 90-91.

This article describes five court cases concerned with applicable standards and the evidence required to determine trial competency, competency to waive other rights, and competency to plead guilty: West Virginia v. Swiger, 336 S.E.2d. 541 (W. Va. S. Ct. 1985); New Mexico v. Coates, 707 P.2d. 1163 (N.M. S. Ct. 1985); Louisiana v. Leason, 477 So.2d. 771 (La. Ct. App. 1985);

Starks v. Indiana, 486 N.E.2d. 491 (Ind. S. Ct. 1985); and Missouri v. Randolph, 698 S.W.2d. 535 (Mo. Ct. App. 1985).

32. **Askwith, J. (1983). The role of social work in enhancing the sexuality of the physically handicapped.** *Journal of Social Work and Human Sexuality, 1*(3), 83-93.

This author claims that the social worker is well suited to be an effective sex educator for people with disabilities if they are educated about sexuality and the individual with disabilities. The author outlines the sources of sexual feelings and presents three case histories that illustrate the relationship between the perception of sexuality and the ability to cope with a sexual dysfunction.

33. **Asrael, W. (1987). The rehabilitation team's role during the childbearing years for disabled women.** *Sexuality and Disability, 8*(1), 47-62.

This article discusses the role of rehabilitation professionals in assisting women with disabilities in childbearing. Topics include the following: education regarding sexuality and disability; information helpful to an obstetrics team, such as information on the role of attitudinal approach and on infant and maternal medical risk; advocacy; resource information; and the rights and responsibilities of a pregnant woman with a disability. A case history is presented.

34. **Atwell, A. A., & Jamison, C. B. (1977).** *The mentally retarded: Answers to questions about sex.* **Los Angeles: Western Psychological Services.**

This book attempts to answer a wide range of questions about sexuality in people with mental retardation. It would provide a useful introduction for parents, teachers, or the general public with interest in this area. It would be a useful reference for those involved in planning sex education for people with developmental disabilities, but it is not really suited for use as a sex education program in itself.

35. **Ayrault, E. W. (1981).** *Sex, love, and the physically handicapped.* **New York: Continuum Publishing.**

This book is an attempt to sexually liberate persons with physical handicaps by broadening the attitude and acceptance of them by people without disabilities. Sexuality shapes the personality of all individuals, develops their emotions, and determines how well they socialize with others. An individual's sexuality is dependent upon that person's attitudes toward him- or herself and his or her relationships with other people. This book discusses the importance of sexuality and the development of sexuality through the early years and into adulthood. It also discusses sexuality and rehabilitation.

•B•

36. **Badgley, R. F. (Chairman). (1984).** *Sexual offenses against children* (Vols. 1 and 2). Ottawa: Canadian Government Printing Centre.

In this report, the committee developed 52 recommendations on incidence and prevalence, which include the following: a) the establishment of an office of Commissioner to implement social and legal reform, b) a national program of public education relevant to the prevention of sexual offenses against children, c) reforms of the Canadian Criminal code relevant to sexual offenses, d) reforms of the principles of evidence, e) measures to strengthen the provision of services, f) the development of relevant information systems, g) the establishment of a national research agenda, h) implementation of specific initiatives against juvenile prostitution, and i) specific measures against child pornography. Statistics presented in this report suggest that one in two females and one in three males have been victims of sexual offenses, with four of five victims experiencing the offense before age 21, and that the majority of cases go unreported. More than half of the incidents occurred in the victims' homes. While the special implications of other potentially handicapping conditions are not addressed (they are beyond the mandate and scope of the report), much of the content has relevance for children. The synthesis of information from a wide variety of sources and the references make this report a valuable reference for researchers and clinicians and indispensable for those involved in public policy.

37. **Baird, P. A., & McGillivray, B. (1982).** Children of incest. *Journal of Pediatrics, 101*(5), 854-857.

Twenty-nine children born of incestuous matings between brother and sister or father and daughter were studied for evidence of negative genetic effects. Of the 21 children referred on the basis of interview data, rather than because of signs or symptoms of dysfunction, 12 had abnormalities. Chromosomal analysis was performed for all children with multiple congenital abnormalities or mental retardation, but no abnormalities were found. Also noted is the association of sudden infant death syndrome (SIDS) with children of incestuous matings. Implications for genetic counseling are discussed.

38. **Bajt, T. R., & Pope, K. S. (1989).** Therapist-patient sexual intimacy involving children and adolescents [Special issue: Children and their development: Knowledge base, research agenda, and social policy application]. *American Psychologist, 44*(2), 455.

This paper discusses the results of a survey of 90 psychologists, 22 of whom reported having been sexually intimate with clients 3 to 17 years of age.

39. **Baker, L. B., Seltzer, G. B., & Seltzer, M. M. (1977).** *As close as possible: Community residences for retarded adults.* Boston: Little, Brown.

These authors conducted a survey of community residences for adults with mental handicaps across the United States. Of interest here is the data obtained on the autonomy of the residents in regard to entertaining nonresidents of the opposite sex within the house. The results showed the following: 5.6% of residences did not allow residents to entertain members of the opposite sex; 27.5% allowed such visits, but only in certain rooms; 7.8% allowed such visits, but only at certain times; 29.4% allowed the visits, with both time and place restrictions; 16.6% had no policy; and 13.1% left the decision up to the resident. In total, 70.3% of the residences had some type of restriction in regard to socializing with the opposite sex. These results point to the lack of autonomy given to many persons with developmental disabilities in the area of social-sexual relationships. The opportunities for developing appropriate relationships with the opposite sex are largely restricted. When combined with an absence of sex education, many residents may be more vulnerable to sexual exploitation.

40. **Baladerian, N. J. et al. (1986).** *Survivor: For people with developmental disabilities who have been sexually assaulted. Booklet I: For those who read best with few words.* Los Angeles: Los Angeles Commission on Assaults against Women. (ERIC Document Reproduction Service No. ED 292 263)

This is the first booklet in a series geared to helping survivors of sexual assault, and it is designed for people who, due to reading difficulties, need to be taken through the booklet by a caregiver. It is written in large print and uses simple words and many illustrations. Topics include body parts, good and bad touching, rape and assault, when the victim should go to the hospital or to the police, and court procedures. The booklet focuses on the victim as a survivor who can learn to feel safe again. Los Angeles area telephone numbers where help can be sought are listed.

41. **Baladerian, N. J. et al. (1986).** *Survivor: For people with developmental disabilities who have been sexually assaulted. Booklet III: For family members, advocates and special care providers.* Los Angeles: Los Angeles Commission on Assaults against Women. (ERIC Document Reproduction Service No. ED 292 264)

This is the third booklet in a series geared to helping survivors of sexual assault, and it is designed to assist people aiding the victim or who are teaching preventative measures. Topics include definition of assault-related terms, statistics on the incidence of assault, signs of an unreported sexual assault, symptoms of rape trauma, confidentiality, reporting requirements, police, hospital, and court procedures, cost reimbursement, understanding the victim's emotional response, how to respond to disclosure, and the steps that should be taken following disclosure. Also included is a list of rape hotlines and counseling resources in the Los Angeles area.

42. **Bancroft, J. (1984). Interaction of psychosocial and biological factors in marital sexuality: Differences between men and women.** *British Journal of Guidance and Counselling, 12*(1), 62-71.

This article examines 100 British men's and 100 British women's clinical presentation of sexual problems, the importance of sexual appetite, and the effects of aging and of physical handicap on sexual relationships. The author concludes that men and women attending sexual problem clinics present their sexual problems in different ways. This article also discusses the consistency principle, sexual interest, aging and sexuality, and disability and sexual dysfunction.

43. **Banning, A. (1989). Mother-son incest: Confronting a prejudice.** *Child Abuse & Neglect, 13*(4), 563-570.

This article discusses the possibility that women are underreported as child sexual abusers. Prejudice against confronting mother-child incest is discussed. Predisposing factors for both women and men are presented. A case study of mother-child incest is presented and used to illustrate prejudice. Two tentative conclusions are put forward: sexual abuse by women is underestimated and that the changing role of both women and men in Western societies may see an increase in female perpetrators.

44. **Barker, D. (1983). How to curb the fertility of the unfit: The feeble minded in Edwardian Britain.** *Oxford Review of Education, 9*(3), 197-211. (ERIC Document Reproduction Service No. ED 293 955)

This article discusses the political and social climate in which eugenics evolved and the strategies employed to prevent "the unfit" from procreating.

45. **Barlow, M. M. (1986). The adult development of middle-aged congenitally blind men.** *Journal of Visual Impairment and Blindness, 80*(6), 810-812.

In this study, ethnographic interviews were conducted with 18 men who were blind from birth. Findings indicate that developmental issues (including sexuality) for these men are similar to sighted men and that these issues operate within a similar time frame.

46. **Barnes, K. (1982). Mother to daughter: Woman to woman talks.** *Exceptional Parent, 12*(6), 47-49.

In this article, the mother of an adolescent with mental retardation discusses how she used mother-daughter nightly talks to help her daughter adapt to her emerging sexuality.

47. **Barnes, K. (1984). Sex education: Let's not pretend.** *Exceptional Parent, 14*(8), 43-44.

In this article, the mother of a 16-year-old discusses how parents of children with disabilities can accept their child's sexuality and help them adapt. Sexuality is viewed as a natural part of adjustment and sex education is viewed as an essential educational component for every child.

48. **Barnett, B. (1985). The concept of "informed consent" and its use in the practice of psychology.** *Educational and Child Psychology, 2*(2), 34-39.

This article describes various types of informed consent. These include educated consent, consent by choice, and consent based on a client's competence. The case of a court decision refusing to allow an 11-year-old girl to be sterilized is discussed in terms of informed consent and consent by proxy.

49. **Baron, R. B. (1985). Love and erotic contact between psychiatrists and patients from the second therapist's point of view: The counter reaction issues.** *American Journal of Forensic Psychiatry, 6*(4), 11-21.

In this article, the author reviews his counter-reactions to seven female psychotherapy patients, 15 to 36 years of age, who had been sexually involved with a previous therapist. Patient characteristics include depression, borderline personality disorder, and histories of parental abandonment, seduction, and brutality. Therapist characteristics include presence of physical disabilities, poor self-esteem, and sexual dysfunction. Recommendations are made regarding the types of interventions that are useful for specific issues and conflicts.

50. **Barowsky, E. I. (1976). The abuse and neglect of handicapped children by professionals and parents.** *Journal of Pediatric Psychology, 1*(2), 44-46.

This article discusses passive means of abuse and neglect of children with handicaps. Sample topics include pediatricians' slowness to refer patients or to pay enough attention to patients on their first visit, pediatricians' over-prescription of psychotropic drugs for behavioral control (e.g., Ritalin), the use of technical skills by untrained personnel (e.g., behavior modification), the use of experimental treatment programs to the exclusion of more proven methods, the placement of any and all children with handicaps in nonhandicapped education facilities, and the failure of parents to comply with necessary medical intervention. The author concludes that the greatest responsibility lies with professionals.

51. **Barowsky, E. I. (1987). Factors affecting the impact of pain and painful experiences on the exceptional child.** *Journal of Special Education, 21*(2), 109-121.

This article discusses pain perception in children with

disabilities. The effect of the attenuation of coping skills on quality of life and educational and psychological functioning is discussed. Intervention and the development of coping skills are also addressed.

52. **Barrett, M. (1984). Resources on sexuality and physical disability.** *Rehabilitation Digest, 15*(1), 15-18.
Much of the growing literature in the field of sexuality for persons with a physical disability now deals with the sexual implications of specific disabilities or conditions. This article lists some of the literature that is available on the topic. The author supplies a brief annotation about each reference.

53. **Barrett, T. R. (1985). Mentally ill and mentally retarded parents. In D. J. Besharov (Ed.),** *Child abuse and neglect law: A Canadian perspective* **(pp. 281-307). Washington, DC: Child Welfare League of America.**
This article addresses the right of people with mental retardation to parent and focuses on the child protective laws of Ontario and the relevant provisions of the Criminal Code of Canada. Topics include Canadian case law, the American legal approach, supervision versus wardship, types of evidence, constitutional rights of people with mental retardation, and critiques and recommendations.

54. **Barrmann, B. C., & Murray, W. J. (1981). Suppression of inappropriate sexual behavior by facial screening.** *Behavior Therapy, 12,* 730-735.
This article discusses the use of facial screening in suppressing the public genital self-stimulation of a 14-year-old nonambulatory boy with severe mental retardation. Facial screening was used in the classroom, school bus, and at home. Following a training period of five days, the target behavior was decreased by an average of 93% over the three locales. During a six month follow-up, virtually no regression was seen. Previous unsuccessful attempts to eliminate the target behavior included DRO, verbal reprimand, overcorrection, extinction, and time-out.

55. **Bartel, N. B., & Meddock, T. D. (1989). AIDS and adolescents with learning disabilities: Issues for parents and educators.** *Reading, Writing, and Learning Disabilities, 5,* 299-311.
The literature suggests that certain behavioral characteristics of adolescents with learning disabilities make them particularly vulnerable to contracting acquired immunodeficiency syndrome (AIDS) and resistant to traditional educational approaches. This article discusses the important role of parents and educators in AIDS education and the need for research on specific populations regarding AIDS education.

56. **Barthell, C. N. (1983). Deaf and gay: Where is my community? [Monograph]** *Readings in Deafness, 9,* 147-157.

This article explores the hearing and hearing impaired populations' attitudes concerning the sexuality of hearing impaired and gay deaf persons, the occurrence of and attitude toward homosexuality in the deaf community, the attitude toward homosexuality reflected in American Sign Language, and support networks among the deaf and gay population.

57. **Baruth, L. G., & Burggraf, M. Z. (1983). Marital counseling: Parents have special needs also.** *Individual Psychology Journal of Adlerian Theory, Research and Practice, 39*(40), 409-418.
This article focuses on the use of Adlerian psychology in the resolution of marital conflict in families with a child with special needs. The four principles of conflict resolution discussed are creation of mutual respect, pinpointing the issue, seeking areas of agreement, and mutual participation in making decisions. An example is used to illustrate the four principles. The importance of sharing the responsibility for decisions is also discussed.

58. **Bauer, H. (1983). Preparation of the sexually abused child for court testimony.** *Bulletin of the American Academy of Psychiatry and the Law, 11*(3), 287-289.
This article describes how a child who has been sexually abused can be prepared for court appearances in order to reduce the risk for psychiatric damage to the child which might be caused by court procedures. Topics include the use of detailed descriptions of courtroom procedures for preschool and primary grade children, visiting the courtroom before appearing in court, the need for the child to understand sexual terms that might be used in cross-examination, and role-playing for latency-age and adolescent children. The author argues that it is unlikely that these techniques will interfere with the course of justice and that they are needed to protect children from procedural assault in the courtroom.

59. **Baugh, R. J. (1984). Sexuality education for the visually and hearing impaired child in the regular classroom.** *Journal of School Health, 54*(10), 407-409.
This article discusses how teachers in regular classrooms can modify teaching methods to assist mainstreamed children with sensory impairments in their psychosocial/sexual adjustment.

60. **Baum, E., Grodin, M. A., Alpert, J., & Glantz, L. (1987). Child sexual abuse, criminal justice, and the pediatrician.** *Pediatrics, 79*(3), 437-439.
In this commentary, the authors discuss the relationship between the pediatrician and the justice system relevant to child sexual abuse. The increased involvement of pediatricians in child sexual abuse cases has increased in frequency and complexity in recent years. The authors stress the role of physicians in minimizing the emotional trauma of the children involved and pro-

viding the best possible evidence. The need for collaborative efforts between the justice system and the medical field is viewed as a key element in the evolution of further efforts to protect children from abuse.

61. Bax, M. (1983). Child abuse and cerebral palsy [Editorial]. *Developmental Medicine and Child Neurology, 25(2), 141-142.*

The causal link between cerebral palsy and child abuse is discussed. Intervention is discussed as being important during the early months of an infant's life since it is during this period that parents' coping mechanisms are most strained. The author concludes that early identification of child abuse may be achieved through regular contact with health professionals.

62. Beck, C. M., & Phillips, L. R. (1983). Abuse of the elderly. *Journal of Gerontological Nursing, 9(2), 97-101.*

This article discusses the dynamics of elder abuse in the home. Stressors acting upon the abusive caregiver are discussed, in particular the effects of confusion in the elderly person. It is estimated that elder abuse occurs in approximately 10% of all families and that confusion in the elderly person compounds the stress acting on the caregiver.

63. Becker, J. V., & Abel, G. G. (1983). Sex and disability: Treatment issues. *Behavioral Medicine Update, 4(4), 15-20.*

This article examines sexual counseling for disabled persons and is based on clinical experience and literature. The authors suggest that information given by a therapist can help the patient find alternative sexual behaviors, enhance sexual functioning, and, given the patient's limitations, be sexually creative. The authors also describe the nature and treatment of the sexual problems associated with diabetes, cardiovascular disorders, rheumatoid disorders, and spinal cord injuries.

64. Beckham, K., & Giordano, J. A. (1986). Illness and impairment in elderly couples: Implications for marital therapy. *Family Relations Journal of Applied Family and Child Studies, 35(2), 257-264.*

This article discusses the impact of disabling illness or impairment in a spouse on marital relations among the elderly. Treatment issues are addressed and include behavioral intervention, therapist barriers, the impact of emerging caregiver roles, and client barriers.

65. Beckmann, C. R., Gittler, M., Barzansky, B. M., & Beckmann, C. A. (1989). Gynecologic health care of women with disabilities. *Obstetrics & Gynecology, 74(1), 75-79.*

In this study, 55 women with acquired and congenital disabilities provided information about their gynecologic health care. Only 18.8% reported having received sexuality counseling, and 64.6% reported receiving information on contraception. Women with paralysis, impaired motor function, or obvious physical deformity were rarely offered information on contraception. The authors suggest that, in particular, patients disabled after menarche require information regarding sexuality and contraception. They also suggest that health professionals must be educated regarding gynecologic health care of people with disabilities.

66. Bell, R. Q., & Pearl, D. (1982). Psychosocial change in risk groups: Implications for early identification. *Prevention in Human Services, 1(4), 45-59.*

This article explores the problems and possible solutions to transactional risk. It defines "risk" and discusses the literature dealing with risk research. The authors examine the psychosocial change in groups of infants and children at risk for schizophrenia, developmental retardation, delinquency, learning disability, substance abuse, child abuse, and hyperactivity and conclude that individuals are likely to move in and out of risk status as far as any given developmental phase is concerned. The authors suggest periodic developmental assessment is more feasible for service providers than for an external screening team.

67. Bellamy, G., Clark, G. M., Hamre-Nietupski, S., & Williams, W. (1977). Implementation of selected sex education and social skills to severely handicapped students. *Education and Training of the Mentally Retarded, 12(4), 364-372.*

A sex education/social skills program for people with severe mental handicaps is described in this article. The sex education component consisted of teaching the student to distinguish gender and body parts as well as self-care skills. The social skills component involved teaching appropriate social behaviors and interactions and social manners. Results of the program showed that the great majority of students mastered the skills taught.

68. Bellett, G. (1985, June 10). Friends of the handicapped seek ways to prevent abuse. *The Vancouver Sun, p. A14.*

This newspaper article reports that the group, British Columbians for Mentally Handicapped People, has urged Attorney-General Brian Smith to give authorities the right to apprehend adults with mental handicaps suspected of being physically or sexually abused. The group is asking for legislation to protect hundreds of people with mental handicaps living in private homes or in centers operated for profit.

69. Belsky, J. (1980). Child maltreatment: An ecological integration. *American Psychologist, 35(4), 320-335.*

This article is based on Bronfenbrenner's (1977) ecological model. The author urges consideration of microsystems (e.g., dyad), exosystems (e.g., the community, institutions, and so forth in which a dyad is embedded), and macrosystems (e.g., overriding cultural beliefs). The author also states that cultural validation of violence is a macrosystem characteristic influencing abuse, and the cultural devaluation of women, children, and people with disabilities encourages abuse.

70. **Benefield, L., & Head, D. W. (1984). Discrimination and disabled women.** *Journal of Humanistic Education and Development,* *23*(2), 60-68.

This article examines society's discrimination against disabled females. It finds that social values equate everything young, beautiful, healthy, and vigorous with "goodness" and that these values create a negative view of the disabled female. It reveals that disabled females may be more socially handicapped by their disability than disabled males. The authors suggest that if counselors are aware of the potential discrimination against females with a disability they can effectively help them, their families, and the institutions serving them.

71. **Benson, B. A., & Laman, D. S. (1988). Suicidal tendencies of mentally retarded adults in community settings.** *Australia and New Zealand Journal of Developmental Disabilities,* *14*(1), 49-54.

In this study, people with mental retardation living in community settings who had either attempted suicide or who had suicidal tendencies were contrasted with nonsuicidal adults with mental retardation referred for out-patient mental health services. Suicide methods were found to be similar to those seen in the general population. Based on an examination of the precipitants of suicide attempts and the presenting problems seen in clinics, the authors identify the types of mental health services needed by this population.

72. **Berkman, A. (1984-86). Professional responsibility: Confronting sexual abuse of people with disabilities.** *Sexuality and Disability,* *7*(3/4), 89-95.

This article examines the health professional's obligations to clients with disabilities and to colleagues regarding sexual abuse. The author notes that most sexual abuse is committed by caregivers, and fear of retribution is a barrier to reporting abuse. The article examines three areas of professional responsibility: clinical, management, and personal. The author claims that prevention of sexual assault is a primary professional obligation, and an outline is offered for developing a systematic approach to deal with the problems of sexual abuse within an institutional setting.

73. **Bernstein, N. R. (1985). Psychotherapy of the retarded adolescent.** *Adolescent Psychiatry,* *12*, 406-413.

This article presents evidence showing the effectiveness of psychotherapy with individuals with mental impairments and claims that in spite of this evidence there is still a strong bias against this population by psychiatrists, psychologists, and social workers. This article examines the successful use of psychotherapy

with three individuals with mental impairments: a 20-year-old male (IQ 62) who was afraid of his sexual impulses; a 15-year-old girl (IQ 55) who was afraid of sexuality; and a 14-year-old girl (IQ 67) who was afraid of streets, elevators, storms, and the dark.

74. **Bernstein, N. R. (1985). Sexuality in mentally retarded adolescents.** *Medical Aspects of Human Sexuality,* *19*(11), 50-61.

This article discusses the sexual functioning and sexual problems of adolescents with mental retardation. It claims that attempts to eradicate the sex drive in these individuals is often caused by lack of parental support for manifested erotic desires and by the problems inherent in providing sex education for this population. The author concludes that the sex life of people with mental retardation can be enhanced by simple direct explanations and directives, including the acceptance of masturbation in private and the use of birth control.

75. **Besharov, D. J. (1987). Reporting out-of-home maltreatment: Penalties and protections.** *Child Welfare,* *66*(5), 399-408.

Amendments to many child abuse laws mandate that real or suspected incidences of child abuse or neglect occurring in out-of-home settings be reported by staff. This article discusses penalties for failure to report as well as protective measures for staff members who do report.

76. **Billick, S. B. (1986). Developmental competency.** *Bulletin of the American Academy of Psychiatry & the Law,* *14*(4), 301-309.

This article reviews the historical development of competency in children and examines current psychiatric and scientific thinking on the subject. It also suggests areas for future research.

77. **Birrell, R., & Birrell, J. (1968). The maltreatment syndrome in children: A hospital survey.** *Medical Journal of Australia, 2,* 1023-1029.

These authors surveyed 42 abused children and found that 25% had physical disabilities prior to abuse. This finding is consistent with many other studies that find a high rate of disability among victims of abuse.

78. **Blacher, J. (1984). Attachment and severely handicapped children: Implications for intervention.** *Journal of Developmental and Behavioral Pediatrics,* *5*(4), 178-183.

This article provides an overview of attachment formation in children with handicaps. Data on attachment formation behaviors demonstrated by 50 children 3 to 8 years of age with severe to profound mental retardation is presented. In 67% of the cases, the children had other handicaps, such as cerebral palsy, seizure disorders, or visual impairment. Implications for pediatric practice are discussed as well as promotion of attachment formation in families with a child who is severely impaired. The author argues that attachment formation can be assessed in children with severe impairment. (Note: Attachment *may* be an important factor in internal inhibition of abuse by parents or caregivers.)

79.   **Blacher, J., & Meyers, C. E. (1983). A review of attachment formation and disorder of handicapped children.** *American Journal of Mental Deficiency, 87*(4), 359-371.
This article examines attachment development and disorder in individuals with handicaps using handicap categories (e.g., Down syndrome, retardation, deafness) and the procedures used to study attachment and analogous behavior. It also discusses some critical methodological issues and describes the implications of studying attachment for developing theory, providing services, and understanding child abuse.

80.   **Blanc, P. M. (1982). La sexualité handicapée.** *Genitif, 4*(7), 5-8.
In this article, the author presents three brief case studies to illustrate the similarities between the sexual behavior of adolescents with mental retardation and sexual pathology seen in adults without mental retardation. Parallels are also found between the sex therapy of adults without mental retardation and the sexual and affective education of people with mental retardation. Intervention is discussed in cognitive, sensorimotor, and relational terms. The need for individualized plans in sex education is discussed.

81.   **Blatt, B. (1980). The pariah industry: A diary from purgatory and other places. In G. Gerbner, C. J. Ross, & E. Zigler (Eds.),** *Child abuse: An agenda for action* (pp. 185-203). New York: Oxford University Press.
This chapter examines institutional abuse in residential facilities for people with mental retardation. In the sample of institutions studied, residents were often 19 years of age or under. While conditions had improved from those seen in a 1965 study, the author concludes that monetary considerations prevail over considerations of the well-being of residents. The author recommends that community-based programs be implemented in place of institutions.

82.   **Blatt, B. (1983). The next hundred years.** *Special Educators, 19*(4), 16-22.
This article discusses the future of services for people with mental retardation given the development of the view that this group of individuals represents a "surplus population." The author discusses an alternative view that is humanistic and ascribes value to all people.

83.   **Blatt, E. R., & Brown, S. W. (1986). Environmental influences on incidents of alleged child abuse and neglect in New York State psychiatric facilities: Toward an etiology of institutional child maltreatment.** *Child Abuse & Neglect, 10*(2), 171-180.
These authors investigated child abuse cases in institutions in the state of New York to determine whether environmental stresses on staff precipitated incidents of child abuse in the same way that parental stress can contribute to incidents of familial abuse. A statistical analysis of the results show that sexual abuse comprised 11% of the total number of abuse cases in institutions, compared to only 3% of total abuse cases taking place outside of institutions.

84.   **Blum, R. W. (1983). The adolescent with spina bifida.** *Clinical Pediatrics, 22*(5), 331-335.
This article discusses the need to consider the broader health and social needs of adolescents with spina bifida and their families. In particular, the article addresses the need for increased professional support, vocational training, and sex counseling.

85.   **Blumberg, M. L. (1979). Character disorders in traumatized and handicapped children.** *American Journal of Psychotherapy, 33*(2), 201-213.
Character disorders represent neurotic behavior disturbances that may have their origin during the early formative years of childhood. Precipitating factors are family crises of death, divorce, violence, and particularly child abuse and neglect. Sexual abuse of the child may create latent, long-range disturbances that will affect future adult adjustment. Stresses of a poor socioeconomic environment, the gang, and school difficulties are further aggravations. Violence in the popular television medium has a profound influence on the viewer, especially in the presence of an existing character disorder or a disturbed personality. Physical handicaps and mental retardation are problems with which children and their families must cope adequately lest they predispose to the development of character disorders. The effects of emotional dysfunction in childhood are often apparent in later life as aberrant adult behavior patterns. Preventive and therapeutic measures should be initiated early and a multidisciplinary approach with follow-up should be adopted.

86.   **Blyden, A. E. (1989). Survival word acquisition in mentally retarded adolescents with multi-handicaps: Effects of color-reversed stimulus materials.** *Journal of Special Education, 22*(4), 493-501.
This article discusses the effects of reversing the color of black/white word cards used to teach survival vocabulary to 32 participants, half of whom had spastic cerebral palsy, the other half of whom were multiply handicapped and had mental retardation. Participants were 12 to 17 years of age. White-on-black cards were found to improve acquisition for both groups, but they did not affect retention.

87.   **Boat, B. W., & Everson, M. D. (1988). Interviewing young children with anatomical dolls.** *Child Welfare, 67*(4), 337-352.
This article presents guidelines for conducting structured interviews using anatomical dolls with child

victims of sexual abuse. The guidelines might be adapted for use with other victims of sexual abuse whose credibility may be in question due to the presence of cognitive deficits and/or problems in communication.

88. **Boat, B. W., & Everson, M. D. (1988). Use of anatomical dolls among professionals in sexual abuse evaluations.** *Child Abuse & Neglect,* *12*(2), 171-179.
This article presents data from a survey on the use of anatomical dolls in child sexual abuse evaluations. The respondents included child protection workers, law enforcement officers, mental health practitioners, and physicians. Although most respondents reported having had little specific training in their use, the use of dolls was found to be fairly widespread. No specific behavior was identified by any group as constituting normal play by children who had not been sexually abused. The need for training resources and normative research is underscored. While special populations are not discussed in the article, the need for training and normative research may be much the same.

89. **Bobek, B. (1984). Use the common senses: Childbirth education for blind and visually impaired persons.** *Journal of Visual Impairment and Blindness,* *78*(8), 350-351.
This article discusses a course on pregnancy and childbirth that uses sound- and touch-oriented materials to educate students in a school for the blind and visually impaired. The course is comprehensive and covers the trimesters of pregnancy, labor and delivery, the post-partum period and breastfeeding, and birth control and parenting. It describes the techniques used, which include films, records, anatomical models and charts, and a comparison of body parts to the other senses and to inanimate objects.

90. **Bolea, A. S. (1986). Treating loneliness in children.** *Psychotherapy Patient,* *2*(3), 15-27.
This article examines two types of loneliness and the effects of therapy on 6- to 11-year-old children. It was predicted that individuals with loneliness associated with central nervous system (CNS) dysfunction (i.e., "learning disability" loneliness, characterized by defensive attitudes) would have low self-disclosure and high self-deception scores on the Pictorial Self-Concept Scale. Conversely, it was predicted that individuals with "silent loneliness" (i.e., typical of physically or sexually abused children) would score high on self-disclosure and low on self-deception, although less than that of a reference group selected for general loneliness. The findings support both hypotheses. This article found that art therapy and family therapy increased disclosure scores of people with learning disability loneliness and the silent type. The author concludes that therapy enhanced the ability to deal with loneliness.

91. **Bopp, J., Jr., & Balch, T. J. (1985). The Child Abuse Amendments of 1984 and their implementing regulations: A summary.** *Issues in Law & Medicine,* *1,* 91-130.*
The Child Abuse Amendments of 1984 required states to implement specific procedures to protect disabled children from passive and active euthanasia measures. The conditions that led to the need for this legislation are discussed, illustrating the double standard that had been in effect prior to that time that allowed rationalization of the starving of children with disabilities when such practices had already been clearly criminalized when applied to children without disabilities. The need for equal protection addressed by this legislation is also apparent in the differences that sometimes exist in seeking legal remedies against other forms of abuse of people with disabilities.

92. **Bourgeois, M. (1975). Sexualité et l'institution psychiatrique [Sexuality and the psychiatric institution].** *Evolution Psychiatrique,* *40*(3), 551-573.
This article reviews problems encountered in psychiatric institutions regarding the sexuality of their patients. Issues discussed include the integration of the sexes, contraception, marriage between patients, sexual tensions in the hospital, sexual behavior in the hospital, official attitudes, staff attitudes, and ethics in the care of people with mental illness.

93. **Bowden, M. L., Grant, S. T., Vogel, B., & Prasad, J. K. (1988). The elderly, disabled and handicapped adult burned through abuse and neglect.** *Burns, Including Thermal Injury,* *14*(6), 447-450.
Of 1152 acute burn patients treated at the University of Michigan Burn Center in a five and one-half year period, 26 adult patients were identified as suspected victims of abuse and neglect. Inflicted injury was suspected in 8 cases, while neglect was suspected in 18 cases. All of the adults were either very elderly or had mental impairments and/or physical disabilities. Of the 26 patients, 7 died from their injury, and 23 were burned in health care facilities or in institutions. Burn patterns were found to be similar to those seen in victims of child abuse. Also, explanations did not correspond to the injury, and medical help was not immediately sought.

94. **Boyle, G., Rioux, M., Ticoll, M., & Felske, A. W. (1988). Women and disabilities: A national forum.** *Entourage,* *3*(4), 9-13.
This article describes a Canadian national three-day conference on women and disability sponsored by the Secretary of State of Canada in Ottawa in June, 1988. The conference addressed the issues of oppression and devaluation of women with disabilities and the struggle toward fully equal participation in society. Some major issues discussed include the following: a) employment, b) education, c) reproductive rights, d) violence against women, e) sexuality, f) motherhood, g) participation of women with disabilities in the women's movement, and h) inclusion in the research and policy agenda. In the discussion of violence against women, it is pointed out

that women with disabilities (especially developmental disabilities) experience increased risk for sexual assault and abuse and that services for victims of abuse are often inaccessible to or intentionally exclude people with disabilities.

95. **Brandwein, H. (1973). The battered child: A definite and significant factor in mental retardation.** *Mental Retardation, 11*(5), 50-51.

This article takes a deductive-speculative approach to answering three questions on the relationship between mental retardation and child abuse: What is the incidence of child abuse, to what extent is child abuse associated with head and brain trauma, and are head and brain trauma related to mental retardation? The author concludes that child abuse contributes to mental retardation.

96. **Brannan, A. C., Sigelman, C., & Bensberg, G. J. (1975). The hearing impaired in state institutions for the retarded: I. Prevalence, characteristics, and diagnosis.** *American Annals of the Deaf, 210*(4), 408-416.

This 1975 mail-out survey involving 181 public institutions for people with mental retardation indicates that 9.5% of residents are deaf or hearing impaired. The authors point out the need for special services for these clients.

97. **Brantlinger, E. A. (1983). Measuring variation and change in attitudes of residential care staff toward the sexuality of mentally retarded persons.** *Mental Retardation, 21*(1), 17-22.

This article discusses the development of an attitude scale on the sexuality of persons with mental retardation and the results obtained from administering it to 29 parents of adults with mental retardation employed in a sheltered workshop, five sheltered workshop staff members, 37 college juniors in a severely handicapped teacher-training program, 19 nursing home employees, 33 workshop participants, 59 group home managers, and 50 persons employed at a large residential institution for people with mental retardation. The scale was found to be sensitive to differences in attitudes within and between groups. It also reveals that sexuality training that promotes the human rights of people with disabilities produces a change in attitude and that attitudes vary according to work setting and personal characteristics.

98. **Brantlinger, E. A. (1985). Mildly mentally retarded secondary students' information about and attitudes toward sexuality and sexuality education.** *Education and Training of the Mentally Retarded, 20*(2), 99-108.

This article investigates 13 students with mild mental retardation, ages 14-17 years, and their knowledge about and attitudes toward sexuality and sex education. The author found that all the subjects had attitudes about sexuality, marriage, and parenting that could cause them problems in adult adjustment in the community. All 13 subjects said they needed more information about sexuality, and 11 wanted sex education in school.

99. **Brantlinger, E. A. (1988). Teachers' perceptions of the parenting abilities of their secondary students with mild mental retardation.** *RASE: Remedial and Special Education, 9*(4), 31-43.

This article examines teachers' perceptions of the parenting abilities of their secondary students with mild mental retardation. Teachers felt that the majority of their students expected to marry and have children and that students varied in their ability to assume a parenting role. This author recommends comprehensive, realistic, practical sex education about sexuality, intimate social relationships, and parenting for students with mild mental retardation in secondary programs.

100. **Brashear, D. B. (1981). Contemporary patterns: Emerging issues of the sexual rights of adolescents in institutions.** In D. A. Shore & H. L. Gochros (Eds.), *Sexual problems of adolescents in institutions* (pp. 17-26). Springfield, IL: Charles C Thomas.

Four specific problems in the area of policy development regarding the sexuality of institutionalized adolescents are discussed: the scope of the policy; the role of staff; determining what rights adolescents have regarding sex education, health care, and sexual self-determination; and the extent to which the institution should ensure these rights. Sample topics include regulation of private sexual behavior, homosexuality, and sexual medical care.

101. **Brauner, A., & Brauner, F. (1982). La puberté des handicapés mentaux vue a travers leurs creations d'expression [The puberty of mentally handicapped as seen through their creative expression].** *Psychologie Medicale, 14*(9), 1385-1391.

This article focuses on the use of drawing and ceramics as an alternative to verbal expression in adolescents with low IQs, psychosis, or autism. Through the use of artistic expression, therapists can better understand the sexual concerns and problems of these adolescent clients.

102. **Bregman, S. (1984). Assertiveness training for mentally retarded adults.** *Mental Retardation, 22*(1), 12-16.

An assertive training program was used to train 128 participants from four rehabilitation centers for people with mental retardation. The program had been adapted from the Elwyn Institute's Adjustment Manual. Locus of control and assertiveness were examined. The Bailer-Cromwell Locus of Control measure and the Chapman Assertiveness Instrument were used. As a result of the training, assertiveness was improved. Increased skills in assertiveness were associated with increased internal locus of control.

103. Bregman, S. (1985). Assertiveness training for mentally retarded adults. *Psychiatric Aspects of Mental Retardation Reviews, 4*(11), 43-48.

This study discusses research evidence that suggests that people with mental retardation tend to have personality characteristics that result in unassertive behavior. The characteristics of assertiveness are discussed as well as how assertiveness can be best taught in a group setting. Techniques for assertiveness training are discussed and include focused instruction, modeling, behavioral rehearsal, and feedback. An assertiveness training program developed specifically for people with mental retardation is presented. Lessons address the following: using appropriate affect; expressing feelings, needs, and desires; and knowing appropriate ways to say no. A training outline is also included.

104. Briar, K. H. (1983). Jails: Neglected asylums. *Social Casework, 64*(7), 387-393.

This article describes how jails have become the repositories of people (e.g., delinquent youths, persons with mental illness, persons with developmental disabilities, and alcoholics) who have been deinstitutionalized in recent decades. The author claims that the relationship of economic insecurity to criminal acts remains a central issue for research and policy and discusses the idea that criminality may mask discrimination, oppression, and victimization of ethnic or minority groups. This author stresses the need for jail social workers to promote linkages between social service and criminal justice systems.

105. Bright, R. W., & Wright, J. M. C. (1986). Community-based services: The impact on mothers of children with disabilities. *Australia and New Zealand Journal of Development Disabilities, 12*(4), 223-228.

This article addresses the need to examine whether the assumptions underlying community-based services for children with disabilities do not in fact reinforce cultural stereotypes for their mothers. This article examines three assumptions: 1) single concept of family, 2) women want and are able to remain at home, and 3) women are the natural and therefore primary caregivers. The authors examine the possibility that mothers of children with disabilities may be denied opportunities that exist for other women.

106. Bristol, M. M., Gallagher, J. J., & Schopler, E. (1988). Mothers and fathers of young developmentally disabled and nondisabled boys: Adaptation and spousal support. *Developmental Psychology, 24*(3), 441-451.

This study examines adaptation and parental roles in families in which a son is either disabled or nondisabled. Measurements include developmental child assessments, in-home ratings of parenting, maternal and paternal self-ratings, and interviews. Fathers of boys with a disability assumed less responsibility for the boy, even in families in which the mother was employed. The father's decreased involvement did not extend to

other children who were not disabled. The degree of noninvolvement appeared to coincide with the severity of the child's atypical behavior. For both groups of families studied, expressive support for the spouse was the best predictor of quality of parenting. Lack of support was a negative predictor of parental adaptation. The authors present a concept of harmonic responsiveness to account for their findings.

107. Bristol, M. M., & Schloper, E. (1984). A developmental perspective on stress and coping in families of autistic children. In J. Blacher (Ed.), *Severely handicapped young children and their families* (pp. 91-142). Orlando, FL: Academic Press.

This chapter provides a good discussion of the stress that families with children with autism experience. It details the nature and extent of stress that the families of many children with disabilities experience.

108. Britt, J. H. (1988). Psychosocial aspects of being female and disabled. *Journal of Applied Rehabilitation Counseling, 19*(3), 19-23.

This review focuses on the vocational rehabilitation setting. Within the context of a general discussion on the status of women with disabilities, self-image and self-acceptance are discussed in relation to women's sexuality.

109. Brodyagg, L., Gates, M., Singer, S., Tucker, M., & White, R. (1975). *Rape and its victims: A report for citizens, health facilities, and criminal justice agencies.* Washington, DC: National Institute of Criminal Justice.

This 360-page report provides police, medical facilities, prosecutors, and citizens' action groups with guidelines for victims' services and law enforcement. General guidelines provide a good starting place, and this report was no doubt influential in shaping current services. No special consideration of victims with handicaps is apparent in the report.

110. Broggini, M., & Torre, D. (1988). [The problem of screening for HIV infection in mentally retarded institutionalized subjects]. *Bollettino Dell Istituto Sieroterapico Milanese, 67*(1), 77-78.

This article is available in Italian only. It discusses the possibility of establishing mandatory AIDS screening programs for people with mental retardation living in institutions.

111. Bronfenbrenner, U. (1977). Toward an experimental ecology of human development. *American Psychologist, 32*, 513-531.

This article lays the groundwork for understanding human development in an ecological model. According to this author, individuals exist within dyads, and families exist within communities and societies. (Note: This model has been used by others, including Belsky as a basis for a model of abuse; see Abstract 69.)

112. **Brookhouser, P. E. (1987). Ensuring the safety of deaf children in residential schools.** *Otolaryngology Head and Neck Surgery, 97*(4), 361-368.

More than one quarter of the children with hearing impairments live in residential schools. These children are at increased risk for maltreatment by surrogate caregivers. Barriers to administrative response include disbelief and fear of public reaction. Health providers must assume a special responsibility in the prevention and detection of abuse and neglect of their child patients with handicaps. Discussion includes the relevant aspects of the American health delivery system, as well as specific strategies for the detection, documentation, and prevention of maltreatment of this particularly vulnerable group of children.

113. **Brookhouser, P. E. (1987). Medical issues. In J. Garbarino, P. E. Brookhouser, & K. J. Authier (Eds.),** *Special children-special risks: The maltreatment of children with disabilities* **(pp. 161-178). New York: Aldine de Gruyter.**

This chapter is addressed to physicians who have children with handicaps as patients. Children with handicaps are at special risk for child abuse because their care is particularly stressful for the parents. The health professional's best strategy for identifying an abused child with handicaps is to maintain a high index of suspicion during routine service encounters. Specifics on identifying the physically and/or sexually abused child are given.

114. **Brookhouser, P. E., Sullivan, P., Scanlan, J. M., & Garbarino, J. (1986). Identifying the sexually abused deaf child: The otolaryngologist's role.** *Laryngoscope, 96,* 152-158.

As a primary physician for most children who are deaf, the otolaryngologist must be able to identify signs and symptoms of sexual abuse. Child sexual abuse is a topic of national concern as epidemiologic data indicate more than 100,000 American children become victims annually. This paper provides an overview of the incidence, demographic characteristics, risk factors, and dynamics of child sexual abuse within both the general population of individuals with handicaps and, specifically, those persons with hearing impairments. Strategies for identifying the sexually abused child who is hearing impaired are delineated, including the physical appearance and behavioral manifestations of child victims as well as the characteristics of abusive caregivers and perpetrators. Case summaries are presented that illustrate these characteristics. A national center specializing in the evaluation and treatment of abused children with handicaps is described.

115. **Bross, D. C., & Davidson, H. A. (1985). Reporting laws, legal and evidentiary issues, and legislative initiatives. In V. L. Vivian (Ed.),** *Child abuse and neglect: A medical community response* **(pp. 45-53). Chicago: American Medical Association.**

These authors stress several areas that would encourage a medical community response to child abuse and neglect: feedback to physicians and other professionals who report child neglect and abuse should be permitted; penalties for failing to report abuse and neglect should be increased; multidisciplinary teams should be developed; whistle-blower protection legislation should be enacted, particularly for institutional settings; interagency cooperation should be mandated; evidence acts should be broadened; and civil and criminal immunity should be extended beyond the reporter to others who are involved in the investigative process.

116. **Brown, H., & Craft, A. (1989).** *Thinking the unthinkable: Papers on sexual abuse and people with learning difficulties.* **London: FPA Education Unit.**

This 84-page book contains five papers, an introduction, and a postscript on sexual abuse as it affects people with learning difficulties. The papers include the following: The need for safeguards (Walmsley); Child sexual abuse and mental handicap: A child psychiatrist's perspective (Vizard); Keeping safe: Sex education and assertiveness skills (Craft & Hitching); Uncovering and responding to sexual abuse in psychotherapeutic settings (Sinason); and Sexual abuse and adults with mental handicap: Can the law help? (Gunn). (Note: These five chapters are individually listed in this annotated bibliography.)

117. **Browning, D. H., & Boatman, B. (1977). Incest: Children at risk.** *American Journal of Psychiatry, 134*(1), 69-72.

A study was conducted reviewing 14 incest cases that constituted 3.8% of new cases over a 14-month period. Four of the children were handicapped, physically or mentally. Excessively high rates of depression in mothers and alcoholism in fathers were cited as contributing to incest. The existence of handicaps among some of the children is seen from a psychiatric viewpoint as increasing their vulnerability: Such children may seek physical affection from parents as an assurance that they are loved.

118. **Bryant, G. (1986). Preventive health care for preschool children or health surveillance.** *Child Care, Health and Development, 12*(3), 195-206.

This article describes the debate regarding health surveillance programs for preschool children in the United Kingdom. It questions the continuance of these programs in their present form as the health of the child population has improved. It discusses disadvantaged children and their health needs and areas of concern in child health and development, which include infectious diseases, congenital malformations, sensory defects, neurodevelopmental disabilities, behavior problems, and child abuse. The author advocates changes in social policy and continued initiatives in providing preventive health care to vulnerable families.

119. **Buchanan, A., & Oliver, J. E. (1977). Abuse and neglect as a cause of mental retardation: A study of 140 children admitted to subnormality hospitals in Wiltshire. *British Journal of Psychiatry, 131*, 458-467.**
This survey of 140 children under 16 years of age in two subnormality hospitals shows that 3% of the children had definitely been rendered mentally handicapped as a consequence of violent abuse and that this number might possibly reach a maximum total of 11%. In 24% of the children, neglect was considered to be a contributory factor in reducing intellectual potential. Impairment of intellect from abuse and neglect, especially in those with "vulnerable" brains due to preexisting abnormality, may be much more common than is generally realized.

120. **Buchanan, S. (1988). Women and disability research forum: An overview. *Resources for Feminist Research, 17*(4), 35-36.**
This short article describes the first Women and Disability Research Forum held from June 2-4, 1988 in Ottawa, Canada. Topics addressed at the forum include the need for community-based research, the need for information-sharing and information networks, gaps in research, sexuality, parenting, sexual abuse, isolation, and solutions.

121. **Bullard, D. G., & Knight, S. E. (Eds.). (1981). *Sexuality and physical disability: Personal perspectives*. St. Louis: C.V. Mosby.**
This book combines information on a wide range of related topics. Its 36 chapters include information on personal experiences and professional issues. Sex education, sex therapy and counseling, sexuality and attendant care, and many other topics are included. Ellen Ryerson's chapter on sexual abuse of people with disabilities was instrumental in raising public awareness of the nature and extent of the problems. There is also a useful list of agencies and a bibliography that is now a bit dated.

122. **Bullard, D. G., Knight, S. E., Radocker, M. M., & Wallace, D. H. (1979). *The sex and disability training project: Final report*. San Francisco: California University. (ERIC Document Reproduction Service No. ED 195 883)**
This final report outlines the result of a project undertaken in 1976 in which professionals and paraprofessionals with and without disabilities were trained as socio-sexual educator-counselors for people with physical disabilities. Evaluation data indicate that trainees met or exceeded project expectations. Project staff and graduates are available to consult with those wishing to establish similar training programs. The program included a practicum.

123. **Bullough, V. L. (1985). Problems of research on a delicate topic: A personal view. *Journal of Sex Research, 21*(4), 375-386.**
This article examines the problems of conducting sex research caused by public ambivalence about sex, and the author claims that this ambivalence has stigmatized those engaged in sex research. The author surveys this stigmatization in the United States during the 19th and 20th centuries and discusses the Federal Bureau of Investigation's interest in his sex research.

124. **Burgdorf, R. L., Jr. (1983). Procreation, marriage, and raising children. In R. L. Burgdorf, Jr. & P. P. Spicer (Eds.), *The legal rights of handicapped persons: Cases, materials, and text: 1983 Supplement* (pp. 371-425). Baltimore: Paul H. Brookes Publishing Co.**
This chapter is a supplement to the 1980 (see Shuger) edition, and it examines the U. S. law on legal rights of people with handicaps regarding procreation, marriage, and raising children. There have not been any important new directions in regard to the rights of persons with handicaps to enter marriage; however, significant judicial development has occurred in regard to sterilization and parental rights. Several courts have found a *parens patriae* authority to order sterilization operations to be performed when proper procedures have been followed to ensure that sterilization is in the best interest of a legally incompetent person with a handicap. Several judicial opinions have recognized and protected the rights of individuals with mental and physical handicaps to retain the custody of their children.

125. **Burgess, A. W., & Hartman, C. R. (Eds.). (1986). *Sexual exploitation of patients by health care professionals*. New York: Praeger.**
This 189-page book provides much information about and discussion of sexual exploitation of patients by health care professionals. It includes case studies as a basis for analysis. Some specific topics include the roles of health care professionals, patients' perspectives on the problem, legal aspects, abuse of patients under anesthesia, abuse of gynecological patients, abuse by pediatricians, abuse by counselors, impact on victims, prevention methods, victim treatment methods, and offender treatment methods.

126. **Burnstein, D. (1986). Sexual malpractice litigation. In A. W. Burgess & C. R. Hartman (Eds.), *Sexual exploitation of patients by health care professionals* (pp. 49-60). New York: Praeger.**
This chapter provides a lawyer's view of cases that he has taken involving charges of sexual malpractice. The cases are used as a backdrop for a discussion of the changing role of the courts.

127. **Bus driver acquitted. (1987, June 23). *Chilliwack Valley Times*, pp. 1, 2.**
This newspaper article states that a Chilliwack bus driver was acquitted in court on a charge of sexual assault against a 35-year-old woman with mental handicaps. The article recounts that the driver stated that the woman approached him and kissed him, while

the woman states that the driver stopped the bus and sexually assaulted her. The judge stated that the difference between her story and the accused is substantial and acquitted the driver.

128. Bus driver charged with sex assault. (1988, September 15). *Edmonton Journal,* **p. G2.**
This newspaper article reports that a Calgary Handi-Bus driver was charged with sexually assaulting a female passenger in her home. Police released this information after a series of reports in the news about sexual misconduct of Handi-Bus employees. A preliminary hearing was scheduled for December 6, 1988.

•C•

129. Caffey, J. (1972). On the theory and practice of shaking infants. *American Journal of Diseases of Children, 124*(1), 161-169.
This study looks at the effects of the habitual, relatively mild shaking of infants and the effects of isolated incidents of violent shaking. Bone lesions characteristic of the two forms of shaking are contrasted. Mental retardation is discussed as an outcome of Whiplash Shaking syndrome.

130. Caffey, J. (1974). The Whiplash Shaken Infant syndrome: Manual shaking by the extremities with whiplash-induced intracranial and intraocular bleedings, linked with residual permanent brain damage and mental retardation. *Pediatrics, 54,* **396-403.**
In this article, four aspects of Whiplash Shaken Infant syndrome are discussed: clinical manifestations; evidence suggesting that many battered babies are actually shaken; the high vulnerability of the infant's brain and eyes to habitual, manual whiplash stresses of ordinary shaking by the extremities; and that manual habitual shaking frequently causes mental retardation and permanent brain damage. Indications are that whiplash shaking is a primary cause of trauma in battered infant syndrome. A national campaign on the dangers of habitual, manual whiplash shaking of infants is warranted.

131. California Attorney General's Commission on Disability. (1989). *Justice and disability: Final report.* **California: Author.**
This report suggests several ways in which the justice system can assist people with disabilities: the Department of Justice should collect and disseminate information on crimes against people with disabilities; legislation should require law enforcement officers to include a notation about apparent disabilities on crime reports; the Attorney General should assist law enforcement agencies in developing policies and procedures for taking crime reports from victims and witnesses with disabilities; support should be provided for community-based protection and prevention programs for people with disabilities; community-based escort services should be established for people with disabilities; local law enforcement agents should be educated about the needs of people with disabilities; guidelines for victim assistance programs for people with disabilities should be developed and disseminated; training on disabilities should be provided to staff in existing witness programs, rape crisis centers, domestic violence shelters, and other victim support agencies; funding should be provided for improving accessibility to existing witness programs, rape crisis centers, domestic violence shelters, and other victim support agencies; law enforcement and judicial agencies should be encouraged to employ people with disabilities where appropriate; agencies responsible for peace officer training should appoint a Committee on Disability to ensure input and ongoing consultation; model law enforcement policies for dealing with victims and witnesses with disabilities should be drafted; and courtrooms should be made fully accessible to witnesses with disabilities.

132. Camblin, L. D., Jr. (1982). A survey of state efforts in gathering information on child abuse and neglect in handicapped populations. *Child Abuse & Neglect, 6*(4), 465-472.
This article reports on a survey of the 50 states and the District of Columbia in regard to reporting of abuse and neglect of children with handicaps. Of 51 respondents, 7 did not have a standardized reporting form. Forty-four states do use either a national or state form. It was found that of this group 18 (40.9%) forms do not mention preexisting handicaps. Much variation in reporting style was found among the 26 states which do gather information on handicapping conditions. Respondents were also asked about accuracy of information submitted by local resources on abuse of children with handicaps. Forty-three percent of state representatives reported that locally collected information was inaccurate. Forty-one percent stated their information was accurate, but not one agency claimed it was precise. The remaining 15.6 % either did not respond or did not know if the information was accurate. The author states the following: In order for the true relationship of handicaps to abuse to be understood, state representatives must ensure that this information is collected in a uniform manner.

133. Cantalician Foundation, Inc. (1985). *Preventing child abuse and neglect in families headed by mentally retarded adults: Final report.* **Buffalo, NY: Author.**
This report describes the Specialized Family Training Program developed for direct service providers working with parents with developmental disabilities living in the inner city. The inner city families involved were

predominantly Black or Hispanic. (Note: Child abuse and neglect have been observed in families headed by parents with intellectual disabilities, but it remains unclear how the incidence of these events are compared with similar events in other families.)

134. **Caparulo, F. (1987).** *A comprehensive evaluation of a victim/offender of sexual abuse who is intellectually disabled.* **Orange, CT: The Centre for Sexual Health and Education, Inc.**
This evaluation was conducted by a sex therapist working with special populations. The purpose of the evaluation was to determine the extent of the evaluee's offending behaviors, to measure the level of risk he or she presents, to evaluate his or her suitability as a candidate for out-patient treatment, and to determine the nature of treatment to be undertaken. Components of the evaluation procedure include a three-hour interview and the administration and interpretation of the Socio-Sexual Knowledge and Attitude Assessment Instrument. Therapist recommendations are presented and discussed. Also included is a discussion of the use of Depo-Provera as a suppressant of libido in sex offenders.

135. **Caplan, P. (1986). Is there a relationship between child abuse and learning disability?** *Canadian Journal of Behavioural Science, 18*(4), 367-380.
It has been suggested that there is a relationship between child abuse and learning disability. Perhaps child abuse causes learning disability; perhaps learning disability places a child at particular risk for being abused; perhaps both are true. No adequate investigation of the possible relationships of child abuse to learning disability can be carried out in the absence of adequate, consensual definitions of "child abuse" and "learning disability," and such definitions have been lacking in the work done thus far. Furthermore, the extant research has been plagued by methodological problems, which further impede a clear view of a possible cause-effect relationship. This paper is a review of the pertinent studies that have been done, with an analysis of their shortcomings. It is concluded that at this time, despite the fact that case reports link child abuse with learning disability in some individual cases, there is no evidence either that abused children are more likely than nonabused children to have a learning disability or that children with learning disabilities are more likely than children without learning disabilities to be abused.

136. *Care of institutionalized mentally disabled persons.* **(1985, April). Joint hearings before the Subcommittee on the Handicapped and the Subcommittee on Labor, Health and Human Services, Education, and Related Agencies. Washington, DC: United States Senate, 99th Congress, First Session, On examining the issues related to the care and treatment of the nation's institutionalized mentally disabled persons. Part 1 and 2. (ERIC Document Reproduction Service No. ED 263 712)**

This 95-page document contains proceedings from public joint hearings and is published in two parts. Part 2 presents the findings from a study of 31 American mental state hospitals and the results of more than 600 interviews held with staff, patients, residents, facility administrators, state and federal officials, and others. Findings suggest that on many wards clients are vulnerable to abuse and serious injury, that hospital staff are at risk for serious physical injury, that often little treatment is provided other than drug therapy, and that in many facilities living conditions are unacceptable. Other sample topics addressed in these proceedings include excessive restriction of patients' liberties, the accreditation and certification of facilities, the role of the American federal government, and the constitutional rights of people with mental retardation. Solutions to problems identified are discussed.

137. **Carr, J., & Purdue, C. (1988). Sexuality education for special needs adolescents.** *Canadian Nurse, 84*(11), 26-29.
This article discusses the development of a sexuality program for use with adolescents with physical disabilities or mental retardation. The program was adapted from the grade 7 level version of the program, *Changing Me,* developed by the Ontario Ministry of Health. The adapted program was implemented with 10 girls and 11 boys, ranging in age from 12 to 17 years old. Ten of the students had physical disabilities, while the other 11 had mental retardation. All of the students with a physical disability used a wheelchair, with 8 being capable of some degree of verbal expression. Of the students with mental retardation, 5 had Down syndrome, and the remainder had severe behavioral and developmental disorders. Program design, implementation, and evaluation are discussed.

138. **Carrick, M. M., & Bibb, T. (1982). Women and rehabilitation of disabled persons: Disabled women and access to benefits and services.** *Report of the Mary E. Switzer Memorial Seminar, 6,* 28-35.
This document discusses general medical and social aspects of being female and disabled. Special topics include the sexuality of women with disabilities and their premarital and postmarital counseling.

139. **Carter, U. E., & McCormick, A. (1983). Whiplash Shaking syndrome: Retinal hemorrhages and computerized axial tomography of the brain.** *Child Abuse & Neglect, 7,* 279-286.
Three cases of Whiplash Shaking syndrome are presented. All three presented with seizures and minimal external injury. Although missed upon initial examination, extensive retinal hemorrhages were discovered after pupillary dilatation, a finding suggestive of a diagnosis of abuse. Skeletal surveys and thorough social histories confirmed this diagnosis. Computerized axial tomography scan, however, showed minimal interhemispheric bleeding. In contrast to the

Battered Child syndrome, the signs of Whiplash Shaking syndrome are subtle and require careful investigation. Extensive retinal examination is a useful diagnostic tool, but it is not often performed by family physicians and medical residents, and the syndrome may be missed.

140. **Carty, E. A., & Conine, T. A. (1988). Disability and pregnancy: A double dose of disequilibrium. *Rehabilitation Nursing, 13*(2), 85-87, 92.**
This article describes the interrelationships between six sources of stress for women who are disabled and pregnant: self-esteem, body image, sexuality, independence, fatigue, and the acceptance of the pregnancy. The role of the rehabilitation practitioner is discussed.

141. **Cash, T., & Valentine, D. (1987). A decade of adult protective services: Case characteristics. *Journal of Gerontological Social Work, 10*(3/4), 47-60.**
This article examines 17,355 reports to the South Carolina Department of Social Services, Adult Protective Services Division made between 1974 and 1984. More than 75% of the reports were proven to be maltreatment: 85.1% involved neglect; 17.2% abuse; and 19.7% exploitation. Generally, victims were ambulatory females with low incomes. Information is provided on sources of referral, application of court action and protective placement, and services provided (including counseling and mental health services).

142. **Caster, J. A. (1988). Sex education. In G. A. Robertson et al. (Eds.), *Best practices in mental disabilities* (Chapter 17). Des Moines, IA: Division of Special Education, Iowa State Department of Public Instruction. (ERIC Document Reproduction Service No. ED 304 845)**
This chapter presents a framework for the initiation and teaching of a sex education program for students with mental retardation. A problem-solving approach to real-life situations is recommended. Topics include the purposes of sex education, the qualities of an effective sex education teacher, resources, the use of resource persons, and student involvement. The author suggests that controversy about the program can be prevented by talking with parents. Relevant background information, guidelines, and resource lists are provided.

143. **Caton, D. J., Grossnickle, W. F., Cope, J. G., Long, T. E., & Mitchell, C. C. (1988). Burnout and stress among employees at a state institution for mentally retarded persons. *American Journal on Mental Retardation, 93*(3), 300-304.**
In this article, stress and burnout are measured among 192 employees of a state institution. Measures included the Maslach Burnout Inventory and the Ivancevich Job Stress Scale. The employees studied included developmental technicians, professional staff (e.g., social workers, psychologists, occupational therapists,

teachers, nurses), educational development assistants, and environmental personnel (e.g., housekeepers, secretaries, food service personnel). Results indicate that, in general, stress and burnout are best considered as separate constructs.

144. **Cavanagh, J., & Ashman, A. F. (1985). Stress in families with handicapped children. *Australia and New Zealand Journal of Developmental Disabilities, 11*(3), 151-156.**
This article examines stressors operating in families in which a child has an intellectual handicap. The article addresses the need for respite care from intensive caregiving. (Note: While stress has been suggested as a factor linking disability to abuse, little empirical research is available supporting this hypothesis. Nevertheless, stress reducing family supports may be extremely valuable in keeping families intact. This, in turn, may contribute to abuse prevention because natural families appear to pose less threat than institutional alternatives.)

145. **Chacko, M. R., Buttler, J. T., & Kirkland, R. T. (1987). Communication and special health care needs of a profoundly hearing impaired adolescent. *Clinical Pediatrics, 26*(8), 395-397.**
This article discusses the case of an 18-year-old Black female with a hearing impairment who required an interpreter when receiving assistance with medical and birth control needs. The authors also discuss the necessity of verbal feedback for understanding sexuality and development concepts.

146. **Chakraborti, D. (1987). Sterilization and the mentally handicapped [Editorial]. *British Medical Journal [Clinical Research], 294*(6575), 794.**
This article discusses a Court of Appeal's decision to authorize the sterilization of a girl with severe mental handicaps weeks before her 18th birthday. The author discusses other forms of birth control and suggests that sterilization must be carefully considered before performing this procedure. This author also states that before deciding on sterilization three factors must be considered: the person's fertility, whether consent will be informed, and the affect on sexual functions.

147. **Chamberlain, A., Rauh, J., Passer, A., McGrath, M., & Burket, R. (1984). Issues in fertility control for mentally retarded female adolescents: I. Sexual activity, sexual abuse, and contraception. *Pediatrics, 73*(4), 445-450.**
This article reports on a study of 87 females with mental retardation, 11 to 23 years of age, with regard to sexual activity, assault, and contraception. Forty-six percent of subjects had mild mental retardation, 27% had moderate mental retardation, and 27% had severe retardation. The results indicate that 34% of subjects had had sexual intercourse (51% mild, 30% moderate, 9% severe mental retardation). Twenty-five percent of

the subjects had a known history of sexual assault (one-third of the females with mild mental retardation, one-quarter of the females with moderate mental retardation, and 9% of the females with severe retardation). Ten percent of the sexually abused females were incest victims. Forty-eight percent of the sample had used birth control. Choice of a method of birth control is a special problem for individuals with mental handicaps since the health care provider has little normative data with which to compare the patient and because patient communication and comprehension difficulties may put up barriers to utilization.

148. **Champagne, M. P., & Walker-Hirsch, L. W. (1982). Circles: A self-organization system for teaching appropriate social/sexual behavior to mentally retarded/developmentally disabled persons.** *Sexuality and Disability, 5*(3), 172-174.

This article discusses the "circle" concept, a self-organization system used in sexuality training with persons with mental retardation/developmental disabilities. The circle concept allows concrete teaching modes to be employed to teach all aspects of human sexual behavior to persons with learning disabilities.

149. **Chapelle, P. A., Roby, B. A., Yakovleff, A., & Bussel, B. (1988). Neurological correlations of ejaculation and testicular size in men with a complete spinal cord section.** *Journal of Neurology, Neurosurgery & Psychiatry, 51*(2), 197-202.

In this study, 135 patients with complete spinal cord section were given physostigmine to facilitate ejaculation. Of the 75 successful cases, 15 resulted in successful pregnancy. The integrity of the T12-L2 metamers largely determined the efficacy of the drug. Measurements of testicular volume correlated with the presence or absence of lesions in the T12 metamer. Findings suggest that the T12 segment may play a role in testicular function in patients with paraplegia.

150. **Chapman, J. W., & Pitceathly, A. S. (1985). Sexuality and mentally handicapped people: Issues of sex education, marriage, parenthood, and care staff attitudes.** *Australia and New Zealand Journal of Developmental Disabilities, 11*(4), 227-235.

This article discusses sexuality, marriage, and parenthood of people with mental retardation within the context of normalization. Along with studies that demonstrate that many individuals with mental impairments are capable of appropriate sexual behavior, marriage, and childrearing, the authors consider the negative attitudes regarding sexual expression by people with mental retardation. They also examine a study that investigated the attitudes of 17 residential and workshop staff toward people with mental retardation involved in social-sexual interactions, contraception, sex education, and marriage. The findings were consistent with other studies, but the study revealed a

considerable degree of conservatism about the expression and practice of sexual behavior. The authors recommend that counselors, care staff, and parents should assist individuals with mental retardation in attaining their rights to engage in sexual activity, marriage, and parenthood. This article also describes teaching techniques used in sex education programs for mentally retarded people and presents examples of programs that deal with psychosexual development, marriage, parenthood, and sexual problems and dysfunctions.

151. **Chellson, J. A. (1986). Retarded offenders: Assessment of trial competency.** *American Journal of Forensic Psychology, 4*(4), 11-14.

This article outlines and discusses current standards of competency to stand trial. Procedures for evaluation of trial competency currently being developed are discussed and critiqued. The author notes the need for greater sophistication in competency evaluations and suggests that increased methodological and philosophical clarity would help the clinician in making meaningful determinations of competency.

152. **Chess, S., & Fernandez, P. (1981). Do deaf children have a typical personality? In S. Chess & A. Thomas (Eds.),** *Annual progress in child psychiatry and child development* **(pp. 295-305). New York: Brunner/Mazel.**

This article discusses a longitudinal study of 171 rubella adolescents who were deaf and 34 normal controls that investigated four personality characteristics often reported as characteristic of adults and children who are deaf: impulsivity, hyperactivity, rigidity, and suspiciousness. This study found that 75% of the adolescents whose only handicap was deafness and 94% of the normal controls did not exhibit any of these characteristics, while only 32% of the adolescents who were deaf and multihandicapped showed none of the characteristics. Self-abuse remained constant in the adolescents who were deaf and multihandicapped, and it decreased over time in the adolescents whose only handicap was deafness.

153. **Child Abuse Amendments of 1984, PL 98-457, 98 Stat. 1749-1764 (1984, October 9).**

This Act extends laws relating to child abuse, neglect, and adoption. Title I of the Act is the Amendments to Child Abuse Prevention and Treatment Act. In regard to people with disabilities, notable changes involve the insertion of "including any employee of a residential facility or any staff person providing out-of-home care" in section 102, section 3, of the previous version of the Act. Part B of Title I addresses changes made to legislation governing services and treatment for infants with disabilities. Title II is Amendments to the Child Abuse Prevention and Treatment and Adoption Reform Act of 1978. Regarding people with disabilities, notable changes involve the specific discussion of infants with life-threatening conditions and a discussion of improved services to facilitate the adoption of children with special needs. Furthermore, the Department of Health and Human Services is to coordinate with other U.S. Federal departments and agencies, including the Bureau of Census, to provide for a national adoption and foster care information data-gathering and analysis system. Title III is the Family Violence Prevention and Services Act. In regard to people who are elderly, the proposal is made that research be conducted to determine the national incidence of abuse, neglect, and exploitation of this group of adults. The National Clearinghouse on Family Violence Prevention is also to include information regarding people who are elderly.

154. Child abuse and cerebral palsy [Editorial]. (1983, May 21). *The Lancet*, p. 1143.

This editorial reviews the findings of a recent study that discusses a disturbing two-way relationship between child abuse and cerebral palsy. The study by Diamond and Jaudes revealed that some cerebral palsy is caused by abuse and that those with cerebral palsy are also at risk for abuse. As a result of these findings, this editorial states that more studies should be done to examine conditions that lead to abuse of cerebral palsy victims.

155. Child abuse by whiplash. (1984). *Emergency Medicine, 16*(15), 71-72.

This article addresses the diagnosis and treatment of whiplash in children. Diagnosis is complicated by the fact that the violent shaking of an infant may not result in obvious head trauma. Nonetheless, such shaking of the child may result in motor and visual impairment, seizures, and death. Often diagnosis is delayed owing to the age of the child and the symptoms being protean. Initial diagnoses often indicate meningitis or bacterial infection. Fundoscopic examinations offer a means for the differentiation of this syndrome from meningitis as 80% of infant whiplash victims show retinal hemorrhage, a strong indication of trauma, and intracranial bleeding. The discovery of fluid in a lumbar or subdural tap will confirm the diagnosis. Attending physicians treating whiplash victims must exercise rigid fluid control and take other measures to decrease intracranial pressure in an effort to prevent secondary injury from cerebral edema or hypoxemia. Long-term prognosis depends on the extent of both primary and secondary injury. Early diagnosis of the syndrome and the prevention of secondary injury will reduce the current high levels of permanent brain damage.

156. *Child abuse: How it affects you* [Video-cassette]. (1983). Marshfield, WI: Marsh-field Clinic, Video Network.

This 24-minute videocassette deals with the detection of abusive families. In it, Dr. G. E. Porter, a pediatrician at the Marshfield Clinic in Wisconsin, examines symptoms of abusive families. Symptoms include hospital shopping, failure to thrive, hyperactivity in children, enjoyment of hospitalization by children, and performance typical of borderline intelligence or retardation in children. It is available on 3/4 inch, synchronized, color videocassette.

157. Child Abuse Prevention and Treatment Act, PL 93-247, 88 Stat. 4-8 (1974, January 31).

The basic goals of this Act are as follows: to provide financial assistance for a demonstration program for the prevention, identification, and treatment of child abuse and neglect and to establish a National Center on Child Abuse and Neglect. This Center shall be responsible for the following: compiling, analyzing, and publishing an annual research summary; developing and maintaining an information clearing house; compiling and publishing relevant training materials; providing technical assistance to public and nonprofit private organizations and agencies engaged in the prevention, identification, and treatment of child abuse and neglect; conducting research into the causes of child abuse and neglect and its prevention, identification, and treatment; and investigating the national incidence of child abuse and neglect and possible future trends. Also discussed is the nature of programs and demonstration projects that may be funded. The guidelines for the establishment of the Advisory Board on Child Abuse and Neglect are discussed.

158. *Children who invite child abuse: The early years: Sensory problems* [Videocassette]. (no date). Eugene, OR: Eugene Public Library, Audio-visual Dept.

In this 30-minute color cassette, Dr. C. Delacato examines which behaviors, on the part of even a very small child, may trigger an abusive response in parents. Based on his experiences in working with autistic children, Dr. Delacato analyzes the child's deviant behavior by looking for distortions in sensory input such that the child's perceptions are affected and result in unusual behavior. He also discusses intervention. (Note: The image conveyed by the title is unfortunate because it may be interpreted to imply that these children and their behavior want to be abused or are somehow responsible for their own abuse.)

159. Chubon, R. A. (1981). Development and evaluation of a sexuality and disability course for the helping professions. *Sexuality and Disability, 4*(1), 3-14.

A graduate level course dealing with sexuality and disability was developed for students in the helping professions. At the end of the course, students' attitudes were found to be enhanced, and they demonstrated increased comfort levels in dealing with sexual matters. Limitations of the study are discussed as well as problem areas regarding enhanced sexual expression among people with disabilities (e.g., institutional constraint on human sexuality).

160. Chwalisz, K., Diener, E., & Gallagher, D. (1988). Autonomic arousal feedback and emotional experience: Evidence from the spinal cord injured. *Journal of Personality and Social Psychology, 54*(5), 820-828.

This article investigates the relationship between the perception of autonomic arousal and experienced emotion using interviews with subjects with spinal cord injuries, other persons with handicaps, and nonhandicapped individuals. Although there was some suggestion that the perception of arousal may enhance the experience of emotional intensity, the findings of this study indicate that the perception of autonomic arousal may not be necessary for emotional experience. The findings also reveal that the group of individuals with handicaps were successfully coping with their disability.

161. Cirrin, F. M., & Rowland, C. M. (1985). Communicative assessment of nonverbal youths with severe/profound mental retardation. *Mental Retardation, 23,* **52-62.**
These authors use natural observation to study the communication functions of nonverbal signers with severe handicaps in an institution. Their low rates of initiation and dependence on others for interaction may provide some clues as to why many victims with disabilities fail to report abuse until they are directly questioned. (Note: Impaired communication skills may be critical to perception of vulnerability which appears to be an important factor in selection of victims by offenders.)

162. Citterio, C., Gualdi, G., & Bianconi, S. (1980). L'infermo di mente vittima di congiunzione carnale violenta [Mental patients as victims of violent rape]. *Lavoro Neuropsichiatrico,* **67(1/2), 27-54.**
This article describes the mental anguish of psychiatric patients who are rape victims. Responses to the experience are examined in relation to three categories of victims: 1) patients with borderline mental retardation, those with combined physical and mental handicaps, and people with epilepsy immediately after a seizure; 2) psychotics, people with epilepsy with frequent severe seizures, and oligophrenics with moderate to severe mental retardation; and 3) psychopathic and psychotic patients. The authors outline the differences in the vulnerability of these three groups and examine the reactions to rape among psychiatric patients, which can include sullen resentment, violent determination for revenge, indifference, and even complacency. They also explore the reactions of victims' relatives and discuss the possibility of false accusations, delusions of sexual assault, and other problems. (This article is available in Italian only.)

163. Clark, K. (1986). *Sexual abuse prevention education: An annotated bibliography* **(1986 revision). Santa Cruz, CA: Network Publications.**
This 66-page bibliography includes many useful resources, including a few directly related to the needs of people with disabilities and many related to the needs of people with and without disabilities. It is divided into several sections: 1) books for adults, 2) books for children, 3) booklets, pamphlets, and so forth, 4) curricula and teachers' guides, 5) audiovisual materials for students, 6) professional training audiovisual materials, and 7) a list of film distributors.

164. Clark, R. E., & Clark, J. F. (1989). *The encyclopedia of child abuse.* **New York: Facts on File.**
This encyclopedia is an invaluable resource for professionals and nonprofessionals alike who work in any area of child sexual abuse. A total of 200 pages of terms are alphabetically presented and defined. Additional sections in the book summarize a variety of useful information. Sample sections include a selection of relevant Canadian and American legislation, trends in child abuse funding, national estimates of child abuse and neglect reports in the United States, selected American state child abuse and neglect reports, types of immunity granted by American states, and an overview of child abuse.

165. Clarke, D. J. (1989). Antilibidinal drugs and mental retardation: A review. *Medicine, Science & the Law,* **29(2), 136-146.**
Topics addressed in this review article include the use of anitlibidinal drugs (drugs that reduce sexual drives) in conjunction with counseling and psychotherapy, the use of various antilibidinal drugs by themselves, and some of the methodological issues in research on the effects of these drugs. The need for controlled, empirical studies is emphasized.

166. Cohen, S., & Warren, R. D. (1987). *Fellowship report: Child abuse, disability, and family support: An analysis of dynamics in England and the United States, with references to practices in other European countries.* **New York: Hunter College of the City University of New York, Programs in Education.**
A university and a national disability service agency participated in generating this report. The report discusses the dynamics of abuse and neglect of children and adolescents with disabilities in England and the United States. The report describes data collection procedures and considers the relationship between child abuse, disability, and family support systems in England. A similar but briefer discussion revolving around other European countries is given. Implications for the United States are put forward.

167. Cohen, S., & Warren, R. D. (1987). Preliminary survey of family abuse of children served by United Cerebral Palsy centers. *Developmental Medicine and Child Neurology,* **29(1), 12-18.**
This article discusses a study that used questionnaire data from 42 preschool programs serving 2,771 children and 14 respite care programs serving 435 children to investigate the connection between child abuse and handicapping conditions. The results of this study suggest a higher incidence of abuse among children with handicaps in preschool programs than in respite care programs. As it appears that some of the abuse is causing disabilities, and much of it is aimed at children who already have handicapping conditions, the authors recommend greater awareness and reporting of abuse in programs for young children with handicaps.

168. **Cohn, A. H. (1986). Preventing adults from becoming sexual molesters.** *Child Abuse & Neglect, 10,* 559-562.

This article presents an argument that prevention efforts should focus more on the prevention of adults becoming perpetrators and not solely on preventing children from becoming victims. Cohn presents an approach to prevention that includes a number of components.

169. **Cole, S. S. (1981). Disability/ability: The importance of sexual health in adolescence. Issues and concerns of the professional.** *SIECUS Report, 9*(5/6), 3-4.

This article discusses sexual health in adolescents with disabilities. Issues that professionals encounter working in this field are discussed. Issues include the institutionalized adolescent's lack of opportunity for participating in social events, distinguishing between the stages of psychosexual development and the stage at which a child has become disabled, considering the commonalties in psychosexual development between adolescents with and without disabilities, and determining the impact of the helping professional's own attitudes toward sexuality on the adolescent.

170. **Cole, S. S. (1983). Disability and intimacy: The importance of sexual health. In G.W. Albee, S. Gordon, & H. Leitenberg (Eds.),** *Promoting sexual responsibility and preventing sexual problems* **(pp. 297-305). Hanover and London: University Press of New England.**

This article examines the impact of the onset of disability on sexuality. Childhood onset disability is contrasted with adult onset disability.

171. **Cole, S. S. (1984-86). Facing the challenges of sexual abuse in persons with disabilities.** *Sexuality and Disability, 7*(3/4), 71-88.

The presence of developmental or physical handicaps adds another dimension to sexual exploitation. The person who is dependent on relatives and care providers for personal care may be unable to distinguish appropriate affectionate behavior and touch from exploitative touch. A first step toward prevention is the acknowledgement that sexual abuse is common. Programs that inform individuals of their rights to their own bodies must also be included. Indicators of sexual abuse are discussed, as are steps to recovery.

172. **Cole, S. S. (1988). Women, sexuality, and disabilities.** *Women and Therapy, 7*(2/3), 277-294.

This article discusses how women with disabilities experience social expectations and misperceptions regarding their sexuality. Guidelines for therapists are discussed.

173. **Cole, T. M., & Cole, S. S. (1976).** *Sexuality and physical disability: Training of second generation trainers.* **Minneapolis: University** of Minnesota Medical School, Department of Physical Medicine and Rehabilitation, Program in Human Sexuality.

This training package is geared toward rehabilitation practitioners and teaches them how to include sexuality in the rehabilitation of people with disabilities. Part one focuses on experiential learning about sex and counseling. Part two addresses the training of trainers and teaches awareness, group interaction skills, instructional problem-solving, curriculum options, and media selection. The package includes evaluation procedures and a complete audiovisual kit. The kit includes movies, slides, videotapes, music, a step-by-step instructor's book, and a resource manual. Trainees taught with the package have been later evaluated. They rated well on knowledge, accountability, honesty, comfort, confidence, concern, and flexibility.

174. **Cole, T. M., & Cole, S. S. (1977). Sexuality and disability: The physician's role.** *Rehabilitation Medicine, July,* 525-529.

Drawing on case reports, these authors identify four types of disability and discuss sexual outcome as a function of these four classes. Types 1 and 2 include disabilities acquired before puberty. Type 1 is nonprogressive in nature, while Type 2 is progressive. Types 3 and 4 include physical disabilities acquired after puberty. Type 3 is nonprogressive in nature and includes sudden onset disabilities. Type 4 includes disabilities that are progressive in nature. A discussion of physician training is also included.

175. **Cole, T. M., & Cole, S. S. (1981). Sexual adjustment to chronic disease and disability. In W. C. Stolov & M. R. Clowers (Eds.),** *Handbook of severe disability* **(Stock No. 017-090-00054-2, pp. 279-287). Washington, DC: U.S. Government Printing Office.**

At the beginning of this article, the relationship between sexuality and intimacy is addressed. Intimacy needs are discussed. This is followed by a thorough discussion of sexual dysfunction in people with and without disabilities. In the section on sexual dysfunction in people with disabilities, the longest section of the article, evaluation and evaluation technique form the focus of the discussion. The last section of the paper examines the levels and types of sexual counseling for people with disabilities.

176. **Coleman, E. M., & Murphy, W. D. (1980). A survey of sexual attitudes and sex education programs among facilities for the mentally retarded.** *Applied Research in Mental Retardation, 1,* 269-276.

These authors conducted a survey to determine the status of sex education and attitudes toward sexuality in facilities for people with developmental disabilities. The response rate was 40%. Of these respondents, 87% had sex education programs. It is possible that facilities that did have sex education programs were more inclined to reply to the survey. Less than half the programs included information on exploitation. The authors note the following: Although the majority of facilities responding to the survey approved of and provided sex education, very few allowed expression of sexuality, except through masturbation. Thus, a mixed message is being given to the residents, which they may find confusing. Further education of the community and health care providers is necessary before people with developmental disabilities will have the opportunities to develop the sexual aspect of their lives.

177. **Collacott, R. A. (1987). Erotomanic delusions in mentally handicapped patients: Two case reports.** *Journal of Mental Deficiency Research, 31*(1), 87-92.

This article discusses the cases of two females with mental handicaps (15 and 44 years of age) who developed delusions of passion, and it examines the relationship of their cases to de Clerambault syndrome as well as their pathogenetic features.

178. **Collins, C. (1974). On the dangers of shaking young children.** *Child Welfare, 53*(3), 143-146.

This article discusses whiplash shaking as a cause of serious injury or death in young children. The effects of shaking in play, burping, or in response to choking are discussed as well as the effects of more violent shaking on the brain and body. Peak incidence of brain clots occurs at age six months and is seen in children up to age 24 months. Premature infants are particularly susceptible. Male infants are twice as likely as females to be victims of this form of abuse. Whiplash Shaken Infant syndrome is cited as a significant and often undiagnosed source of mental retardation and brain damage.

179. **Colorado State Department of Social Services, Interagency Project on Preventing Abuses, State Institutional Abuse and Neglect Advisory Committee. (1987).** *Specialized training in the investigation of out-of-home child abuse and neglect: Trainer's manual.* **Denver, CO: Author.**

This training manual presents instructions for trainers using a curriculum for technical assistance by the American Institutional Abuse and Neglect Advisory Committee. Goals are to increase the awareness of participants about the vulnerability of children in out-of-home care, to educate participants about their responsibilities, and to provide an overview of the investigative process. An agenda is presented for an audience of investigators of abuse and neglect in out-of-home care. Objectives and lecture material are included as well as activities for use in training sessions. A second, briefer agenda is offered for those who review investigations. This curriculum clarifies the role of the child protection team members in the investigation of institutional abuse and neglect.

180. **Comarr, A. E., Cressy, J. M., & Letch, M. (1983). Sleep dreams of sex among traumatic paraplegics and quadruplegics.** *Sexuality and Disability, 6*(1), 25-29.

This article discusses the role of the study of sex dreams occurring before and after injury in sex counseling.

181. **Comfort, M. B. (1978). Sexuality in the institutionalized patient. In A. Comfort (Ed.),** *Sexual consequences of disability* **(pp. 249-253). Philadelphia: George F. Stickley Co.**

This article discusses the issues around promoting and supporting sexual expression among long-term institutionalized persons with disabilities. Staff attitudes and comfort levels are discussed as well as the need for people with disabilities themselves to be brought into discussions regarding policies and guidelines involving their sexual needs. The role of sexual visitors is discussed.

182. **Comfort, R. L. (1985). Sex, strangers and safety.** *Child Welfare, 64,* **541-545.**

This article advocates more involvement of parents in teaching personal safety skills to young children. The author also stresses the need for age-appropriate content and provides some specific suggestions for making children feel safe.

183. **Competency in court proceedings discussed. (1984).** *Mental and Physical Disability Law Reporter, 8*(2), 108-109.

This article describes five court cases concerned with the competency of people with mental disabilities to testify in court: Connecticut v. Valeriano, 468 A.2d. 936 (Conn. S. Ct. 1983); Jones v. Alabama, 439 So.2d. 1338 (Ala. Crim. App. 1983); Sivils v. Sivils, 659 S.W.2d. 525 (Mo. Ct. App. 1983); Illinois v. Spencer, 457 N.E.2d. 473 (Ill. App. Ct. 1983); and Louisiana v. Peters, 441 So. 2d. 403 (La. Ct. App. 1983). It discusses the competency of persons with mental disabilities with regard to jury service and impeachment as witnesses in New Mexico v. Gilbert, 671 P.2d. 640 (N.M. S. Ct. 1983) and Robinson v. Maryland, 468 A.2d. 328 (Md. Ct. App. 1983), and describes Garcia v. Texas, 659 S.W.2d. 843 (Tex. Ct. App. 1982), which upheld the conviction of a defendant who raped a woman with mental disabilities because her mental condition rendered her incapable of appraising or resisting intercourse.

184. **Conine, T. A., & Quastel, L. N. (1983). Occupational therapists' roles and attitudes toward sexual habilitation of chronically ill and disabled children.** *Canadian Journal of Occupational Therapy, 50*(3), 81-86.

The authors of this article suggest that long-term hospitalization or institutionalization may interfere with normal psychosexual development. They surveyed occupational therapists to find out if they believed they should carry out tasks related to facilitation of psychosexual development. Although most agreed that these tasks were an important program component, few actually carried out these tasks, and most felt that their preparation for carrying out these tasks was inadequate.

185. **Conseil du Statut de la Femme. (1986). *Rapport et propositions sur la prévention des abus sexuels à l'égard des enfants [The prevention of child sexual abuse: Report and recommendations].* Québec City: Conseil du Statut de la Femme du Gouvernement du Québec.**

The general focus of this document is on the analysis of sexual abuse occurring in the family and on resources for prevention. An inventory of recommendations formulated by various public organizations is presented as well as a discussion of needs as identified by people working in intervention. Regarding prevention, the emphasis is placed on sex education, particularly in the school, where increased awareness on the part of students and school personnel can be fostered. (This document is available in French only.)

186. **Convention on the rights of the child. United Nations. General Assembly. November, 1989. A/Res/44/25.**

This manuscript describes the United Nations' position on the rights of children and states the following: all children are entitled to protection against all forms of discrimination; the best interest of the child is of paramount importance in all state actions involving children; the child may only be separated from parents when it is in the best interest of the child; the child has the right to be heard in any judicial or administrative hearing affecting the child; states are responsible for protecting children from all forms of violence and abuse while in the care of parents or any other person, and such protective measures should provide the necessary support for identification, reporting, referral, investigation, and treatment; if a child is removed from the natural family in the child's best interest, then the state shall provide special protection, assistance, and care; states shall recognize the right of a child with a disability to a full and decent life, and assistance shall be provided free of charge whenever possible to ensure access to education, training, health care, rehabilitation, vocational preparation, and recreation in "a manner conducive to the child's achieving the fullest possible social integration and individual development;" children placed in any form of care are entitled to an annual review of treatment and placement; children have a right to education; educations should be directed toward the development of the child's personality, talents, and abilities, have respect for human rights, the child's parents and his or her culture, should prepare the child for life in a free society, and should show respect for the environment; states shall protect children from all forms of sexual exploitation and sexual abuse; children shall not be subjected to any cruel or unusual punishment, incarceration, or detention without due process and then only as a last resort, and if deprived of liberty, a child shall be treated with humanity and respect, and every child deprived of liberty shall have a right to prompt access to legal and other appropriate forms of assistance; and states shall take all appropriate measures to promote the physical and psychological

recovery and social reintegration of all abused children.

187. **Conway, A. (1977). Normalization: A beginning without an end. *Special Children, 3*(3), 39-45, 50.**

This author briefly outlines the history of institutionalization of people with mental retardation in the United States. The attitude of the general public toward people with mental handicaps is reflected in studies confirming institutionalization as the means to deal with such individuals. With the modern trend toward normalization of people with handicaps, the public has not adequately decided about sex education for this population. At one time, it was thought best that people with handicaps should be sterilized, but the courts and some of the public were unwilling to enforce such a measure. The issue of sexuality and people with handicaps has to be defined for the future because modern programs for devalued or deinstitutionalized persons should set goals to ensure success and not leave them open-ended, thereby inviting failure.

188. **Cook, J. W., Altman, K., Shaw, J., & Blaylock, M. (1978). Case histories and shorter communications. *Behavior Research and Therapy, 16*, 131-134.**

In this study, public masturbation by a 7-year-old boy with moderate multiple handicaps and severe mental retardation was successfully controlled through the use of contingent lemon juice being sprayed into his mouth. Previous attempts to modify his behavior had proven ineffective and included saying, "No," in a loud voice, hand spanking, and ignoring the behavior. The intervention with lemon juice proved effective in 13 to 16 days across both home and school environments. The method was used without difficulty by a parent, a teacher, and a paraprofessional. Private masturbation in the boy's bedroom, bathroom, or in the school restroom was not considered inappropriate and so intervention was not used. (Note: The alternatives discussed are aversive. Since the time of this publication greater emphasis has been placed on more positive approaches.)

189. **Coon, K. B., Beck, F. W., & Coon, R. C. (1980). Implications for evaluating abused children. *Child Abuse & Neglect, 4*, 153-156.**

This article reports results of a study of identified child abuse victims. School records were obtained with regard to behavioral problems, suspensions, and referral to special education classes. Results show that all students had normal grades. Suspensions were in line with the rest of the school population. Eleven of 55 students were referred for special education evaluation. Two of these were found to have no learning problems. Of the other nine students, two were designated as emotionally disturbed, two were educable with mental retardation, three had learning disabilities, and two were slow learners. The authors conclude that a "strong possibility" has been raised that earlier in-house outcome studies of abused children overestimated the percentage of developmental disabilities.

190. Cooney, M. H. (1986). *Meeting the social and sexual needs of disabled students: A counseling challenge.* (ERIC Document Reproduction Service No. ED 290 248)

This paper discusses how counselors can help students with disabilities to recognize and work toward fulfilling their sexuality. The human and social needs of the developing person are described at three stages: infancy to 5 years; 6 to 13 years; and 14 to 19 years. Counseling strategies include awareness of students' social and sexual needs, self-awareness regarding one's own attitudes and beliefs, encouraging interaction between a student's counselor and his or her special education instructors, parents, and other family members, and encouraging interaction between students with and without disabilities.

191. Corin, L. (1984-86). Sexual assault of the disabled: A survey of human service providers. *Sexuality and Disability, 7*(3/4), 110-116.

This paper describes an informal survey of human service providers in order to uncover the depth of the problem of sexual abuse of adults and children with disabilities. The results revealed a great deal of concern but few statistics to record the incidence of abuse. Following the survey, a petition was organized for legislation to establish a commission for protection of persons with disabilities in Massachusetts.

192. Cornelius, D., Chipouras, S., Makas, E., & Daniels, S. M. (1982). *Who cares? A handbook on sex education and counseling services for disabled people.* Baltimore: University Park Press.

This handbook presents a careful compilation of available information on the need for and the provision of sex education/counseling services. It includes recommendations, based on research, for greater availability and increased applicability of these services to the particular needs of individuals who happen to be disabled. The handbook is organized into sections, providing foundation information first, more specific information for particular populations next, and finally supplemental material and resource listings. Section I, *Sexuality & Disability*, is the foundation of the handbook and should be read first. It provides the current state of the art and research results. Sections II through V assume that the reader is familiar with the information presented in Section I. They provide more specialized information that applies to consumers with disabilities, counselors and other service providers, trainers, and policymakers. Included in these sections are discussions of specific issues that are relevant to the above populations. Appendices A through H provide a resource listing, survey report, bibliographies, and other supplemental material. These sections are intended to be used as reference guides to additional information in the area of sexuality and disability.

193. Corrigan, J. P., Terpstra, J., Rurrow, A. A., & Thomas, G. (1981). Protecting the rights of

institutionalized individuals. In *Proceedings of the Fifth National Conference on Child Abuse and Neglect* (pp. 181-194). Milwaukee: University of Wisconsin, Region V Child Abuse and Neglect Resource Center.

Child abuse and neglect are reviewed in this series of papers from a workshop on protecting the rights of children who are institutionalized. The prevention activities of the Administration of Children, Youth, and Families are described. Sample topics include developing a definition of institutional abuse and neglect, principles for the reduction of abuse, the impact of the U.S. Civil Rights of Institutionalized Persons Act, changes in parent's and children's rights, and the erosion of the state's authority in child management.

194. Court participation. (1986). *Mental and Physical Disability Law Reporter, 10*(2), 109.

This article describes three cases—Frank v. Iowa, 376 N.W.2d. 637 (Iowa Ct. App. 1985); Merkwan v. Leckey, 376 N.W.2d. 52 (S.D. S. Ct. 1985); and Keeney v. Lawson, 484 N.E.2d. 745 (Ohio Ct. App. 1984)—that consider courtroom participation of people with mental disabilities and describe these individuals in the role of a witness in a criminal case, a plaintiff suing for civil damages in a rape case, and a putative father in a paternity matter.

195. Court participation. (1986). *Mental and Physical Disability Law Reporter, 10*(3), 181-182.

The courtroom participation of people with mental disabilities in criminal cases as defendants, witnesses, and as a plaintiff suing for damages in a civil case is considered in six cases: Kansas v. Pursley, 710 P.2d. 1231 (Kan. S. Ct. 1985); Moran v. Blackburn, 781 F.2d. 444 (5th Cir. 1986); Blackshear v. Florida, 480 So.2d. 207 (Fla. Dist. Ct. App. 1985); Tennessee v. Barnes, 703 S.W.2d. 611 (Tenn. S. Ct. 1986); DiBattisto v. Florida, 480 So.2d. 169 (Fla. Dist. Ct. App. 1985); and Whisnant v. Coots, 337 S.E.2d. 766 (Ga. Ct. App. 1986).

196. Courts review participation of mentally disabled persons in criminal justice system. (1984). *Mental and Physical Disability Law Reporter, 8*(3), 289-290.

This article describes four cases that discussed the capacity of people with mental disabilities to participate in the criminal court system: 1) Eddings v. Alabama, 443 So.2d. 1308 (Ala. Crim. App. 1983); 2) Louisiana v. Brown, 445 So.2d. 456 (La. Ct. App. 1984); 3) Pickens v. Alaska, 675 P.2d. 665 (Alaska Ct. App. 1984); and 4) United States v. Gutman, 725 F.2d. 417 (7th Cir. 1984). Specific issues discussed include waivers of constitutional rights, voluntariness of confessions, and witness or victim submissions to psychiatric examinations.

197. Cozzolino, J. P. (1977). Criminal justice and the mentally retarded. *Dissertation Abstracts International, 38*(6A), 3751-3752.

This dissertation examines how courts in the United States decide the issue of criminal responsibility when faced with a defendant with mental retardation.

198. Craft, A., & Craft, M. (1978). *Sex and the mentally handicapped.* **London: Routledge & Kegan Paul.**

This book includes a basic discussion of sexuality issues as they relate to people with developmental disabilities. Emphasis is placed on sex education and on normalizing sexuality. There is some discussion of people with intellectual disabilities as sexual offenders.

199. Craft, A., & Craft, M. (1983). *Sex education and counselling for mentally handicapped.* **England: Costello.**

These authors review the research and literature on sex education and counseling of people with mental handicaps. Suggestions are made as to the direction that must be taken in terms of counseling, birth control techniques, and the special role in training professional and paraprofessional staff who work with people with mental handicaps. Such vital issues as marriage, reproduction, institutional policies, sterilization, and consent from people with developmental handicaps are covered. There are practical suggestions provided for implementing seminars and workshops designed for training professional and paraprofessional staff.

200. Craft, A., & Hitching, M. (1989). Keeping safe: Sex education and assertiveness skills. In H. Brown & A. Craft (Eds.), *Thinking the unthinkable: Papers on sexual abuse and people with learning difficulties* **(pp. 29-38). London: FPA Education Unit.**

This chapter provides a discussion of the need for sex education and assertiveness training for individuals with learning difficulties to help reduce the chance of sexual abuse or exploitation. The authors include some general and specific suggestions for curriculum and instructional strategies.

201. Crain, L. S., & Millor, G. (1980). Forgotten children: Maltreated children of mentally retarded parents. In J.V. Cook & R.T. Bowles (Eds.), *Child abuse: Commission and ommission* **(pp. 395-399). Toronto: Butterworth.**

This chapter is based on a case study of a family in which both parents were developmentally disabled. Problems encountered in assisting this family are discussed, and they reflect the need for increased services for parents with developmental disabilities and for increased community support.

202. Crime victim with muscular dystrophy. (1989). *Mental and Physical Disability Law Reporter,* ***13*(5), 472.**

A Florida appeals court reversed and remanded a father's conviction for the sexual battery of his 13-year-old daughter with muscular dystrophy on the grounds that she could have told her father to stop, yelled for help,

hit him, was able-bodied apart from the effects of her disease, and had strong arms from using her wheelchair.

203. Crittenden, P. M., & Bonvillian, J. D. (1984). The relationship between maternal risk status and maternal sensitivity. *American Journal of Orthopsychiatry,* ***54*(2), 250-262.**

This article examines a study that measured the relationship between parental risk status and the parents' sensitivity to their infants' (9-18 months old) cues in 1 father-infant and 59 mother-infant dyads. The 60 pairs constituted 6 groups of 10 dyads each: 1) 10 neglecting mothers (20-30 years old); 2) 10 abusing mothers (15-27 years old); 3) 10 mothers with mental retardation (16-49 years old); 4) 10 low income mothers (18-26 years old); 5) 10 parents who are deaf; and 6) 10 middle-class mothers (22-36 years old). The study found that different types of parental risk conditions exert different degrees and types of impact on maternal sensitivity. When compared with the middle-class subjects, deaf and low income parents showed the least reduction in sensitivity. Even though the parents with mental retardation showed a wide range in performance, their mean percent of sensitivity was significantly lower than that of the deaf and low income groups. Many of the parents with mental impairments performed in the maltreating range, and abusing and neglecting parents showed the least sensitivity to their infants' cues. However, it should be noted that the patterns of insensitive responses differed considerably between these two groups: neglecting mothers were uninvolved and passive, and abusing mothers were more active and interfering.

204. Crossmaker, M. (1986). *Empowerment: A systems approach to preventing assaults against people with mental retardation and/or developmental disabilities.* **Columbus, OH: National Assault Prevention Center.**

This book is designed to increase the safety of and respect for people with disabilities. Part I examines assault in historical and societal contexts. Part II presents the Assault Prevention Training (APT) program. Part III describes the curricula and examines the individual and organizational responsibility for changing the conditions that foster assaults. (Note: This source is recommended for those developing institutional abuse prevention procedures. National Assault Prevention Center, P. O. Box 02005, Columbus, OH 43202.)

205. Cruz, V. K., Price-Williams, D., & Andron, L. (1988). Developmentally disabled women who were molested as children. *Social Casework: The Journal of Contemporary Social Work,* ***69*(7), 411-419.**

This article addresses the need for expanded treatment programs for women with developmental disabilities who were molested as children. Topics include treatment issues and the parental relationships of this group of women. Recommendations are made.

206. Csesko, P. A. (1988). **Sexuality and multiple sclerosis.** *Journal of Neuroscience Nursing, 20*(6), 353-355.

This article discusses the need for health care workers to address the sexual concerns of patients with diseases such as multiple sclerosis. Physical and psychological aspects are addressed as well as implications for nursing practice. Health care workers must help lift taboos preventing discussion of altered sexuality with patients.

207. Cullen, J. l., & Boersma, F. J. (1982). **The influence of coping strategies on the manifestation of learned helplessness.** *Contemporary Educational Psychology, 7,* 346-356.

Thirty fourth grade boys with learning disabilities and thirty normally achieving fourth grade boys experienced failure on a problem-solving task, following which they received either tutor assistance, self-instructional training to induce success in coping with failure, or a no-training condition. Training effects were assessed on a subsequent problem-solving task and a measure of continuing motivation. Tutor-assistance training was more effective than self-instructional training for decreasing the number of problems on which boys with learning disabilities gave up prior to solution. Compared with their untrained controls, subjects with learning disabilities with tutor assistance training gave up less often and solved more problems. Continuing motivation increased with the boys with learning disabilities who received tutor-assistance training and normally achieving boys without training. Untrained normal achievers attributed failure to adoption of specific task strategies, while untrained boys with learning disabilities attributed failure to task difficulty. It was suggested that characteristics of learned helplessness were apparent in the impaired performance of the boys with learning disabilities. Normal achievers appeared to have developed active and independent strategies for coping with failure. Relevant implications suggest that training may reduce learned helplessness in populations with disabilities and may be useful in reducing vulnerability to abuse.

•D•

208. Dale, F. (1983). **The body as bondage: Work with two children with physical handicap.** *Journal of Child Psychotherapy, 9,* 33-45.

This article is based on two case studies that involve a child with severe congenital difficulties. The focus of the article is on the impact of bodily physical damage on self-image and object relations. The skin is seen as a boundary between the external and internal worlds.

209. Daley, M. R., & Piliavin, I. (1982). **"Violence against children" revisited: Some necessary clarification of findings from a major national study.** *Journal of Social Service Research, 5*(1/2), 61-81.

This article discusses the methodological problems in D. Gil's (1970) major study on violence against children and J. R. Seaberg's reanalysis of Gil's child abuse data. Reanalysis of Gil's data indicates a strong role for child-related variables in predicting abuse severity, and these include the child's age, physical problems (e.g., infirmity, chronic illness, or disability), rejection by the perpetrator, or misbehavior immediately preceding the abuse. The data suggest that the abuse of adolescents may be caused by different factors than those that result in the abuse of young children, and this analysis may help practitioners identify children who are at risk for physical injury.

210. Daniel, A. E., & Menninger, K. (1983). **Mentally retarded defendants: Competency and criminal responsibility.** *American Journal of Forensic Psychology, 1*(4), 11-22.

People with mental retardation make up a significant portion of defendants referred for psychiatric evaluation to determine competency to stand trial and criminal responsibility. The authors argue that this group of defendants have special needs within the American legal and mental health systems that have often been ignored. Also, the relatively permanent nature of intellectual impairment may result in a finding of incompetency, increasing the likelihood that a defendant will be permanently confined in a state hospital. Sample topics include the lack of clear judicial guidelines regarding competency, the clinician's attitudinal bias, and confusion among health professionals regarding competency standards and tests of criminal responsibility. The authors offer guidelines for professionals in making meaningful recommendations to the court.

211. Daniels, S. M. (1978). **Correlates of attitudes toward the sexuality of the disabled person in selected health professionals.** *Sexuality and Disability, 1*(2), 112-126.

The aim of this study is to clarify the relationship between attitudes toward sexuality, disability, and sexual behavior in people with disabilities. Fifty-three health professionals from three rehabilitation centers completed a series of questionnaires measuring attitude. Findings indicate that attitudes toward disability do not correlate with sexual knowledge or attitudes, nor with attitudes toward sexual behavior in people with disabilities. Attitudes toward premarital sex, extra-marital sex, and autoeroticism were the best predictors of attitudes toward sexual expression in people with disabilities. The author emphasizes the need for programs designed to change the attitudes of professionals toward sexual expression in people with disabilities and to focus on attitudes rather than simple knowledge.

212. Daniels, S. M., Cornelius, D., Makas, E., & Chipouras, S. (1981). Sexuality and disability: The need for services. *Annual Review of Rehabilitation, 2,* 83-112.
The need for services regarding the sexual development and sexual function of people with disabilities is discussed. Topics include types of services that consumers identify as most needed, the roles of various professionals, and how services might be delivered.

213. Darty, T. E., & Potter, S. J. (1983). Sexual work with challenged women: Sexism, sexuality, and the female cancer experience. *Journal of Social Work and Human Sexuality, 2*(1), 83-100.
This article discusses social work with female cancer patients. The trauma of cancer is examined in terms of fear of death or disability, disruption of normal activity, cancer treatment, assault to sexuality and sexual image, and victimization and stigmatization. The authors attempt to define the problem of female cancer in order to discover feasible social work interventions, and they uncover two issues that they consider to be essential: the sexual politics of medicine and the psychosocial trauma of cancer.

214. D'Aubin, A. (1986). *Disabled women's issues: A COPOH discussion paper.* Winnipeg: Coalition of Provincial Organizations of the Handicapped.
This 41-page document presents information on reproductive rights, sexual exploitation by male therapists, unethical experimentation on women with disabilities, the over-medication of women with disabilities, feminist therapy, negative experiences of women with disabilities taking the contraceptive Depo Provera, and violence and abuse. The following deficiencies are identified: few statistics exist documenting the incidence of violence toward women with disabilities, women's shelters are often inaccessible to women with disabilities, violence within institutions is a particular problem for women with mental disabilities, charges of rape or assault may not be taken seriously, and social services are at times provided in a way that promotes violent situations. Suggestions for change include increased monitoring of the extent of sexual abuse of women with disabilities, increased research funding and the wide publication of research results, increased accessibility to programs and services, and increased recognition of women with disabilities by the feminist movement.

215. Daugherty, W. E. (1988). Implications of Acquired Immunodeficiency Syndrome for professionals in the field of visual impairments and blindness. *Education of the Visually Handicapped, 20*(3), 95-108.
This article addresses the AIDS-related education of children who are visually impaired or blind. Sample topics include the legal and policy issues of concern to schools and service agencies and the impact of AIDS on vision.

216. Dave, A. B., Dave, P. B., & Mishra, K. D. (1982). Child abuse and neglect practices in Durg District of Madhya Pradesh. *Indian Pediatrics, 19*(11), 905-907, 910-912.
One thousand children in Madhya Pradesh, India with nonaccidental injuries were studied. Injuries were sexual, physical, and emotional in nature. Child abuse and neglect were seen at the individual, societal, and institutional levels. Victims of sexual abuse constituted 9.3% of the group studied. Physical, intellectual, and emotional sequelae are described.

217. Davies, M. (1986). Sex education for young disabled people. *Adoption and Fostering, 10*(1), 38-40.
This article states that a sex education program for youngsters with disabilities should include the effect of particular disabilities on sexual functioning, overcoming the practical problems that arise from a physical disability in a sexual relationship, coping with menstruation, choosing a contraceptive method, genetic counseling, artificial insemination by donor, masturbation, and developing a positive self-image. The author also provides a list of organizations, books, and audiovisual training materials.

218. Davies, R. K. (1979). Incest and vulnerable children. *Science News, 116,* 244-245.
This author found that 77% of a sample of 22 incest victims had abnormal electroencephalographic readings, and 27% of the sample exhibited overt seizure activity. These rates were 3 to 4 times higher than those present in a control group of other hospital admissions.

219. Davies, R., & Johnston, P. R. (1986). Relationship education for people who live with mental handicaps [Special issue]. *Sieccan Journal, 1*(2), 43-46.
This article addresses sexuality and mental retardation in a social framework. The authors describe The Sexuality Development Index (published by Sex Information and Education Council of Canada), an assessment tool developed in order to establish baseline information about the learning needs of a given student in relation to gender identity, socio-sexual behaviors, and sexual knowledge. Assessment outcomes are described and point to a need for sex education. One finding was that many of the trainees reported identifying more closely with children than adults. Also included is a brief discussion of the use of group sexuality counseling, an informal evaluation of sex education courses designed by the authors, and a life span framework for relationship education.

220. Davis, L. (1988). Who knows best? *Nursing Times, 84*(4), 48.
In this article, the director of a service center for children with mental handicaps and their families queries the advisability of sterilizing people with mental handicaps in order to facilitate caregiving.

221. Davis, L. F. (1976). Touch, sexuality and power in residential settings. *British Journal of Social Work, 5*(4), 397-411.

This article examines areas of concern surrounding touch, sexuality, and associated power in residential establishments. The place of touch and the expression of sexuality are considered in relation to residents and staff. The article specifically examines five residential groups: people with physical handicaps, individuals with mental retardation, elderly persons, adolescents, and members of the staff. The author expresses the belief that the rights of these groups should be no less than those of their peers who are not similarly situated. The current practice is to not allow these groups control over their own sexuality. The author does not make a demand for unfettered freedom, but makes a plea for an examination of the rights that care workers or the general public assume they acquire over others merely because residentially confined groups are forced to live in buildings and situations for which the care worker or general public have responsibility.

222. Dealing with sexual abuse. (1987, April 27). *The Edmonton Sun*, p. 22.

This newspaper article discusses the problem of sexual abuse of children with handicaps. It suggests the need for sex education for people with handicaps.

223. De Champlain, J., & Messier, C. (1984). *La protection sociale des victimes d'abus sexuels...où en sommes-nous au Québec? [The protection of victims of sexual abuse...What does it mean in Quebec?].* Québec: Gouvernement du Québec, Comité de protection de la jeunesse.

The first section of this document addresses the definition of sexual abuse and its different forms. According to a 3-year study, the number of cases of sexual abuse has more than doubled (i.e., 379 in 1978; 806 in 1981). Profiles of offenders and victims are delineated. Forty percent of the children identified as having suffered sexual abuse were already known to a social services centre, and almost one quarter were in foster care. More than 50% of abused children were victims of incest. The incest that was identified almost always involved a father and his daughter. Regarding accessibility of services, the authors found that a number of child sexual abuse cases were not adequately treated, were not treated quickly enough, or were completely ignored. The authors also present intervention and treatment models. A shortened 69-page version of this document is also available. (This document is available in French only.)

224. DeHaan, C. B., & Wallander, J. L. (1988). Self-concept, sexual knowledge and attitudes, and parental support in the sexual adjustment of women with early- and late-onset physical disability. *Archives of Sexual Behavior, 17*(2), 145-161.

This article examines a study that compared three groups of college women with late-onset physical disability, early-onset physical disability, and no disability according to sexual experiences, sexual satisfaction, self-concept, sexual attitudes and knowledge, and parental support for sexual development. The study collected data using an extension of the Sexual Interaction Inventory, the Tennessee Self-Concept Inventory, the Sexual Knowledge and Attitude Test, and questionnaires developed for this study. This article discusses group differences in sexual adjustment in terms of functional, emotional, and social implications. The authors recommend that further research should include following the social development of women with late-onset conditions, comparing the social skills and cognitions of the two groups with disabilities, and assessing men who have established intimate relationships with women with disabilities.

225. Delseries, J., & Uso, T. (1982). Adolescence handicapée, un monde sans amour? [Handicapped adolescence, a world without love?] *Genitif, 4*(9), 16-23.

The onset of puberty and adolescence is described in adolescents with handicaps taking part in a day hospital program. Although their reactions may be more intense, their developmental adjustment was found to be similar to that seen in adolescents without handicaps. Acting-out is discussed as well as the importance of flexibility and patience in working with this population.

226. Demetral, G. D., Driessen, J., & Goff, G. A. (1983). A proactive training approach designed to assist developmentally disabled adolescents deal effectively with their menarche. *Sexuality and Disability, 6*(1), 38-46.

This article describes a procedure that was used successfully to prepare 12 8- to 14-year-old females with developmental disabilities (IQs 23-79) for menstruation and to teach them how and when to use sanitary pads prior to their first menstrual period.

227. Denkowski, G. C., & Denkowski, K. (1985). The mentally retarded offender in the state prison system: Identification, prevalence, adjustment, and rehabilitation. *Criminal Justice and Behavior, 12*(1), 55-70.

In a survey of 48 state adult correction systems, it was found that 36 prison systems routinely assess incoming inmates for mental retardation. The average prevalence of mental retardation in prison systems was 2%. The majority of respondents reported that inmates with mental retardation are victimized by other inmates and that they were disproportionately placed into menial jobs. Thirty-three of the responding states did not provide any special services for inmates with mental retardation.

228. Denkowski, G. C., Denkowski, K. M., & Mabli, J. (1983). A 50-state survey of the current status of residential treatment programs for mentally retarded offenders. *Mental Retardation,*

21(5), 197-203.

The authors conducted a survey of state residential programs for offenders with mental retardation. They found that 14 states have such programs. The authors estimate that 95% of the population that requires residential programming will be unable to secure it. As well, 100% of all adolescent and adult offenders with mental retardation will find no services in 24 and 21 states, respectively. The authors also discuss program and treatment characteristics.

229. **Denmark, J. C. (1985). A study of 250 patients referred to a department of psychiatry for the deaf.** *British Journal of Psychiatry, 146,* 282-286.

Participants in this study were randomly selected. Findings underscore the need for specialized services for patients of all types who are deaf, not only those who communicate through the use of their hands. Difficulties involved in the management of a supra-regional service are discussed.

230. **Department of Health and Welfare. (1978).** *Child abuse and neglect in residential Institutions: Selected readings on prevention, investigation, and correction* **(O H D S Publication No. 78-30160, 9-13, 36-42). Washington, DC: Author.**

These proceedings from a working seminar on developmental handicaps focus on defining comprehensive and concise definitions of abuse in the institutional setting. The goal of deinstitutionalization is discussed as well as the means of attaining it.

231. **Desserprit, A. (1982). Structures temporelles et vie sexuelle [Temporal structures and sexual life].** *Genitif, 4*(7), 17-22.

This article discusses the perception of time in people with mental handicaps and how this affects subjective emotional experience and sexual relationships. Resulting potential difficulties in maintaining sexual relationships are discussed. (This article is available in French only.)

232. **Deutsch, H., & Bustow, S. (1982).** *Developmental disabilities: A training guide.* **Boston: CBI Publishing.**

Chapter ten deals with the general sequence of sexual development of people with developmental disabilities. It discusses the types of social and sexual education necessary to prepare a person with mental retardation for the least restrictive expression of his or her sexuality. It discusses specifically the areas of masturbation and homosexual behavior in people with disabilities. Suggestions for sex-educators as to teaching methods in the area are given.

233. **DeVault, S. (1987). Assessment of adaptive behavior in helping to determine competence. Third Annual Symposium in Forensic Psychology of the American College of Forensic Psychology (1987, Monterey, California).** *American Journal of Forensic Psychology, 5*(3), 45-53.

This article discusses two cases in which the Vineland Adaptive Behavior Scales were used to evaluate accusations and confessions of two individuals of tested borderline intelligence.

234. **Developmental Disabilities Act of 1984, PL 98-527, 98 Stat. 2662-2685 (1984, October 19).**

This Act revises and extends programs for people with developmental disabilities. Title I is Programs for People with Developmental Disabilities. In section 110, Rights for the Developmentally Handicapped, a closing statement has been added that states that the rights of people with developmental disabilities discussed in section 110 exist in addition to any constitutional or other rights otherwise afforded to all persons. Part C of Title I is entitled Protection and Advocacy of Individual Rights and expands upon earlier legislation. Changes include the following: the particular states ensuring the protection and advocacy of the rights of people with developmental disabilities are entitled to (with the exception provided in subsection [b]) obtain access to a resident's records if (i) a complaint has been lodged by or on behalf of a resident with developmental disabilities, and (ii) the resident does not have a legal guardian or the state, or the designee of the state, is the legal guardian. In section 153, it is noted that applications for opening new facilities must be accompanied by reasonable assurances that client's human rights and the rights of people with developmental disabilities will be protected. Section 161, Part E, Special Project Grants, describes the basic goal of the program as funding demonstration projects to increase and support the independence, productivity, and integration into the community of people with developmental disabilities. Underserved groups, such as people with multiple handicaps, native Americans, and native Hawaiians, are identified as requiring particular attention. Other projects that will be considered include those that aim at improving or expanding protection and advocacy services relating to the state protection and advocacy system as well as projects geared at the evaluation and assessment of the quality of services (see section 162 for specific criteria). Section 3a of section 163 describes the goals of a report to be prepared for Congress. The report addresses the operation of Intermediate Care Facilities for the Mentally Retarded. Recommendations for improving services are sought.

235. **Developmental Disabilities Project, Seattle Rape Relief Crisis Center. (1979).** *A curriculum for developing an awareness of sexual exploitation and teaching self-protection techniques.* **Seattle: Author.**

This curriculum is designed for teachers and other workers to teach an awareness of sexual exploitation and self-protection techniques. The curriculum is intended for use with students with moderate to borderline mental handicaps; suggested alterations are included for use with people with visual impairments, learning impairments, orthopedic handicaps, learning disabilities, and behavioral disorders (emotionally disturbed). The kits include a teacher's guide, body map, filmstrips, and brochures for parents which describe the course. The Level I curriculum is designed for use with elementary level children ages 6 to 11. This portion of the curriculum does not address the issue of rape or forced sexual assault. The lessons at this level emphasize distinguishing between family, friends, and strangers, precautions to take with strangers, recognition of inappropriate touching by authority figures and relatives, saying "no" assertively, and reporting exploitation. The Level II curriculum is designed for adolescents age 12 to 19 as well as adults with mental handicaps. Students functioning at this level learn self-protective behaviors in a variety of situations. They are introduced to male-female rape and male-male rape. Students learn to recognize potentially exploitative situations and exploitative touching. Exercises teach assertive verbal and behavioral responses to potentially exploitive home, social, and travel situations. Also addressed are the following issues: avoiding sexual exploitation by authority figures; avoiding sexual exploitation as an exchange for favors or gifts; dealing with obscene phone calls and indecent exposure; and reporting sexual exploitation. Both levels include guidelines for parental involvement and information on prerequisite concepts that the students will need to have acquired before taking the course. Each unit contains an introduction, a list of unit goals and objectives, outlines of activities and materials for meeting objectives, and pretests and post-tests. Transcriptions for slides and audiotapes used with the units are provided, as are vignettes describing potentially exploitative situations and appropriate and inappropriate responses to them.

236. **Developmental Disabilities Project, Seattle Rape Relief Crisis Center. (1983).** *Teacher training manual: Sexual abuse of persons with disabilities: Techniques for planning and implementing a self protection program.* **Seattle: Author.**

This manual provides a systematic approach to developing a special education program concerning sexual exploitation within a school system. The manual includes guidelines for training special education administrators, teachers, counselors, nurses, other professionals, and parents concerning awareness about sexual exploitation of individuals with handicaps. The manual is divided into six units. Unit 1 provides basic information concerning sexual abuse, including laws, statistics, and dynamics. Unit 2 provides information concerning how to inform school administrators and elicit their support in developing a program on sexual exploitation. Unit 3 provides suggested formats for educating parents as well as gaining their support for introducing a program into the schools. A "parent attitude survey" is included which can be used to measure the parents' receptivity to sexuality and sex

exploitation education. Units 4 and 5 concern teacher training and include detailed training formats. Unit 6 provides bibliographies of curricula which are appropriate to teach children with handicaps about sexuality and sexual exploitation. Several curricula are suggested. Some curricula are tailored to the needs of students with specific handicapping conditions.

237. **Developmentally Disabled Assistance and Bill of Rights Act, PL 94-103, 89 Stat. 486-507 (1975, October 4).**

The purpose of this Legislation is to amend the Developmental Disabilities Services and Facilities Construction Act and to extend the programs authorized by this act. Title I is Extension and Revision of the Developmental Disabilities Services and Facilities Construction Act. Part D, Special Projects Grants, describes various types of projects that are eligible for funding. Title II of the act is Establishment and Protection of the Rights of Persons with Developmental Disabilities. A large portion of this act addresses the right of people with developmental disabilities to treatment, services, and habilitation. The delivery of these services is identified as being properly delivered in those settings that are least restrictive to the individual's personal liberty. Institutions identified as not being eligible for funding include, among others, those that use physical and/or chemical restraint as punishment or as a substitute for habilitation. In the case of chemical restraint, funding will be withheld if chemicals are used in quantities that interfere with services, treatments, or habilitation. Also, funding will be withheld from institutions that do not permit a client's close relatives to visit at a reasonable hour without prior notice. Also, all programs for persons with developmental disabilities have the onus placed upon them to protect patients' rights, and habilitation plans should be reviewed at least annually. Title II also includes a new section, section 113, entitled Protection and Advocacy of Individual Rights, that requires each state to create a system to protect and advocate for the rights of persons with developmental disabilities. This system has the authority to pursue legal, administrative, and other appropriate remedies to ensure the protection of the rights of people with developmental disabilities who are receiving treatment, services, or habilitation within the state in question. This system is to operate independently of any state agency serving people with developmental disabilities. Section 204, Studies and Recommendations, suggests that standards and quality assurance mechanisms be developed for residential facilities and community agencies. The need for the enforcement of mechanisms is identified. Title III of the act is Miscellaneous and addresses the definition of the term developmental disabilities for the purposes of the act and recommends that the definition of this term be reviewed annually.

238. **Dewis, M. E., & Thornton, N. G. (1989). Sexual dysfunction in multiple sclerosis.** *Journal of Neuroscience Nursing, 21*(3), 175-179.

This article reviews sexual dysfunction in people with multiple sclerosis. Findings suggest that sexual dysfunction is an early symptom of the disease. Major organic and psychogenic effects of the disease on sexual functioning are discussed. Topics also include associated physical problems and implications for fertility, pregnancy, and birth control. Guidelines for intervention by neuroscience nurses working with these couples are presented.

239. de Young, M. (1982). *The sexual victimization of children.* Jefferson, NC: McFarland & Co.

This book covers a range of topics relevant to child sexual abuse. The author cites other studies along with her own data relevant to the prevalence of handicapping conditions among children who have been sexually abused. The author cites several studies that suggest that daughters with neurological handicaps and a variety of other disabilities are more likely to be victims of incest. The author also notes that mental retardation was a rare finding in her study of pedophile offenders.

240. Diamond, L. J., & Jaudes, P. K. (1983). Child abuse in a cerebral-palsied population. *Developmental Medicine and Child Neurology, 25,* 169-174.

Of children with cerebral palsy seen in one care center over a 12-month period, 17 had been subject to child abuse. Eight of these children's cerebral palsy was a result of abuse. The findings suggest that there is a high incidence of child abuse among children with cerebral palsy. There is a "double indication" for abuse, both as a cause and a result of cerebral palsy.

241. Dickens, B. M. (1982). Retardation and sterilization. *International Journal of Law and Psychiatry, 5*(3/4), 295-318.

This article investigates whether nonconsensual sterilization of persons with mental retardation poses a threat or offers an opportunity. It examines judicial decisions which appear to protect persons who are incompetent against nonconsensual elimination of fundamental reproductive rights and the decisions that view sterilization as a choice that should not be denied solely because persons with mental retardation and who are incompetent cannot express consent.

242. Dickin, K. L., & Ryan, B. A. (1983). Sterilization and the mentally retarded. *Canada's Mental Health, 31*(1), 4-8.

This article examines the legal and moral issues that surround the involuntary sterilization of people with mental retardation. It presents two extreme positions held by mental health and legal professionals: One position believes that sterilization limits the sexuality and parenthood experiences that some persons with mental retardation could otherwise enjoy, and the other position is in favor of legislation that would permit sterilization without personal consent. This article also discusses alternatives to these extreme positions, which include mandatory contraception, segregation by sex,

removal of children born to people with mental retardation, or legislation allowing a third party to give consent for sterilization.

243. Dickman, I. R. (Ed.). (1975). *Sex education and family life for visually handicapped children and youth: A resource guide.* New York: Sex Information and Education Council of the United States and American Foundation for the Blind, Inc.

This book is divided into three sections, with each addressing a crucial aspect of teaching sexuality. Part I covers basic philosophical issues about sex education for people with visual impairments. Part II is a developmental sequence of suggested learning activities and concepts. Part III is an especially helpful resource and information guide, with sections on printed, audiovisual, braille, and large-type materials. Addresses of various agencies, services, and manufacturers are also included.

244. Disabled adult may not be sterilized. (1986). *Mental and Physical Disability Law Reporter, 10*(2), 103-104.

This document discusses a case in which the California Supreme court denied parents the additional powers necessary to have their adult daughter with developmental disabilities sterilized.

245. Disabled women more likely to be battered, survey suggests. (1987, April 1). *Toronto Star,* p. F9.

This newspaper article reports on the finding that women with disabilities are more likely than nondisabled women to be victims of battering and sexual assault, especially when they are young. The report, based on a survey of 62 women by the Ontario Ministry of Community and Social Services, discovered almost half of those women with disabilities had been sexually assaulted as children, compared to 34% for nondisabled. Sixty-seven percent of women with disabilities reported being battered as children, while only 34% of nondisabled women reported abuse during childhood. Thirty-three percent of women with disabilities reported they have been battered during their adult years, mostly by husbands, while only 22% of nondisabled women reported similar abuse. For sexual abuse, the survey found more nondisabled women (31%) reported being sexually assaulted as adults, compared with 23% of women with disabilities.

246. DisAbled Women's Network Toronto. (1987). *Violent acts against disabled women* [Research report]. Toronto: Author.

This report determined the incidence of violent assault against women with disabilities. The study was conducted with 30 participants with disabilities and 32 nondisabled participants. Each of the participants was given a questionnaire to complete. The questionnaire was divided into eight sections: background information, child physical abuse, child sexual abuse, adult physical abuse, adult sexual abuse, medical assault, and a section for comments. Under the section on background, the report collated results on the types of disability, living situation, financial status, and marital status of women with disabilities. Under the other sections, the report collated results of the frequency, duration, and identification of the assailant. The report found that over two thirds of the women with disabilities reported that they had been battered as children. Almost half of the women with disabilities had been sexually abused as children. One-third had been battered as adults. Almost one-quarter had been sexually assaulted during adult-hood. Almost two-thirds had been medically assaulted. Not only is the incidence of violence against women with disabilities extremely high, but the figures also indicate that women with disabilities are more likely to be assaulted or abused than nondisabled women. The only exception to this is in the area of adult sexual assault where about 10% more nondisabled women are assaulted.

247. Distad, L. (1987). A personal legacy. *Phi Delta Kappa, 68*(10), 744-745.
In this article, a remedial classroom reading specialist discusses her view that many children with learning disabilities are victims of child abuse. The need of these children for guidance and guardianship in the classroom is discussed as well as the need for educators and administrators to help assume children's fundamental right to protection.

248. Diverse rulings on disabled offenders. (1987). *Mental and Physical Disability Law Reporter, 11*(3), 169-170.
This paper describes a variety of issues concerned with offenders with mental disabilities, including their dangerousness, sentencing issues, and the use of hearsay evidence: Oregon v. Huntley, 730 P.2d. 1234 (Or. S. Ct. 1986); United States v. Blade, 811 F.2d. 461 (8th Cir. 1987); Pericola v. Florida, 499 So.2d. 864 (Fla. Dist. Ct. App. 1987); and Massachusetts v. Tucker, 502 N.E.2d. 948 (Mass. Ct. App. 1987).

249. Dixon, H. (1988). *Sexuality and mental handicap: An educator's resource book.* **Cambs, England: Learning Development Aids.**
This curriculum guide is intended as an aid to teachers. It provides basic outlines and activities for lessons in sexuality. It includes sections on decision-making and on saying "no."

250. Docherty, J. (1989). *Indicators of abusive residential care facilities.* **Toronto: James Docherty & Associates.**
This author suggests guidelines for reducing abuse in residential care facilities: all clients and their advocates must be fully informed of their rights and how to report alleged abuse; clients must not be restricted from their families and friends; clients must not be restricted from open communication with the outside world; clients should attend school and other community

facilities that are independent of their residential institution; and institutions and other agencies should provide complete cooperation and support for investigations by law enforcement officials and child welfare agencies.

251. Docherty, J. (1989). *Investigating child abuse in residential care settings.* **Toronto: James Docherty & Associates.**
This author suggests several guidelines for investigating child abuse in residential care settings: clear definitions of abuse must be available in each agency; all alleged abuse must be reported, and where any ambiguity exists, the rule must be to report; any person who has knowledge of child abuse should be required to report by law; no protocol or agency policy may be used to restrict individual responsibility for reporting; all reports must be made to Child Welfare or law enforcement agencies (internal reporting within agencies does not substitute for this responsibility); investigation of abuse within an agency should be based on an assumption of the veracity of the allegation until the allegation is proven false; allegations should not be dismissed based solely on assumed motivation to lodge a false report; investigation should collect essential information from the informant at the earliest possible time and maintain written or other permanent records of all information while the investigation is active; assessment of the risk for the victim in the setting should be made immediately, and any necessary steps should be taken to remove the source of risk; the victim may be moved to a safer setting only if this move is clearly in the victim's best interest; the police should be notified and consulted whenever a crime is alleged; investigations should proceed as soon as possible; appropriate measures should be taken to isolate the alleged abuser from the victim; alleged abusers should be informed that any contact with the victim during the course of the investigation shall be considered misconduct; the family or personal advocate of any alleged victim should be notified of the allegation and investigation; police should investigate all allegations of crimes; abuse allegations in institutional settings should be investigated by the police, child welfare agencies, placing agencies, and the institutional administration; protocols should be developed and implemented that clarify the responsibility of the police, child welfare agencies, placing agencies, and the institutional administration in conducting investigations; effective staff supervision should be provided; staff should be provided with opportunities for counseling; the setting should be as open and accessible as possible; client-staff ratios should be reduced; police checks should be used to screen all new employees; clear policies on appropriate and inappropriate client-staff interaction and intimacy should be established; an atmosphere of open discussion of concerns and issues should be created; responsibilities for overnight supervision should be rotated; appropriate staff training should be provided; clear policies for treating problem behavior should be established; ongoing external monitoring, supervision, and, when

required, investigation should be provided; clients should be encouraged to maintain contacts with individuals and agencies outside the institution; and open community involvement should be encouraged.

252. Donovan, A. M. (1988). Family stress and ways of coping with adolescents who have handicaps: Maternal perceptions. *American Journal on Mental Retardation, 92*(6), 502-509.

This study investigates stress in 72 mothers of adolescents with autism or mental retardation. Mothers reported greater family stress if their child was autistic. The contribution of autistic children's limited relational and communication skills to increased family stress is discussed. Child-related stress was found to have a negligible effect on the mothers' marital adjustment.

253. Dorner, S. (1977). Sexual interest and activity in adolescents with spina bifida. *Journal of Child Psychology and Psychiatry and Allied Disciplines, 18,* 229-237.

Sixty-three families with an adolescent with spina bifida were interviewed regarding psychological and social problems. Interview topics included the adolescent's sexual development, interest in the opposite sex, capacity for sexual pleasure, and attitudes toward marriage and parenting. Handicaps were categorized as either mild, moderate, or severe. The authors found that sexual interest was almost universally acknowledged and that programs for group and individual counseling are needed.

254. Doucette, J. (1986). *Violent acts against disabled women.* **Toronto: DAWN (DisAbled Women's Network) Canada.**

This report includes information on sexual and physical violence against women with disabilities based on a study of 30 women with disabilities and 32 nondisabled women. In the group with disabilities, 67% had experienced physical abuse in childhood, compared to 34% in the nondisabled group. Women with disabilities were also more likely to have experienced sexual abuse in childhood. In the group with disabilities, 47% had experienced sexual abuse, compared to 34% in the nondisabled group. Thus, the rate for physical abuse of women with disabilities was 1.97 times higher than for the nondisabled women, and the rate for sexual abuse of women with disabilities was 1.38 times higher than for the nondisabled group.

255. Doucette, J. (1988). *Sexual assault & the disabled woman: Disabled? Sexually assaulted? Need help?* **Toronto: DAWN (DisAbled Women's Network) Canada.**

This author provides straightforward information to women with disabilities who have been sexually assaulted about what to do and how to report a sexual assault. The author includes telephone numbers and hours of police, medical, and counseling services along with information on accessibility relevant to individuals with various disabilities.

256. Downes, M. (1982). Counseling women with developmental disabilities [Special issue: Current feminist issues in psychotherapy]. *Women and Therapy, 1*(3), 101-109.

The focus of this paper is on women with developmental disabilities and their counseling needs. The purpose of this paper is to offer clinicians insight and increased awareness of the counseling needs of women with developmental disabilities. The paper gave the responses of three women with developmental disabilities to a questionnaire. Given the various living situations, intellectual abilities, and emotional stability of the three women, the author concludes from the survey that what these women know and do not know regarding sex reflects the attitudes of the general population (i.e., regarding attitudes about birth control, masturbation, dating, and marriage). It seems to confirm further that which most of the public already knows: Sex is difficult for people to talk about. The message to the helping professional is that the person with a developmental disability is a person first, with the same basic needs for love and acceptance that others have. Their capacity for finding resources to help meet these needs is often limited, and women in this population are at particular risk for exploitation and other related difficulties. Given the appropriate educational and therapeutic environment, a woman with developmental disabilities can live out her sexuality in a physically and emotionally healthy way.

257. Drakes, O. (1984). Spina Bifida and motherhood. *Special Education: Forward Trends, 11*(1), 16-18.

This article discusses two women with spina bifida who gave birth to healthy babies. The article identifies the need for young girls with spina bifida to have counseling about sexual relationships and parenting in order to prepare them for decisions about sexuality and parenting.

258. Dreyer, L., & Haseltine, B. (1987). *The Woodrow Project: A sexual abuse prevention curriculum for the developmentally disabled.* **Fargo, ND: Red Flag Green Flag Resources, Rape and Abuse Crisis Center. (Exceptional Child Education Resources Clearinghouse accession number EC 20 2190)**

This facilitators' manual is used in conjunction with a videotape and presents a comprehensive guide to organizing and implementing a sexual abuse prevention curriculum for use with people with developmental disabilities. The target groups include young adults, ages 15 to 25 years old, with an IQ range of 40-70. The authors suggest that the curriculum might also be effectively used with people whose IQ falls in the 70-80 range and possibly with children as young as 10 years of age. The curriculum is divided into eight sections and emphasizes reinforcement, small group instruction, and role-playing. Appendices include a sample letter to parents and outlines for meetings with teachers and parents. (Copies of this manual are available from Red Flag Green Flag Resources.)

259. Drouet, M., & Rouyer, M. (1986). *L'enfant violenté; des mauvais traitements à l'inceste [Children who suffer violence: From mistreatment to incest].* **Paris: Le Centurion.**
This book consists of two chapters: The first chapter addresses the different forms of child abuse, while the second chapter focuses on incest. The discussion of incest focuses on the origins and profile of the incestuous family. Incest is defined as any relationship of a sexual nature between a child and an adult having a parental role toward the child. The consequences of incest are presented as well as the various forms of treatment. (This book is available in French only.)

260. Drummond, H. P. (1987). *Sex offenses: Medical and psychological subject analysis with bibliography.* **Washington, DC: Abbe Publishers.**
This bibliography is comprised of 287 articles dealing with a wide range of sexual offenses. The titles are numbered and can be located with the use of a subject index that is keyed on the most important or unique word in the title. Sample topics include treatment, theory, detection, the physician's role, child abuse, and paraphilias. Particular attention has been given to the detection of sexually transmitted diseases in children. Only one title addresses sexual abuse of people with disabilities: in this case, an adolescent with mental retardation.

261. Dubé, R., Heger, B., Johnson, E., & Hébert, M. (1988). *Child sexual abuse prevention: A guide to prevention programs and resources.* **Montréal: Services des Publications.**
This publication offers a short discussion on the nature of child sexual abuse and its prevention in the general population. This discussion is followed by an overview of 59 prevention programs operating in Canada. The programs are listed according to province, and information on the client target group, the format type (curriculum versus conference), the language (English or French), a short one-paragraph description of the program, and an address including the name of a contact person is presented. Target-group categories include preschoolers, 5-12 year olds, adolescents, parents, teachers, and a "others" category. None of the programs deals specifically with people with disabilities. In a separate section, audiovisual materials and books are described in a similar fashion. Distributors are listed. Also included are a short annotated bibliography and a short description of the findings of studies evaluating sexual abuse prevention programs.

262. Duncan, D., & Canty-Lemke, J. (1986). **Learning appropriate social and sexual behavior: The role of society.** *Exceptional Parent, 16(3),* 24-26.
The authors argue that just as society must provide people with mental retardation with appropriate feedback as to whether social behavior is acceptable or not, people with mental retardation need direction in sexual behavior. People with mental retardation need to learn to distinguish between public and private behaviors. Since this group frequently is required to engage in familiar activities (e.g., hugging) with relative strangers, they also require information about who is a stranger and who is a friend.

263. Dunn, M. (1983). **Sexual questions and comments on a spinal cord injury service.** *Sexuality and Disability, 6(3/4),* 126-134.
This article discusses the results of a preliminary survey in which psychologists, social workers, and nurses working in spinal cord injury settings identified which sexual interaction situations with patients cause them the highest levels of discomfort (e.g., a sexual advance by a patient). For certain items, staff also rated their ability to deal with the situation. Interrelationships between the various ratings and demographic variables and professional disciplines are discussed. The author proposes that the areas identified be further researched with the aim of developing staff sex education courses.

264. Dupras, A. (1982). Sexualité et déficiences mentales: L'opinion des bénéficiaires [Sexuality and mental deficiency: The beneficiaries' opinions]. *Genitif, 4(9),* 3-8.
This article discusses interviews conducted with five females and three males with mental retardation, 19-32 years old, living in the community, in order to uncover their attitudes toward sexuality. This study found that the subjects were dissatisfied with their sexual education and were apprehensive about romantic and sexual relationships. The author also discusses ethical and clinical problems with birth control among people with mental retardation.

265. Dupras, A., Lévy, J. J. et. al. (1984). *Sexualité et difficulté d'adaptation: Actes du symposium tenu à Montréal. Les 15, 16, et 17 Octobre, 1982 [Sexuality and difficulty in adaptation: Proceedings from a symposium held in Montréal, October 15,16, and 17, 1982].* **Longueuil, Québec: Editions IRIS, Institut de recherches et d'informations sexologiques, Inc.**
The first part of this book consists of summaries of opinion polls on the sexuality of people who have adaptation problems. Several authors participated in editing this volume, and each author addresses one aspect of sexuality in people with handicaps. Major topics include the sterilization of people with mental handicaps and their experiences of sexuality. Practical aspects of sex education among people with physical handicaps are presented. (This book is available in French only.)

266. Dupras, A., Lévy, J. J., & Samson, J. M. (1984). **Les attitudes des Québecois et Québecoises a l'égard de la sexualité des jeunes personnes en difficulte d'adaptation [Attitudes of the Québecois with regard to young persons with**

adjustment difficulties]. *Apprentissage et Socialisation, 7*(2), 118-126.

This article discusses a survey of a representative sample of the citizens of Quebec done during the summer of 1982 in order to discover their attitudes concerning the sexuality of people with adjustment difficulties. The survey found that the highest rate of acceptance concerned sexual expression among people with physical handicaps, was somewhat lower for young delinquents, and was lowest for people with mental retardation. It also found that sexual conservatism, sexism, and racism were correlated with attitudes concerning the sexuality of persons with adjustment problems. The authors suggest that any attempt to establish recognition of the sexual rights of these individuals must include public education.

267. **Dupras, A., Lévy, J. J., & Tremblay, R. (Eds.). (1978).** *Education sexuelle des personnes en difficulté d'adaptation [Sex education of people experiencing difficulty in adaptation].* **Montréal: Conseil du Québec de l'enfance exceptionnelle.**

This monograph consists of documents written by various people with an interest in the sexuality of people with handicaps. The first part of the book is composed of theoretical essays that address, among other topics, the development of the sexuality of people with intellectual impairments as well as the issue of the control of reproduction. The second part consists of empirical research, while the third section focuses on the practical aspects of sex education. The discussion on sex education is geared as much to people with mental handicaps as to people with physical handicaps. The personal accounts of people with handicaps are presented and recommendations are offered. (This monograph is available in French only.)

268. **Dupre la Tour, M. (1982). Interrogation sur la demande d'information sexuelle de certain groupes d'adolescents à retard scolaire [Sexual education for learning-disabled students].** *Genitif, 4*(8), 18-21.

This author claims that providing sex education to students with learning disabilities contains three inherent challenges: the presentation of information in a manner that is comprehensible to the student, the provision of sufficient information for students' future protection, and the teacher's maintenance of an attitude of confidence and friendliness so that students will call on family planning professionals when future needs arise.

269. **Dykes, L. J. (1986). The Whiplash Shaken Infant syndrome: What has been learned?** *Child Abuse & Neglect, 10*(2), 211-221.

The article reviews the literature on Whiplash Shaken Infant syndrome. Findings indicate that many studies focus on the use of CAT scans in the diagnosis of head injury in infants. The author notes that Caffey's 1974 recommendations that the ocular fundi in all babies be examined regularly and that a public educational program on the hazards of shaking infants be implemented have not yet been carried out.

•E•

270. **Edmonson, B., McCombs, K., & Wish, J. (1979). What retarded adults believe about sex.** *American Journal of Mental Deficiency, 84*(1), 11-18.

The Socio-Sexual Knowledge and Attitudes Test was administered to two groups of males and females with mental handicaps, those institutionalized and those in the community. The results indicate that knowledge scores were related to the respondents' gender and place of residence and reflected differences in experiences, instruction, and interest. Institutionalized women had the highest scores on dating, marriage, intercourse, menstruation, and birth control, but they had the lowest scores on intimacy, homosexuality, and community risks and hazards. Institutionalized men had the lowest scores on seven categories and the highest on none. Community women scored higher than the other groups on intimacy, community risks, and venereal disease and lowest on intercourse and masturbation. Community men scored highest on anatomy, masturbation, homosexuality, and alcohol and drugs and scored the lowest on marriage, menstruation, and birth control. The authors state that in view of the sexual stimuli from television, magazines, peers, and neighbors trying to preserve the naivete of people with handicaps is unrealistic. The data from the study indicate that people with handicaps can acquire facts and attitudes that make up responsible behavior but that most respondents were poorly prepared for such knowledge.

271. **Edwards, J. P. (1976).** *Sara and Allen: The right to choose.* **Portland, OR: Ednick Communications.**

This short book is geared toward parents of children with mental retardation who wish to address the social-sexual needs of their children. Topics include moral-ethical concerns, socialization, masturbation, sublimation, pornography, exhibitionism, homosexuality, menstruation, wet dreams, sterilization, contraception, marriage, and parenthood.

272. **Edwards, J. P., & Elkins, T. E. (1988).** *Just between us: A social sexual guide for parents and professionals with concerns for persons with developmental disabilities.* **Portland, OR: Ednick Communications.**

This book provides guidance for parents and

professionals in discussing social-sexual needs with children with mental retardation or developmental disabilities. Topics include socialization, normalization, dignity, morality and ethics, menstruation, pelvic exams, parental concerns (e.g., masturbation, homosexuality, pornography, exhibitionism, sublimation, voyeurism), building self-esteem, sterilization, contraception, marriage and parenthood, and how to avoid sexual exploitation. Lists of resource materials and references are included as well as an example of a group home board of directors' policy statement regarding social-sexual issues.

273. **Edwards, J., Wapnick, S., Mock, P., & Whitson, L. (1982).** *Feeling free...A social/sexual training guide for those who work with the hearing and visually impaired.* **Portland, OR: Ednick Communications.**
This guide is written for a wide variety of people working with people with sensory impairments. It can be used with people with severe handicaps or individuals with mild handicaps. It was field tested in classrooms with children ages 6-12, ages 12-20, and in workshops and group homes for young adults ages 18-36. The guide focuses on teaching responsible decision-making. Topics include administration, working with parents, class size, and so forth. Part III focuses on curriculum preparations and includes assessment tools, materials for working with parents, curriculum examples, and lesson plans. The appendices list resource materials for classroom instruction, audiovisual resources, and a short bibliography.

274. **Egeland, B. (1985). The consequences of physical and emotional neglect on the development of young children. In** *Child Neglect Monograph: Proceedings from a Symposium, November 10, 1985* **(pp. 7-19). Washington, DC: Clearinghouse on Child Abuse and Neglect Information.**
This paper discusses the impact of neglect on childhood development. Using data from the Minnesota Mother-Child Project, the author found the following: Of the 24 families identified as neglecting, all the neglected children suffered from severe developmental consequences. As the assessments accrued from infancy through kindergarten, these children's performance was seen to deteriorate.

275. **Egley, L. C. (1982). Domestic abuse and deaf people: One community's approach.** *Victimology, 7(1-4),* **24-34.**
This article describes the activities of a task force in Minneapolis-St. Paul which provides services for domestic abuse victims with hearing impairments. It discusses some unique barriers to individuals with hearing impairments seeking help, such as the lack of emergency services with 24-hour telecommunication devices for people who are deaf and a lack of community acceptance of these population. The author states that it is essential for people who are deaf and organizations

involved with this population to take the lead in creating domestic violence services that meet their needs.

276. **Eisen, P. (1986). Adolescence: Coping strategies and vulnerabilites: Seminar on Psychiatric Vulnerability in Adolescence (1984, Newcastle, Australia).** *International Journal of Adolescent Medicine and Health, 2(2),* **107-117.**
This article discusses adolescent coping strategies and vulnerability using a developmental framework that examines biological, psychological, and social growth and maturation. The author identifies coping strategies and factors that may increase vulnerability to psychiatric disorders, including developmental disabilities, abuse, and socioeconomic deprivation.

277. **Elder, B. P. (1983). Rehabilitation: The double bind for blind women.** *Journal of Visual Impairment and Blindness, 77(6),* **298-300.**
This article discusses the rehabilitation process in relation to women who are blind. The need for sexuality counseling is discussed.

278. **Eldredge, E., Chadwick, D. L., & Kerns, D. L. (1985). Model program: California. In V. L. Vivian (Ed.),** *Child abuse and neglect: A medical community response* **(pp. 209-221). Chicago: American Medical Association.**
These authors note that professional standards are required for evidentiary examination of physically and sexually abused children, post-mortem examination of children who may have been abused, investigation of sexual abuse, preparation of abuse cases for court action, relative value of various treatments and services, and the conduct and decision-making of judges. They suggest that law reform should allow a modification of the requirements for presenting evidence, allowing videotape and the use of special interviewers, should reconcile the statutory requirements to report and maintain confidentiality, should forbid the publication of the names of victims of sexual abuse, and should provide independent legal counsel for all children under state guardianship. They conclude that evidentiary examinations should be government funded, that programs to increase public consciousness of abuse are required, and that funding for research should be increased.

279. **Elgar, S. (1985). Sex education and sexual awareness building for autistic children and youth: Some viewpoints and considerations.** *Journal of Autism and Developmental Disorders, 15(2),* **214-216.**
This article investigates the feasibility, appropriateness, and ramifications of providing sex education to individuals with autism. The author points out that sex education must be individually oriented and related to levels of ability, understanding, and social maturity and that explicit training for most persons with autism

would be meaningless and, for some of these individuals, confusing and a possible instigator of socially unacceptable behaviors that would not be easily corrected. Consequently, the author states that providing knowledge necessary to complete an act of sexual intercourse without stressing the significance of the act is irresponsible and that intercourse in this context would not help individuals with mental handicaps with their emotional and social problems. The author concludes that sex education would not be appropriate for or in the best interests of the majority of people with autism.

280. Elias, S. F., & Sigelman, C. K. (1980). Interview behavior of and impressions made by mentally retarded adults. *American Journal of Mental Deficiency, 85*(1), 53-60.
In this study, 38 institutionalized adults with mental impairments were interviewed in order to identify verbal and nonverbal behaviors that create positive or negative impressions on others. Participants were videotaped. Ratings of these videotapes reveal that participants whose verbal speech was understandable were more likely to make positive impressions.

281. Elias-Burger, S. F., Sigelman, C. K., & Danley, W. E. (1981). Teaching interview skills to mentally retarded persons. *American Journal of Mental Deficiency, 85*(6), 655-657.
In this study, 88 institutionalized adults with mental retardation were interviewed with the goal of identifying verbal and nonverbal behaviors that create positive or negative impressions on others. Participants were videotaped. Ratings of the videotapes reveal that participants whose verbal speech was understandable were more likely to make positive impressions.

282. Elkins, T. E., Gafford, L. S., Wilks, C. S., Muram, D., & Golden, G. (1986). A model clinic approach to the reproductive health concerns of the mentally handicapped. *Obstetrics & Gynecology, 68*(2), 185-188.
This article describes an interdisciplinary model clinic approach to the reproductive health and sexuality concerns of a noninstitutionalized population with mental handicaps. It discusses some of the common concerns of this population and examines a program for menstrual hygiene control developed using a combination of hormonal medication and home-based behavior modification training. The authors also examine the use of group sexuality counseling for both patients and their families for enhancing the avoidance of sexual abuse, the understanding of sexual development, and intrafamily communication.

283. Elkins, T., Spinnato, J., & Muram, D. (1987). Sexuality and family interaction in Down syndrome: Parental responses. *Journal of Psychosomatic Obstetrics and Gynaecology, 6*(2), 81-88.
This article describes an attitude survey concerning

sexuality, contraception, and sterilization in people with mental handicaps conducted with 92 parents of individuals with Down syndrome. Findings of this study include 19% of the parents agree that parents should make decisions about treatment of newborns with Down syndrome, 40% of parents want the sole right to authorize sterilization for their family member with Down syndrome, 19% want legal authorization from a court to sterilize a person with Down syndrome, 85% desire legal protection for newborns with handicaps, 10% think all persons with Down syndrome should be sterilized, and 77% desire some form of birth control for their children.

284. Elliott, F. A. (1982). Biological contributions to family violence. In J. C. Hansen & L. R. Barnhill (Eds.), *Clinical approaches to family violence* (pp. 35-58). Rockville, MD: Aspen Systems.
Neurological examinations were given to 286 adult patients with a history of repeated intrafamilial violence. Examinations were directed at uncovering evidence of temporal lobe seizures and minimal brain dysfunction syndrome. Organic deficits were found in 94% of this nonrandom sample. The contribution of biological factors to abusive behavior is discussed (e.g., syndrome of explosive rage). The need for further research using a random sample of abusers is stressed.

285. Elliott, M. (1985). *Preventing child sexual assault: A practical guide to talking with children.* London: Bedford Square Press.
This book is designed for parents and teachers. It provides suggestions on how to prepare children to prevent sexual abuse. It stresses the importance of physical abilities to resist or run away and communication skills to report events to appropriate authority figures. The implications for children unable to carry out these functions are not discussed. This book also fails to address sexual abuse and assault by parents or teachers, which appears to occur much more frequently than offenses by strangers.

286. Ellis, J. W. (1990). Criminal justice system: News and notes. *American Association on Mental Retardation, 3*(2), 3.
This article discusses the treatment and mistreatment of people with mental retardation by the criminal justice system. The author discusses his request to amend a proposed bill requiring the American Attorney General to gather statistics on hate-crimes aimed at minorities. He requests that people with physical or mental disabilities be added to the list of minorities studied and cites the example of keeping statistics on fire-bombings of group homes.

287. Ellis, J. W., & Luckasson, R. A. (1987). *Testimony of American Association on Mental Deficiency and Association for Retarded Citizens of the United States to the United States Sentencing Commission.* Washington,

DC: American Association on Mental Retardation.

This 42-page document contains excerpts from testimony before the United States Sentencing Commission. The authors address criminal issues related to both offenders and victims with mental disabilities. They suggest that sentences be increased for offenders whose victims are mentally disabled if the situation involves one or both of the following: 1) the victim's vulnerability due to disability was exploited, or 2) the offender was in a position of authority in relation to the victim. They also suggest that sentences be decreased for offenders with mental disabilities since their abilities to understand the consequences of their actions may be impaired.

288. Ellis, M. (1988). *Surviving procedures after a sexual assault* (3rd ed.). Vancouver, B.C: Press Gang.

This book is a practical guide for women victims of sexual assault and the procedure that they may follow after an assault has occurred. The book does not deal specifically with people with handicaps; however, it would be of value to anyone who is not knowledgeable about the court system, including people with disabilities, their caregivers, and advocates. It explains the choices and the process of the police and court system after a sexual assault. This 3rd edition incorporates the 1988 amendments to the Canadian Criminal Code.

289. Ellison, P. H., Tsai, F. Y., & Largent, J. A. (1978). Computed tomography in child abuse and cerebral contusion. *Pediatrics, 62*(2), 151-154.

In this 1978 article, the use of computer tomography (CAT scan) is suggested as a means to diagnose child abuse. The authors suggest that a high index of suspicion of abuse warrants the use of this test.

290. Elmer, E., & Gregg, G. S. (1967). Developmental characteristics of abused children. *Pediatrics, 40*(4, Pt. I), 596-602.

A group of 50 children admitted to hospitals for injuries due to physical abuse were evaluated years later regarding their development. Of the original 50 children, five could not be studied because they had been admitted to institutions for people with mental retardation. It could not be determined whether their severe mental retardation preceded or followed their injuries as the developmental level of the children was not systematically evaluated at the time of admission to hospital. Overall, the reevaluation showed that 50% of the children now were classified as having mental retardation; however, due to the absence of information gathering on admission to the hospital, it was not possible to state whether the intellectual impairment occurred due to abuse or precipitated the abuse. In either case, the authors predicted that due to their impairments one-quarter of these children will become wards of the state and several others may only be able to remain in the community if kept in a sheltered environment.

291. Elonen, A. S., & Zwarensteyn, S. B. (1975). Sexual trauma in young blind children. *New Outlook for the Blind, 69*, 440-442.

This article focuses on sexual abuse of children who are blind. Records of children who are severely disturbed and blind and who were referred for psychological and psychiatric counseling reveal that this sample suffered a broad range of sexually traumatic experiences. Topics discussed by the authors include age-inappropriate fondling of maturing children by adults, the child's restricted ability to detect cues regarding socially appropriate behavior, and the children's reactions, ranging from mild pleasure to psychotic breakdown. The authors also discuss how the gross psychiatric pathology following abnormal sexual experience can be prevented by alleviating isolation through social stimulation, physical activity, and emotional enrichment.

292. Embry, L. H. (1980). Family support for handicapped preschool children at risk for abuse. *New Directions for Exceptional Children, 4*, 29-57.

This author states that "young handicapped children and their families are at much greater risk for severe family dysfunction, which may exhibit itself in its most extreme form, child abuse." The increased stress on the family with a handicapped preschool child appears to be due to the interactive effects of dealing with a child who lacks the behaviors that normal children use to elicit caregiving and attention, to unappealing behaviors, to the social isolation of the family, and to a developmental history that may disrupt the maternal attachment process. Consequently, the task of intervention becomes more sophisticated, and the risks of nonintervention become more serious. Although much data has been accumulated on sociological, psychological, and personality variables of the family at risk for abuse, there is much less that can be used to develop intervention strategies that will be successful in improving family relationships. Therefore, the next steps needed are the examination of family interaction patterns from a perspective of which factors impede or enhance the development of successful family relationships and the development of assessment and intervention strategies for individual families that are tailored to their needs.

293. Ende, A. (1983). Children in history: A personal review of the past decade's published research. *Journal of Psychohistory, 11*, 65-88.

This article reviews the historical literature dealing with children, particularly works concerned with European families and children, and it discusses topics which include infanticide, sexism, child abuse, mental and physical handicaps, infant mortality, and sexual abuse. The author claims that parental care is an expression and not a cause of childcare, and in order to change childcare, the questions of why parents are and are not able to develop caring qualities must be explored.

294. Endicott, O. (1986). Does litigation make a difference? *Entourage, 1*(4), 12-15.
This article provides a discussion of the role of litigation in securing the rights of people with disabilities and focuses on the specific litigation actions of the Canadian Association for Community Living. A review of cases indicates that the second most common issue was assault against people with disabilities (the most common issue was the right to an appropriate education). The author suggests that these cases have had important effects that go beyond the individuals directly involved.

295. Endicott, O. (1987). All about "Eve." *Entourage, 2*(1), 21-24.
This article gives a brief description of the findings of the Supreme Court of Canada in Re: Eve, and it discusses implications of this ruling. The decision generally affirmed the right of an individual, regardless of developmental disability, to make her own decision not to have a nontherapeutic sterilization. The court found that a substituted consent was not appropriate.

296. Endicott, O. (1987). To tell the truth. *Entourage, 2*(2), 23-25.
This author claims that Canadians with handicaps and intellectual impairments have been denied equal protection under criminal law, which is specifically provided for under the Canadian Charter of Rights and Freedoms. The author notes that there is a bill (Bill C-15) before Parliament that may remove the barrier and admit the testimony of persons with mental handicaps. The author maintains that this reform is overdue. (Note: Although reforms to the Canada Evidence Act did allow some flexibility in how the evidence of children could be introduced in court, these changes have not been extended to adults with disabilities.)

297. Engman, K. (1989, May 26). Law keeps disabled from testifying. *Edmonton Journal,* p. B7.
This newspaper article discusses a Canadian conference on sexual assault and abuse of people with disabilities. It focuses on the drafting of a petition that would allow fuller participation of victims with disabilities in court proceedings. This is viewed as providing more equal protection for people with disabilities.

298. Engman, K. (1989, May 26). Mentally disabled fall through gaps in act. *Edmonton Journal,* p. B7.
This newspaper article points out that although Canadian law now makes special provision for children to act as witnesses in cases of child sexual abuse these provisions are unavailable to adults with cognitive or communication deficits.

299. Enos, W. F., Conrath, T. B., & Byer, J. C. (1986). Forensic evaluation of the sexually abused child. *Pediatrics, 78*(3), 385-398.
Results of a forensic study of 162 cases of sexual abuse are presented along with a protocol for forensic examination. Victims were 82.1% female. Alleged incest accounted for 21.9% of female and 3.3% of male cases.

300. Eppler, M., & Brown, G. (1977). Child abuse and neglect: Preventable causes of mental retardation. *Child Abuse & Neglect, 1,* 309-313.
In this retrospective case study analysis of 436 documented cases of mental retardation seen between 1957 and 1977, 65 of the cases showed evidence of abuse and neglect prior to the diagnosis of mental retardation. Higher rates of abuse and neglect were found among Aleuts, Inuits, and Natives than among Caucasians. The authors conclude that child abuse is a preventable cause of mental retardation.

301. Evans, A. L., & McKinlay, I. A. (1988). Sexual maturation in girls with severe mental handicap. *Child Care, Health and Development, 14*(1), 59-69.
This article discusses a study that investigated the mean age of menarche in 153 girls with severe mental handicaps (ranging in age from 8 years to 19 years 10 months), including 44 girls with Down syndrome. The study found that menarche occurred about 11 months earlier in the Down syndrome girls and about 21 months later in girls without Down syndrome than in the general population (mean age 13.02 years). The authors also discuss the implications for sex education.

302. Evans, A. L., & McKinlay, I. A. (1989). Sex education and the severely mentally retarded child. *Developmental Medicine and Child Neurology, 31*(1), 98-103.
This article provides an overview of sex education for children and adolescents with disabilities. The authors found that menstrual hygiene and inappropriate masturbation are among the most commonly covered topics in sex education for these populations. They note that the crisis-oriented approach still prevails over encouraging adolescents with disabilities to understand themselves and their social relationships.

303. Evans, J. (1985). Performance and attitudes of occupational therapists regarding sexual habilitation of pediatric patients. *American Journal of Occupational Therapy, 39*(10), 664-670.
Seventy registered occupational therapists responded to a questionnaire measuring attitudes toward sexual habilitation and task performance related to the sexual development of children with disabilities. Positive attitudes did not correlate with the reported low rates of actual task performance. Therapists educated in sexual habilitation and rehabilitation performed significantly more tasks than those without the benefit of such education.

304. Evans, J., & Conine, T. (1985). Sexual habilitation of youngsters with chronic illness

or disabling conditions. *Journal of Allied Health, 14*(1), 79-87.

This article describes a model for identifying impediments to the development of healthy sexuality and provides interventions for overcoming these impediments. This article also raises and answers questions of who is responsible for incorporating sexual habilitation into treatment and when intervention should begin, and it discusses the potential problem of securing parental cooperation.

•**F**•

305. Fantuzzo, J. W., Wray, L., Hall, R., Goins, C., & Azar, S. (1986). Parent and social-skills training for mentally retarded mothers identified as child maltreaters. *American Journal of Mental Deficiency, 91*(2), 135-140.

This article examines the effectiveness and generality of a parent- and social-skills training program for three Black mothers with mild mental retardation (IQs 60, 57, 54) identified as child maltreaters. The program was conducted by one trainer in a community-based facility and, using a simple board game, dealt with: a) individualized performance standards, b) response-specific feedback, c) self-monitoring, and d) group rewards. The training was evaluated using a multiple-baseline design across parenting- and social-skill areas. Response maintenance was assessed using pre- and post-generalization tests in the home setting and a follow-up probe in the treatment setting. Findings of this investigation show that the game effectively increased these mothers' ability to identify the most effective action to take in common problematic parenting and social situations.

306. Father convicted of molesting deaf daughter. (1984). *Mental and Physical Disability Law Reporter, 8*(5), 477-478.

This discussion discribes the case California v. Younghanz, 202 Cal. Rptr. 907 (Cal. Ct. App. 1984), a case in which a man was convicted of child molestation against his daughter who is deaf and has borderline mental retardation. A California appeals court upheld the constitutionality of the mandatory disclosure requirement of the state of California's Child Abuse Reporting Act. The father had self-disclosed to a student counselor working at a clinic regarding his sexual activity with his daughter. The clinic's director informed him of the law regarding the mandatory reporting of child abuse. The father continued to seek treatment regarding his sexual abuse of his daughter and was reported. The father claimed that the Child Abuse Reporting Act interfered with his right to seek

treatment. The court rejected this claim and the claim that the father had been denied his right to confront an opposing witness, his daughter, because of the "inherent unreliability of the sign language method used at trial." The court also rejected the claim that the court's failure to videotape the victim's sign language testimony deprived him of a complete record for consideration on appeal. The court held that he did not allege any errors in translation, that he was fluent in sign language, and that he testified that he understood his daughter.

307. *Federal assistance to states to prevent the abuse of children in child care facilities.* (1985). Hearings before the Subcommittee on Juvenile Justice of the Committee on the Judiciary. United States Senate, 98th Congress, Second Session (April 11 and September 18, 1984). Washington, DC: Congress of the U. S., Senate Committee on the Judiciary. (ERIC Document Reproduction Service No. ED 274 412)

This 197-page report is comprised of the text from congressional hearings on the proposed American Senate Bills S. 521 and S. 1924. Bill S. 521 is designed to protect institutionalized children from abuse. Bill S. 1924 allows the creation of a central federal file of sexual assaults and child molesting arrests and convictions. The possibility of using the federal file in screening applicants wishing to work with children is discussed. Testimony was obtained from politicians, district attorneys, directors of clinics and child care centers, members of professional associations, and parents. Also included are materials related to the proposed Bills and other pertinent materials.

308. Federal Bureau of Investigation and Metro-Dade Police Department. (1983). *Proceedings: Forensic Science Symposium on the Analysis of Sexual Assault Evidence.* Quantico, VA: Forensic Science Research and Training Center, Laboratory Division, FBI Academy.

These conference proceedings include 10 lectures, 24 short presentation abstracts, summaries of three workshops, two panel presentations, and two special presentations. The presentations cover a variety of topics. While they discuss many of the limitations of physical evidence, they suggest that a well-developed scientific body of knowledge can provide powerful evidence of sexual abuse, especially when a victim is unable to fully communicate or when a victim's testimony is doubted. Information included in these proceedings points toward the importance of forensic examination immediately after incidents of suspected sexual abuse.

309. Feinmann, J. (1988). Corridors of fear. *Nursing Times, 84*(39), 16-17.

This article discusses women's claims of sexual harassment, rape, and abduction in psychiatric institutions. The focus of the article in on patient-patient abuse. Possible solutions are discussed.

310. **Feutl, R. (1987, April 27). Sex education is for everyone.** *The Edmonton Sun*, p. 22.
This article is the last of a two-part series on the problems with sexuality faced by people with mental handicaps. The article deals with teaching this population about sex and their right not to be abused.

311. **Fidone, G. S. (1987). Homosexuality in institutionalized retardates [Letter to the editor].** *Infection Control, 8*(6), 231.
In this letter, the director of a department of mental health and mental retardation discusses the prevalence of biological markers of hepatitis B and AIDS among institutionalized people with mental retardation and the prevalence of homosexual behavior in this group. The author discusses findings that suggest that a significant portion of ambulatory adolescent and adult males with mental retardation returning to the community constitute another small subgroup at increased risk of sexually transmitted disease. In the case of homosexually active hepatitis B carriers, pertinent information could be confidentially transmitted to local health professionals, thereby protecting the recipient, schools, and communities. Also, upon readmission to an institution, repeat antibody screening would serve to detect new cases of infection and protect other clients in the institution. The author also discusses possible parallels between patterns of homosexual behavior in this population and in prisoners. The author suggests that the prevalence of homosexual behavior and of sexually transmitted diseases in institutionalized people with mental retardation should be studied using a broad database.

312. **Fifield, B. B. (1984-86). Ethical issues related to sexual abuse of disabled persons.** *Sexuality and Disability, 7*(3/4), 102-109.
This author focuses on ethical issues for health professionals and, in particular, on how ethical standards may be applied when one is confronted with situations involving sexual abuse of persons with disabilities.

313. **Fine, M. J. (1986). Intervening with abusing parents of handicapped children.** *Techniques, 2*(4), 353-363.
This article discusses a systems-ecological orientation for understanding and intervening with abusive families. As abuse of a child with handicaps is viewed as a dysfunction within the family, it is suggested that intervention be focused on the family. The author uses an example of a child with mild handicaps and his family to illustrate the dynamics of abuse and proposes a multilevel intervention model that integrates intervention at the levels of information input, belief/attitude change, skill acquisition, and behavior change. The author also stresses the need for ongoing family support and a sympathetic view of the parents.

314. **Finkel, P., Fishwick, M., Nessel, K. L., & Solz, D. (1981). Sexuality and attendant care: A panel discussion.** In D. G. Bullard & S. E. Knight (Eds.), *Sexuality and physical disability: Personal perspectives* (pp. 111-123). St. Louis: C.V. Mosby.
This chapter provides personal perspectives on the intimacy of relationships between personal care attendants and the people for whom they provide care. The ambiguity of roles created by supposed physical detachment and close personal contact often creates problems. Some people who require personal care attendants establish overt sexual relationships with their caregivers that may be rewarding for both parties, but the level of dependence of one partner on the other for care creates potential power inequalities that may threaten the relationship.

315. **Finkelhor, D. (1984).** *Child sexual abuse.* New York: Free Press.
This author proposes the following Four Preconditions Model of Sexual Abuse: 1) a potential offender had some motivation to abuse a child sexually, 2) the potential offender had to overcome internal inhibitions against acting on the motivation, 3) the potential offender had to overcome external impediments to committing sexual abuse, and 4) the potential offender or some other factor had to undermine or overcome a child's possible resistance to the sexual abuse. With regard to precondition three, factors predisposing to overcoming external inhibitors include a mother who is not close to the child, social isolation of family, or unusual opportunities to be alone with the child. Factors predisposed to overcoming a child's resistance (precondition four) include a child who is emotionally deprived, a child who lacks knowledge about sexual abuse, a situation of unusual trust between child and offender, and coercion. All of the above predisposing factors are applicable to children with handicaps, although the author does not specifically make this connection. He does, however, point out in his suggestions for further research that physical or emotional handicaps may compromise the child's ability to avoid abuse.

316. **Finkelhor, D. (1986). The prevention of child sexual abuse: An overview of needs and problems.** In B. Schlesinger (Ed.), *Sexual abuse of children in the 1980's: Ten essays and an annotated bibliography* (pp. 16-29). Toronto: University of Toronto Press.
In the 1980s, dozens of child sexual abuse educational prevention programs have appeared. This article discusses the need for such programs based on two factors: 1) the percentage of all children likely to suffer abuse, and 2) the likelihood that those who are abused will not receive treatment. The prevention programs have been directed at a very broad spectrum of children based on the realization that boys are victimized as well as girls, children are victimized at an early age, and children with handicaps are also victimized. Some prevention education has been aimed at parents. The author discusses some of the problems that have arisen with parents as educators. The article also discusses the common concepts that are in the prevention programs.

317. Finkelhor, D., & Baron, L. (1986). Risk factors for child sexual abuse. *Journal of Interpersonal Violence, 1*(1), 43-71.

This article reviews a number of surveys that examine the relative risk of persons from various backgrounds who have experienced sexual abuse during childhood. Although differences according to social class or race have not been found, community studies show that a child has a higher risk for abuse under the following conditions: a) the child lives without one of the biological parents, b) the mother is unavailable to the child as a result of employment, disability, or illness, c) the parents' marriage is unhappy and full of conflict, d) the child has a poor relationship with the parents or is subject to extremely punitive discipline or child abuse, and e) the child has a stepfather. The authors discuss the implications of these findings and recommend ways to improve subsequent studies of risk factors. (Note: There is little available information to determine if any of the factors described in this article may be more common among families with children with disabilities.)

318. Finkelhor, D. et al. (1988). *Sexual abuse in day care: A national study. Executive summary.* **Durham, NH: New Hampshire University, Family Research Lab. (ERIC Document Reproduction Service No. ED 292 552)**

This 18-page summary describes a study aimed at identifying and analyzing all cases of sexual abuse occurring in day care settings reported in the United States between January, 1983 and December, 1985. Findings address incidence, perpetrators, victims, disclosure, risk factors, dynamics, impact on the child, and the experiences of investigators and prosecutors. The authors offer general recommendations on how to respond to sexual abuse of children as well as specific recommendations regarding prevention, detection, investigation, and intervention. Abusers in the day care setting were not found to conform to prevalent stereotypes about people who sexually abuse.

319. Fischer, H. L., & Krajicek, M. J. (1974). Sexual development of the moderately retarded child: Level of information and parental attitudes. *Mental Retardation, 12*(3), 28-30.

A group of children with moderate mental retardation (10 to 17 years of age) were interviewed about their knowledge of sexual matters. The parents of the children observed the interview from behind a one-way mirror. The parents were then asked to fill out a questionnaire. Results show that all children had no problem in distinguishing males and females, but they did have greater inability to name sexual body parts. When viewing pictures of people hugging, kissing, and engaging in intercourse, the vast majority of children gave accurate answers as to what the pictures showed; however, when asked to explain why people engage in such behaviors, fewer children gave accurate responses. The results from the parents' questionnaire show that the number one concern of the parents of both boys and girls was that their child might be taken advantage of

sexually. The authors conclude that parents must take the initiative in raising the issue of sexuality with their children as the opportunities to do so exist during bathing and toileting, while watching love scenes on television, or when pregnant females are observed.

320. Fischer, H. L., Krajicek, M. J., & Borthick, W. A. (1973). *Sex education for the developmentally disabled: A guide for parents, teachers, and professionals.* **Baltimore: University Park Press.**

This book gives a very brief introduction to sex education for people with developmental disabilities. A structured interview with line drawings of various sexual concepts, functions, and structures is included. The chapters on parent involvement and teacher/ professional workshops include some helpful questionnaires and organizational tips. A bibliography is also included.

321. Fischler, R. S. (1985). Child abuse and neglect in American Indian communities. *Child Abuse & Neglect, 9*(1), 95-106.

This article discusses the recent discovery of significant child maltreatment in American Native communities. Although little is known about the clinical spectrum of Native maltreatment, the psychodynamics, effective treatment modalities, cultural misunderstanding, modernization, poverty, situational stress, poor parenting skills because of the early break-up of Native families, alcoholism, unusual perceptions of children, children with handicaps, and divorce are factors associated with maltreatment in the cases cited. The old solution of removing children from families has been found to be largely inappropriate and ineffective, and it is being replaced by local efforts to develop foster homes, supportive family services, and legal procedures to protect children. The author points out that the lack of communication between the agencies involved and mistrust of outsiders plus a lack of trained personnel and available community resources pose major barriers to effective treatment and prevention efforts. The author also states that although recent federal policies and laws clearly place the responsibility for child welfare in the hands of the Native tribes and tribal courts, the health professional who is not a Native has an important role in providing technical expertise and in aiding the development of community resources.

322. Fisher, N. W. (1985-86). Multimodal sex therapy with a blind man suffering from retarded ejaculation [Special issue: Social work practice in sexual problems]. *Journal of Social Work and Human Sexuality, 4*(1/2), 95-107.

This article describes a multimodal sex therapy with a man with visual impairment suffering from retarded ejaculation. It presents the psychodynamic issues and the treatment plan for a 35-year-old man with visual impairment in order to illustrate how this concept operates and discusses the problems involved in living with limited vision from birth, including distortions of psychological development that may give rise to a sexual dysfunction. The treatment program included intrapsychic, systems, and behavioral methods that furthered the separation/individuation process and enhanced the patient's self-esteem.

323. **Fisher, G., & Behrns, C. (1985). *Self-protection for the handicapped.* (ERIC Document Reproduction Service No. ED 263 705)**
This curriculum is designed to meet the needs of students with moderate to severe handicaps. It was adapted from the special education curriculum on sexual exploitation for students with mild mental retardation. The curriculum consists of 11 units: identifying relationships; precautions to take with strangers; private body parts; saying "no"; protecting information; travel safety; social situations; home safety; authority figures; exploitation for favors, gifts, and kindnesses; and reporting exploitation. The authors recommend a minimum of 6 hours of inservice training for learning the curriculum. The material can be presented in 1-, 2-, or 3-day programs. Trainees may include teachers, parents, and others.

324. **Fitz-Gerald, D., & Fitz-Gerald, M. (1986). *Information on sexuality for young people and their families.* Washington, DC: Gallaudet College, Pre-College Programs. (ERIC Document Reproduction Service No. ED 294 407)**
This book is written for young people who are hearing impaired or have difficulty with reading and language skills. The language used is straightforward. Illustrations are composed of line drawings. Numerous aspects of sexuality are addressed, including sexually transmitted diseases, abortion, sexual abuse and assault, and building relationships with others. A glossary of 175 terms and expressions is included. Other resource materials listed include books for parents, preteens, teens, and children 7 to 10 years old, and a list of 11 free or inexpensive materials.

325. **Fitz-Gerald, M., & Fitz-Gerald, D. (1983). How to develop and implement a comprehensive sex education program for the deaf. *Perspectives for Teachers of the Hearing Impaired, 1*(3), 8-12.**
In this discussion of the development and implementation of a sex education program for students who are deaf, the following points are addressed: reviewing state guidelines, enlisting the support of policymakers and instructors, providing training for instructors and the child's parents, developing curriculum and materials, and evaluating and revising developed programs on an ongoing basis.

326. **Fitz-Gerald, M., & Fitz-Gerald, D. R. (1987). Parents' involvement in the sex education of their hearing impaired children. *Volta Review, 89*(5), 96-110.**
This article describes a practical guide for parents and those who work with parents for providing sex education to children with hearing impairments. Information provided includes helping parents feel better about themselves as the primary sex educators of their children, helping parents better understand their children's sexual growth and development, suggesting some ways that parents can initiate and respond to sexual issues in the family, and identifying where sex education resources can be found. As the most frequent problems in parent-child communication about sex include embarrassment, lack of knowledge, unresolved personal values, fear of encouraging sexual acts, and insufficient communications skills to initiate and maintain a discussion of sex, the authors discuss the major landmarks of normal sexual development from birth to adolescence and suggest a list of books for family communication.

327. **Fletcher, D., & Ogle, P. (1981). A realistic approach to sex education for the developmentally disabled: The human growth and development curriculum. *Journal for Special Educators, 17*(4), 316-325.**
Little agreement exists concerning what actually constitutes an adequate, appropriate sex education program for people with developmental disabilities. Traditionally, most sex education programs talked around sex rather than about sex. The newly developed program focuses on teaching the biological facts of human sexuality. The program is taught separately from the rest of the regular educational curriculum. A curriculum outline is presented to show how the biological facts of human sexuality can be appropriately integrated into the regular curriculum through a human growth and development approach which then logically becomes an integral part of the total life adjustment curriculum for those with developmental disabilities. The six levels of the curriculum outline are presented in developmental sequence. The categories of social identity, physiological identity, and health and hygiene are presented at each of the six levels. Chronological and mental ages are purposefully omitted from the outline because people with developmental disabilities enter the sequence at whatever level they are currently functioning, regardless of age.

328. **Fletcher, D., & Ogle, P. (1986). *Being human: A handbook in human growth and development for the developmentally disabled.* Tallahassee: Developmental Services Program Office, Florida Department of Health and Rehabilitative Services. (ERIC Document Reproduction Service No. ED 280 235)**
This handbook is a guide to establishing and organizing a Human Growth and Development program in agencies and facilities that offer training to people with developmental disabilities. Sex education is addressed. Legal aspects are discussed in terms of Florida law. Specific methods for teaching the program are described. The first chapter addresses a wide matrix of factors in human growth and development. Chapter two addresses

policies and support systems and describes sample policy statements on masturbation and privacy. The third chapter discusses legal considerations and includes a discussion of client rights, competency, and consent. The appendix includes relevant Florida statutes.

329. Flinn, S. (1982). Preparing teachers of the deaf to teach sex education. *Sexuality and Disability, 5*(4), 230-236.

This article describes an inservice model used to prepare professionals working with people with hearing impairments to teach the concepts of elementary human growth and development, including basic family relationships, sex differentiation, health and personal hygiene, social attitudes, habits and problems, and growth, development, and reproduction. The article places special emphasis on the problems in communicating with people who are deaf, and the author notes that the model is intended for training professionals who have no extensive preparation in sexuality or sex education.

330. Floor, L., & Rosen, M. (1975). Investigating the phenomenon of helplessness in mentally retarded adults. *American Journal of Mental Deficiency, 79*(5), 565-572.

These authors compared institutionalized and noninstitutionalized adults with mild to moderate developmental disabilities to nondisabled adults for scores on the Helplessness Test, an instrument designed to assess coping ability in a problem-solving situation that included a passive dependency scale and a locus of control questionnaire. Both institutionalized and noninstitutionalized adults with disabilities were significantly more passive and externally controlled. The results support the notion that adults with disabilities exhibit more signs of helplessness than other members of society. Test scores did not discriminate between institutionalized and noninstitutionalized adults with disabilities; therefore, the etiology of the helplessness behavior was unclear.

331. Floorian, V. (1983). Sex counseling: Comparison of attitudes of disabled and nondisabled subjects. *Archives of Physical Medicine and Rehabilitation, 64,* 81-84.

This article reports the results of a survey comparing the attitudes of 103 respondents with orthopedic disabilities to those of 124 nondisabled respondents. Generally, both groups were similar in their attitudes regarding counseling on sexuality, but some differences existed in when and how and by whom they felt counseling should be provided. The author interprets some of the differences as increased anxiety in the group with disabilities. Regardless of this interpretation, the findings suggest that some adaptation of generic counseling may be required to ensure appropriate service to individuals with disabilities.

332. Flor, H., Turk, D. C., & Scholz, O. B. (1987). Impact of chronic pain on the spouse: Marital, emotional and physical consequences. *Journal of Psychosomatic Research, 31*(1), 63-71.

This study examines the effects of chronic illness on marital relationships. Emotional and physical health were examined in chronic pain patients and their spouses as well as in a control group of spouses married to people with diabetes. The authors found that the level of chronic pain experienced did not predict poorer marital adjustment; rather, they found that patients' and spouses' manner of coping predicted the quality of marital adjustment. As compared to the spouses of people with diabetes, the spouses of chronic pain patients reported significantly more pain symptoms that were related to elevated levels of depressed moods.

333. Flynn, M. C. (1986). Adults who are mentally handicapped as consumers: Issues and guidelines for interviewing. *Journal of Mental Deficiency Research, 30*(4), 369-377.

This article investigates the difficulties inherent in interviewing individuals with mental handicaps. This article includes a consideration of the findings of previous research and a list of guidelines for interviewing. It explores consent procedures and issues pertaining to the measurement of satisfaction, and the author suggests examining the work of C. K. Sigelman (1981), which underlines some of the difficulties associated with interviewing adults with mental handicaps and suggests some procedures that enhance response validity.

334. Flynn, M. C., Reeves, D. J., Speake, B., & Whelan, E. (1986). Staff's estimations of the performance of mentally handicapped adults on a test of moral knowledge. *Journal of Mental Deficiency Research, 30,* 41-48.

These authors investigate whether staff in an adult training center could estimate the performance of adults with mental impairments on a test of moral knowledge. The results indicate that staff are unable to estimate accurately and that they tend to overestimate client knowledge in this area. The authors suggest that staff in adult training centers need training in assessment criteria prior to entry of clients into specific training programs.

335. Flynn, R. J. (1981). Normalization, social integration, and sex behavior: A service approach and evaluation method for improving rehabilitation programs. In A. Sha'ked (Ed.), *Human sexuality and rehabilitation* (pp. 37-66). **Baltimore: Williams & Wilkins.**

This article discusses the normalization principle and sexuality in the rehabilitation of people with physical or mental disabilities. The normalization-based program evaluation tool entitled Programs Analysis of Systems (PASS) is examined. PASS is used to evaluate quality of service in the fostering of normative sex behavior in clients. The author offers suggestions for making agency programs and client interpretations more normalizing and more supportive of normative sexual behavior.

336. Flynt, S. W., & Wood, T. A. (1989). Stress and coping of mothers with children with moderate mental retardation. *American Journal on Mental Retardation, 94,* 278-283.

This article reports research on mothers' coping behavior. Stress levels were found to be more closely tied to the characteristics of the mothers than to the characteristics of their children with disabilities. This finding casts doubt on the hypothesis that disability creates dependency and dependency creates stress that causes abuse.

337. Foon, D. (1985). *Am I the only one?* Vancouver: Douglas & McIntyre.

This book deals with individual stories of sexual assault. One of the stories concerns Vicki, who is deaf. It relates the fear of telling someone about the attack because Vicki thinks no one will believe her.

338. Forget, C. A. (1980). The mentally retarded person in the criminal justice system. *Journal of Offender Counseling, Services and Rehabilitation, 4*(3), 285-295.

Research indicates that more than 30% of criminal offenders can be classified as having mental retardation, yet the judicial system is ill-prepared to work effectively with this population. Advances made in this area are discussed as well as recommendations.

339. Forrester, R. G., & Huggins, J. (1981). Homosexuality and homosexual behavior. In D. A. Shore & H. L. Gochros (Eds.), *Sexual problems of adolescents in institutions* (pp. 154-166). Springfield, IL: Charles C Thomas.

The focus of this chapter is on the effects of homosexual behavior on adolescents in institutions. Sample topics include policy issues, segregation of the sexes as precipitating homosexual behavior, the need for human sexuality training for staff, consistency and clarity in dealing with problems of a sexual nature, and recognition of residents' need for intimacy and privacy.

340. Foxx, R. M., & McMorrow, M. J. (1985). Teaching social skills to mentally retarded adults: Follow-up results from three studies. *Behavior Therapist, 8*(4), 77-78.

In this study, the authors evaluate whether social skills learned six to eight months previously by adults with moderate mental retardation would generate to social situations in a simulated environment. The initial training involved the use of the game *Sorry,* and it focused on social skills in one of three areas: vocational, general, or sexual. Participants were found to have maintained their original levels of skill acquisition and, in some cases, surpassed them. The role of positive social consequence on social skill acquisition is discussed.

341. Foxx, R. M., McMorrow, M. J., Fenlon, S., & Bittle, R. G. (1986). The reductive effects of reinforcement procedures on the genital stimulation and stereotype of a mentally retarded adolescent male. *Analysis and Intervention in Developmental Disabilities, 6*(3), 239-248.

This article reports on the use of positive reinforcement with a 16-year-old male with severe mental retardation. Results include the finding that rewarding with edibles was sufficient to maintain reductions in genital stimulation but that withholding edibles had little effect.

342. Foxx, R., McMorrow, M. J., Storey, K., & Rogers, B. (1984). Teaching social/sexual skills to mentally retarded adults. *American Journal of Mental Deficiency, 89*(1), 9-15.

A social-sexual skills training program for institutionalized adults with mental retardation was evaluated. The target behaviors involved a verbal action or reaction within six skill areas and were taught using a commercially available table game, *Sorry,* and a specially designed deck of cards. The program featured response-specific feedback, self-monitoring, individualized reinforcers, and individualized performance criterion levels. A multiple baseline across two groups (n=3 per group) reveals that there were increases in all skill areas. Generalization occurred in individual and group tests conducted by a peer with mental retardation. The program appears to be an effective method of training social-sexual skills because it produces effects that generalize.

343. Frankish, P. (1989). Meeting the emotional needs of handicapped people: A psycho-dynamic approach. *Journal of Mental Deficiency Research, 33,* 407-414.

This article discusses emotional development from the theoretical standpoint of normal development and applies it to people with mental handicaps. Case studies are described, including treatment procedures using a psycho-dynamic approach. Implications for care models, education, and further research are discussed.

344. Frederick, C. J. (1986). Post-traumatic stress disorder and child molestation. In A. W. Burgess & C. R. Hartman (Eds.), *Sexual exploitation of patients by health care professionals* (pp. 133-142). New York: Praeger.

This chapter presents information on 15 male victims (ages 10-18) of two male health care professionals who sexually abused them. All 15 suffered from post-traumatic stress disorder. The offenders selected victims who showed signs of emotional difficulty and vulnerability. Fear and exercise of authority over the victims were used as methods to obtain compliance with sexual exploitation.

345. Freeman, S. T., & Conoley, C. W. (1986). Training, experience, and similarity as factors of influence in preferences of deaf students for counselors. *Journal of Counseling Psychology, 33*(2), 164-169.

In this study, 96 college students with hearing impairments responded to descriptions of counselors made in terms of their training, experience, and similarity. Participants indicated their willingness to see the counselor. Findings indicate that counsellors described as experienced were given lower ratings if the counselor was reported as using a sign language interpreter. The authors discuss the importance of learning sign language for counselors who wish to work with clients who are deaf.

346. **Frey, K. S., Fewell, R. R., & Vadasy, P. F. (1989). Parental adjustment and changes in child outcome among families of young handicapped children.** *Topics in Early Childhood Special Education, 8*(4), 38-57.

Parental adjustment was studied in 48 couples with children with handicaps (ranging from 8 months to 12 years of age). Factors studied include parent and child competencies and characteristics and supports available to the family. The child's skill in communication and the sex of the child were found to be related to parental adjustment. The impact of the father's view of his child is also discussed.

347. **Friedrich, W. N., & Boriskin, J. A. (1976). The role of the child in abuse: A review of the literature.** *American Journal of Orthopsychiatry, 46*(4), 580-590.

This paper reviews the literature and discusses the role of the child in abuse, with special attention to identification of particular types of children who may be most at risk. Those children who are at risk include premature children and children with mental and physical handicaps. The authors review the literature on the incidence of mental retardation among battered and neglected children. The literature is also reviewed on abused children with physical handicaps.

348. **Friedrich, W. N., & Boriskin, J. A. (1978). Primary prevention of child abuse: Focus on the special child.** *Hospital and Community Psychiatry, 29*(4), 248-256.

These authors review the literature on child abuse and present evidence demonstrating that children who are born prematurely, who are sickly, or who are mentally or physically handicapped are at high risk for child abuse. The authors do not define child abuse and neglect in the article, and it is unclear whether the definition includes sexual abuse. The authors describe ways to identify such children and suggest a number of primary prevention techniques that can reduce parental stress and help prevent child abuse. The techniques include programs providing day care for children with handicaps, mothers' social clubs, and lay health visitors to give support and impart proper maternal attitudes.

349. **Friedrich, W. N., Cohen, D. S., & Wilturner, L. S. (1987). Family relations and marital quality when a mentally handicapped child is present.** *Psychological Reports, 61*(3), 911-919.

This study assesses the quality of family relationships and marital satisfaction in 131 families with a child with a handicap. Measures included the Marlowe Crown Social Desirability Scale and the Beck Depression Inventory. Questionnaires were also administered measuring cognitive coping resources, marital adjustment, and family environment. Positive family relationships were predicted by greater marital satisfaction, less maternal depression, and greater internal locus of control.

350. **Frisch, L. E., & Rhoads, F. A. (1982). Child abuse and neglect in children referred for learning evaluation.** *Journal of Learning Disability, 15*(10), 538-541.

During the 1977-78 school year, 430 children from the island of Oahu, Hawaii, were referred to a central school problem clinic for evaluation of learning problems. The proportion of these children (6.7%) who had been independently reported to the state child abuse agency was compared, after age adjustment, to the rate of such reporting for all children on the island and was found to be 3.5 times higher. The types of abuse and/or neglect reported were similar for the children with learning problems and for other island children. These findings strengthen the argument for a link between child maltreatment and developmental disabilities.

351. **Frodi, A. M. (1981). Contribution of infant characteristics to child abuse.** *American Journal of Mental Deficiency, 85*(4), 341-349.

This review suggests that atypical infants/children (with mental, physical, or behavioral abnormalities) are at greater risk for child abuse than other children. An explanatory model of abuse is outlined, and several studies are described whose findings provided support for the model. Some infants or infant attributes are especially likely to be perceived as aversive by parents or other caregivers and, as such, may serve as aggression-facilitating stimuli. Other factors that contribute to the probability of abuse are dispositions of the parent, such as hyperreactivity to noxious stimulation. Such dispositions may be constitutional or may have developed during negative transactions with the child. The author claims that characteristics of the child and of the caregiver, as well as the social ecology in which they exist, all affect the likelihood of abuse of children, including those with disabilities.

352. **Fryer, G. E., Kraizer, S. K., & Miyoshi, T. (1987). Measuring children's retention skills to resist stranger abduction: Use of the simulation technique.** *Child Abuse & Neglect, 11*, 181-185.

These authors present follow-up data from their earlier study using potential abduction simulation procedures to evaluate effects of abuse prevention training. All of the children who refused to go with strangers after initial training refused again after six months. Two of four children who failed in initial acquisition passed after retraining. Students in the initial control group were trained and passed the simulation test after training.

353. Fryer, G. E., Kraizer, S. K., & Miyoshi, T. (1987). Measuring the actual reduction of risk to child abuse: A new approach. *Child Abuse & Neglect, 11,* 173-179.

These authors attempted to measure actual effects of abuse prevention training by creating covert simulations in which children had the opportunity to leave the building with a stranger. They correlated results with other program evaluation data. Results indicate that higher self-esteem prior to training and higher knowledge and attitude scores after training were predictive of less vulnerable responses to the covert simulation procedure.

354. Fugl-Meyer, A. R., & Sjogren, K. (1983). Sexuality of health care students. *Scandinavian Journal of Rehabilitation Medicine, 15*(2), 47-53.

This article examines the sexual experiences together with the parameters of sexual function and sexual performance-orientation of 283 students in various branches of the health profession commonly involved in physical medicine and rehabilitation. The results of this study indicate that sexual performance-orientation, frustration, and dysfunction are common features for the students. When these findings were related to attitudes toward sexuality of subjects with disabilities, it was found that sexual performance-orientation was associated with alienation toward the sexuality and the sexual counseling needs of people with disabilities. The authors recommend that the curricula of these students should include sexual education and possibilities for sexual counseling.

355. Fujii, K. (1985). Child sexual abuse and family background. *Journal of Mental Health, 32,* 27-37.

This article reviews 12 cases of sexually abused children (11-14 years old) whose assailants were natural or stepfathers or friends of fathers. The author found that the fathers were either mentally retarded, alcoholic, or had personality disorders and that the victims were emotionally disturbed and maladjusted to school life. Interestingly, the author also found that the children had not lost hope that they would find an accepting and supportive adult.

•G•

356. Gabinet, L. (1983). Child abuse treatment failures reveal need for redefinition of the problem. *Child Abuse & Neglect, 7*(4), 395-402.

This article attempts to prove that current modalities for treating child abuse are not working because many high-risk and abusive families do not get help and identified families represent only a small part of the population at risk for child abuse. This article presents statistics, obtained by the Cleveland Parenting Program for the Prevention of Child Abuse, on the number of high-risk parents who refuse treatment and who fail to profit from therapy: sociopathic-addictive, grossly immature or infantile, mild mental retardation-infantile personalities, moderate or severe mental retardation, psychotic, and hard-core premeditated abusers. This article describes a larger population that is at risk of child abuse because of the parents' early experiences of violence as well as other emotional and educational deprivations. The author concludes that primary prevention of child abuse can only be addressed effectively if programs are designed to help both groups: people identified as being at risk and the larger, unidentified at-risk population.

357. Gallo, L. G. (1983). Child abuse: Who is involved? *New York State Dental Journal, 49*(2), 77-78.

This article discusses the interaction between parent, child, and environmental factors in child abuse as well as the implications of child abuse and neglect reporting laws for dentists. Head and facial areas are the most frequent injuries found in physically abused children.

358. Garbarino, J. (1987). The abuse and neglect of special children: An introduction to the issues. In J. Garbarino, P. E. Brookhouser, & K. J. Authier (Eds.), *Special children-special risks: The maltreatment of children with disabilities* (pp. 3-14). New York: Aldine de Gruyter.

This chapter looks at the social context of abuse in order to determine ways in which the factors that produce or prevent abuse in the lives of nonhandicapped children operate for children with handicaps. If being handicapped elicits greater nurturance, surveillance, and resources being brought to bear upon a child's family, then the child in such a situation might be at less risk than a nonhandicapped child in the same family. Nevertheless, comprehension and communication difficulties and greater dependence on caregivers might make a handicapped child less able to seek protection from maltreatment when it does occur. Therefore, in looking at the problem, this author is interested in knowing what differences do the differences make, not just "what are the differences?" It must be recognized that handicapping conditions may be linked to other factors that are the real cause of maltreatment. Research has identified five broad categories of risk: 1) characteristics of parents; 2) characteristics of the child; 3) aspects of the relationship between a particular adult and child that produce a deteriorating pattern of interaction; 4) elements of the immediate situation that stimulate abuse; and 5) any feature of the culture or society that encourages maltreatment or permits it to occur. Children with handicaps may be at risk for abuse because of any or all of these factors. The goal of this chapter is to protect children with handicaps by preventing conditions under which they are at special risk and by correcting problems when they do occur.

359. **Garbarino, J., & Authier, K. (1987). The role of the educators. In J. Garbarino, P. E. Brookhouser, & K. J. Authier (Eds.),** *Special children-special risks: The maltreatment of children with disabilities* **(pp. 69-81). New York: Aldine de Gruyter.**

Child abuse could not occur without a social context that will permit it. Our society offers support in law and custom for violence against children and permits isolation of parent-child relations from prosocial support systems. Schools could have an important role to play in the human ecology of abuse and neglect. By modeling nonviolent interpersonal relations, the behavior of present and future generations could be shaped. By acting as a support system, the school could be a force in breaking down barriers of isolation and building social networks.

360. **Garbarino, J., Brookhouser, P. E., & Authier, K. J. (Eds.). (1987).** *Special children-special risks: The maltreatment of children with disabilities.* **New York: Aldine de Gruyter.**

This comprehensive book contains chapters relating to the following topics: 1) factors that contribute to maltreatment of children with handicaps, 2) the way in which supporting and strengthening families contributes to preventing maltreatment, 3) the relationship of the child with handicaps with nondisabled siblings and peers and their potential effects on the child's well-being and development, 4) the role of educators in prevention and identification of maltreatment, 5) the incidence of abuse in residential settings and implications for its prevention, 6) the role of the federal government in regard to legislation affecting children with handicaps who are abused, 7) therapeutic issues, including a discussion of the long-term effects of abuse, intervention, the client, the therapist, and therapeutic methods, 8) medical issues, including indicators of physical and sexual abuse, 9) special legal problems in protecting children with handicaps, 10) children within the criminal justice system, and 11) a discussion of model community approaches for bringing together the concerns, knowledge, resources, and efforts of the systems that may separately address the problems of child abuse and handicapping conditions. The issue of sexual abuse is discussed briefly in terms of detection, effects, reporting, and prevention.

361. **Garbarino, J., & Stocking, S. H. (1980). The social context of child maltreatment. In J. Garbarino & S. H. Stocking (Eds.),** *Protecting children from abuse and neglect: Developing and maintaining support systems for families* **(pp. 1-14). San Francisco: Jossey-Bass.**

These authors state that solutions to child maltreatment must consider the social context in which families live. Understanding and change can only take place if abuse is viewed in an ecological model that recognizes context and community influence, provides a habitable social environment, allows for mutual accommodation between individuals and society, recognizes second order effects (e.g., the effect of community values on intra-familial interactions), considers cross contextual dyads (e.g., parent-child interactions at home and in public) and ecological transitions (e.g., movement from one environment to another), and utilizes a life course perspective (e.g., immediate, intermediate, and long-term effects).

362. **Gardner, N. E. S. (1986). Sexuality. In J. A. Summers (Ed.),** *The right to grow up: An introduction to adults with developmental disabilities* **(pp. 45-66). Baltimore: Paul H. Brookes Publishing Co.**

This article discusses sexuality and socialization, sex education, how to design a sex education program, the role of service providers in socio-sexual development and in working with parents, sexual exploitation and abuse, and policy implications for service providers. The section on sexual abuse includes a discussion of prevention, the vulnerability of adults with disabilities, and working with victims. The section on policy implications includes practical questions that policy-makers can ask themselves when addressing such issues as privacy, social opportunities, respect for choice and sexuality, and the protection of legal rights. Also included is an appendix of sexuality training materials, including curricula and resource guides for planning sexuality training programs, materials for parents, materials for people with disabilities, a list of films and filmstrips, and other resources.

363. **Garfinkel, L., Gorka, C., Murphy, C., Goldberg, P. F., Goldberg, M., Bergdahl, M., Harrington, A., Greenberg, S., & Linafelter, G. T. (1986).** *A resource manual on child abuse: PACER'S Let's Prevent Abuse Program.* **Minneapolis, MN: Pacer Center, Inc. (ERIC Document Reproduction Service No. ED 283 345)**

This 115-page resource manual is directed at professionals who have regular contact with children, both with handicaps and those without (e.g., teachers, child care workers, and so forth). The manual overviews child abuse, abuse of children with handicaps, institutional abuse, the child protection system, prevention strategies, and it lists resources, including printed materials, audiovisual materials, and agencies.

364. **Garmise, R., Guggenheim, P. D., & Schuster, R. (1984). Diagnostic and Statistical Manual-III: A perspective from family court.** *Journal of Forensic Sciences, 29*(4), 1127-1139.

The Diagnostic and Statistical Manual-III (DSM III) is evaluated from the perspective of forensic science in the family court setting. This manual is the standard source for defining and categorizing psychological and psychiatric impairments. The limitations of the Diagnostic and Statistical Manual-III criteria for application of diagnostic categories to people with developmental disabilities are discussed.

365. **Gartell, N. K., Olarte, S., & Herman, J. L. (1986). Institutional resistance to self-study: A case report. In A. W. Burgess & C. R. Hartman (Eds.), *Sexual exploitation of patients by health care professionals* (pp. 120-128). New York: Praeger.**
This chapter discusses efforts by some members of the American Psychiatric Association to study sexual abuse of patients by therapists. The issue was deemed to be controversial, and although there was some support within the organization and the study was found to be sound, the organization refused to sponsor the study. This response was viewed by the authors as a resistance to study the problem.

366. **Gath, A. (1988). Mentally handicapped people as parents. *Journal of Child Psychology and Psychiatry and Allied Disciplines*, 29(6), 739-744.**
This article reviews articles addressing the parenting skills of people with various degrees of learning disability. Severe learning difficulties are seen to result in limited opportunities in the areas of sexuality and parenting. The author discusses the interaction between degree of learning disability and such variables as the inability to organize, the presence of personality disorder, and having a history of long-standing deprivation. The article addresses issues in the treatment of problems in parenting, sex, and marriage. The right to sex education is emphasized.

367. **Geist, C. S., Knudsen, C., & Sorenson, K. (1979). Practical sex education for the mentally retarded: What the rehabilitation counselor needs to know. *Journal of Applied Rehabilitation Counseling*, 10(4), 186-189.**
These authors discuss the need to develop a comprehensive approach to teaching sex education to people with moderate mental retardation. A discussion of birth control and the individual with mental handicaps is followed by suggestions on how to present topics and materials on sex education and some implications for the rehabilitation counselor.

368. **Geist, R. F. (1988). Sexually related trauma. *Emergency Medical Clinics of North America*, 6(3), 439-466.**
This article details the types of sex-related injuries treated by physicians. The prevalence rate of various forms of sexual violence and sex differences are discussed. Topics include post-traumatic psychological syndrome following rape, sexual child abuse, and other bodily injury associated with sexual injury. The author stresses that physicians must be educated and vigilant regarding sex-related injuries as patients tend to delay treatment and provide misleading histories out of embarrassment.

369. **Gerring, J. P., & McCarthy, L. P. (1988). *The psychiatry of handicapped children and adolescents: Managing emotional and behavioral problems*. Boston: College-Hill Press.**
This book aims at acquainting nonpsychiatric specialists with the psychiatric problems of youths with disabilities and the treatment of these problems. Chapter one discusses the definition of handicaps within the framework of PL 94-142, the role of the public school system, and the organization of multidisciplinary teams. Chapter two describes the psychiatric symptoms and disorders commonly seen in children with handicaps. Chapter three focuses on adolescents, while chapter four focuses on psychotherapy and drug therapy. Chapter five addresses the behavioral assessment and treatment of youths with handicaps. Chapters six and seven address educational issues. Chapter eight discusses the family's response and adaptation to a new member with a handicap. Sexuality and sexuality counseling are addressed briefly in this book. Sexual and physical abuse are not addressed.

370. **Giami, A. (1986). La prise en compte du cadre et des processus dans un dispositif de recherche [Making the psychoanalytic setting and processes part of the objects of a research project]. *Bulletin de Psychologie*, 39(16/18), 769-775.**
This study includes an examination of institutional analysts on a psychological research team who were studying the structure, function, and meaning of sexuality of institutionalized patients with mental handicaps. While observing the patients, the analysts were themselves observed by external researchers. Topics include the institutional environment and patient-analyst interactions.

371. **Giami, A. (1987). Coping with the sexuality of the disabled: A comparison of the physically disabled and the mentally retarded. *International Journal of Rehabilitation Research*, 10(1), 41-48.**
This article examines attitudes toward the expression of sexuality by people with physical disabilities and people with mental retardation. The author claims that procreation is supported for people with physical disabilities, but it is discouraged for people with mental retardation.

372. **Giami, A., Humbert-Viveret, C., & Laval, D. (1983). *L'ange et la bête; représentation de la sexualité des handicapés mentaux par les parents et les éducateurs [The angel and the beast: Sexuality of people with mental handicaps as seen by parents and educators]*. Paris: Les publications du CTNERHI (Centre technique national d'études et de recherches sur les handicapes et les inadaptations).**
This document presents the opinions of the parents of children with mental handicaps as well as those of their educators regarding the sexuality of people with mental

handicaps. In general, the results indicate that parents desexualize people with mental handicaps. Although educators share a viewpoint that is close to that of the parents, they maintain that young adults with mental handicaps are incapable of having a full sexual relationship. Only masturbation is perceived as a sign of sexual potential, with individual and/or group masturbation remaining the predominant form of sexuality in people with mental handicaps. (This document is available in French only.)

373. **Gibbens, T. C., & Robertson, G. (1983). A survey of the criminal careers of hospital order patients.** *British Journal of Psychiatry, 143,* 362-369.
This article reports on a survey that followed up all men receiving hospital orders (Section 60) in the United Kingdom in the year 1963-64 (excluding those receiving restriction orders [Section 60/65]) over a 15-year period with regard to the following: 1) subsequent offenses and convictions, 2) hospital admissions, and 3) death. The findings reveal that 9% of the patients involved could not be traced, 16% had died by 1978 (a quarter of them by suicide), 4% of those with mental illness subsequently committed serious offenses (manslaughter, wounding, homicide, robbery, rape, or arson), 4% committed assaults repeatedly, 7% of those who were mentally subnormal committed serious sex crimes subsequent to committal, 9% were considered to be persistent sex offenders, and 9% were judged to be persistently violent. The authors claim that the best predictor of subsequent offenses is the number of previous offenses: This was especially true for acquisitive offenses committed by the young.

374. **Gibson, D. E. (1984). Hospice and the new devaluation of human life.** *Mental Retardation, 22*(4), 157-162.
This article contends that the hospice literature contains cost containment and quality-of-life arguments sometimes used to justify nontreatment or killing of people with mental retardation. The author suggests that hospice concepts and practices pose indirect and direct threats to people with mental retardation.

375. **Gigeroff, A. K. (1968).** *Sexual deviation in the criminal law, pedophilic offenses.* **Toronto: University of Toronto Press.**
Forty-five percent of child sexual abusers studied were heavy drinkers. The author suggests that economic stress is associated with an increased incidence of child sexual abuse.

376. **Gil, E. (1981). Protecting the rights of children in institutions. In National Legal Resources Center for Child Advocacy and Protection Staff (Eds.),** *Protecting children through the legal system* **(pp. 303-323). Washington, DC: American Bar Association.**
This article focuses on child protection laws for children in institutions and recent trends in the laws that recognize children's rights. Institutional abuse is defined. Problem areas discussed include lack of monitoring systems, inability to enforce existing regulation, insufficient staff training, poor screening of caregivers, and the inaccessibility of children in institutions. The author suggests the establishment of an independent monitoring system for the investigation of complaints and violations.

377. **Gil, E. (1982). Institutional abuse of children in out-of-home care. In R. Hanson (Ed.),** *Institutional abuse of children and youth* **(pp. 7-13). New York: Haworth Press.**
Seventy-seven percent of abuse reports were physical abuse, and 23% were sexual abuse. Unfortunately, actual incidence and prevalence is unclear as underreporting is a major problem.

378. **Gilbert, T. (1989, June 3). Legal deck stacked against victims of care-givers.** *Calgary Herald,* pp. D1-D2.
This newspaper article reports on information presented at a Canadian conference on sexual assault and abuse of people with disabilities. It points out that although sexual offenses against people with disabilities are common, conviction of offenders is rare. It quotes several experts who indicate that crime victims with disabilities are disadvantaged in the Canadian court system and fail to receive equal protection under Canadian or American law.

379. **Gilbert, T. (1989, June 3). Offenders unpunished for assaults.** *Calgary Herald,* p. D1.
This newspaper article discusses the vulnerability to abuse of people with disabilities and quotes researchers and other experts on a number of measures that might assist in better prevention, detection, law enforcement, and treatment.

380. **Giles, K. (1987). Sex education for pupils with severe learning difficulties: Research supplement.** *British Journal of Special Education, 14*(3), 107-111.
Findings from a survey of eight British special schools are applied to the following areas: curriculum, staff development, parent involvement, school policy, local police policy, and resources.

381. **Gillan, P. (1980). Psychological methods in sex therapy for the disabled.** *Sexuality and Disability, 3*(3), 199-202.
This paper provides a short discussion of social skills training and methods to reduce social anxiety in people with disabilities who are seeking to establish a sexual relationship. Systematic desensitization and role-playing with feedback are contrasted.

382. **Gillberg, C. (1984). Autistic children growing up: Problems during puberty and adolescence.** *Developmental Medicine and Child Neurology,*

26(1), 125-129.

This study indicates that children with autism experience a substantial increase in neuropsychiatric problems during puberty. The author suggests that services for adolescents in puberty be planned so as to engender minimal stress during this time.

383. **Glaser, D., & Bentovim, A. (1979). Abuse and risk to handicapped and chronically ill children.** *Child Abuse & Neglect, 3,* **565-575.**
Weekly meetings have been held since 1973 in the Hospital for Sick Children (London) to discuss children thought to be at risk for or actually abused through nonaccidental injury, neglect, rejection, or nonmedical failure to thrive. During the years 1973-1977, a total of 189 children were discussed at regular meetings. Fifteen children were excluded from this group because of insufficient information being documented or because on review the committee felt there was little evidence of abuse or the presence of risk factors. In this group of children feared to be at risk for or actually abused, there were two clear subdivisions: those children who were handicapped prior to abuse and those children who were previously nonhandicapped. Patterns of abuse and age distribution between these two groups have been found to differ considerably. Within the handicapped group, it appeared that beyond a moderate degree of illness or handicap increasing severity does not contribute materially to the degree of abuse. The degree of social/emotional stress is the important varying factor. One of the most disturbing factors seems to be the enduring nature of abuse of children with disabilities. After the age of 5, while 9% of nonhandicapped children were abused, 29% of the children with handicaps were abused.

384. **Glisson, C. A. (1981). Correctional facilities. In D. A. Shore & H. L. Gochros (Eds.),** *Sexual problems of adolescents in institutions* **(pp. 180-199). Springfield, IL: Charles C Thomas.**
This chapter addresses the following sexual problems of incarcerated adolescents: correctional institutions provide a stifling and problematic environment for the development of healthy sexuality; disturbed sexual norms may be passed on to adolescents; and inmate subculture may lead to an aversion to sexual expression. The chapter also focuses on treatment strategies.

385. **Glueckauf, R. L. (1983). Sex counseling training programs for rehabilitation personnel.** *Sexuality and Disability, 6*(2), **106-110.**
This article discusses the effectiveness of sex counseling courses for rehabilitation personnel. It notes that there is little quantitative research on the efficacy of such courses, and the author recommends that future research develop standardized instruments to assess rehabilitation workers' attitudes and knowledge about sexuality and disability, behavioral measures of counseling skills, and measures assessing the effectiveness of service delivery by course participants to disabled consumers. The author concludes that the use of behavioral measures

and the collection of patient outcome data may substantially enhance the quality of research in sex counseling training.

386. **Gochros, H. L., Gochros, J. S., & Fischer, J. (1986).** *Helping the sexually oppressed.* **Englewoods Cliffs, NJ: Prentice-Hall.**
This book discusses the sexual oppression of various populations and how professionals and family can help. Part I discusses social control, the components of sexuality, counseling, and social system interventions. Part II is made up of articles written by various authors on the needs of specific groups, including women, men, children and adolescents, the elderly, the poor, ethnic minorities, gay men, lesbians, the unattractive, people with terminal illnesses, and victims. Three papers address the needs of people with developmental disabilities, people with physical disabilities, and institutionalized people with mental illnesses. Virginia Satir provides the epilogue to the book.

387. **Goerdt, A. (1986). Social integration of the physically disabled in Barbados.** *Social Science & Medicine, 22*(4), **459-466.**
This study focuses on the social integration of adults with physical disabilities among the nonelite, Black population of Barbados, West Indies, and it examines the role of 30 adults with physical disabilities in Barbadian society. The study found the following: Although village Barbadians do not expect people with physical disabilities to fulfill normative adult roles, some individuals with disabilities do perform adult activities such as maintaining employment and engaging in sexual relationships. In spite of this finding, very few people with disabilities participate in the relationships through which village Barbadians achieve status and "respect" as adults.

388. **Goldberg, B. (1986). Broken noses, sex abuse and devils on shoulders: A twenty-five year experience with mentally disabled adolescents.** *International Journal of Adolescent Medicine and Health, 2*(3), **179-191.**
This article describes an interdisciplinary model used to diagnose, evaluate, and treat children with mental retardation at a regional center in London, Ontario, Canada. It presents three cases in order to illustrate this model and considers community-oriented treatment and some current ethical issues affecting treatment.

389. **Goldstein, H. (1988). Menarche, menstruation, sexual relations and contraception of adolescent females with Down Syndrome.** *European Journal of Obstetrics, Gynecology and Reproductive Biology, 27*(4), **343-349.**
Fifteen female adolescents with Down syndrome and 33 female controls were surveyed on age of menarche, menstruation, sex relationships, and contraception. Data were collected from the controls personally, while data regarding the young people with Down syndrome were collected from parents, foster-parents, and the staff who

were caring for them. Thirteen of the young people with Down syndrome were reported as never having had sexual intercourse. Data were not available for the remaining two. Significant differences were found between the group with Down syndrome and the controls regarding the use of contraceptives.

390. **Gomes-Schwartz, B., Horowitz, J. M., & Sauzier, M. (1985). Severity of emotional distress among sexually abused preschool, school-age, and adolescent children.** *Hospital and Community Psychiatry, 36*(5), 503-508.

In a study aimed at evaluating the emotional response of children to sexual abuse, 112 sexually abused children were examined. Emotional distress was measured by the Louisville Behavior Checklist. Results show that 20% of the preschool children had serious deficits in intellectual, physical, and social development. The authors state that it is unlikely that the immaturity or lack of awareness of social norms observed in some of these victims was only a reaction to the sexual experience. Rather, it is more probable that many of the children had long-standing developmental difficulties that made them more vulnerable to coercion and intimidation by sexual offenders.

391. **Goodman, L. (1973). The sexual rights of the retarded—A dilemma for parents.** *The Family Coordinator, 22,* 472-474.

Affirming the sexual rights and the sexuality of children with developmental disabilities presents a dilemma for parents. Many are influenced by their own unresolved conflicts on sexuality, lack of knowledge, and discomfort in discussing the topic with their child. The author describes the spectrum of responses that parents may have to the sexuality of a child with developmental disabilities. These attitudes range from the belief that these children have the same entitlement to sexual expression as anyone else to the belief that sex is sinful. Professionals working with these parents and their children must be aware of which concerns are realistic and which are "lingering vestiges of arbitrary outmoded concepts." Working with these parents successfully involves using factual material, clarification, and interpretation only at those points in the contact where it can be productively utilized.

392. **Goodman, R. E. (1980). Sex aids and the disabled.** *Sexuality and Disability, 3*(3), 232-235.

This short article discusses the utility of sex aids for people with disabilities and offers suggestions on practical improvements that might be made to sexual devices for use by people with handicaps. Also presented are the satisfaction ratings of 10 men with secondary impotence who had been offered a Blakoe ring or a special aid.

393. **Goodwin, J. (1985). Family violence: Principles of intervention and prevention [Special issue: Women and health].** *Hospital and Community Psychiatry, 36*(10), 1074-1079.

This article suggests that failure to explore family violence may lead to underdiagnosis of dissociative disorders and overdiagnosis of depressive disorders in victims. It discusses three types of interventions— verbalization, violence-prevention strategies, and advocacy and support—that are useful with victims, abusers, other family members, and "battered professionals" who handle these cases. It also describes a comprehensive intervention program and the necessary services for treating family violence.

394. **Goodwin, L. R., & Holmes, G. E. (1988). Counseling the crime victim: A guide for rehabilitation counselors.** *Journal of Applied Rehabilitation Counseling, 19*(2), 42-47.

This article provides a guide for rehabilitation counselors working with crime victims with disabilities. It suggests that crime victims, especially those subject to violent crime, may be disrupted psychosocially, medically, vocationally, educationally, and financially and that such adverse effects can jeopardize rehabilitation efforts and plans. The authors also discuss evaluation methods and interventions.

395. **Goodwin, O., Zouhar, M. S., & Bergman, R. (1982). Hysterical seizures in adolescent incest victims. In J. Goodwin (Ed.),** *Sexual abuse: Incest victims and their families* **(pp. 101-108). Littleton, MA: John Wright-PSG, Inc.**

This chapter discusses six cases of hysterical or conversion seizures occurring in female adolescents who had been victims of incest. All experienced sexual problems, had histories of running away from home, and had attempted suicide. All experienced relief from the hysterical seizures as a result of psychodynamic intervention. The hysterical movements repeated actions related to sexual stimulation and actions related to resisting sexual assault. The defensive functions of hysterical seizures are discussed. The authors recommend that physicians take a complete sexual history when pseudoseizures are in the differential diagnosis. A complete neurological examination including electroencephalography is also recommended.

396. **Gordon, S. (1979).** *Sex education and the library: A basic bibliography for the general public with special resources for the librarian.* **Syracuse, NY: ERIC Clearinghouse on Information Resources. (ERIC Document Reproduction Service No. ED 180 504)**

This bibliography is preceded by arguments in favor of the dissemination of sex education information. The issues that should, at minimum, be addressed in a quality sex education program are listed. The author discusses the role of parents, the role of librarians, and public opinion on sex education. Approximately 260 titles are listed, and they are grouped by categories such as age and special interest, for example, religion and sexuality or history of sexual attitudes. Eleven books are listed under the heading "Sexuality and People with Handicaps."

397. Gostason, R. (1985). **Psychiatric illness among the mentally retarded: A Swedish population study.** *Acta Psychiatrica Scandinavica, 71*(Suppl 318), 1-117.

This article discusses a study that investigated the frequency of severe and mild mental retardation in a primary sample of 145,049 Swedish adults (20-60 years old). Once the individuals with mild and severe mental retardation were identified, the study focused on social conditions in the two mental retardation groups and in a control group representing the rest of the population. The three groups were compared using the Comprehensive Psychopathological Rating Scale, by classifying any mental illness according to the Diagnostic and Statistical Manual (DSM-III), and by determining the intake of psychotropic drugs and antiepileptics. The individuals with mild mental retardation and the control groups were also compared with respect to neuroticism and extraversion-introversion using the Eysenck Personality Inventory.

398. Gothard, T. W., Runyan, D. K., & Hadler, J. L. (1985). **The diagnosis and evaluation of child maltreatment.** *Journal of Emergency Medicine, 3*(3), 181-194.

Child maltreatment continues to be one of the most common and difficult problems seen in the emergency room. An early estimate indicated that up to 10% of children under age 6 seen in emergency departments have some form of nonaccidental injury. Recent data suggest that approximately 1% of the child population are victims of maltreatment each year. Many of these cases involve only subtle signs and have great potential to pass undetected. The article points out that past reports have suggested that prematurity, mental retardation, physical handicaps, and being a twin all place the child at increased risk for maltreatment. The definition of maltreatment in the article is wide enough to include sexual abuse. This article provides a review of the various forms of maltreatment, with emphasis on the key points involved with the patient's history, physical examination, and management. The protocol for evaluating maltreatment from the North Carolina Memorial Hospital is presented. This framework will aid the physician in the crucial first step of identifying maltreatment, which, along with diligent follow-up and the assistance of the available social services, offers the best hope for further prevention.

399. Gottlieb, B. H. (1981). **The role of the individual and social support in preventing child maltreatment.** In J. Garbarino & S. H. Stocking (Eds.), *Protecting children from abuse and neglect: Developing and maintaining support systems for families* (pp. 37-60). San Francisco: Jossey-Bass.

This author states that a consumer definition of child maltreatment is essential for effective solutions, a consumer definition of solutions is essential for effectiveness, social support networks provide powerful counter-control, family members require skills to tap into social support networks, and formalized social supports may encourage interaction with agencies at the expense of less formal social support networks.

400. Gowen, J. W., Johnson-Martin, N., Goldman, B. D., & Appelbaum, M. (1989). **Feelings of depression and parenting competence of mothers of handicapped and nonhandicapped infants: A longitudinal study.** *American Journal on Mental Retardation, 94*(3), 259-271.

This study examines feelings of maternal depression and parenting competence in mothers with children with handicaps and in mothers with children without handicaps. In mothers parenting children with handicaps, caregiving difficulty predicted maternal depression, and quality of family relations predicted feelings of parenting competence. In mothers parenting children without handicaps, both feelings of depression and feelings of parental competence were predicted by child irritability and quality of family relations. Although the infants differed significantly in level of functioning and difficulty of caregiving, measures of feelings of maternal depression and feelings of parenting competence did not differ for the two groups.

401. Graff, D. (1983). **Teacher preparation: The key to effective sex education for the mentally retarded.** *Health Education, 14*(3), 25-27.

This article points out the need for sex educators to be provided with additional training when working with students with mental retardation. Included is a discussion of techniques sex educators can use with this population of students.

402. Grant, L. J. (1984). **Assessment of child sexual abuse: Eighteen months' experience at the Child Protection Center.** *American Journal of Obstetrics & Gynecology, 148*(5), 617-620.

This article assesses 157 cases of alleged child sexual abuse. The data were analysed according to age, sex, relationship to assailant, and type of assault, and the analysis corroborates other published data. The assessment found that referrals were usually made through a parent and that concomitant social work and police investigation are necessary, especially in complex cases. The author also found that in many cases initial screening enables the scheduling of appointments for medical assessment.

403. Gravel, S. (1985). *Le traitement judiciare des délits d'agression sexuelle dans le district de Montréal [Judicial response to sexual abuse offenses in the Montréal area].* Montréal: Université de Montréal.

This research illustrates the differential judicial treatment of crimes involving sexual aggression as compared to other violent crimes. This is due to the unique characteristics of sexual aggression and the influence of various associated myths and stereotypes. People accused of sexual aggression toward children or adolescents more often plead guilty only once the victim becomes an adult. However, in the first case, sentencing is less severe than in the second case as physical violence is less frequently used when the victim is a child. (This document is available in French only.)

404. Green, A. H. (1978). Psychopathology of abused children. *Journal of the American Academy of Child Psychiatry, 17*(1), 92-103.

This study details the principle types of psychopathology and behavioral deviancy observed in 20 physically abused children who took part in clinical research and treatment programs. The children were 5 to 14 years old, 70% were black, two-thirds were boys, and most had been abused on a recurring basis during the first two years of life. Problems included impaired ego functioning associated with intellectual and cognitive deficits, traumatic reactions with acute anxiety states, pathological object relations characterized by failure to trust, excessive use of defenses (e.g., denial, projection, introjection, and splitting), impaired impulse control, impaired self-concept, masochistic and self-destructive behavior, difficulties with separation, and problematic adjustment to school.

405. Green, A. H. (1988). Special issues in child sexual abuse. In D. H. Schetky & A H. Green (Eds.), *Child sexual abuse: A handbook for health care professionals* **(pp. 125-135). New York: Brunner/Mazel.**

This chapter discusses several issues: male victims, sibling incest, female offenders, grandfather-grandchild incest, ritualistic abuse, and institutional abuse. The section on institutional abuse points out that child sexual abuse was considered a family problem until 1984 when institutional settings began to receive attention. Vulnerability of children with disabilities and the high rates of abuse in institutional settings are discussed. The author makes reference to a study that found more than 50% of staff working in day care agencies in New York City had arrest records and that many were for child abuse.

406. Green, A. H., Gaines, R. W., & Sandgrund, A. (1974). Child abuse: Pathological syndrome of family interaction. *American Journal of Psychiatry, 131*(8), 882-886.

A study of mothers of 60 abused children was conducted to determine the characteristics of abusing parents, the abused child, and environmental stress factors. Characteristics of a child that contribute to abuse were found to be of 2 types: 1) extreme physical or psychological deviance (e.g., psychoses, mental retardation, brain damage); and 2) normal traits that are misperceived by or have special significance for the abusive parent, such as a child who resembles a hated ex-husband. In combination with the low self-esteem of abusive parents, "defective" children are seen as further proof of the parent's inadequacy. The poor impulse control of these parents allows aggression against the child to occur.

407. Green, A. H., Voeller, K., Gaines, R W., & Kubie, U. (1981). Neurological impairment in maltreated children. *Child Abuse & Neglect, 5*(2), 129-134.

In this study, 60 physically abused children were compared to 30 neglected children and 30 normally reared children on neurological competency. Most of the children were Black or Hispanic. Neurological examinations were conducted, developmental histories taken, and psychological tests administered. Blind ratings by a pediatric neurologist placed more than 50% of the abused children in the moderately to severely impaired group, which is high when compared to 37% of the neglected group and 14% of the adequate-care group. The authors suggest that child abuse be conceptualized within its environmental context.

408. Green, B., & Paul, R. (1974). Parenthood and the mentally retarded. *University of Toronto Law Journal, 24*(2), 117-125.

This paper is a draft of a model statute delineating the conditions under which parents may seek sterilization for their child with mental retardation. The statute is based on two assumptions: a) sterilization is non-criminal, and b) the procedure may be made available only to the child with retardation and only if the parents are truly well-intentioned. The conditions pertaining to these assumptions are discussed as well as the legal means to protect children from overeager parents.

409. Green, D. T. (1983). A human sexuality program for developmentally disabled women in a sheltered workshop setting. *Sexuality and Disability, 6*(1), 20-24.

This author describes a human sexuality program at a sheltered workshop for women with emotional and mental disabilities. Because of their limited reading skills, many people with mental handicaps do not have the opportunity to learn about general sexual information on their own. The program described involves discussion of such issues as personal hygiene, menstruation, reproduction, birth control, dating, marriage, venereal disease, and personal values. Directions are given where necessary, such as in the use of birth control devices or breast self-examinations. Repetition of instructions is an important aspect of the program. Dialogue between participants also helps to facilitate learning and relieve anxiety about the topics. An open format including both men and women is used for the topics of dating, marriage, and parenting.

410. Green, F. C. (1977). What will it cost the child if I don't report? In M. A. Thomas (Ed.), *Children alone: What can be done about abuse and neglect* **(pp. 61-67). Reston, VA: Council for Exceptional Children.**

This author discusses the physical, developmental, and socioemotional consequences of failing to report child abuse. Physical injuries that are not treated may result in scarring due to burns, misshapen or shortened limbs from unattended fractures, or neurologic deficits that accrue from repeated head injuries. Children who remain in maltreatment situations may suffer from developmental delays or damage (e.g., failures in social, language, and motor development), which in turn may require long-term intervention and, at worst, long-term institutionalization. Child abuse and neglect is a cyclical syndrome, which means that children who are abused will grow to become abusing parents. In the interim, such children may be hostile, isolated, and have difficulty establishing relationships with others. As they act out and their behavior becomes socially unacceptable, society may label them as delinquent and criminal. This leads to segregating them in institutions with other sociopaths, which reinforces antisocial behavior. The author concludes that the costs of failing to report child abuse are so great that failure to report is intolerable.

411. Greengross, W. (1976). *Entitled to love: The sexual and emotional needs of the handicapped.* London: Malaby Press.
The aim of this book is to establish that people with handicaps have a right to love and to be loved. At present, the public, parents, and educators are not permitting people with handicaps the right to express love through their sexuality. The book discusses marriage, the role of the parent and staff careworkers, and sex education for people with handicaps. As well, the special problems of people with mental handicaps are discussed with respect to sex.

412. Greenland, C. (1983). Sex law reform in an international perspective: England and Wales and Canada. *Bulletin of the American Academy of Psychiatry and the Law, 11*(4), 309-330.
This article discusses the proposal for sex law reform in Canada, England, and Wales. It reviews laws dealing with sexual conduct, rape and spousal immunity, age of consent, incest, protecting people with mental retardation, homosexuality, and bestiality, and the author concludes that governments encourage the motions of reform without actually allowing substantive changes to occur.

413. Greydanus, D. E., Demarest, D. S., & Sears, J. M. (1985). Sexuality of the chronically ill adolescent. *Medical Aspects of Human Sexuality, 19*(12), 36-49.
This article discusses how sexual dysfunction may result from chronic illness in adolescents. Problems that may result include difficulties in gaining independence from parents, noncompliance with treatment, legal issues, and poor self-image. The authors suggest that physicians should provide special counseling and treatment for this group of adolescents regarding sexual function. and its relation to specific disabilities. Some specific chronic illnesses and disabilities are addressed (e.g., cystic fibrosis and spinal cord injuries).

414. Griffiths, D., Hingsburger, D., & Christian, R. (1985). Treating developmentally handicapped sexual offenders: The York Behaviour Management Services Treatment Program. *Psychiatric Aspects of Mental Retardation Reviews, 4*(12), 49-52.
This article examines the prevalence, causes, and treatment of sex offenders with developmental handicaps and describes the York Behaviour Management Services treatment program, a comprehensive treatment program designed specifically for paraphilics with developmental handicaps. The main principles of this program include the prevention of a reoffense, creation of a specialized treatment plan to decrease direct arousal and to provide the individual with the skills needed to pursue normal adult relations and sexual interactions, and a holistic approach that addresses the individual's psychosocial needs. This program involves sensitization, sexual education, social skills training, instruction on strategies for coping, and creation of a support network. The benefits of this program include being cost-effective, having a preventive nature, having a holistic view of the person with developmental handicaps, and being a minimally intrusive and restrictive method of providing a safety net for the community in which individuals who are at risk live. The article discusses a case history to illustrate the type of success achieved by this program.

415. Griffiths, D.M., Quinsey, V.L., & Hingsburger, D. (1989). *Changing inappropriate sexual behavior: A community-based approach for persons with developmental disabilities.* Baltimore: Paul H. Brookes Publishing Co.
This book describes principles and a specific program for treating sexually inappropriate behavior in clients with developmental disabilities. It provides a general introduction, reviews relevant literature, and furnishes examples to acquaint the reader with some of the underlying issues concerning inappropriate sexual behavior by people with developmental disabilities. The authors state that inappropriate sexual behavior is a problem found in some people with developmental disabilities (as it is in other segments of the population), and they suggest that differences in life experience and learning styles may require differences in intervention. They describe the assessment and treatment planning process. Assessment is broken into a preliminary survey, an environmental assessment, an assessment of sexual knowledge, an assessment of social competence, and an analysis of sexual preferences. Treatment planning follows to alter the clients environment, increase appropriate skills and knowledge, and (when required) alter deviant sexual preferences. They also cover measures to maintain appropriate behavior and prevent relapse. Several appendices are also included: Social L.I.F.E. (Social Learning of Independence through Functional Experience), a game for teaching appropriate social skills, is described in detail; a case study is provided as an example of program design; terms of reference for the program advisory

committee are included; and consent procedures and related issues are discussed. In addition to the appendices, suggested readings and materials are listed along with references and an index.

416. Gripton, J., & Valentich, M. (1983). Assessing sexual concerns of clients with health problems. *Journal of Social Work and Human Sexuality,* **2(1), 53-66.**

This article investigates the process of assessing the sexual concerns of clients with health problems. It examines the interaction of sex, impairment, disability, and handicap and classifies the various ways disability affects sexuality. The basic components of a sexual assessment are discussed and include helping clients to gain a realistic perception of disabling impairments on sexual performance, exploring and evaluating their potential for sexual satisfaction, dealing effectively with strains in sexual relationships, and minimizing sexual handicaps by asserting their sexual rights. The authors also consider the timing and guidelines for assessment interviewing.

417. Grob, G. N. (1980). Abuse in American mental hospitals in historical perspective: Myth and reality. *International Journal of Law and Psychiatry, 3,* **295-310.**

In this article, the author takes a historical perspective on the evolution of mental institutions and questions critics' attacks on these facilities.

418. Gross, M. (1979). Incestuous rape: A cause for hysterical seizures in four adolescent girls. *American Journal of Orthopsychiatry, 49(4),* **704-708.**

Four cases of hysterical seizures in adolescent girls are discussed. The seizures were related to incestuous father-daughter relationships. Three of the girls attempted suicide, and one attempted to run away. Psychotherapy was used in all cases, hypnotherapy in three cases, and family therapy in two cases. Findings indicate that the girls felt anxiety due to the constant threat as well as guilt over arousing phallic drives. The hysterical seizures served as a means to escape threatening parents.

419. Grossman, R., & Sutherland, J. (Eds.). (1983). *Surviving sexual assault.* **New York: Congdon & Weed.**

This book deals generally on how to survive a sexual assault. It has a short section on the myths and realities of sexual assault of people with handicaps. Some suggestions are offered for treatment of people with handicaps after assault.

420. Groth, N. (1979). *Men who rape.* **New York: Plenum.**

This is a classic book that explores the psychology of 500 sex offenders. It includes interesting information on the dynamics of power and the need for control. It may implicitly suggest some of the factors that encourage offenders to choose victims with disabilities.

421. Grothaus, R. S. (1985). Abuse of women with disabilities. In S. Browne, D. Connors, & N. Stern (Eds.), *With the power of each breath* **(pp. 124-128). Pittsburgh: Cleis Press.**

This author discusses the problem of abuse of women with disabilities. It is a personal problem as well as a political problem. Women with disabilities are discriminated against not only based on their disability but also on their gender. The author makes 10 recommendations as a starting point for discussion and potential corrective action: 1) increased attention by policymakers; 2) increased enforcement of disability nondiscrimination laws; 3) increased funding for programs; 4) education by people with disabilities of workers in all violence-oriented programs; 5) development of resource lists in programs that provide specialized assistance; 6) better education of staff in medical facilities; 7) provision of adequate equipment in medical facilities; 8) recognition by the disability civil rights movement that women with disabilities face double discrimination; 9) recognition by the feminist movement that women with disabilities are being excluded by inaccessible meeting places and by ignorance; and 10) agitation by women with disabilities to demand that their concerns be considered and that their needs be met.

422. Gruson, L. (1987, March 27). Prosecutors to ask death penalty in torture case. *New York Times,* **p. A12.**

This article is one of a series discussing the arrest and prosecution of Gary Heidnik, a licensed practical nurse, who was charged with kidnapping, raping, and torturing four young women and the brutal murder of two others in the basement of his Philadelphia home. A self-styled minister, Mr. Heidnik held services for people with physical or mental handicaps in his home. The accused met some of his victims with the aid of a friend working at a treatment center for people with mental handicaps. Others he picked up near the center. Spokesmen for the center had complained to police that Mr. Heidnik was preying on people with mental handicaps. Also charged was Cyril Brown, a man with mental retardation who participated in the crimes. In 1988, despite an insanity plea by his lawyer, Mr. Heidnik was sentenced to death by electrocution. In order to prevent eligibility for parole in the event that the death sentence was overturned, in 1989, he received an additional sentence of 320 years in prison. In 1983, Mr. Heidnik had been released from a Pennsylvania hospital for the criminally insane for kidnapping a woman with mental retardation and holding her prisoner in a coal bin. Victims' reports of forced cannibalism were not substantiated although human remains were found in the kitchen. Police came under criticism in this case for not responding sooner to neighbors' repeated complaints of foul smells coming from the house and of unusual late-night activities. Heidnik's brother stated that they had been raised in an atmosphere of violence and racial prejudice. All of Heidnik's known victims were Black. His brother also stated that Mr. Heidnik's suicide attempt, made one week following his arrest, is one of several made over the years. Three weeks prior to his arrest, Mr. Heidnik had visited a Veteran's Administration mental health clinic. Newspaper coverage includes *Time*, *Newsweek*, *U.S. News and World Report*, *The London Times*, *The Washington Post*, and *Facts on File*.

423. **Guarnaschelli, D., Lee, U., & Pitts, F. W. (1972). Fallen fontanelle (Caida de Mollera): A variant of the battered child syndrome.** *Journal of the American Medical Association, 222(12), 1545-1546.*

This article alerts doctors serving Mexican-Americans to the dangers of a folk-medicine practice used in the treatment of the folk syndrome, "Caida de Mollera," in which the anterior fontanel is believed to have dropped, causing feeding difficulties. The cure is violent and involves whiplash shaking. The article discusses a case study describing the folk treatment and subsequent death of a 2-month-old boy.

424. **Gudjonsson, G. H., & Gunn, M. (1982). The competence and reliability of a witness in a criminal court: A case report.** *British Journal of Psychiatry, 141, 624-627.*

This article examines the law relating to the use of a 22-year-old female victim with mental handicaps as a prosecution witness in a criminal trial. The main problem involved the victim's competence to act as a witness and the reliability of her evidence. The authors discuss the results of psychological testing which provided guidelines by which the court could distinguish the reliable and the unreliable areas in her evidence.

425. **Guess, D., Helmstetter, E., & Turnbull, H. R., III (1987).** *Use of aversive procedures with persons who are disabled: An historical review and critical analysis.* **Seattle: The Association for Persons with Severe Handicaps.**

This monograph provides a discussion of the use of punishment and negative reinforcement procedures, particularly as applied to people with severe intellectual impairment. It suggests that these procedures have been frequently used to increase compliance and that the procedures have been used more frequently with individuals with mental handicaps than with prisoners or individuals with psychiatric impairments because people with severe intellectual disabilities have been less able or less effective in protesting against their use. It reports a number of studies in which electric shock, slaps, or other aversive stimuli are used as "treatment" to gain more compliant behavior.

426. **Gunn, M. (1989). Sexual abuse and adults with mental handicap: Can the law help? In H. Brown & A. Craft (Eds.),** *Thinking the unthinkable: Papers on sexual abuse and people with learning difficulties* **(pp. 51-73). London: FPA Education Unit.**

This chapter provides a legal discussion of sexual abuse

of adults with mental handicaps under English law. Many of the specific issues addressed do not generalize to other legal systems, but the more general implications are of universal concern. Concerns and limitations of the law are discussed. The author also presents alternative and proactive strategies that might reduce the risk for abuse or at least stop abuse where prosecution is difficult.

427. **Gunner, A. (1988). Are we handicapped by our prejudices?** *Professional Nurse, 3, 436-438.*

This article discusses the need of people with mental handicaps to express sexuality and the traditional societal response of denying them opportunities to express sexuality. Special attention is paid to the attitudes of nurses. It discusses the myth that sexual behavior should not be exhibited by people with mental handicaps because they do not fully understand the physiology or some other detailed aspect of their sexuality. The author suggests that this reasoning is equivalent to requiring people to fully understand the mechanics and physics of motorized transportation before allowing them to drive a car. The author also suggests that nurses must be comfortable with their own attitudes about sexuality and tolerant of others. She also suggests that "sex education" should focus more on developing mutually satisfactory human emotional and physical relationships while focusing less on clinical details. She points out the role of inadequate sex education and deprivation of appropriate sexual relationships in contributing to vulnerability to sexual abuse.

•H•

428. **Haavik, S. (1986). Marriage and parenthood. In J. A. Summers (Ed.),** *The right to grow up: An introduction to adults with developmental disabilities* **(pp. 67-90). Baltimore: Paul H. Brookes Publishing Co.**

This chapter discusses marriage and parenthood among people with developmental disabilities. Opening topics include attitudes of parents and caregivers and the prevalence of marriage, divorce, and marital maladjustment. The author concludes that people with developmental disabilities require more assistance in maintaining stable and satisfactory marriages than do people without disabilities. The discussion then moves on to address the use of workable alternative living arrangements and premarital training programs in assisting couples. The last section in the article addresses parenthood. Topics include attitudes of parents and caregivers, family size, quality of child care, intelligence and achievement in offspring, and alternatives for maximizing growth and development. The discussion topics on alternatives include the use of screening procedures for identifying families who may require assistance before they have children, education programs, and parent training.

429. Haavik, S.F., & Menninger, K. A., II. (1981). *Sexuality, law, and the developmentally disabled person.* **Baltimore: Paul H. Brookes Publishing Co.**

This book provides a good history and overview of sexual behavior, marriage, parenthood, and sterilization of people with developmental disabilities. It discusses law and ethical issues relevant to each of these topics. It also includes practical information on sex education programs, and it raises the difficult issue of balance between protection from sexual exploitation and allowing freedom of sexual expression.

430. Haddock, M. D., & McQueen, W. M. (1983). Assessing employee potentials for abuse. *Journal of Clinical Psychology, 77(6), 296-297.*

In this study, questionnaires were administered to 21 abusive and 21 nonabusive employees working in residential facilities in an effort to identify factors associated with potential for institutional abuse. The authors discuss the need for developing this type of assessment tool in the screening of staff working with children with developmental disabilities and children cared for outside the home.

431. Haight, S. L., & Fachting, D. D. (1986). Materials for teaching sexuality, love and maturity to high school students with learning disabilities. *Journal of Learning Disabilities, 19(6), 344-350.*

In this study, six 15- to 17-year-old students with learning disabilities and six 15- to 17-year-old average students were given an instructional unit on love, sexuality, and maturity. Post-test scores ranged between 90%-100% for the students with learning disabilities. Their pretest scores had been in the 58% to 84% range.

432. Haines, A. (1983). Legal studies and developmentally disabled persons. *Australia and New Zealand Journal of Developmental Disabilities, 9(3), 129-133.*

The focus of this study was to determine the effectiveness of a legal studies program used to teach 12 adolescents with "EMR" (mild to moderate mental retardation) in a special school. Follow-up scores were significantly greater than pretest scores, though not as high as post-test scores. The author argues that legal studies should be included in the curricula of special schools.

433. Hakim-Elahi, E. (1982). Contraceptive of choice for disabled (handicapped) persons. *New York State Journal of Medicine, 82(11),* 1601-1608.

This article describes a new medical classification of disabilities for use when providing contraception for people with handicaps. The categories of disability include mobility impairment, blindness, deafness, deaf-blind combination, mental impairment, chemical dependency, speech disorders, disabling birth defects, disabilities (e.g., learning disabilities), ostomies, major chronic diseases, and other disabling disorders (e.g., leprosy). The author explores the effect of disability on menstruation, fertility, and sexual function and discusses the contraceptive of choice for each group.

434. Hall, J. E. (1979). Sexuality and the mentally retarded person. In R. Green (Ed.), *Human sexuality: A health practitioner's text* **(pp. 165-174). Baltimore: Williams & Wilkins.**

This author discusses two common problems that parents of children with developmental disabilities bring to health professionals. The first is sterilization of females to avoid menstrual hygiene and the possibility of pregnancy. The author notes that only in sexual matters is it suggested that bodily structures be removed. Such a drastic procedure would not be recommended for a nondisabled girl so that she would not have to learn menstrual hygiene. Although it may require more patience and repetition to teach a girl with developmental disabilities to take care of her health and personal hygiene during menstruation, it generally can be done in an acceptable manner. In terms of sterilization as protection against pregnancy in the case of molestation, the author notes that it will not actually prevent molestation, and in any case, contraception is a better method of preventing unwanted pregnancy. The author feels that the alternative of abortion is available should unwanted pregnancy occur, and it would be preferable to such a final measure as hysterectomy. The second concern of parents of children with developmental disabilities is whether their child is homosexual. The author lists questions that parents should ask to guide them in assessing the sexual orientation of their child.

435. Hall, J. E., & Morris, H. L. (1976). Sexual knowledge and attitudes of institutionalized retarded adolescents. *American Journal of Mental Deficiency, 80(4), 382-387.*

These authors compared noninstitutionalized and institutionalized adolescents with mental handicaps on their sexual knowledge, self-concept, and attitude. The institutionalized adolescents had considerably less knowledge on socio-sexual topics. The amount of knowledge appeared to decrease with longer institutionalization, although residents in coed facilities have greater knowledge than those in same-sex housing. Although subjects in both groups knew what menstruation, pregnancy, and intercourse were, less than half knew what venereal disease, family planning, and birth control were. This lack of knowledge points to increased vulnerability of these adolescents to sexual exploitation and abuse.

436. **Hall, M. H. (1975). A view from the emergency and accident department. In A. W. Franklin (Ed.),** *Concerning child abuse: Papers presented by the Tunbridge Wells Study Group on non-accidental injury to children* **(pp. 7-20). New York: Churchill Livingstone.**
In this paper, a physician extensively involved in managing a busy emergency department discusses child abuse cases seen in the emergency room. Topics include early recognition of physically abused children, diagnosis, the need for exchange between pathologists and clinicians, prevalence, a five category classification system for abuse, and a discussion of problems and difficulties, including managing effective relationships between doctors, the police, and social workers. In his own case, the author has succeeded in establishing a valuable and fruitful link with the police. The author supports the view that the decision to return a child to parents who abused the child should be made on the basis of consultation between social agencies, medical professionals, and the police, rather than on the basis of unilateral decisions where one agent alone determines recommendations to the court.

437. **Halliday, S., & Stradiotti, J. (1986). Sexual health services: A formalized approach to sexuality and disability within health care agencies.** *Sieccan Journal, Special Issue: Proceedings of the Canadian Sex Research Forum, 1*(2), 40-42.
This article discusses the Sexual Health Care Service operating at Shaughnessy Hospital, Vancouver, British Columbia. Clients include both young and old with physical disabilities. The article is divided into four sections: background, major areas of sex-related concerns, assessment, and management.

438. **Halliechuk, R. (1989, November 25). Law society rules sex-abuser won't be allowed to be lawyer.** *Toronto Star*, p. A1.
This article discusses the case of a man who was refused the right to practice law in Ontario because the Law Society of Upper Canada ruled that he lacked "good character" after he had been convicted of sexually abusing his two-year old daughter and an eight-year-old child who was deaf and who rode on a school bus that he drove. The man had argued that he should be allowed to practice law because he would restrict his practice to real estate and business law, that he believed at the time of the assaults that these acts were not morally wrong, and that these were not serious crimes because he only was jailed for two months for these offenses..

439. **Hallingby, L. (1985). A human sexuality and sex education information service and library.** *Behavioral and Social Sciences Librarian, 4*(4), 43-48.
This article describes the Mary S. Caldrone Library of Sex Information and Education Council of the United States (SIECUS). Information on collections, services, and computerization plans is included.

440. **Halpern, R. (1986). Home-based early intervention: Dimensions of current practice.** *Child Welfare, 65*(4), 387-398.
This article claims that in recent years the practice of home-based early intervention (HBEI) has been influenced by four factors: changes in family composition and roles, increases in the numbers of single parent households, increases in births to unmarried mothers, and increases in births to very young mothers. The author examines the dynamics, contradictions, ambiguities, and unique strengths of HBEI and suggests that the most appropriate purpose for HBEI will evolve in response to perceived needs and changing social and scientific priorities.

441. **Halstead, L. O., & Halstead, K. (1983). Disability SARs and the small group experience: A conceptual framework.** *Sexuality and Disability, 6*(3/4), 183-196.
This article describes Sexual Attitude Reassessment (SAR) workshops held for people with physical disabilities, health care professionals, and interested community members. The major goal was the promotion of the reassessment of sexual attitudes and the development of increased comfort regarding sexuality, both in the personal and in the professional realm.

442. **Hammond, D. B., & Bonney, W. C. (1985). Results of sex education for support persons working with the elderly [Special issue: Sex education: Past, present, future].** *Journal of Sex Education and Therapy, 11*(2), 42-45.
This article examines the acquisition of knowledge and change in attitudes of 28 participants in a course on sexuality and aging. The course covered developmental stages, cultural differences, myths and facts, institutionalization, handicaps, and counseling. The authors found a significant increase in knowledge about sexual aging, a trend toward a more liberal viewpoint, and an ability to deal openly with elderly people when helping them with sexual problems.

443. **Hamre-Nietupski, S., & Ford, A. (1981). Sex education and related skills: A series of programs implemented with severely handicapped students.** *Sexuality and Disability, 4*(3), 179-193.
This article describes a program in which students with severe handicaps (mental/physical handicaps) were given training in sex education and related skills. Reproduction, birth control, and self-care were covered as part of the training. Students who received the training are now using the skills, and the data show that skills have generalized to situations in which direct training was not given.

444. **Hamre-Nietupski, S., & Williams, W. (1977). Implementation of selected sex education and social skills to severely handicapped students.** *Education and Training of the Mentally Retarded, 12*(4), 364-372.

A sex education/social skills program for people with severe mental handicaps is described in this article. The sex education component consisted of teaching the student to distinguish gender and body parts as well as self-care skills. The social skills component involved teaching appropriate social behaviors and interactions and social manners. Results of the program show that the great majority of students mastered the skills taught.

445. Hanke, G. C. (1987). Sexuality of clients with mental retardation/developmental disability. *Asha, 29*(12), 31, 33.

This article provides a brief and very basic discussion of sexuality of people with developmental disabilities. The author suggests that most residential programs deal with sexual expression on a "situational intervention basis: they stop it when they see it."

446. Hansen, C. (1980). Child abuse: A cause and effect of mental retardation. In M.K. McCormack (Ed.), *Prevention of mental retardation and other developmental disabilities* (pp. 549-568). New York: Dekker.

This article reviews the literature linking cerebral palsy to abuse. The long-term effects of abuse and neglect on children are also discussed.

447. Hanson, R. (Ed.). (1982). *Institutional abuse of children and youth*. New York: Haworth Press.

This book is comprised of 14 articles written by various authors on topics related to the abuse and neglect of children in out-of-home care situations. The first section deals with defining institutional abuse and includes articles that address out-of-home care using a family systems perspective and the role of defining children's rights in the prevention of abuse. The second section discusses the relationship between religious values and child abuse. It also addresses the newspaper coverage of corporal punishment in schools. The third section deals with in-patient treatment and includes articles addressing the neglect of the health needs of juveniles, children's rights upon entering therapeutic institutions, and abuse resulting from attempting to treat the untreatable. The fourth section discusses responses to the problem of abuse in institutional settings. Article topics include offering advice to would-be reporters of institutional abuse, the attitudes of direct-care workers toward the use of physical force on children, and the use of standards in prevention. The last section deals with meta-abuse, the inadvertent re-abuse of children by professional helping agencies.

448. Harrell, S. A., & Orem, R. C. (1980). *Preventing child abuse and neglect: A guide for staff in residential institutions* (DHHS Publication No. ADM 80-30255). Washington, DC: U. S. Department of Health & Human Services.

Institutionalized children have a common characteristic: They are children with whom their families or the community cannot cope. In most cases, institutionalization results from mental retardation, physical handicap, emotional disturbance, incorrigibility, or delinquency. The authors further state that all of these children "are more likely than other 'normal' children to be maltreated," even when they are living with their own families. Therefore, the community, when institutionalizing these children, is admitting that they cannot be handled in a more normal environment. However, the institutions in which they are placed are expected to cope with them, treat their problems, and not to abuse or neglect them. Characteristics of institutionalized children that may make them difficult to cope with include the following: a) they may be severely handicapped, either mentally or physically, with well-documented frustration and very little observable response or "progress," even over long periods of time; b) they may exhibit bizarre behavior that does not respond to methods of rewards, reinforcements, and punishments; c) they can be dangerous, based on their demonstrated behavior; and d) they may be unable to show staff any warmth or appreciation, at least until after a period of treatment.

449. Harris, V. S., & McHale, S. M. (1989). Family life problems, daily caregiving activities, and psychological well-being of mothers of mentally retarded children. *American Journal on Mental Retardation, 94*, 231-239.

This article compares 30 mothers of children with mental handicaps to 30 mothers who only had children without disabilities. The mothers of children with disabilities differed in the degree of maternal involvement and time spent in child-oriented activities, but there were no overall differences in maternal well-being between the groups. This finding casts some additional doubt on the hypothesized disability-dependency-stress-abuse cycle that is often used to explain increased abuse of children with disabilities.

450. Harrison, D. F. (1986). The institutionalized mentally ill. In H. L. Gochros, J. S. Gochros, & J. Fischer (Eds.), *Helping the sexually oppressed* (pp. 191-209). Englewood Cliffs, NJ: Prentice-Hall.

In this chapter, the kinds of interventions available for ensuring the sexual rights of institutionalized people with mental illness are discussed. Research and practical implications are briefly addressed. Topics include the following: patient advocacy; indications and contra-indications of clinical treatment of sexual problems in a hospitalized population; individual, couple, or group treatment formats; an overview of techniques that can be used for sexual problems in psychiatric hospitals; broadscale intervention; the range of sex-related problems; and the scope of sexual oppression.

451. Harry, B. (1984). A deaf sex offender. *Journal of Forensic Sciences, 29*(4), 1140-1143.

This article discusses the case of a sex offender who is deaf which illustrates discretionary handling within the criminal justice system and suggests an altered psychosexual development. The author examines several characteristics in the development and lives of people who are deaf that may contribute to an altered psychosexual development and an increased likelihood of committing sex offenses.

452. Hartman, C., MacIntosh, B., & Englehardt, B. (1983). The neglected and forgotten sexual partner of the physically disabled. *Social Work, 28*(5), 370-374.

This article discusses some treatment methods for the problems of the partners of people with physical disabilities. The authors claim treatment must include knowledge of the prior relationship and the sexual expectations that have guided the couple since the disability. They examine the implications for social workers involved in the health care of people with physical disabilities and their partners and suggest reviewing the present rehabilitation process, researching the impact of the trauma on other partners of the individual with disabilities, and educating those within the profession as well as outside it. The authors conclude that support groups for the able-bodied partner, in conjunction with individual and conjoint therapy, can enrich the treatment process.

453. Harvey, M. A. (1989). *Psychotherapy with deaf and hard-of-hearing persons: A systemic model.* Hillsdale, NJ: Lawrence Erlbaum Associates.

This book describes a systemic approach to the treatment of clients with hearing handicaps. Sample topics include life span development of deaf and hearing impaired ecosystems, treatment issues, family treatment, the use of interpreters, and deaf parents' children who can hear. Sexuality and sexual abuse are not discussed.

454. Harvey, W., & Watson-Russell, A. (1986). *So, you have to go to court.* Toronto: Butterworth.

This booklet is designed to help parents, teachers, counselors, or other adults to prepare children (5 to 8 years old) to participate in court as witnesses. It is also intended to be read by older children (9 to 12 years old) to prepare them to serve as witnesses. It has been used by police departments and victims' services agencies for this purpose. It uses simple language with boldface for essential statements that may be used exclusive of the remaining text for very young children. With some modification, the book may also be suitable for use with older individuals with impaired learning or communication skills.

455. Hastings, M. M. (1986). The long-term care puzzle and mental health policy: Putting the pieces together. *American Behavioral Scientist, 30*(2), 143-173.

This article examines the long-term care of elderly people and people with disabilities in light of the rapid growth in the older population. The author claims that the state, now the main policymaker, will face complex issues as regulator, purchaser, and service provider and will need creativity and vision in policy formulation for long-term care. The author also considers public and private financing mechanisms.

456. Haugaard, J. J., & Emery, R. E. (1989). Methodological issues in child sexual abuse research. *Child Abuse & Neglect, 13*, 89-100.

This article discusses issues related to sexual abuse methodology, suggesting ways in which results may be influenced by methodology. Measures of incidence and prevalence have reported highly variable results. The authors point out that the highest rates come from sampling women in urban households, intermediate rates come from national surveys, and lower rates come from college students. The lack of a standard definition of sexual abuse also contributes to differences. For example, some definitions include noncontact offenses and others do not, and differences in age ranges describing children may substantially influence rates. The authors include results from their own study of 1089 female and male undergraduate university students that was designed to test the effects of some methodological variables. The order of testing personality variables before or after asking about sexual abuse experiences did not prove significant. High response rates did not necessarily produce more accurate estimates of prevalence. Some individuals did not respond to surveys because recounting their experiences was too painful. Others did not respond because they did not find it relevant as nonvictims. Since the errors introduced by these two groups biased results in opposite directions, the relative representation of these two groups in the sample may influence the direction of bias. The definition of sexual abuse used had a significant effect on the prevalence rate, which was only 1.7% with the most conservative definition, but which increased to 9.3% when the broadest definition was used. The narrowest definition was, however, associated with the most severe impact on the victim.

457. Haugaard, J. J., & Reppucci, N. D. (1988). *The sexual abuse of children: A comprehensive guide to current knowledge and intervention strategies.* San Francisco: Jossey-Bass.

This book provides an overview and discussion of child sexual abuse. It includes a substantial discussion of definitions, incidence, detection, treatment, prevention, and the legal process. The authors point out that although prevention programs have been shown to increase knowledge about sexual abuse there is a significant lack of data supporting their actual ability to prevent abuse.

458. Hawkins, W. E., & Duncan, D. F. (1985). Children's illnesses as risk factors for child abuse. *Psychological Reports, 56*, 638.

This study assessed whether children with chronic physical or mental health problems were overrepresented among victims of child abuse and neglect. Risk factors examined included prior abuse, mental retardation, congenital physical handicaps, other physical handicaps, chronic illness, emotional disturbance, excessive crying, feeding problems, and hyperactivity. When substantiated cases were compared to unsubstantiated cases, five risk factors were significantly more common among the former: chronic illness, emotional disturbance, hyperactivity, mental retardation, and other physical handicaps. Emotional disturbance and mental retardation were most often indicated for substantiated abuse cases.

459. Hebert, P. (1986, August). Our justice system is lacking [Letter to the editor]. *Spokesman*, p. 4.
The director of Edmonton's Disabled Victims of Violence writes that often the criminal justice system and courts are not aware of the response of people with disabilities to specific situations. In some circumstances, a person with disabilities will react to stress by laughter, which in a courtroom can be construed against the victim. The author states that the criminal justice system and the courts have to have an understanding of the person with the disability if a fair trial is to be given.

460. Helfer, R. E. (1980). Developmental deficits which limit interpersonal skills. In R. E. Helfer & R. S. Kempe (Eds.), *The battered child* (3rd ed., pp. 36-48). Chicago: University of Chicago Press.
This chapter addresses the need for service providers to understand the basic developmental traits seen in young adults reared in neglectful or abusive circumstances. Unless treated, maladaptive traits are passed on to offspring. Maladaptive traits include poor interpersonal skills, poor understanding of the emotional needs of others, inability to accept responsibility for their actions, a tendency to reverse child-parent roles, poor decision-making and problem-solving skills, and confusion over the relationship between feelings and actions.

461. Helfer, R. E. (1980). Retraining and relearning. In R. E. Helfer & R. S. Kempe (Eds.), *The battered child* (3rd ed., pp. 391-400). Chicago: University of Chicago Press.
This chapter focuses on teaching young parents with deficient childhood skills in effectively interacting with each other and with their children. Teaching methods include teaching small subsets of the skill, positive modeling by the instructor, the use of small and logical progressive steps, and rapid and logical feedback. The unlearning of maladaptive behaviors is also critical. The author emphasizes that knowing what to do usually precedes knowing how to do it. Other topics include the need for active participation in learning, the difficulty of starting, the reawakening of disturbing memories in students, and the progression of skills learning from the context of the individual to the group context.

462. Helfer, R. E., & Kempe, R. S. (Eds.). (1987). *The battered child* (4th ed.). Chicago: University of Chicago Press.

This fourth edition of a classic text on child abuse is composed of articles by a wide range of authors and is organized into four sections: context, assessment, intervention and treatment, and prevention. Sample topics include the history of child abuse, cultural factors, the short- and long-term effects of child abuse and neglect on normal development, psychodynamic factors, the therapeutic relationship, assessment by child protection teams, assessment by child psychologists, protective services, incest and sexual abuse, malnutrition and growth retardation, therapy for the offender, the role of law enforcement, legal issues in child protection, the promotion of positive parent-infant relationships, American national priorities for prevention, and future directions. Abuse of people with disabilities does not form a focus for discussion.

463. Hensey, O., Ilett, S. J., & Rosenbloom, L. (1983, August 13). Child abuse and cerebral palsy [Letter to the editor]. *The Lancet*, p. 400.
This letter to the editor is in response to an editorial that stated the results of a recent study by Diamond and Jaudes (1983) on child abuse and cerebral palsy. In the study by Diamond and Jaudes, the following is suggested: In as many as 20% of children with cerebral palsy, child abuse was a cause of or a response to the handicapping condition. Drawing on their experience, the authors of this letter to the editor suggest the following: Although child abuse is a cause of handicaps, it is not as common a cause as stated by Diamond and Jaudes.

464. Herman, J. (1983). Recognition and treatment of incestuous families. *International Journal of Family Therapy*, 5(2), 81-91.
This article discusses incest as a major mental health problem, describing both its prevalence and morbidity. It suggests that the possibility of incest should be considered when a family includes a violent father, a mother with a disability, a child in an adult maternal role, or an "acting out" adolescent girl. It advocates active cooperation between mental health professionals and mandated child-protective and law-enforcement agencies for effective treatment. It describes group therapy and affiliated self-help programs as the treatment modality of choice and concludes that rehabilitation of the family is based on restoration of the mother-daughter bond as a guarantee of safety for the child.

465. Herrenkohl, E. C., & Herrenkohl, R. C. (1981). *Explanations of child maltreatment: A preliminary appraisal.* Durham: New Hampshire University, Center for Social Research, National Conference for Family Violence Researchers.
The causes of child maltreatment are discussed in terms of the findings of two studies, one of which was a follow-up study. Findings suggest that there is a positive relationship between the total number of stressors on a family, as perceived by the parent, and the

total number of abusive incidents. Further analyses were done on 826 incidents of physical abuse, and the results indicate that abuse often occurs in reaction to difficult, but not unusual, childrearing situations.

466. Heshusius, L. (1982). Sexuality, intimacy, and persons we label mentally retarded: What they think—what we think. *Mental Retardation, 20*(4), 164-168.

This article reviews naturalistic research in which people with mental impairments discussed their perceptions of intimacy and sexuality. It describes normal sexual development and the beneficial effects of sexual contact. It includes cultural comparisons and discusses the psychological and anthropological data on the importance of touch and sexual expression in human development. The author suggests that ideas about sex and people with mental retardation as well as professional practices and attitudes should be reexamined.

467. Hewitt, S. E. (1987). The abuse of deinstitutionalized persons with mental handicaps. *Disability, Handicap and Society, 2*(2), 127-135.

This article advocates for the humane treatment of people with mental handicaps who are deinstitutionalized. It examines the strong likelihood of the abuse of these individuals, especially sexual abuse, and it reviews legislative efforts to protect people with mental handicaps, paying special attention to a 1986 Massachusetts law that established a Disabled Persons Protection Commission.

468. Hill, G. (1987). Sexual abuse and the mentally handicapped. *Child Sexual Abuse Newsletter, 6,* 4-5.

This author discusses the importance of self-protection education for people with mental handicaps. Such education greatly reduces the chances of being exploited. Materials have been developed specifically for teaching sexuality concepts and self-protection to people with mental handicaps. The Seattle Rape Relief Developmental Disabilities Project is one such program. Level 1 is designed for children ages 6-11 and addresses incest and molestation. Level 2 is designed for ages 12 and up. Self-protection in social and home situations is the focus, along with assertiveness training. The article states that 88% of people with mental handicaps are exploited and that only 12% are exploited if they have received self-protection education. Based on these figures, the suggestion is made that education is the key.

469. Hingsburger, D. (1987). Sex counseling with the developmentally handicapped: The assessment and management of seven critical problems. *Psychiatric Aspects of Mental Retardation Reviews, 6*(9), 41-46.

The author of this article works with clients with developmental disabilities who engage in inappropriate sexual behavior. In this article, he discusses seven problems identified in providing sex counseling to

people with mental handicaps: 1) confused self-concept, 2) isolation from peers, 3) lack of sexual knowledge, 4) sexuality as furtive behavior, 5) negative sexual experiences, 6) inconsistent socio-sexual environments, and 7) lack of personal power. In regard to negative sexual experiences, the author points out the following: In his clinic, all clients who had lived in institutions had been molested or coerced into sexual activity, and many had later become perpetrators of deviant sexual acts. The author briefly explains each of these problems and offers suggestions on therapeutic intervention for professionals who provide sex counseling for people with mental handicaps.

470. Hingsburger, D. (1988). Clients and curriculum: Preparing for sex education. *Psychiatric Aspects of Mental Retardation Reviews, 7*(3), 13-17.

This article examines how counselors can prepare their clients with intellectual and developmental handicaps for sex education. The author emphasizes respecting the client's history, the beliefs of his or her family, and discovering what the client may already know about sex and using this information to differentiate between moral beliefs and misinformation, providing education where necessary. Counselors are advised to make sure the client knows that sex is a positive aspect of life, that the counseling sessions are private, that any idea the client may have will not meet with disapproval in counseling sessions, and that he or she is free to make autonomous decisions about sexual beliefs and behavior. The author also recommends encouraging clients to make decisions that are safe and that will be reinforced with success at home.

471. Hingsburger, D., & Griffiths, D. (1986). Dealing with sexuality in a community residential service. *Psychiatric Aspects of Mental Retardation Reviews, 5*(12), 63-67.

Using an example of a program implemented with eight male clients, this article demonstrates how sexuality can be included in a counseling program for residents in an agency serving people with developmental handicaps. Components of the program include establishing a consistent value system, educating staff to accept clients' sexuality, educating clients on bodily sexual functions, and counseling clients in a nonjudgmental manner. Resulting public relations issues were handled well, and the program resulted in increased client and staff comfort with the issue of client sexuality. Homosexuality as a result of institutional life also is discussed.

472. Hirayama, H. (1979). Management of the sexuality of the mentally retarded in institutions: Problems and issues. In D. Kunkel (Ed.), *Sexual issues in social work* **(pp. 105-130). Honolulu: University of Hawaii, School of Social Work.**

This chapter is a discussion of the nature and sources of conflicts and dilemmas in the development of policies and practices relating to the management of sexuality of people with mental retardation in institutions. Topics addressed include the following: a) the lack of knowledge about the sexuality of people with mental retardation, b) the dilemma created by wanting to help people with mental retardation meet their sexual needs, but fearing exploitation may result, c) the consequences to people with mental retardation when sexual policies are lacking in the institution, d) sexual attitudes of parents and staff, e) components of human sexuality, and f) the application of the normalization principle to institutions.

473. **Hirschbach, E. (1982). Children beyond reach? In R. Hanson (Ed.),** *Institutional abuse of children and youth* **(pp. 99-107). New York: Haworth Press.**
This chapter is based on the premise that child abuse in institutions is caused by asking workers to treat the untreatable. Inaccessible children should be identified early and given treatment that recognizes their inability to be restored to health. These children include those who have experienced early and prolonged physical and emotional deprivation and show most of the characteristics of chronic neglect, those who manifest severe character disorder and are asocial and lack a super-ego, and those children whose ability to relate to others has been systematically destroyed through multiple placements. The author discusses psychiatrists', social workers', and child care workers' reluctance to recognize the untreatability of some profoundly damaged children. The problem of labeling children as untreatable is discussed.

474. **Hobbs, C. J., & Wynne, J. M. (1989). Sexual abuse of English boys and girls: The importance of anal examination.** *Child Abuse & Neglect,* *13,* **195-210.**
This article describes results from a study of 1,368 referrals for neglect and abuse, including 608 cases of suspected sexual abuse. A wide variety of anal injuries and abnormalities were found in many of the sexually abused children and were absent in the great majority of the children who were not sexually abused. The anal signs were particularly common in children under 5 years of age. The authors conclude that anal examination should be an essential part of evaluation whenever sexual abuse is suspected. This and other physical examination evidence of abuse may be especially critical for children whose impaired ability to communicate prevents disclosure of abuse or when the validity of a child's disclosure is questioned.

475. **Hochstadt, N. J., Jaudes, P. K., Zimo, D. A., & Schachter, J. (1987). The medical and psychosocial needs of children entering foster care.** *Child Abuse & Neglect, 11*(1), **53-62.**
In this study, 149 children entering foster care in Illinois were screened on medical and psychosocial parameters. The children were found to have a higher incidence of chronic medical conditions, to weigh less, be shorter in height, have a high incidence of developmental delays, and show deficits in adaptive behavior.

476. **Hoffman, N. D. (1984). Conjugal psychiatric hospitalization.** *Canadian Journal of Psychiatry, 29*(4), **344-346.**
Contrary to ward staff expectations, the conjugal hospitalization of a 41-year-old paranoid schizophrenic man with his 36-year-old girlfriend with mild mental retardation and behavior-disorders proved to be beneficial both to the couple and to the ward where they had their room.

477. **Hohenshil, T. H., & Szymanski, E. M. (1989). Introduction to special feature.** *Journal of Counseling & Development, 68,* **138-139.**
This introduction to a special feature on counseling people with disabilities raises a question regarding the progress of the last 10 years in this area. The authors conclude that significant progress has been made but that many unresolved problems remain. They suggest that the next challenge is the application of recent advances to professional training and practice.

478. **Holbrook, T. (1989). Policing sexuality in a modern state hospital.** *Hospital & Community Psychiatry, 40*(1), **75-79.**
This article examines the legal and clinical issues that were raised by a 1985 grand jury investigation into conditions at the Rochester (New York) Psychiatric Center following the center's decision not to notify police of the sodomy of a patient by another patient. As a result of the investigation, the hospital instituted a stringent policy requiring extensive investigation and physical examination of patients found having sex. The article discusses the impact of public scrutiny on the policing of patient sexuality and the negative aspects of overreporting sexual activity at a state hospital.

479. **Holder, V. (1976). The battered child at school.** *Health and Social Service Journal, 86*(4472), **71-72.**
The academic difficulties of children who have been physically or emotionally abused are examined in this article. Abuse resulting in perceptual difficulties and difficulties with perceptual motor skills are discussed. Also, severe anxiety resulting in a child's inability to focus is addressed. Other topics include parents' unfulfilled dependency needs, unrealistically high parental expectation, and school failure as an expression of anger that acts to trigger parental violence.

480. **Hopper, C. E., & Allen, W. A. (1980).** *Sex education for physically handicapped youth.* **Springfield, IL: Charles C Thomas.**
This book provides basic sex education material addressed to adolescents with physical handicaps. It combines factual information about sexual mechanics with motivational content on developing a positive self-concept and mutually supportive relationships with others. It does not deal directly with issues of sexual abuse.

481. Hopper, D. (1989). Intellectually handicapped victims of abuse: Doubly victimized? *Autism Society Canada, 7*(4), 1, 3.

This article discusses a case in Canada in which a victim of sexual assault with a mental handicap was not allowed to testify in court on her own behalf. Although the offender confessed, the case will not go to court.

482. Horowitz, R. M. (1984). *The legal rights of children.* Monterey, CA: Shepard's/McGraw-Hill.

This book is written primarily for lawyers who work with children, but it may be valuable to other professionals and advocates working with children. Sections on child protection and children as witnesses are of particular interest.

483. Hosie, T. W., Patterson, J. B., & Hollingsworth, D. K. (1989). School rehabilitation counselor preparation: Meeting the needs of individuals with disabilities. *Journal of Counseling & Development, 68,* 171-176.

This article addresses the need for preparing school and rehabilitation counselors to work with clients with disabilities. A number of challenges to the field are discussed, and relevant accreditation standards are considered.

484. Hoxter, S. (1986). The significance of trauma in the difficulties encountered by physically disabled children. *Journal of Child Psycho-therapy, 12*(1), 87-102.

This article is of interest to therapists and counselors. The focus is on the counter-transference that is experienced when working with children who have experienced external trauma. Particular reference is made to children with disabilities.

485. Hucker, S., Langevin, R., Wortzman, G., Bain, J., & Handy, L. (1986). Neuropsychological impairment in pedophiles. *Canadian Journal of Behavioural Science, 18*(4), 440-448.

In this study, neuropsychological examinations were administered to heterosexual, homosexual, and bisexual pedophiles as well as to a control group made up of nonviolent sex offenders. As compared to the nonviolent control group, the three pedophile groups showed significantly more impairment on all measures. Also, left temporo-parietal pathology was more common in pedophiles. The findings suggest that a neuropychological examination can prove useful in the clinical assessment of pedophilia.

486. Hughes, H. M., & DiBrezzo, R. (1987). Physical and emotional abuse and motor development: A preliminary investigation. *Perceptual and Motor Skills, 64,* 469-470.

A study was conducted that compared children temporarily residing in a women's shelter who had reportedly been abused with a comparison group of nonabused children in the same shelter. The mothers of the children were interviewed about learning difficulties experienced by their children. Twelve percent of nonabused and 22% of physically abused children were reported to have language delays. Eleven percent of nonabused and 23% of physically abused children were reported to have learning difficulties. The authors conclude that further research using standardized measures of motor development and skills would be valuable.

487. Hughes, R. C., & Rycus, J. S. (1983). *Child welfare services for children with developmental disabilities* [Monograph]. New York: Child Welfare League of America, Inc.

This 1983 monograph addresses the need for child welfare services to be modified to meet the needs of children with disabilities. Sample topics include description of specific developmental disabilities, the early identification of children with developmental disabilities through the child welfare system, myths and misconceptions about developmental disabilities, and specific service needs. Proposed modifications include formal changes to screening procedures, staff training in making referrals to resources available to people with disabilities, the inclusion of respite care in substitute care operations, the inclusion of children with disabilities in foster care and adoption services, and the establishment of new services. New services might include parent education programs and advocacy programs. Sample parent education programs include behavior management, home management, sexual issues, nondisabled siblings, and negative attitudes toward disability.

488. Hulnick, M. R., & Hulnick, H. R. (1989). Life's challenges: Curse or opportunity? Counseling families of persons with disabilities. *Journal of Counseling & Development, 68,* 166-170.

Disability is viewed from the perspective of presenting a positive opportunity for reframing life experiences. Assuming responsibility for outcomes is seen as a step toward adjustment and empowerment. Specific techniques for facilitating adjustment and empowerment are discussed.

489. Humes, C. W., Szymanski, E. M., & Hohenshil, T. H. (1989). Roles of counseling in enabling persons with disabilities. *Journal of Counseling & Development, 68,* 145-150.

This article discusses the roles of counselors serving clients with disabilities. It also provides some guidelines for counselors working with these clients. Some of these basic guidelines include the following: 1) avoiding disabling language, 2) considering the effects of perceptions, environments, and expectations, 3) emphasizing abilities and not disabilities, and 4) consulting specialists in the complexities of specific disabilities. The authors surveyed state departments of education and found that the development of

Individualized Education Programs, transitional planning, and rehabilitation counseling were important roles. They emphasize transdisciplinary teamwork as a method for best meeting client needs.

490. Hunter, R. S., Kilstrom, N., & Loda, F. (1985). Sexually abused children: Identifying masked presentations in a medical setting. *Child Abuse & Neglect, 9*(1), 17-25.

These authors studied 50 sexually abused children whose initial symptoms masked the abuse (masked group) and compared them to 31 sexually abused children for whom the abuse was the chief complaint (overt group). In cases where abuse was masked, genital symptoms were the most common complaints, followed by psychosomatic/behavioral disorders (e.g., stomach pain, drug overdose, anorexia). Victims in the masked group were much more likely to reveal past incidents of sexual abuse, whereas, victims in the overt group were more likely to be reporting the initial incident of abuse. In masked cases, the perpetrator was more likely to be a member of the victim's immediate family than in overt cases. The authors state that their findings put the average age at which sexual abuse is most likely to occur at two years younger than reported in the literature. When masked cases are considered, the rate of victimization for males is increased (i.e., 16% of masked victims compared with only 3% of overt victims). Health care professionals working with children must be aware of the possibility that sexual abuse is being masked by other ailments in order to identify abuse at the earliest stages.

491. Hurley, A. D., & Hurley, F. J. (1986). Counseling and psychotherapy with mentally retarded clients: I. The initial interview. *Psychiatric Aspects of Mental Retardation Reviews, 5*(5), 22-26.

This article discusses the intake procedure for clients with mental retardation when the therapist must determine the suitability of the client for counseling or psychotherapy. Intake tasks include introductions, problem identification, the assessment of cognitive functioning, and client education. Procedures for establishing a fruitful therapeutic alliance are presented. The need for adapting the interview procedure to the specific needs and personality of the client is emphasized.

492. Hurley, A. D., & Hurley, F. J. (1987). Psychotherapy and counseling: II. Establishing a therapeutic relationship. *Psychiatric Aspects of Mental Retardation Reviews, 6*(4), 15-20.

This article offers guidelines on how to establish a therapeutic alliance with a client with mental retardation. The authors suggest that the trust learned through the alliance will generalize to other relationships.

493. Hurley, A. D., & Sovner, R. (1982). Phobic behavior and mentally retarded persons. *Psychiatric Aspects of Mental Retardation Newsletter, 1*(11), 41-44.

This article reviews studies on the treatment of phobia in people with mental retardation and outlines various treatment methods, including graded exposure, counter-conditioning, systematic desensitization, flooding, modeling, and stimulus fading. Phobias include fear of separation, animals, unknown adults, community-based activities, riding a school bus, and fear related to natural events. Note that this article is a fairly old one, and aversive methods such as flooding have come into question.

494. Hurley, A. D., & Sovner, R. (1982). Use of the Rorschach technique in mentally retarded patients. *Psychiatric Aspects of Mental Retardation Newsletter, 1*(2), 4-7.

This article discusses the utility, administration, and interpretation of the Rorschach Test when used with people with mental retardation. The Rorschach Test can assess capacity and efficiency in cognitive functioning, cognitive complexity and response style, creativity and organizational ability, and affective functioning. The test can also identify the presence of an active psychosis, specific habilitation needs, and the need for further neuropsychological testing.

495. Hurley, A. D., & Sovner, R. (1983). Treatment of sexual deviation in mentally retarded persons. *Psychiatric Aspects of Mental Retardation Newsletter, 2*(4), 13-16.

These authors state that the first step in assessing treatment needs for offenders with mental retardation is to determine whether the behavior is really deviant or just labeled as such by others. Since giving direct education about sexuality may be all that is needed, the problem should be discussed candidly with the client in simple terms that he or she can understand. If intervention through direct discussion is inadequate, behavioral techniques may be used to eliminate the undesirable behavior. The article gives examples of clients treated by the authors. The case examples include pedophilia, public masturbation, public disrobing, exhibitionism, and fetishism. The behavioral treatments used are described.

496. Hurley, A. D., & Sovner, R. (1985). Paradoxical interventions with mentally retarded clients. *Psychiatric Aspects of Mental Retardation Reviews, 4*(10), 39-42.

This article outlines the use of paradoxical intention with clients with mental retardation. This technique should only be used after other techniques have failed or been identified as unsuitable. Clients with mild to moderate developmental disabilities respond better to this intervention than people with more severe impairments. The client must have a rudimentary understanding of interpersonal dynamics. The use of this intervention in a residential setting must involve the participation of an experienced therapist and the approval of the human rights committee. Case studies are presented.

497. Hurley, A. D., & Sovner, R. (1985). The use of the Thematic Apperception Test in mentally retarded persons. *Psychiatric Aspects of Mental Retardation Reviews, 4(3), 9-12.*

This article describes the use of the Thematic Apperception Test (TAT) with clients with mental retardation. The need for concrete and explicit instructions is discussed. Illustrative studies are cited and include the use of the test in understanding clients from broken homes, clients' motivation for achievement, the psychodynamics of clients diagnosed as having psychopathic personalities, and the aggressive fantasies of clients with criminal records. The authors highly recommend the use of this personality test with people with mental retardation.

•I•

498. Immunity found in parental termination action. (1984). *Mental and Physical Disability Law Reporter, 8(5), 476-477.*

This paper describes the Sixth Circuit court's ruling, in Kurzawa v. Mueller, 732 F.2d. 1456 (6th Cir. 1984), that all individuals professionally associated with the prosecution of child neglect and delinquency proceedings are entitled to absolute immunity from lawsuits that result from their various duties.

499. Innovations in the habilitation and rehabilitation of deaf adolescents. (1986). *Selected proceedings of the National Conference on the Habilitation and Rehabilitation of Deaf Adolescents (Afton, Oklahoma, April 28-May 2, 1986).* **Little Rock: Arkansas University, Rehabilitation, Research and Training Center on Deafness and Hearing Impairment. (ERIC Document Reproduction Service No. ED 296 547)**

This document includes 24 papers addressing the habilitation and rehabilitation of adolescents who are deaf. The paper entitled "Approaches to Sexual Abuse Interventions and Suicide Prevention" is the only article addressing the issues of sexuality and sexual assault. This article discusses the treatment of victims, sexual health policies, and intervening with suicidal adolescents who are deaf.

500. Institute of Information Studies, National Rehabilitation Information Centre. (1982). *Intimacy and disability.* **Washington, DC: Author.**

This 90-page guide is written for people with disabilities who want information on how to develop and maintain relationships, both sexual and nonsexual. Topics related to sexual intimacy include self-image, body image, meeting prospective partners, developing a sexual relationship, sexuality, and exploring sexual options. A bibliography of books, films, and tapes is included.

501. Institute of Law Research and Reform. (1986). *Sterilization: Minors and mentally incompetent adults.* **Edmonton, Alberta: Author.**

The Institute of Law Research and Reform has presented a discussion paper on the subject of sterilization of minors and people who are mentally incompetent. The purpose of the study was as follows: to ascertain the present law of sterilization; to ascertain how often, on whose decision, and for what reasons sterilizations are being performed on minors and adults who are mentally incompetent in Alberta; and to decide whether the present law adequately protects the interest of the minor or the adult who is mentally incompetent being sterilized and the physician performing the operation and, if it does not, to recommend change. The existing law is unclear about who may make what sterilization decision for what purposes in what circumstances for minors and adults who are mentally incompetent. The report details past and present sterilization laws. The repeal of the Sexual Sterilization Act in 1972 left Alberta without a statute on sterilization. In the absence of specific legislation, the authority for sterilization from guardians or parents has been argued to come from three possible sources of law: 1) the law places a duty on parents and guardians to make provision for persons in their charge; 2) the law permits a parent or guardian to substitute his or her consent for the consent of a minor or adult who is mentally incompetent to beneficial treatment; and 3) the law confers supervisory and protective jurisdiction on the courts. It is uncertain whether any of these sources is broad enough to cover contraceptive procedures and hygienic hysterectomies. There are also Charter considerations that may affect the issue of sterilization of people with mental handicaps. The paper discusses the various pertinent sections. The position of the law in England and the United States and the findings of the Law Reform Commission of Canada Study and Recommendations are also discussed. From the examination of these sources, the Institute makes some tentative recommendations. The recommendations are divided into two parts: The first part identifies the persons and sterilization purposes that should be made subject to appropriate substantive and procedural safeguards, and the second part suggests what those safeguards should be. The Institute does not recommend any change in the law of consent by an adult who is mentally competent to his or her own sterilization (that is, an adult who is mentally competent can give valid consent to medical treatment, contraceptive procedures, or a hygienic hysterectomy). The Institute does not recommend a contraceptive procedure or hygienic hysterectomy for a minor who is mentally incompetent and is reasonably likely to become competent with maturation or on an individual who is mentally incompetent who may become competent. For a person who is permanently mentally incompetent (minor or adult), sterilization for the above purpose should be available based on the equality of rights argument, but the sterilization decision should be subject to the imposition of stringent procedural safeguards to ensure that sterilizations are performed in appropriate circumstances and that the power to authorize the performance of sterilization on people who are permanently mentally incompetent is not abused. The safeguards that should be implemented were divided into a majority and a minority viewpoint. The report discusses each.

502. Institute of Law Research and Reform. (1988). *Sterilization decisions: Minors and mentally incompetent adults.* **Edmonton, Alberta: Author.**

This paper presents the current laws on sterilization of minors and people with mental handicaps and makes recommendations for changes to the law in Alberta. The recommendations are based on four guiding principles: 1) a sterilization should be performed only where it is in the best interests of the person to be sterilized and not where its purpose benefits others; 2) a sterilization should be a last resort, other alternatives having been shown to be inadequate for the intended purpose; 3) the dignity, welfare, and total development of the person with a mental disability for whom the sterilization is being considered should be respected at all times; and 4) the procedure for decision should ensure the protection of the other principles.

Recommendations for a new sterilization law include the following: 1) a judge may make an order authorizing either an elective sterilization or a hysterectomy for menstrual management on an adult who is not competent to consent to the proposed sterilization; 2) a judge shall not make an order (of elective sterilization or hysterectomy) unless he or she is satisfied that the proposed sterilization would be in the best interests of the person to be sterilized or refuse to make an order as above merely because the sterilization is not necessary for the protection of physical or mental health; 3) before making an order authorizing elective sterilization, the judge shall consider the mental condition of the person to be sterilized, her physical capacity to reproduce, the likelihood that she will engage in sexual activity, the risks to her physical health with or without sterilization, the risks to her mental health, the alternatives to sterilization, the likelihood that she will marry, the risk of disability in a child that may be born, her ability to care for a child, other care available for the child, the effect of undergoing or foregoing sterilization on the care available for her, and on her opportunities for satisfying human interaction, her wishes and concerns, the wishes of her family and other caregivers, and any other relevant matter; and 4) where a hysterectomy for menstrual management is sought, the

factors to be considered should include consideration of the alternative means of menstrual management and such other factors in the list for elective sterilization as the judge considers relevant.

503. Institution-based litigation. (1986). *Mental and Physical Disability Law Reporter, 10*(1), 22-24.

This paper describes court case decisions that deal with the rights of institutionalized people with mental illness and residents with mental retardation, including federal class action certification, payment for care, eligibility for grounds passes and increased privileges, and patient abuse: Rights, Equality Always at Letchworth, Inc. v. Cuomo, 84 Civ. 4163 (CES) (S.D.N.Y. Nov. 1, 1985); In re R.M., 697 S.W.2d. 205 (Mo. Ct. App. 1985); K.P. v. Albanese, 497 A.2d. 1276 (N.J. S. Ct. App. Div 1985); and Watassek v. Michigan Department of Mental Health, 372 N.W.2d. 617 (Mich. Ct. App. 1985).

504. Interstate Consortium on Residential Child Care, Inc. (no date). *Trigger stories: Preventing institutional child abuse through the development of positive norms for staff.* **Trenton, ND: Author.**

This package uses stories to open up discussion by staff of child care issues in secure care facilities for juveniles. Some story topics include sexual abuse, physical abuse, emotional abuse, failure to provide adequate supervision, sleeping on duty, the possibility of false accusations of abuse by a resident, and racism. The stories are designed for use at staff meetings and to increase reports of questionable incidents. Discussion questions are provided.

505. An introduction to the National Legal Center for the Medically Dependent and Disabled, Inc. (1985). *Issues in Law and Medicine, 1,* 1-12.

A basic description of the National Legal Center for the Medically Dependent & Disabled, Inc. is provided, indicating its mission and basic procedures. It includes information on some specific cases of interest to the Center. The Center is a nonprofit, publicly supported foundation in the United States with four major purposes: 1) to ensure the right to beneficial medical treatment, 2) to increase the understanding of the legal services community about the issues related to persons who are medically dependent, 3) to gather and disseminate relevant educational materials, and 4) to coordinate efforts of legal services attorneys in the field.

506. Irvine, A. C. (1988). Balancing the right of the mentally retarded to obtain a therapeutic sterilization against the potential for abuse. *Law and Psychology Review, 12,* 95-122.

This article examines the history, controversies, and needs surrounding the sterilization of people with mental retardation. It argues that people with mental retardation have no method by which to obtain therapeutic sterilization. The author recognizes the need to protect people with mental retardation from the abuse of routine eugenics sterilization programs and proposes a model statute allowing a narrow avenue to sterilization.

507. Is there a difference? (1984). *Rehabilitation Digest, Spring,* 8-9.
This article was written by a young man who became a C-5 quadruplegic after a diving accident at the age of 19. He discusses his experience of sex education in rehabilitation centers and ways in which sexual relationships between people with disabilities and people without disabilities can be developed and maintained.

•J•

508. Jacobson, A. (1989). Physical and sexual assault histories among psychiatric outpatients. *American Journal of Psychiatry, 146*(6), 755-758.
In this study, the author uses a semi-structured interview to gather complete histories of experience of physical and sexual assault in the lives of 31 psychiatric out-patients. Of this group, 68% report having experienced major physical and/or sexual assault. Most of the assaults had not been disclosed to past therapists. Discussion includes a comparison of assault histories in out-patients and in-patients. Findings are related to clinical practice.

509. Jacobson, A., Koehler, J. E., & Jones-Brown, C. (1987). The failure of routine assessment to detect histories of assault experienced by psychiatric patients. *Hospital and Community Psychiatry, 38*(4), 386-389.
In this study, structured interviews were used to uncover incidences of sexual or physical abuse among psychiatric patients. Of 151 assaults reported, only 9 were recorded in patients' charts. Also, the information given in the chart often did not provide information about the assault beyond the fact that it occurred. The authors suggest that underreporting is due to not actively questioning patients about assault.

510. Jacobson, A., & Richardson, B. (1987). Assault experiences of 100 psychiatric inpatients: Evidence for the need for routine inquiry. *American Journal of Psychiatry, 144*(7), 908-913.
One hundred psychiatric in-patients were interviewed regarding their history of physical and/or sexual assault.

Assault scales were used and detailed histories taken. Eighty-one percent of patients reported having experienced major physical and/or sexual assault. The authors suggest that routine inquiry be made into patients' assault history.

511. Jacobson, J. W., & Ackerman, L. J. (1988). An appraisal of services for persons with mental retardation and psychiatric impairments. *Mental Retardation, 26*(6), 377-380.
This article summarizes the results of a survey completed by administrators and psychologists. The questionnaire dealt with population, system, and program issues regarding people with mental retardation or with a psychiatric impairment. Results support the belief that services are not readily available to these populations and that enhanced administrative and clinical resources are needed.

512. Jailed for sexual assault. (1986, February 11). *The Upper Islander.* (Campbell River, British Columbia)
This newspaper article states that a man was sentenced to four years in prison for sexually assaulting a female with mental handicaps over a period of three years, a period of time when he was on probation for previous molesting offenses. The attacker also had two previous convictions of indecent assault on two young girls.

513. James, B., & Nasjleti, M. (1983). *Treating sexually abused children and their families.* Palo Alto: Consulting Psychologists Press.
Chapter three (pp. 25-33) presents profiles of mothers of incest victims: the passive child-woman mother; the intelligent, competent, distant mother; the rejecting, vindictive mother; and the psychotic mother or mother with severe mental retardation. A mother with severe mental retardation with no awareness of the inappropriateness of incestuous behavior may condone and actively participate in molestation of her own children. In such cases, the mother should not have custody of the child.

514. Janicki, M. P., Jacobson, J. W., Zigman, W. B., & Gordon, N. H. (1984). Characteristics of employees of community residences for retarded persons. *Education and Training of the Mentally Retarded, 19,* 35-44.
This study reports data from 2800 community residence workers serving clients with mental retardation. Staff development related to human sexuality was considered the greatest need for staff training by 19.5% of these workers. This training need ranked fifth, higher than first aid or communication programming.

515. Jaudes, P. K., & Diamond, L. J. (1985). The handicapped child and child abuse. *Child Abuse & Neglect, 9*(3), 341-347.
For children with handicaps, growth and development can be affected by abuse (including sexual abuse) and neglect. By examining the experience of 37 children

with cerebral palsy who have been maltreated and reviewing the literature in related areas, the authors identified the following four problems as crucial to the study of abuse and neglect of the child with handicaps: 1) abuse that causes handicaps, 2) abuse that occurs to the handicapped child, 3) compromises in care that can occur when the child with handicaps becomes involved with the medical and legal systems, and 4) arrangements for foster care or other out-of-home placement for the child with handicaps. The authors conclude that the very systems designed to protect and care for the child often fail, leaving the child with handicaps without opportunity to reach developmental potential. In light of these observations, they recommend that the pediatrician not only be aware of the existence of abuse and neglect in the population of children with handicaps, but they should also serve in the dual role of coordinator of services and advocate for these children.

516. **Jaudes, P. K., & Diamond, L. J. (1986). Neglect of chronically ill children.** *American Journal of Diseases of Children, 140,* 655-658.
This article describes results of a retrospective chart review (1977-1984) of a Chicago Hospital. Sixty-one children with chronic illnesses had been reported to the State Protection Agency as neglected. Forms of neglect included the following: a) medical care neglect (65%), b) educational neglect (8%), c) abandonment (14%), d) emotional neglect (4%), and e) physical neglect (9%). Although the nature of the data does not allow estimates of incidence, the authors conclude that neglect is a serious concern for many children with chronic illnesses.

517. **Jerrell, J. M., & Larsen, J. K. (1986). Community mental health services in transition: Who is benefiting?** *American Journal of Orthopsychiatry, 56*(1), 78-88.
This article describes a study of changes in 71 mental health centers (MHCs) in 15 states that had been previously federally funded. Findings include the following: 1) state policy and funding guidelines have designated people with chronic mental illness and severe, acute illness as priority groups for program development and service in local centers, and the amount and range of service to this group has increased; 2) other client groups are receiving substantially less attention and support; 3) there is little state support for establishing a comprehensive range of children's services or for addressing the discontinuity of care issues characteristic of these services; and 4) current funding policies for alcohol and drug abuse services have separated these programs from the mental health services at the local level, except for the prevention activities still performed by many community health centers.

518. **Johnson, G. S. (1989). Emotional indicators in the human figure drawings of hearing-impaired children: A small sample validation study.** *American Annals of the Deaf, 134*(3), 205-208.
This study examines the concurrent validity for the Kappitz scoring technique in a sample of 7- to 12-year-old students with hearing impairments. The technique shows a positive correlation with emotional status as measured on the Stress Response Scale and is particularly useful in detecting impulsive and passive-aggressive response modes.

519. **Johnson, J. D. (1981). Institutional groups and human sexuality: Threatening or therapeutic? In D. A. Shore & H. L. Gochros (Eds.),** *Sexual problems of adolescents in institutions* (pp. 139-153). Springfield, IL: Charles C Thomas.
This chapter addresses the impact of group norms on institutionalized adolescents living without parental sexual role models and often within settings that hamper normal sexual development, and it discusses the possibility of using therapeutic groups to deal with the sexual concerns of adolescents. Guidelines are provided for leading various types of groups. Group modalities include educational, skill-building, support, problem-solving, behavioral, and treatment.

520. **Johnson, W. R. (1975).** *Sex education and counseling of special groups: The mentally and physically handicapped, ill and elderly.* Springfield, IL: Charles C Thomas.
The first segment of this book deals with cultural norms and expectations in relation to sexuality and special groups. One chapter discusses precautions in sex education and counseling. The second portion of the book discusses various aspects of sex counseling. Each topic is discussed first in terms of the general population of nondisabled people and then in terms of various special groups. Topics include physical contact, nudity, circumcision, masturbation, sex play with own and other sex, menstruation, "dirty" words, homosexuality, incestuous wishes and behavior, child molestation, venereal diseases, pornography, sex with and without intercourse, contraception, abortion, co-recreational activities and dating, sexual inadequacy, paid sexual companions, marriage, and parenthood.

521. **Jones, C. O. (1981). Characteristics and needs of abused and neglected children. In K. C. Faller (Ed.),** *Social work with abused and neglected children* (pp. 79-83). New York: Free Press.
This article addresses the impact of abuse and neglect on personality and behavior. While abuse and neglect do not result in a specific neurological or personality profile, certain trends can be seen. Victims develop different kinds of problems related to development and socialization. Feeding problems are common among abused and neglected infants. A lack of social response or variation is seen in abused children ages 6-12 months. Abused and neglected preschool children tend to either become withdrawn, compliant and apathetic, or they become aggressive and action-oriented. School age children are reluctant to discuss the abuse or to ascribe guilt to their parents. Expecting punishment or

criticism, these children are reluctant to trust adults and are concerned with having the limits defined in any new setting. They tend to have difficulty expressing their feelings and have a restricted ability to play or enjoy themselves. Many of these children put their energy into creating order and security for themselves and in struggling with identity problems.

522. Jones, D. P. H., & McQuiston, M. (1985). *Interviewing the sexually abused child.* **Denver: C. H. Kempe Center for the Prevention and Treatment of Child Abuse and Neglect.**
This 42-page document provides basic principles for interviewing children who have been or who may have been sexually abused. Information is also included on resources, supplies, and equipment.

523. Jones, T. R. (1983). Treatment approaches to sexual problems with dual diagnosis clients. *Journal of Social Work and Human Sexuality,* **2(1), 113-130.**
This article discusses treatment approaches to the sexual problems of clients with both a mental and developmental disability. Treatment of sexual problems include behavioral programming, counseling, social skills training, and sex education. It provides case examples in order to illustrate these treatment modalities, and it claims that personal sexual issues of people with mental and developmental disabilities cannot be separated from society or its regulations and infringements. The author also states that clinicians must be aware of oppressive social and institutional factors that can influence the clinical picture.

524. Joseph, B., & Standish, M. (1981). Legal Issues. In D. A. Shore & H. L. Gochros (Eds.), *Sexual problems of adolescents in institutions* **(pp. 51-55). Springfield, IL: Charles C Thomas.**
Legal issues regarding the sexuality of institutionalized adolescents are examined. The need for courts and child care institutions to recognize children's rights to sexuality is discussed. Sample topics include pregnancy, abortion, and the repression of sexuality.

•K•

525. Kaeser, F., & O'Neill, J. (1987). Task analyzed masturbation instruction for a profoundly mentally retarded adult male: A data based case study. *Sexuality and Disability,* **8(1), 17-24.**
This article discusses the instruction of a safe masturbation technique to a 29-year-old man with profound mental retardation who was otherwise at risk

for injuring himself. The instruction method adopted was a task-analysed approach.

526. Kaminer, Y., Feinstein, C., & Barrett, R. P. (1987). Suicidal behavior in mentally retarded adolescents: An overlooked problem. *Child Psychiatry and Human Development,* **18(2), 90-94.**
These authors suggest that suicide and suicidal behavior are overlooked in people with mental retardation. Three cases of suicidal behavior in in-patient adolescents with mental retardation are discussed. The authors note that cognitive deficits do not imply a decreased risk for suicide.

527. Kaplan, S. J., & Pelcovitz, D. (1982). Child abuse & neglect and sexual abuse. *Psychiatric Clinics of North America,* **5(2), 321-332.**
These authors discuss child abuse and sexual abuse in terms of the theory that abuse occurs as a result of interaction between a psychologically vulnerable parent, a child who is in some way "special," and environmental factors. The authors state that while some researchers have theorized that "specialness" of the child may contribute to abuse it is difficult to determine whether physical or mental handicap is the cause or effect of abuse. Environmental factors contributing to abuse include stress and social isolation. In terms of treatment, the authors note that although the abused child is at risk for serious emotional and developmental disorders most often the perpetrator is the focus of treatment.

528. Kastner, T. A., De Lotto, P., Scagnelli, B., & Testa, W. R. (1990). Proposed guidelines for agencies serving persons with developmental disabilities and HIV infection. *Mental Retardation,* **28(3), 139-145.**
This article discusses the development of procedural guidelines for agencies serving people with developmental disabilities living in the community who are infected with HIV. Discussion includes the need for ethics in making decisions and universal infectious disease recommendations that allow for the provision of these services in the "least restrictive" environment.

529. Kastner, T. A., Hickman, M. L., & Bellehumeur, D. (1989). The provision of services to persons with mental retardation and subsequent infection with human immunodeficiency virus (HIV). *American Journal of Public Health,* **79(4), 491-494.**
This article presents the first reported cases of persons with mental retardation who have become infected with HIV. The article discusses implications for agencies providing services to people with mental retardation. Ethical review committees are proposed as a means of settling conflicts that may face service agencies.

530. Katz, I., Glass, D. C., Lucido, D. J., & Farber, J. (1977). Ambivalence, guilt, and the denigra-

tion of a physically handicapped victim. *Journal of Personality, 45*(3), 419-429.

This study replicates an experiment in which subjects denigrated a black victim more than a white victim and demonstrated the highest levels of denigration toward the black confederates when the subject had a racial attitude that was ambivalent rather than clearly positive or negative. In the present study, 60 female subjects delivered either mild or noxious stimuli to a female confederate either confined to a wheelchair or not. Both before and after this task, subjects were asked to rate the confederate's personality. While variations in the preratings were constant, post-ratings duplicated earlier findings. The confederates in the wheelchair condition were given the least favorable personality ratings. Denigration was greatest among subjects who were ambivalent about people with handicaps in general; however, denigration bore no relation to whether the subject initially had a positive or negative attitude toward people with handicaps. These findings are discussed in terms of an ambivalence-guilt-response amplification hypothesis regarding reactions to people who are stigmatized.

531. Kazak, A. E. (1987). Families with disabled children: Stress and social networks in three samples. *Journal of Abnormal Child Psychology, 15*(1), 137-146.

Two groups of more than 100 parents were compared on three variables: personal stress, marital satisfaction, and social network size and density. One group of parents cared for children who were either chronically ill or had handicaps. The other group was comprised of matched controls. Only the mothers of special needs children experienced higher levels of stress. They also had higher density networks. No differences in marital satisfaction were found.

532. Kazak, A. E., & Clark, M. W. (1986). Stress in families of children with myelomeningocele. *Developmental Medicine and Child Neurology, 28*(2), 220-228.

Three stress measures in 56 families with a child with myelomeningocele and in 53 matched control families were compared. On the Piers-Harris Children's Self-Concept Scale, children with a disability scored lower than controls. Their siblings, however, did not follow this pattern. Overall, a good marital relationship was found to be predictive of greater adjustment in families with a child who has a disability.

533. Keall, B. (1982). Sexuality and the disabled: A training programme for physiotherapists. *The New Zealand Journal of Physiotherapy, 10*(1), 5.

This article is a short description of a teaching program developed for use in training physiotherapists working with people with disabilities in a hospital or health care setting. The article discusses the assumptions made before planning the course, the aims of the course, a description of the experiment group (composed of 12 registered physiotherapists), the program (consisting of 12 1-hour sessions), an evaluation of the program, and conclusions. Conclusions include the recognition of the need for a resource person to lead role-play sessions and to help staff deal with their own personal sexual issues. The utility of having back-up counselors and sex therapists was also identified. The program was developed in response to a 1979 survey that indicated that 85% of patients wanted information on sexuality and/or sex counseling.

534. Kearns, A., & O'Connor, A. (1988). The mentally handicapped criminal offender: A 10-year study of two hospitals. *British Journal of Psychiatry, 152*, 848-851.

This article discusses a 10-year study of 92 patients (ages 15+ years) in two mental handicap hospitals. The study compared the general criminal population with these offenders and found that their ages were higher, the ratio of male to female offenders was similar, and the proportion of married people was lower. It also found that the greatest number of offenses against property and public order occurred in the subgroup whose intelligences were in the mentally handicapped range. The authors conclude that the presence of so many subjects in the group classified as dull-normal or borderline suggests that factors other than intelligence testing, such as social skills, were considered in their admission to the hospitals.

535. Keilitz, I., & Dunivant, N. (1986). The relationship between learning disability and juvenile delinquency: Current state of knowledge. *RASE Remedial and Special Education, 7*(3), 18-26.

This article describes a multiyear learning disability-juvenile delinquency project that examined the relationship between learning disability and delinquency and the effectiveness of intervention. The results of this study suggest a causal relationship between learning disability and juvenile delinquency and confirm the school failure theory, the susceptibility theory, and the differential treatment theory. The authors also evaluated an academic treatment program and found that remedial instruction improved the academic skills and decreased the delinquency of a youth with learning disabilities.

536. Kelleher, M. E. (1987). Investigating institutional abuse: A post substantiation model. *Child Welfare, 66*(4), 343-351.

This article describes a post-substantiation model for the investigation of institutional abuse. The model is applied to a cottage-based group care facility for children. Discussion includes evaluation and the development of an evaluation team. The case of a sexually abused male is also discussed. Future policy developments are addressed.

537. Keller, R. A., Cicchinelli, L. F., & Gardner, D. M. (1989). Characteristics of child sexual abuse

treatment programs. *Child Abuse & Neglect, 13,* 361-368.

This article provides data from a survey of 533 American child sexual abuse treatment programs. More than 88% of programs focused on the victims of abuse, and most used a family-based form of treatment. Many programs offered a variety of other related services: information and referral (98%), abuse reporting (94%), consultation (92%), advocacy (90%), training (87%), service coordination (83%), parent education (83%), sex education (72%), diagnostic services (71%), transportation (49%), abuse hotline (47%), technical assistance (43%), self-image classes (37%), parent aide service (30%), medical services (27%), child care (26%), and legal services (18%).

538. Keller, S., & Buchanan, D. C. (1984). Sexuality and disability: An overview. *Rehabilitation Digest, Spring,* 3-7.

In this article, the psychological and physical aspects of sexuality and disability are discussed. The emphasis is on identifying practical solutions to common problems. Specific disabilities discussed include multiple sclerosis, spinal cord injury, brain dysfunction, coronary dysfunction disease, and chronic obstructive lung disease. The discussion addresses current research, social skills training, religious and sexual attitudes, intervention strategies, assessment in sexuality counseling, and intervention strategies. Also included is a short discussion of available resources for people with disabilities seeking sexuality counseling and of resources for people seeking training in sex therapy.

539. Kelley, S. J. (1986). Learned helplessness in the sexually abused child. *Issues in Comprehensive Pediatric Nursing, 9*(3), 193-207.

This author discusses child sexual abuse in terms of the theory of learned helplessness. The child is in an unequal power position with the adult and thus feels incapable of refusing. The abuse is repetitive and controlled by the adult, and the child learns that his or her attempts at avoidance do not affect the outcome. Realizing that resistance has been ineffective in the past, the child may discontinue resistance. The child then tends to attribute the cause of abuse to his- or herself rather than to the adult, who is seen as infallible. The child also believes that nothing he or she can do will stop the abuse from occurring in the future. The balance of the article concerns intervention for nurses who are caring for abused children.

540. Kellogg, R. C. (1987, June). *Dormitory program review: A model for external analysis.* **Paper presented at the Joint Meeting of the Convention of American Instructors of the Deaf and and the Conference of the Deaf Inc. (ERIC Document Reproduction Service No. ED 293 245)**

This paper presents a model developed at the Nebraska School for the Deaf for the systematic review of dormitory programs at residential schools for people who are deaf. One area of particular concern is the allegations of sexual misconduct and child abuse. Sample recommendations include the importance of each dormitory program having a policy and procedures manual that is part of the overall school policy system and the need to keep accurate records regarding disciplinary actions and procedures applied to students. The author also addresses sex education and administrative procedures. A bibliography and a list of resources are included as well as a number of examples of Individualized Action Plans, which are used to coordinate liaison between the dormitory and the school.

541. Kempe, C. H., Silverman, F. N., Steele, B. F., Droegemueller, W., & Silver, H. K. (1974). The battered-child syndrome. In J. E. Leavitt (Ed.), *The battered child: Selected readings* **(pp. 4-11). Morristown, NJ: General Learning Corporation.**

In this article, the findings from 71 hospitals participating in a survey on Battered Child syndrome are described. Statistics are presented on the incidence of death and permanent injury. In one-third of the cases, proper medical diagnosis of child abuse resulted in legal action. Signs of the Battered Child syndrome are discussed. Physicians have a duty to fully evaluate child patients who may be victims of abuse and ensure that these children will not be subjected to new instances of trauma.

542. Kempton, W. (1977). The mentally retarded person. In H. L. Gochros & J. S. Gochros (Eds.), *The sexually oppressed* **(pp. 239-256). New York: Association Press.**

In this chapter, the author discusses the sexual oppression of people with developmental disabilities. She states that this group has had rigid controls imposed due to fears of the public that if their sexuality were not suppressed people with developmental disabilities would "prolifically reproduce, or their sexual impulses would emerge in uncontrollable bursts of violence." The author discusses the factors that contribute to this suppression. One of these factors is that people with developmental disabilities have characteristics that make them more sexually exploitable than non-handicapped people. A child with developmental disabilities is more likely to: a) trust strangers, b) lack the ability to determine appropriate behavior, c) not know how to judge the motivation for others' behavior, d) do what he or she is told, e) show and receive affection more readily, f) be unable to defend his- or herself, and g) be unable to communicate or report the incident effectively. The author states that the fear of exploitation results in overprotection which deprives the individual of sexual rights and freedom. Instead of treating people with developmental disabilities as perennial children who will never be able to fend for themselves, the author believes they should receive prevention training and be supervised only when necessary.

543. Kempton, W. (1977). The sexual adolescent who is mentally retarded. *Journal of Pediatric Psychology, 2*(3), 104-107.

Adolescents with mental retardation are described, and the current trend of accepting them as social-sexual persons in comparison to past practices of suppressing their freedom because they are not considered to be sexual is discussed. The importance of sex education is emphasized, and the author states that it should be included in a broader program of preparation for skills in social living because of the recent innovations in mainstreaming people with mental retardation into the community. Issues on birth control are discussed, and methods of teaching sex education are outlined.

544. Kempton, W. (1978). Sex education for the mentally handicapped. *Sexuality and Disability, 1*(2), 137-146.

This article discusses the results of an evaluation of a slide series on sex education for people with mild to severe mental retardation. The series was evaluated by 110 teachers and other professionals working in institutions, schools, and agencies for people with mental retardation. In general, sex education for people with mental retardation was found to be positive and to not result in deleterious effects.

545. Kempton, W. (1983). Teaching retarded children about sex. *PTA Today, 8*(6), 28-30.

This article discusses how parents can prepare children to cope with their emerging sexuality, not only in terms of biology, but in terms of emotional and social development.

546. Kempton, W. (1988). *Sex education for persons with disabilities that hinder learning: A teacher's guide.* **MA: Duxbury Press.**

Like its popular predecessor, this new edition is based on the experiences of professionals working with people with disabilities. A new feature is the incorporation of materials for people with learning disabilities. Chapter topics include characteristics of the student, perspectives on sex education, attitudes toward sexuality, characteristics of the sex educator, teaching techniques, the teacher as counselor to the student, the teacher as counselor to parents, and the sex education program, including information regarding very young children, prepubertal children, adolescents, and adults. Other sample topics include information on sex myths, sexual responsibility, and the slide series *Life Horizons*. Each chapter is followed by a practice exercise. The bibliography includes the following: books on sexuality for professionals, caregivers, and parents; books and articles on sexuality for people with any of a large range of disabilities; a list of guides and manuals, including curriculum guides; a list of audiovisual materials used in the training of caregivers and parents as well as for training students; a list of visual aids, including dolls and cards; a list of organizations; and a list of sources for obtaining training and instructional materials.

547. Kempton, W., & Carelli, L. (1981). Mentally handicapped. In D. A. Shore & H. L. Gochros (Eds.), *Sexual problems of adolescents in institutions* (pp. 210-222). Springfield, IL: Charles C Thomas.

This chapter provides a general overview of the treatment of adolescents with intellectual impairment in institutions. Much of the material is covered in more detail in other places, but there are a number of interesting issues addressed in this well-organized chapter. For example, the authors address the routine sterilization of residents in the past and suggest the following: In spite of sexual segregation and attempts at enforced celibacy, sexual activity among people with intellectual impairments living in institutions is not a new phenomena.

548. Kempton, W., & Gochros, J. S. (1986). The developmentally disabled. In H. L. Gochros, J. S. Gochros, & J. Fischer (Eds.), *Helping the sexually oppressed* (pp. 224-237). Englewood Cliffs, NJ: Prentice-Hall.

This chapter discusses the problem of sexual oppression of people with mental retardation and the changes needed in the various services offered to them as deinstitutionalization and mainstreaming become the norm. Topics include factors contributing to sexual oppression, a discussion of direct services, and sex education.

549. Kennedy, M. (1987). Occupational therapists as sexual rehabilitation professionals using the rehabilitive frame of reference. *Canadian Journal of Occupational Therapy, 54*(4), 189-193.

This article describes how the rehabilitative frame of reference may be used to assist adults with physical disabilities in their sexual adjustment. By way of example, the framework is applied to men and women with rheumatoid arthritis and secondary osteoarthritis. Topics include a discussion of sexual positions that decrease stress on painful joints. The role of the occupational therapist is discussed within an interdisciplinary context. Recommendations for the development of sexual rehabilitation are made.

550. Kent, D. (1983). Finding a way through the rough years: How blind girls survive adolescence. *Journal of Visual Impairment and Blindness, 77*(6), 247-250.

This article describes the problems encountered by female adolescents who are blind regarding peers, role models, dating, fashion, and make-up. The author draws on her own experience as well as that of seven other women. In reviewing the literature, the author finds that blind teenagers often feel isolated from peers.

551. Kent Public Schools. (1985). *Self-protection for the handicapped: A curriculum designed to teach handicapped persons to avoid exploitation.* **Seattle: Author. (ERIC Docu-**

ment Reproduction Service No. ED 263 705)
This curriculum is a modification of the Curriculum for Developing an Awareness of Sexual Exploitation and Teaching Self-Protection Techniques developed by the Developmental Disabilities Project of Seattle Rape Relief Center. The Self-Protection curriculum contains one level instead of the two that the original curriculum has: The intent being that younger children (ages 8-13) or students with more handicaps would be taught the first five units only during the first few times the curriculum is taught. Vocabulary has been simplified and some lessons omitted, while others have been added. Where possible, third person characteristics have been changed to first person in the narrative stories, making them easier to identify with. References to rape and sexual exploitation have largely been omitted for two reasons. First, the self-protection curriculum deals with exploitation in general rather than specifically with sexual exploitation. Second, since many students have little knowledge of sexual intercourse, the concept of rape would have no meaning. Where the original curriculum refers to a victim as being raped, the self-protection curriculum refers to the victim as being "hurt." Also, appropriate and inappropriate touching is discussed. The curriculum has been evaluated and selected as a model program for use in the state of Washington.

552. **Kerr, D. L. (1989). Forum addresses HIV education for children and youth with special educational needs.** *Journal of School Health,* *59*(3), 129.
This article provides a brief account of the National Forum on HIV/AIDS Prevention Education for Children and Youth with Special Needs. The three main objectives included the following: 1) to determine the extent of risk, 2) to determine the most appropriate approaches to prevention curriculum, and 3) to determine the extent to which the HIV prevention and general health education needs of these students are being met. The forum determined that students with special needs are at increased risk for HIV infection because of increased likelihood of being sexually abused along with several other factors.

553. **Kester, B. L., Rothblum, E. D., Lobato, D., & Milhous, R. L. (1988). Spouse adjustment to spinal cord injury: Long-term medical and psychosocial factors.** *Rehabilitation Counseling Bulletin, 32*(1), 4-21.
In this study, 25 female partners of men with spinal cord injuries completed a life change events schedule and a comprehensive questionnaire composed of subscales. They also took part in semi-structured interviews designed to assess adjustment to the impact of the spinal cord injury. A group of out-patients and nurses acted as a control group. Findings indicate that the adjustment process was very stressful and resulted in major psychological and medical consequences.

554. **Kiernan, K. E. (1988). Who remains celibate?** *Journal of Biosocial Science, 20*(3), 253-263.
In this study, life history data for a British cohort born in 1946 is used to identify characteristics of people who are single in their mid-30s. An important minority are people with handicaps, who tend to be cared for by their families, particularly by elderly parents.

555. **Kirkham, M. A., Schilling, R. F., Norelius, K., & Schinke, S. P. (1986). Developing coping styles and social support networks: An intervention outcome study with mothers of handicapped children.** *Child Care, Health and Development, 12*(5), 313-323.
This article describes a pilot intervention program designed to teach coping techniques for the reduction of stress and to assist parents in developing social support networks. Five instruments were administered to four mothers of children, ages 7-9 years, with cerebral palsy, autism, blindness, or learning disabilities. The instruments measured the mothers' resources, stress levels, quality of life, social support, and communication skills. Eight 2-hour group sessions were held and focused on personal coping skills, communication skills, problem solving, and social support enhancement. As compared to pre-intervention scores, post-intervention scores indicate that three of the mothers experienced improvement and three had increased stress levels at post-test. Results are discussed in terms of building on the traditional services offered to families with children with developmental disabilities.

556. **Kirkham, M. A., Schinke, S. P., Schilling, R. F., Meltzer, N. J., & Norelius, K. L. (1986). Cognitive-behavioral skills, social supports, and child abuse potential among mothers of handicapped children.** *Journal of Family Violence, 1*(3), 235-245.
This article examines cognitive-behavioral skills, social support networks, and the risk for child abuse in 92 mothers (23-50 years of age) of children with developmental disabilities. The authors found that the subjects at highest risk for child abuse scored low on cognitive skills, social support networks, and life satisfaction. They also found that single mothers had significantly different scores than married mothers on child abuse potential, relationship satisfaction, community involvement, and loneliness.

557. **Klein, D. M. (1980). Central nervous system injuries. In N. S. Ellerstein (Ed.),** *Child abuse and neglect: A medical reference* (pp. 73-93). New York: John Wiley & Sons.
This article addresses diagnostic issues. Chronic organic disability and death as a result of child abuse are most often linked to assault to the central nervous system (CNS). Injury patterns are often related to the unique structural features of infants and young children. While infant subdural hemotoma is often associated with abuse, it is cerebral contusion that much more frequently results in neurologic disability and death.

Intrinsic disease can sometimes be differentiated from trauma to the CNS by the presence of multiple injuries and inadequate explanations for injury. The author suggests that moral and legal considerations should be excluded from the intensive care environment and that medical personnel should communicate with the victim's family in a dignified, impartial, and compassionate way.

558. Kline, D. F. (1977). *Child abuse and neglect: A primer for school personnel.* **Reston, VA: Council for Exceptional Children.**

The purpose of the book is to provide teachers, administrators, school-board members, and parent-teacher organizations with basic information regarding child abuse and neglect. Children with handicaps are only referred to briefly as inviting abuse more frequently than nonhandicapped children; however, the author states that there is no way to identify which one among several children in a family will be abused. The book discusses generally the legal and professional responsibilities of teachers, identification of the problem, reporting procedures and report forms, and prevention methods.

559. Kline, D. F. (1982). *The disabled child and child abuse.* **Chicago: National Committee for Prevention of Child Abuse.**

The relationship between child abuse and disability is discussed. The problems of multiple placements are addressed. In the United States, there are an estimated 8 million children with handicaps, 7% of whom acquired the handicap after birth. Sample topics include educational neglect, the relationship between abuse and the presence of a child with a handicap in the family, prevention, and help for parents.

560. Knappett, K., & Wagner, N. (1976). Sex education and the blind. *Education of the Visually Handicapped, 8*(1), 1-5.

A review of the literature indicated that sex education in the schools is of particular importance to people who are blind because other avenues of receiving sexual information are generally not available. However, due to a combination of attitudes about people who are blind and about sex education, it has only been in the last 3 or 4 years that sex education has been seriously considered. It was concluded that positive changes in the attitude of society toward sex education of people who are blind is largely dependent upon changes in the view that society takes of sexuality in general.

561. Knight, S. E. (1986). The physically disabled. In H. L. Gochros, J. S. Gochros, & J. Fischer (Eds.), *Helping the sexually oppressed* **(pp. 238-249). Englewood Cliffs, NJ: Prentice-Hall.**

This chapter is a guide in the development and refinement of therapeutic techniques used in sex therapy for people with disabilities. Topics include broadscale interventions, counseling issues (such as lifelong disability, acquired disability), issues of the partners of people with disabilities, and social skills issues. Peer counseling is touched on in the conclusion.

562. Knopp, F. H. (1984). The sex offender unit & the social skills unit correctional treatment programs. In F. H. Knopp (Ed.), *Retraining adult sex offenders: Methods and models* **(pp. 185-209). Syracuse, NY: Safer Society Press.**

This author describes a program for sex offenders who appear to be low functioning (most of whom do not have mental retardation). The basic goals of the program are to increase the offender's level of social coping skills and to reduce his or her criminality. The treatment modalities employed include cognitive restructuring, behavioral techniques, Depo Provera, and group therapy. A heavy emphasis is placed on social skills development. The director of this program believes that low-functioning sex offenders may have a better prognosis of controlling their behavior than high-functioning offenders.

563. Koller, H., Richardson, S. A., & Katz, M. (1988). Marriage in a young adult mentally retarded population. *Journal of Mental Deficiency Research, 32*(2), 93-102.

This article examines marriage in a population of young adults with mental impairments. Findings include the following: females with mental retardation had significantly more problems in their marriages than nonretarded comparison subjects, including physical abuse and financial difficulties; almost half the women with mild retardation appeared to have successful marriages; men with mental retardation were not significantly different from nonretarded comparison subjects; and there were many problems in marriages in which both partners had mental retardation.

564. Koller, H., Richardson, S. A., & Katz, M. (1988). Peer relationships of mildly retarded young adults living in the community. *Journal of Mental Deficiency Research, 32*(4), 321-331.

This article examines peer relationships and opposite sex relationships in young adults with mental retardation. Half of the group studied were attending centers for adults with mental retardation, and half were no longer receiving mental retardation services. Those not receiving services socialized less and had fewer opposite sex relationships.

565. Korbin, J. E. (1987). Child abuse and neglect: The cultural context. In R. E. Helfer & R.S. Kempe (Eds.), *The battered child* **(pp. 23-41). Chicago: University of Chicago Press.**

At one point, this article suggests that Euro-American studies have focused more on the characteristics of abusive parents than on the characteristics of the abused child. In turning to the cross-cultural literature, the author found better information on the categories of children who are vulnerable to abuse and neglect and concludes that, overall, child abuse and neglect are less likely in cultures in which children are highly valued for their economic utility, as bearers of cultural or religious continuity, or as sources of emotional satisfaction. The author also found that some categories of children are at increased risk for maltreatment across cultures, including children with handicaps.

566. Kratochvil, M. S., & Devereux, S. A. (1988). Counseling needs of parents of handicapped children. *Social Casework: The Journal of Contemporary Social Work, 69*(7), 420-442.
In this article, experts debate whether the bereavement experienced by parents of children with handicaps is of a relatively brief or of a chronic/periodic nature. The need for professional services by well-adjusted parents who identify periods of recurring grief is discussed.

567. Krausz, S. (1980). Group psychotherapy with legally blind patients. *Clinical Social Work Journal, 8*(1), 37-49.
This article discusses difficulties patients who are blind may encounter in accepting their disability. Methods mental health professionals may use to help them achieve this acceptance are discussed. The advantages of group therapy over individual therapy are described. The author notes that the therapist's attitude toward the disability profoundly influences the patient's evolving attitude toward it.

568. Krausz, S. (1988). Illness and loss: Helping couples cope. *Clinical Social Work Journal, 16*(1), 52-65.
In this article, the author proposes that serious illness or disability in a spouse may pose a threat to marital and family functioning. A developmental framework is presented that addresses some of the special adjustment issues faced by these couples over time. Sample topics include adaptations that promote optimal family functioning, the role of the therapist, and relevant intervention strategies.

569. Kreigsman, K. H., & Bregman, S. (1985). Women with disabilities at midlife [Special issue: Transition and disability over the life span]. *Rehabilitation Counseling Bulletin, 29*(2), 112-122.
This article discusses issues unique to women who have physical disabilities at midlife. Various aspects are addressed, such as employment and relationship issues. Part of the discussion focuses on the need to share concerns with other women who are disabled and on the need to work with intense feelings regarding sexuality and disability. The role of individual and group counseling and the role of community and organizational education efforts are discussed. The role of three-fold devaluation based on disability, sex, and age is also addressed.

570. Krenk, C. J. (1984). Training residence staff for child abuse treatment. *Child Welfare, 63*(2), 167-173.
As a result of the increased number of reported incidents

of sexual abuse of children with disabilities, a pilot staff training program was undertaken in a residential center for children with emotional disorders. This article describes the identification of training needs as well as the coordination and implementation of training. Training took place over a 5-month period. Outcomes were positive and included the initiation of individual and group therapy within the facility for trauma that was related to sexual abuse. Some initial concern that discussion of sexual molestation would result in sexual acting out by residents proved to be unfounded.

571. Krents, E., Schulman, V., & Brenner, S. (1987). Child abuse and the disabled child: Perspectives for parents. *Volta Review, 89*(5), 78-95.
This article focuses on the problem of physical and sexual child abuse. Providing a general background on this widespread problem, the article describes the particular vulnerability to exploitation and abuse experienced by children with disabilities. Active roles that schools and parents can assume to effectively confront and deal with this issue are described in detail. The need to intensify efforts to ensure that children with disabilities are provided both accurate information on sexual abuse and the necessary skills to protect themselves from victimization is stressed.

572. Krug, R. S. (1989). Adult male report of childhood sexual abuse by mothers: Case description, motivations and long-term consequences. *Child Abuse & Neglect, 13*, 111-119.
This article presents eight case histories of adults who had been sexually abused by their mothers as children or adolescents. The author suggests that this form of sexual abuse may be more common than current reports would suggest, that victims are likely to suffer in adult social and sexual adjustment, and that many victims experience depression and substance abuse.

573. Krugman, R. D. (1985). Preventing sexual abuse in day care: Whose problem is it anyway? *Pediatrics, 75*, 1150-1151.
This author suggests that the value of prevention programs in actually enabling children to resist abuse has not been demonstrated. The author stresses the need for parents and pediatricians to recognize signs of abuse and suggests that they are responsible for prevention.

574. Kunkel, O. D. (1981). In-service training programs for staff. In D. A. Shore & H. L. Gochros (Eds.), *Sexual problems of adolescents in institutions* (pp. 71-89). Springfield, IL: Charles C Thomas.
This chapter discusses the need for staff training on sexuality in institutions serving adolescents. Although the primary focus of the training described is to develop more accepting attitudes of clients' sexuality, staff training may also be valuable in the prevention,

detection, and treatment of sexual abuse and assault. Elements to specifically address abuse and assault should be incorporated into a more comprehensive sexuality training program.

575. Kurtz, P. D. (1979). Early identification of handicapped children: A time for social work involvement. *Child Welfare, 58*(3), 165-176.

This 1979 article discusses the role of the social worker in the early identification of handicapping conditions in children. Sample topics include counseling skills, referral procedure, advocating for early detection, training nonsocial workers in early identification and screening techniques, organizing and coordinating community-wide developmental check-ups, and ensuring a continuity of service for clients.

576. Kusinitz, M. (1984). Health professionals work for sexual rights of disabled persons: Part 1. *New York State Journal of Medicine, 84*(3), 140-142.

This article examines the legal, social, educational, and physical obstacles that hinder the sexual fulfillment of people with handicaps, and it discusses ways of overcoming these conditions. It discusses the societal obstacles to the sexual lives of single and married people with handicaps and suggests that treatment approaches must recognize that people with handicaps are sexual beings and are entitled to sexual fulfillment. This article also describes techniques and seminars designed to educate patients with handicaps and health professionals.

•L•

577. LaBarre, A. (no date). *Sexual abuse! What is it?* St. Paul, MN: Hearing Impaired Health and Wellness.

This book is written for adolescents and young adults with hearing impairments in an effort to prevent sexual abuse by giving them important information about safety issues. The book covers topics such as: a) what is sexual abuse, b) what are some of the safety issues to be aware of, c) who are the offenders, and d) what to do if it happens to someone. The book is written in a very simple and easily understood style. There are many illustrations that support the concepts presented. The book is a resource for parents to share with their adolescent with hearing impairments, and it also serves as a helpful educational tool for educators, counselors, and other professionals working with individuals with hearing impairments.

578. Lafrance, G. (1975). De la sexualité des handicapés et des autres minorités [The sexuality of people with handicaps and of other minorities]. *Feux verts, 3.*

This article uncovers the prohibitions and prejudices that still constrain the sexuality of people with handicaps and that of other minorities. Written by a person with a handicap, this article condemns the negative attitudes of society that consider people with handicaps to be asexual. In order to realize their sexuality, people with handicaps must transcend stereotypical myths regarding physical beauty and be ready to love and feel loved. The author also addresses the problem of sexual repression in institutions. (This article is available in French only.)

579. Lakin, K. C., & Bruininks, R. H. (1985). Social integration of developmentally disabled persons. In K. C. Lakin & R. H. Bruininks (Eds.), *Strategies for achieving community integration of developmentally disabled citizens* (pp. 3-25). Baltimore: Paul H. Brookes Publishing Co.

This chapter contains statistics regarding the movement away from institutionalization of people with developmental disabilities. Between 1966 and 1981, public school systems in the United States expanded special education services from 2.1 million to 3.9 million children with handicaps. The total population of large state institutions for people with developmental disabilities decreased from 194,650 to 119,335 between 1967 and 1982. During the same period, the number of people with developmental disabilities in private and state facilities decreased from 130.4 to 106.3 per 100,000 of United States population. Finally, between 1969 and 1982, the number of people with developmental disabilities in smaller, privately operated placements grew from 24,355 to 115,032. As more and more people with developmental disabilities live in the community at large, a greater number of incidents of sexual abuse may come to the attention of various community agencies.

580. Lamond, D. A. P. (1989). The impact of mandatory reporting legislation on reporting behavior. *Child Abuse & Neglect, 13*(4), 471-480.

In 1987, in New South Wales, Australia, teachers and other school professionals were included among professionals required by law to report suspected cases of child sexual abuse to the Department of Family and Community Services. A significant increase in the number of reports made by teachers resulted.

581. Lane, M. E. (1982). *The legal response to sexual abuse of children: A review of current procedural and legal practices in the child welfare and criminal justice systems.* Toronto: Metropolitan Chairman's Special Committee on Child Abuse.

This background paper examines the legal context of

child sexual abuse. More particularly, the focus is on the child welfare and criminal justice systems, which together have primary responsibility for mobilizing the legal response to the problem. The review was commissioned by the Special Committee on Child Abuse in an attempt to understand the experience of children involved in either child welfare or criminal justice proceedings as a result of sexual abuse. As such, the results provide valuable direction in reshaping those legal policies and procedures that inadvertently place child victims in further jeopardy. The first section reviews the legal context of child sexual abuse and examines law and procedures in both child welfare and criminal jurisdictions. Next, the response of the child welfare system is reviewed, including a review of relevant literature, current practices, and the opportunities presented by the forthcoming omnibus legislation on children's services. The last section examines child sexual abuse in the context of the criminal justice system, including a review of practices related to investigation, laying charges, treatment of the victim and accused, convictions, and sentencing.

582. Lang, R. E., & Kahn, J. V. (1986). Teacher estimates of handicapped student crime victimization and delinquency. *Journal of Special Education, 20*(3), 359-365.

In this American study, 75 special education teachers identified the most common violent and property crimes among their special education students. They also provided estimates of crime victimization and delinquency among these students. Findings indicate a need for more federal and state crime reporting methods and a need for education aimed at reducing the risk that students with handicaps, will become victims or perpetrators of crimes.

583. Lang, R. E., & Kahn, J. V. (1989). Effects of an experimental special-education crime-prevention intervention: A time-series study. *Journal of Clinical Child Psychology, 18*(3), 263-270.

In this study, 42 students in special education enrolled in four elementary schools were studied at four different times. Students either had learning disabilities, educable mental retardation, or behavior disorders. Following crime-prevention intervention, the students' violent and property crime victimization and criminal exploitation rate dropped significantly over time. The authors emphasize the need for this type of education for this group of children.

584. Laszlo, K., Mindel, E. D., & Jabaley, T. (Eds.). (1981). *Deafness and mental health.* **New York: Grune & Stratton.**

This book discusses various aspects of mental health in relation to people who are deaf. The book is comprised of articles written by various authors and is broken into three sections: the child who is deaf, the adult who is deaf, and societal issues. Assessment and treatment are addressed. One article by Sy Dubrow and Larry J.

Goldberg discusses legal strategies to improve mental health services to people who are deaf. Sexuality is not addressed.

585. LeGrand, C. (1984). Mental hospital regulation and the safe environment. *Law, Medicine & Health Care, 12*(6), 236-242.

This article addresses the emerging legal issue of institutions that fail to protect staff and clients from sexual assault. The author suggests that institutions are liable for sexual assaults only if they contributed to the assault through negligence. Courts focus on whether the institution had any specific information about the assailant or victim that made the attack foreseeable and preventable. At least seven such lawsuits by clients raped in mental institutions have been heard. In three successful lawsuits, regulatory infractions were cited as contributing factors.

586. Lehne, G. K. (1984-86). Brain damage and paraphilia: Treated with medroxyprogesterone acetate. *Sexuality and Disability, 7*(3/4), 145-158.

This article reviews the literature on hypersexuality and atypical sexual interests as a result of brain damage. The case of a man who developed a paraphilia for his step-daughter's breasts following traumatic frontal lobe damage is presented. His successful treatment with drug therapy is discussed.

587. Levine, S. B., Risen, C. B., & Althof, S. E. (1990). Essay on the diagnosis and nature of paraphilia. *Journal of Sex and Marital Therapy, 16*(2), 89-102.

This article discusses the definition and diagnosis of paraphilia. Psychodynamic viewpoints are discussed, most notably the definition of paraphilia as a disorder of sexual identity development, often solely of the intention component. Paraphilia is also briefly discussed as a disorder of self-regulation and as a dramatic impairment in the capacity to love. The article also addresses two rarely recognized issues that complicate the nosology of paraphilia: Many related sexual problems are often confused with paraphilia, and some paraphilias manifest themselves as variations in gender identity and object choice. Also addressed are the defensive functions of paraphilia.

588. Levitt, C. J. (1986). Sexual abuse in children: A compassionate yet thorough approach to evaluation. *Postgraduate Medicine, 80*(2), 201-204, 213-215.

This article presents guidelines for physicians for completing a history and physical examination in cases of alleged sexual abuse. The author explains that irrefutable and conclusive physical findings are often absent and that a well-documented history may be essential in evaluating physical findings.

589. Levy, J. M., Levy, P. H., & Samowitz, P. (1988). *AIDS: Teaching persons with disabilities* *to better protect themselves.* **New York: The Young Adult Institute.**

The Young Adult Institute in New York, which serves people with disabilities, developed and used a program geared to teach clients how to better protect themselves from acquiring AIDS. The program comes with a manual and a videotape and is particularly useful in working with higher-functioning clients requiring less supervision. Program objectives include defining AIDS and its dangers, the identification of high-risk populations and how the disease is transmitted, the identification of risky sexual behaviors, the identification of safer sexual behaviors, teaching clients to resist social pressure to engage in unsafe sex, and the demonstration of the use of a condom with the aid of a videotape. Dilemmas possibly arising from AIDS training, such as parental objections, are discussed. Policy statements are discussed, such as the need for clients to be trained in terms of their level of cognitive functioning.

590. **Lewark, C. A. (1983).** *The developmentally disabled child as a victim of child abuse.* **(ERIC Document Reproduction Service No. ED 233 545)**

Records from a 1972-1982 period documenting the abuse or neglect of 95 children with disabilities were studied. Findings indicate that the families experienced serious multiple problems in nearly every case and that none seemed aware of the abuse or neglect. The author judges the connection between abuse and disability to be minimal. Major problems identified are the fragmentation of services and the lack of a coordinating agency in handling these families.

591. **Lewis, K. C. (1985). Health education and the hearing impaired.** *AEP Association of Educational Psychologists Journal, 6*(5, Pt. 2, Suppl.), 15-19.

This article discusses the development of health education (including information on sex education), particularly in special schools. It examines the difficulties of teaching health education to students with hearing impairments, and it suggests that the difficulties can be divided into three problem areas: naivete, confused knowledge, and unusual attitudes or beliefs resulting from information obtained from uninformed or poorly informed sources.

592. **Liability to patients. (1985).** *Mental and Physical Disability Law Reporter, 9*(5), 366-369.

This article describes eight cases involving suits brought by people with mental disabilities against state facilities and includes decisions on issues of burden of proof (Saporta v. Nebraska, 368 N.W.2d. 783 [Neb. Sup. Ct. 1985]), expert testimony (Rudy v. Meshorer, No. 202449 [Ariz. Ct. App. May 1, 1985]), standard of care (Nesbitt v. Community Health of South Dade, Inc., 467 So.2d. 711 [Fla. Dist. Ct. App. 1985]), false imprisonment (Gonzalez v. New York, 488 N.Y.S.2d. 231 [N.Y. App. Div. 1985]), emergency commitment

(Temple v. Marlborough Division of District Court Department, 479 N.E.2d. 137 [Mass. S. Jud. Ct. 1985]), constitutional rights (Gann v. Schramm, 606 F.Supp. 1442 [D. Del. 1985]), state agency immunity (Rubacha ex rel. Rubacha v. Coler, 607 F.Supp. 477 [N.D. Ill. 1985]), and assault by a state hospital aide (United States v. Dise, 763 F.2d. 586 [3d Cir. 1985]).

593. **Liebow, P. R. (1984). The new-look school nurse.** *Journal of Psychosocial Nursing and Mental Health Services, 22*(3), 37-41.

This article examines the role of the school nurse in providing preventive services to schoolchildren with emotional disabilities. It describes the characteristics of children with emotional disorders and the three most common emotional disorders: conduct, anxiety, and depressive types. The author suggests several nursing interventions: inducing relaxation and imaging, counselling, active listening, educating teachers about such things as childhood suicide, breathing exercises, discussions with parents about medication noncompliance, referrals of family problems to social workers, and nutrition education.

594. **Light, J., Collier, B., & Parnes, P. (1985). Communicative interaction between young nonspeaking physically disabled children and their primary caregivers.** *Augmentative and Alternative Communication, 1,* 74-83.

These authors studied communication functions in children with physical handicaps. Overall low rates of communication, especially of initiation, suggest that many victims of abuse with disabilities would be unlikely to report the incident unless directly asked.

595. **Lightcap, J. L., Kurland, J. A., & Burgess, R. L. (1982). Child abuse: A test of some predictions from evolutionary theory.** *Ethology and Sociobiology, 3*(2), 61-67.

This article analyzes data from R. L. Burgess and R. D. Conger's study of 24 two-parent households with at least one known victim of child abuse using an evolutionary model of social behavior. Findings include: 1) stepparents and their stepchildren were much more at risk to child abuse than were parents and their offspring, 2) parents were much more likely to abuse their stepchildren than their own children, 3) males were more likely than females to be abusers, 4) children with handicaps were more likely than nonhandicapped children to be abused, and 5) the youngest child was less likely to be abused than any other child in the family. Although results of this analysis were as predicted, the findings do not represent a strong test of evolutionary models of social behavior.

596. **Lister, L. (1981). Chronically ill and disabled. In D. A. Shore & H. L. Gochros (Eds.),** *Sexual problems of adolescents in institutions* **(pp. 223-235). Springfield, IL: Charles C Thomas.**

This discussion of adolescent sexuality is based on a case study of an adolescent with a chronic illness and disabilities living in a hospital. A social worker, a tutor, and an occupational therapist worked with the boy. The author identifies three spheres of sexuality that must be addressed in this type of intervention: the biological and the reproductive; gender identity and sex role behavior; sex drive influences, including eroticism and sensuality; and sexual activities. Each patient must be considered individually. The place of sexuality throughout their life cycle must be considered. In the study discussed, intervention focused on the patient's talents and interests as a means to afford him entry back into his peer group.

597. Livneh, H. (1982). On the origins of negative attitudes toward people with disabilities. *Rehabilitation Literature, 43*(11/12), 338-347.

This article examines the study of attitudes toward people with disabilities and offers a new classification scheme for conceptualizing these attitudes. It classifies factors that should help professionals deal more effectively with the feelings of clients with disabilities: sociocultural, childhood, psychodynamic, and religious influences; anxiety as the result of an aesthetic aversion; supposed threat to the nondisabled person's body image; disability as a reminder of death; and demographic variables.

598. Llewellyn, M. H., & McLaughlin, T. F. (1986). An evaluation of a self-protection skills program for the mildly handicapped. *Child and Family Behviour Therapy, 8*(4), 29-37.

This article discusses the outcome of a self-protection curriculum taught to 10 junior high school special education students. Skills taught include the identification of strangers, the identification of unsafe situations, the use of refusal skills, and the understanding of acceptable and unacceptable touch. Acquired skills were found to be stable over time.

599. Lloyd-Bostock, S., & Shapland, J. (1986). The Police and Criminal Evidence Act, 1984: Some continuing questions for psychologists. *Bulletin of the British Psychological Society, 39,* 241-245.

This article discusses psychology's contribution to the United Kingdom's Police and Criminal Evidence Act of 1984 and describes interrogation, tape-recording of suspects, and the interviewing of people with mental handicaps and other disadvantaged groups.

600. Lombana, J. H. (1989). Counseling persons with disabilities: Summary and projections. *Journal of Counseling & Development, 68,* 177-179.

This author summarizes the findings and discussions of several other articles included in a special section on counseling persons with disabilities. A number of areas of concern are identified, but sexual abuse and sexual assault counseling are not among those specifically named. The author makes several predictions about future directions of counseling people with disabilities.

601. Longo, R. E., & Gochenor, C. (1981). Sexual assault of handicapped individuals. *Journal of Rehabilitation, 47,* 24-27.

These authors explore the relationship between handicaps and assault. They point to statements by convicted sex offenders who say they have selected victims on the basis of their perception of how vulnerable the potential victim would be.

602. Lorber, R., Felton, D. K., & Reid, J. B. (1984). A social learning approach to the reduction of coercive process in child abuse families: A molecular analysis. *Advances in Behavior Research & Therapy, 6,* 29-45.

This article discusses the role of social learning theory in the victim-offender cycle of abuse. The authors found abuse victims were more likely to be violent, aggressive, or disruptive than nonabused controls. This disparity is viewed as the result of learned behavior. Social learning theory suggests that violent and aggressive behavior is learned primarily through imitation of a model.

603. Love, E. (1983). Parental and staff attitudes toward instruction in human sexuality for sensorially impaired students at the Alabama Institute for Deaf and Blind. *American Annals of the Deaf, 128*(1), 45-47.

This article examines parental and staff attitudes toward sex education for students with sensory impairments at the Alabama Institute for Deaf and Blind. Data included information on instruction, grouping of students by sex, and person(s) responsible for instruction. In spite of the idea that parents of children with sensory impairments are resistant to sex education for their children, findings show strong agreement between parents and staff about the need for instruction in human sexuality.

604. Luiselli, J. K., Helfen, C. S., & Pemberton, B. W. (1977). The elimination of a child's in-class masturbation by overcorrection and reinforcement. *Journal of Behavior Therapy and Experimental Psychiatry, 8,* 201-204.

In this study, overcorrection was used to successfully eliminate masturbation in the school setting. The client is an 8-year-old boy with mental retardation and behavior disorders. After eight days of using the overcorrection technique, the target behavior ceased. At follow-up 1 month, 6 months, and 12 months later, the boy's gains were found to be intact.

605. Lukoff, D., Gioia-Hasick, D., Sullivan, G., Golden, J. S., & Nuechterlein, K. H. (1986). Sex education and rehabilitation with schizophrenic male outpatients. *Schizophrenia Bulletin, 12*(4), 669-677.

This article describes a sex education program for recent onset male schizophrenic patients attending an outpatient clinic and the program objectives, which were to provide information, to clarify values, to overcome sexual dysfunction, and to enhance intimacy skills. It also discusses the techniques used, which included role-playing, modeling, group exercises, and the use of explicit sex therapy audiovisual material.

606. Lund, J. (1985). The prevalence of psychiatric morbidity in mentally retarded adults. *Acta Psychiatrica Scandinavica, 72*(6), 563-570.
This article describes an examination of 302 adults with mental retardation with regard to handicaps, behavior, skills, and psychopathology using a handicap, behavior, and skills schedule developed by Wing (1980) and a list of psychiatric items. Findings include the following: psychiatric disorder was diagnosed in 85 subjects (27.1%), behavior disorder (10.9%) and psychosis of uncertain type (5%) were the most common disorders, dementia and early childhood autism were of equal prevalence (3.6%), neurosis was rare (2%), schizophrenia (1.3%) and affective disorder (1.7%) occurred at about the same rates as found in comparable investigations, and no cases of alcohol or drug abuse were noted.

607. Lundervold, D., & Bourland, G. (1987). Behavioral treatment of bisexual aggression of an adult with developmental disabilities. *Sexuality and Disability, 8*(4), 216-220.
This short case study describes the suppression of inappropriate sexual behavior in a 22-year-old man with severe mental retardation living in an eight-resident unit for the treatment of severe behavior problems. The two overcorrection methods used were restitution and positive practice. Restitution involved washing and drying the hands for 5 minutes based on the logic that physical contact is unhygienic. Positive practice involved shaking hands with the victim and others nearby for 15 minutes following handwashing. The intervention was successful. The article briefly mentions the need for training in multiple environments, the potential difficulty in determining when a victim is in fact a consenting partner, and the desirability of comprehensive intervention plans that address sexual preference and appropriate as well as inappropriate sexual behavior. These authors conclude that behavioral interventions are a viable alternative to the use of drugs in the treatment of sexual aggression in people with developmental disabilities.

608. Luterman, D. (1984). *Counseling the communicatively disordered and their families.* Boston: Little, Brown.
This book discusses a number of basic approaches to counseling as they are applied to clients who are deaf and their families. The effects of communication disorders are discussed in relation to life and marital adjustment. The author recommends training communication disorder therapists in counseling methods.

609. Lutzer, V. D. (1983). Modification of inappropriate sexual behaviors in a mildly mentally retarded male. *Sexuality and Disability, 6*(3/4), 176-182.
This article describes a program for modifying the inappropriate social behaviors of a man with mild mental retardation with a history of socially unacceptable verbal and sexual behaviors. A systems perspective was used to analyze interview, test, and observational material from the subject, work supervisor, and parents. The program employed reframing techniques and positive reinforcement. The program eliminated inappropriate verbal and nonverbal behaviors, but it did not generalize regarding inappropriate behavior unaffected by the reframing procedure. Reframing should be further studied as a promising tool in modifying the social system of a person with a mental handicap.

•M•

610. MacDonald, A. (1987, November 5). Adult Protection Act pleases committee. *Journal Pioneer.*
This newspaper article discusses the presentation of the Ad Hoc Committee on Adults in Need of Protection, a subcommittee of the P.E.I. Inter-Agency Committee on the proposed Adult Protection Act, to a special legislative committee holding hearings on the act. The proposed act is designed to recognize responsibility for the provision of assistance and protection services to adults who are dependent, who cannot care for themselves, or who are abused or neglected by caregivers. The committee's presentation discusses the recognition of the problem of abuse and neglect of dependent adults (includes people who are elderly and people who are mentally and physically frail). The committee sees the act as a tool for public education, reinforcement of responsibility, and granting legal power to intervene in extreme cases of neglect or abuse. Strategies must be developed to aid in identification, crisis intervention, education, and advocacy for adults who are dependent and their caregivers. The committee identified some problems with the legislation: a) the act does not make reporting mandatory, b) the act could penalize individuals financially if they have to bear the cost of medical attention and legal action, and c) the act takes all responsibility away from health professionals and institutions for treatment by removing liability.

611. MacDonald, J. M. (1973). *Indecent exposure.* Springfield, IL: Charles C Thomas.
Although the majority of this book does not address disability, in one paragraph, the author discusses exhibitionists with mental retardation. He cites studies that show a slightly higher incidence of offenders with mental retardation than in the general population. He states that this might be due to the greater likelihood of detection and arrest of offenders with mental retardation than of nonhandicapped offenders rather than a genuine increase in incidence.

612. MacEachron, A. E. (1979). Mentally retarded offenders: Prevalence and characteristics. *American Journal of Mental Deficiency, 84*(2), 165-176.
This author examined literature and prison records in order to determine the prevalence and characteristics of offenders with mental retardation and concludes that the prevalence rate of male adult offenders with mental retardation is only slightly higher than prevalence of adult males with mental retardation in the general population. The author also found that social rather than legal characteristics predict offense severity and that social and legal characteristics separately predict sentence length and past recidivism.

613. MacKeith, R. (1975). Speculations on some possible long-term effects. In A. W. Franklin (Ed.), *Concerning child abuse* (pp. 63-68). Edinburgh, Scotland: Churchill Livingstone.
In the United Kingdom, no adequate cause of disability could be found in 50% of children with cerebral palsy and in 50% of children with mental retardation. Speculation on incomplete data suggests the following: Each year, abuse may cause up to 6% (90) of all new cases of cerebral palsy, one-quarter of new cases of severe mental handicap, and up to 3000 new cases of personality disturbance.

614. Macleod, S. (1985). *For one and all: Sexuality and your disabled child.* Halifax, NS: Planned Parenthood Nova Scotia.
This 23-page booklet discusses what parents of children with disabilities can do to help their children develop a positive attitude toward themselves and sexuality. It points out that overprotection is actually a disservice to children as it leaves them unprepared to deal with new people and situations. The booklet has a short bibliography, including materials on talking to children and teens about sex, disabilities in general, and sexuality and people with disabilities.

615. Malloy, G. L., & Herold, E. S. (1988). Factors related to sexual counseling of physically disabled adults. *Journal of Sex Research, 24,* 220-227.
In this study, 226 Canadian physicians, nurses, and therapists responded to a questionnaire on the likelihood of their providing sex counseling to patients with physical disabilities. Nine variables were measured and subjected to a multivariate analysis. Findings indicate that inadequate preparation, rather than negative attitudes, resulted in the respondents not providing sex counseling to these patients.

616. Man cleared. (1987, May 11). *Kamloops News.* (Kamloops, British Columbia)
A 41-year-old man was cleared of sexually assaulting a teenager with mental retardation because he said she was willing. The judge described the occurrence as outrageous and unforgivable, but he said he had to acquit the man because the accused believed there was consent, a legal defense against the charge. (Note: The "honest belief" defense contends that if the alleged perpetrator honestly believes that consent is given, there is no sexual assault, even if this belief is in error.)

617. Mandatory AIDS testing. (1989). *Mental and Physical Disability Law Reporter, 13*(2), 149.
The Eastern Nebraska Community Office of Retardation (ENCOR) adopted an infectious disease policy requiring certain of its direct care workers to be tested for AIDS and hepatitis B. An American federal district court struck down the requirement as a violation of the employees' fourth amendment rights. In the present ruling, the Eighth Circuit upheld the district court ruling, rejecting ENCOR's assertion that clients who bite and scratch risk infection. Sexually transmitted diseases were not addressed.

618. Man jailed for attack on disabled woman. (1987, July 9). *Toronto Star,* p. A2.
This newspaper article reports that a man who sexually assaulted a one-armed, 73-year-old woman on her way to morning prayers received a sentence of 18 months in jail. The attacker was known to be abused in his own childhood and had schizophrenia.

619. Man judged not guilty of sex assault. (1987, June 26). *Comox District Free Press,* pp. 1, 3.
This newspaper article states that a part-time group home "parent" working with or supervising residents was found not guilty of sexually assaulting three men with mental handicaps. The trial was taken up by determining whether the three complainants were mentally competent and whether they were competent to take an oath. It was also noted that the judge relied on the psychologist's opinion that there is a tendency on the part of people with mental handicaps to want to please, and thus, if they sense that a person questioning them is seeking the answer "yes" or "no," they might give that answer in error. The psychologist also testified that people with mental handicaps may have poorer than normal memories and also might have difficulty determining the sequence of events. During the trial, all three of these points became evident.

620. Marchetti, A. (1987, May). *Abuse of mentally retarded persons: Characteristics of the abused, the abuser, and the informer.* Paper presented at the 111th Annual Meeting of the American Association on Mental Deficiency, Los Angeles, CA. (ERIC Document Reproduction Service No. ED 286 313)
In this paper, the author discusses possible causes of abuse of people with mental retardation living in institutions by residence staff. The database comprised all abuse cases reported between January, 1984 and September, 1986 in residential facilities in the state of Alabama. The abused group is identified as having higher IQs and demonstrating more adaptive behavior compared to nonabused residents. Age, sex, and racial factors yielded no significant differences. Staff profiles suggest

that the abuse was committed primarily by direct care personnel who are less educated and less well-paid than other staff members. Abuse tended to be reported by professionals and administrative staff. The author suggests that direct care staff should receive more instruction regarding behavior management and aggression control techniques and that staff should be rotated on a regular basis to less stressful areas of the residence. Also, more professional and administrative staff should be assigned to residential areas, and abuse should be reported and tracked.

621. Margolin, K. N. (1988). Risk of privacy policy by residential institutions for handicapped adolescents. *Journal of Rehabilitation, 54*(2), 50-54.

This article discusses information on the legal risks associated with residential institution policies that provide privacy for adolescents with intellectual, learning, or physical disabilities. The article is based on a day-long seminar held for 200 professionals to discuss this topic. Most agreed that adolescents in institutional care should have the same right to privacy and sexual exploration as adolescents living with their families in the community; however, many concerns (particularly those related to potential institutional liability for pregnancy and sexual assault) were raised regarding the implementation of this policy. Court decisions related to the rights of adolescents to privacy and control over their own bodies are discussed. Potential liability is discussed in reference to general institutional responsibility cases and specifically to hypothetical cases involving adolescent sexuality. The author presents guidelines for minimizing liability risks while implementing a privacy policy.

622. Marion, R. L. (1981). *Educators, parents, and exceptional children.* Rockville, MD: Aspen Systems.

This book describes roles that teachers can adopt to fulfill meaningful functions while seeking to involve parents of exceptional children and youths in special education. The definition of an exceptional child includes a child with mental or physical handicaps as well as a child with learning disabilities. Chapter 8 deals specifically with teachers becoming involved with families of abused exceptional children. There are three major contributing factors to child abuse: a parent, a child, and a situation. The characteristics of abuse-prone parents and abuse-prone situations are discussed. Special or exceptional children have been identified as at higher risk for abuse. The special educator's responsibility is to identify and report the abused child and to work with the parents of the abused child. The educator should develop specific skills for the parent involvement program. These necessary skills are discussed.

623. Marker, G., & Friedman, P. R. (1973). Rethinking children's rights. *Children Today, 2*(6), 8-11.

This article urges that children's rights be recognized and ensured by the legal system. Rights include having a supportive and nurturing environment, adequate medical care, appropriate education, protection from severe abuse and neglect, and having one's own best interest adequately presented. These rights are held as being basic to the healthy development of the child. The article also discusses three precedent-setting United States court cases in which these rights were expanded to include institutionalized children, exceptional children, and children with mental retardation.

624. Martin, H. (1972). The child and his development. In C. H. Kempe & R. E. Helfer (Eds.), *Helping the battered child and his family* (pp. 93-114). Philadelphia: J. P. Lippincott.

In this classic article, a study is described in which 42 abused children were followed for 3 years. Child abuse was correlated with mental retardation. Of the children with handicaps, 93% had a history of severe head trauma. Findings indicate that treatment of children with neurological impairments can result in increased IQ scores.

625. Martin, H. P. (1976). Neurologic status of abused children. In H. P.Martin (Ed.), *The abused child: A multidisciplinary approach to developmental issues and treatment* (pp. 67-82). Cambridge, MA: Ballinger Publishing Co.

This article describes a 5-year follow-up study of 58 abused children. This sample of children represented less severely injured children than many other studies done around this time. Of the children with no previous history of head injury, 43% manifested some neurological trauma. The author emphasizes the importance of using a multidisciplinary approach.

626. Martin, H. P. (1980). The neuro-psycho-developmental aspects of child abuse and neglect. In N. S. Ellerstein (Ed.), *Child abuse and neglect: A medical reference* (pp. 95-119). New York: John Wiley & Sons.

This chapter focuses on the psychological sequelae to child abuse. The neurological damage, developmental delays, and psychological problems seen in abused children may result from at least three basic causes: physical damage from assault or neglect, aberrant patterns of parent-child relationships, or iatrogenic complications of intervention. The author proposes that all abused children be screened for neurological deficits and developmental delays and that parenting skills must be addressed.

627. Martin, H. P., Beezley, P., Conway, E. F., & Kempe, C. H. (1974). The development of abused children, Part 2: Physical, neurologic, and intellectual outcome. *Advances in Pediatrics, 21,* 44-73.

Fifty-eight abused children were assessed for physical and intellectual development at a mean of 4.5 years after abuse. In 53% of the cases, there was some neurologic abnormality, with 31% falling in the moderate to severe range. Of the 58 children, 5% were microcephallic. Implications for treatment indicate that children should not be returned to high-risk families.

628. **Martin, M., & Forchuk, C. (1987). Sexuality and the developmentally handicapped: Health education strategies.** *B. C. Journal of Special Education, 11*(2), 101-108.
This article describes a sex education program designed for use with small groups of adolescents and young adults with developmental handicaps. Topics include body parts, acceptable social behavior, birth control, sexually transmitted diseases, and assertiveness.

629. **Martin, M., & Forchuk, C. (1987). Sexuality and the developmentally handicapped: Health education strategies.** *Canadian Journal of Special Education, 3*(2), 181-189.
This article describes the HEALTH (Health Education And Learning for The Handicapped) program. The sex education components include group discussion, role-playing, and the use of visual aids such as films. Group sessions are one hour long and are given over a period of 12 to 14 weeks to 6 to 12 participants. Topics addressed include sexually transmitted diseases, anatomy, acceptable social behavior, birth control, and assertiveness.

630. **Martorana, G. R. (1985, June). Schizophreniform disorder in a mentally retarded adolescent boy following sexual victimization [Letter to the editor].** *American Journal of Psychiatry, 142*(6), 784.
This letter to the editor is a comment on an earlier article in the journal about three female adolescents who developed psychoses after sexual assault and their subsequent treatment. The writer tells of a case involving a 14-year-old male with mental retardation who was sexually assaulted and developed a psychosis after the attack. The writer describes the child's subsequent treatment and recovery.

631. **Mastrocola-Morris, E. (1989).** *Woman abuse: The relationship between wife assault and elder abuse.* **Ottawa: National Clearing House on Family Violence.**
This literature review presents information that suggests that female victims of elder abuse may have been battered wives in their younger years. This suggests that the victim's role is learned. Also, debilitation may reduce personal power and increase the likelihood of abuse.

632. **Masuda, S. (1988). 22 million for transition houses—But can we use them.** *Thriving, 1*(1), 1. **(Thriving is a publication of DAWN Canada.)**
This article points out that although the Canadian government is undertaking an initiative to create more shelters for battered women there is no requirement that these shelters are accessible to women with disabilities.

633. **Masuda, S. (in press).** *Meeting our needs.* **Vancouver: DAWN (DisAbled Women's Network) Canada.**
This document includes the following: 1) background information about sexual, physical, and emotional abuse of women with disabilities, 2) a survey of accessibility of Canadian transition houses for battered women, and 3) guidelines for improving the accessibility of transition houses. An introduction, written by Jillian Ridington, includes information on the nature and prevalence of offenses committed against women with disabilities. The accessibility survey includes useful ratings of shelters in each province and territory. The guidelines for improving accessibility include much useful information to assist service providers. (Note: This document was reviewed in draft form. The final report is expected to be released in Spring, 1990, by DAWN Canada and may be significantly revised from the current draft. However, the document has been included here because of its great practical value.)

634. **Matek, O. (1981). Administrative concerns. In D. A. Shore & H. L. Gochros (Eds.),** *Sexual problems of adolescents in institutions* **(pp. 36-50). Springfield, IL: Charles C Thomas.**
This chapter discusses sexual issues of institutionalized adolescents. The focus is on normal sexual development. The impact of resident peer groups upon each other is addressed. Group norms influence adolescent behavior to a large degree. The sexual values held by different members of the institution may vary greatly. As a result of these varied influences, the adolescent's sexuality may develop in ways that are socially unacceptable outside the institution.

635. **Matson, J. L. (1987). Trends and developments in behavioral assessment and treatment of mentally retarded persons.** *School Psychology Review, 16*(4), 566-581.
This article examines the field of mental retardation and discusses advances in: 1) support and lobbying efforts of parent groups, 2) development of psychometric assessment methods, and 3) development of behavioral assessment and training strategies. It explores recent trends in vocational training, parent training, sensory extinction, and enhancement of self-control through self-evaluation and monitoring. It identifies education and habilitation of people with mental retardation in schools and sex education of people with handicaps as areas for future research, and it concludes that the emphasis on teaching adaptive skills requires consultation between teachers and school psychologists who have more training in teaching adaptive behavior.

636. **Matson, J. L., & Barrett, R. P. (Eds.). (1982).** *Psychopathology in the mentally retarded.* **New York: Grune & Stratton.**
This book is comprised of articles written by various authors on such topics as treatment services, assessment and diagnosis, current models of psychopathology, anxiety disorders, affective disorders, psychosis,

pharmacotherapy, and behavior therapy. Sexuality is not addressed.

637. Matthews, G. F. (1984). Voices from the shadows. *Rehabilitation Digest, Spring*, 10, 21.
This article is an excerpt from the book *Voices from the shadows: Women with disabilities speak out*, which explores the lives and experiences of women with disabilities. The article addresses the feelings of women with disabilities about their sexuality and is based on material drawn from interviews. The author herself became physically disabled at the age of sixteen.

638. Mayer, A. (1985). *Sexual abuse: Causes, consequences and treatment of incestuous and pedophilic acts.* Holmes Beach, FL: Learning Publications.
This book deals with incestuous and pedophilic acts and the causes, consequences, and treatment of these acts. It specifically deals with sexual abuse of children with handicaps in the section on children who are at risk (p. 35). The author states that children who are handicapped are at risk because there is less likelihood that they will disclose the fact that abuse is occurring.

639. Mayer, T., Walker, M. L., Johnson, D. G., & Matlak, M. E. (1981). Causes of morbidity and mortality in severe pediatric trauma. *Journal of the American Medical Association, 245*(7), 719-721.
A two-year study was undertaken at a United States children's medical centre to determine the nature of injuries sustained by a total of 160 patients with multiple trauma and neurologic injury as rated by the Modified Injury Severity Scale and the Glascow Coma Scale. Neurologic injury was found in 80% of patients. A total of 126 patients had head injuries. Child abuse was the third most frequent cause of injury (6%). Mortality among patients with head injuries was 16%, nearly three times as great as among patients without head injury.

640. McAfee, J. K., & Gural, M. (1988). Individuals with mental retardation and the criminal justice system: The view from States' attorneys general. *Mental Retardation, 26*, 5-12.
This article deals primarily with people with mental retardation who are accused of criminal offenses; however, some of the problems cited with defendants also are of concern to victims. The authors conclude that police, prosecutors, and judges typically lack information about people with disabilities.

641. McArther, S. (1989). Crime Risk Education is Essential for the Disabled. *Rehabilitation Digest, 19*(4), 20-21.
In this article, crime prevention materials designed for use by people with disabilities are described. Materials addressed include the following: the need for accessibility to 911 emergency services; Ontario laws regarding physical, verbal, and sexual abuse; how to get help; residential security; and safety in the streets. The materials were developed by Crime Risk Education is Essential for the Disabled (CREED). CREED was developed by the Ontario Federation for the Cerebral Palsied (OFCP). This article also makes reference to a crime survey conducted by CREED in the Toronto area, a crime survey which indicates that people with disabilities are more often victimized than people without disabilities. Mention is also made of workshops held by CREED throughout Ontario and CREED's coordination for the Ontario Women's Directorate of an education program entitled *Local Sexual Assault Education Initiatives.*

642. McCaffrey, M. (1979). Abused and neglected children are exceptional children. *Teaching Exceptional Children, 11*(2), 47-50.
This article discusses the role of a teacher when child abuse or neglect is suspected. According to this author, the teacher has the responsibility to report suspected cases of child abuse (including sexual abuse) and neglect. The teacher also has a professional responsibility. A teacher should find out the resources that are available to him or her both in and out of school. The school staff should be given inservice training on the problem of child abuse and neglect. The teachers can organize policy development or program development even without inservice training. The staff should provide follow-up assessment and evaluation and support services once a case has been reported. The teacher should recognize children in potential high-risk situations. These are children who are premature, disruptive, or have disabilities.

643. McCay, V. (1984, September). Sexual abuse [Editorial]. *American Annals of the Deaf, 129*(4), 351.
This editorial discusses the issue of sexual abuse of children who are deaf. The opinion is expressed that the best approach to the problem is prevention. Careful hiring procedures of staff is the first step since in most cases the attacker is a member of the staff. It is imperative that once the incident has been discovered it is brought to the attention of the administration and handled appropriately.

644. McCelland, C. O., Rekate, H., Kaufman, B., & Persse, L. (1980). Cerebral injury in child abuse: A changing profile. *Child's Brain, 7*(5), 225-235.
This paper presents case review data on 21 children admitted to the hospital over a 1-year period with skull or cerebral injury as the result of child abuse. A broad profile of resultant central nervous system sequelae is described. Injuries include Whiplash Shaken Infant syndrome, cerebral contusions, severe spinal cord injuries resulting in paresis, skull fractures, and miscellaneous injuries. Computer tomography (CAT scan) has proved to be valuable in the location of subdural-intracerebral hematomas and posterior fossa lesions as well as in providing longitudinal assessment of sequelae

related to head trauma. The role of the child protection team is discussed.

645. McClellan, M. C. (1987). *Child abuse.* **Bloomington, IN: Phi Delta Kappa. (Exceptional Child Education Resources Clearinghouse accession number EC 20 2172)**

This book addresses the complex nature of child abuse and is of particular interest to teachers. Topics include the following: how teachers can meet their legal responsibilities regarding child abuse; defining, recognizing, and reporting child abuse; contributing factors to child abuse; interacting with victims; incest; myths associated with child abuse; the need for the increased recognition of the sexual abuse of boys; evidence that links sexual abuse to deviant adolescent behavior; prevention and intervention; and the consequences of abuse, including learning disabilities, lack of self-concept, and behavioral and emotional problems. (Copies of this book are available from Phi Delta Kappa.)

646. McClennen, S. (1988). Sexuality and students with mental retardation. *Teaching Exceptional Children, 20*(4), 59-61.

This article offers suggestions on how appropriate sexual behavior may be taught to students with moderate and severe mental retardation. Strategies include showing respect for privacy, asking permission before touching a student, teaching appropriate social interaction, and presenting information on sexuality and social interaction.

647. McCown, D. E. (1981). Father-daughter incest: A family problem. *Pediatric Nursing, 7*(4), 25-28.

This article deals generally with the problem of father-daughter incest. The article provides a composite description of the incestuous family. The child victim of incest is usually the eldest daughter living at home. There is a higher rate of incest reported in girls who are deaf, disfigured, seizure-disordered, or illegitimate. The author describes the long-term effects of incest, the law regarding incest, the treatment of incest, and preventive measures.

648. McCrone, W. P., Ziezula, F. R., & Robinson, D. (1985). Preventing child abuse. *Perspectives for Teachers of the Hearing Impaired, 3*(5), 11-13.

This article contains a bibliography of 78 resources relating to child abuse. Included are references on sexual and institutional abuse, legal aspects, personnel training, and prevention and protection programs.

649. McDowell, W. A., Bills, G. F., & Eaton, M. W. (1989). Extending psychotherapeutic strategies for people with disabilities. *Journal of Counseling & Development, 68,* 151-154.

This article discusses the application of psychotherapeutic techniques developed by Milton Erikson in

counseling people with disabilities. It stresses methods of building rapport, use of therapeutic imagery, reframing, and other "paradoxical" techniques.

650. McEwen, E., & Anton-Culver, H. (1988). The medical communication of deaf patients. *Journal of Family Practice, 26*(3), 289-291.

In this study, adults who are deaf adults and adults studying English as a second language at the grade 3 to 5 level were compared in their ability to communicate with their physicians. Patients who are deaf were found to have the greater difficulty and re-explained themselves less frequently when misunderstandings occurred. The authors conclude that as a subset of patients who do not speak English, patients who are deaf are at increased risk for poor patient-physician communication. (Note: Poor communication with health care providers may be related to increased risk for abuse by these service providers and to symptom masking which results in a lower probability of detection of sexual abuse for people with impaired communication within the health care system.)

651. McFadden, E. J., Ziefert, M., & Stovall, B. (1984). *Preventing abuse in foster care: Instructor's manual.* **Washington, DC: National Center on Child Abuse and Neglect. (ERIC Document Reproduction Service No. ED 265 940)**

This manual provides training instructors with teaching approaches to be used with a 10-unit curriculum for foster care staff. Considered in the curriculum are the dynamics of child abuse in foster families, the need for prevention activities on a systems level, the worker's task in handling abuse in foster care placements, and the worker's role of helping foster parents with behavior management. The introduction suggests teaching approaches likely to be effective with child welfare staff and discusses the class's physical setting, classroom procedures, and curriculum theme. The first session presents data on child abuse in foster care, and the second identifies the high-risk child and stress within the foster family. Two sessions on prevention focus on family structure and risk-assessment techniques, overloaded foster families, matching, and monitoring, with attention to indicators pointing to a child at risk. The session on the worker's educational role interprets the difference between discipline and punishment and indicates discipline expectations for foster parents. Other units explore ways to work with the foster family in assessing and managing the child's behavior, staff placement of adolescents, indicators of adolescent abuse, and methods of interviewing adolescents. The final two sessions focus on prevention of child abuse in the home.

652. McFarlane, A. C. (1988). Posttraumatic stress disorder and blindness. *Comprehensive Psychiatry, 29*(6), 558-560.

Four cases of post-traumatic stress disorder in blind clients are discussed. Topics include the importance of visual imagery in the processing of traumatic events and the disruption of selective attention in post-traumatic stress disorder.

653. McGregor, B. M. S., & Dutton, D. G. (1988). *Child sexual abuse within populations that require health system intervention: What is known about its prevalence and service costs?* **Vancouver: University of British Columbia, Department of Psychology.**

This report of a Health and Welfare Canada study reviews literature related to the history of child abuse among eight specialized populations. Increased prevalence in these groups is considered evidence of the damaging effects of abuse, but this prevalence may also represent increased risk among special populations. The authors report studies indicating 44% to 62% of female psychiatric patients have been sexually abused. Among patients with dissociative disorders, rates of 60% to 83% are reported. Prevalence rates for male sex offenders who were child sexual abuse victims are 50% to 56% for juvenile offenders, 23% to 59% for incarcerated rapists, and 32% to 57% for convicted child molesters (3% to 16% reported among normal males). A history of child sexual abuse by female family molesters was more common among rapists, while abuse by a male outside the family was more common among child molesters. A history of childhood incest was noted as a possible risk factor in mothers who abused their children or married men who abused their children. Tentative data also suggest that a history of childhood incest increases the risk of being raped or battered for women as adults. Many (52% to 73%) female prostitutes were previous victims of child sexual abuse. A circular relationship between alcohol abuse and incest is also discussed. The authors discuss two theoretical perspectives explaining these relationships: post-traumatic stress response and social learning theory. An annotated bibliography is included.

654. McKown, J. M. (1984-86). Disabled teenagers: Sexual identification & sexuality counseling. *Sexuality and Disability, 7*(1/2), 17-27.

This article discusses nursing literature concerned with the teenager's with disabilities process of sexual self-identification and physical management of emotional and sexual care. It describes practices and myths that influence body image and discusses distortions attributable to physical disabilities. It outlines an institutionally-based model (i.e., one person takes responsibility for counseling the person with the disability) and a community-based model (i.e., classes on body image/sexuality, parents as sex educators, and adolescent sexuality). The author also discusses nursing implications.

655. McLaren, J. (1989). Childhood problems associated with abuse and neglect. *Canada's Mental Health, 37*(3), 1-6.

This article reviews relevant literature and discusses the effects on children who have been abused or neglected.

Many effects associated with physical abuse and neglect may mimic, exacerbate, or cause disability. Some identified effects of sexual abuse (e.g., depression, sexually inappropriate behavior, sleep disturbances, somatic complaints, withdrawal, school problems, multiple personalities) also may have these effects.

656. McNab, W. L. (1978). The sexual needs of the handicapped. *Journal of School Health, 48*(5), 301-306.

One of the basic needs of life for people with handicaps, as well as to all individuals, is the understanding of one's own sexuality. Sex education can help people with handicaps find sexual satisfaction and may foster self-responsibility, maturity, and positive actions toward other rehabilitation goals. Traditionally, teaching sexuality to people with handicaps has run into objections resulting from society's negative attitude toward this population and parental apprehension regarding the decision-making skills of their children in relation to acceptable and unacceptable sexual behaviors; however, the Education for All Handicapped Children Act of 1975 (PL 94-142) has provided a way for parents and health professionals to put pressure on local, state, and federal programs to allocate funds for the development of a sound sex education program. As professionals in health education, it is our challenge and responsibility to see that the sexual needs of people with handicaps are not forgotten.

657. McPherson, C. (1984, February 6). Vulnerable victims of assault. *Toronto Star,* pp. B1, B2.

This newspaper article gives an overview of the problem of sexual assault on persons with handicaps. While there are virtually no statistics on the rate of assault and crime against people with handicaps, most experts say that crime against this population is no more frequent than crime against able-bodied people. But people with disabilities are clearly more vulnerable. Further, attacks on people with disabilities can have more severe consequences than on an abled-bodied person. People with handicaps cannot communicate to authorities as readily as able-bodied persons can, especially if the victim is deaf or blind. Further, there is a fear felt by the victim that if the crime is reported that there may be repercussions, such as losing a job or some other benefit. People with disabilities also have a poor self-image. Generally, if a person with disabilities is sexually assaulted, the chance for a conviction is low. In court, a victim with mental retardation has his or her credibility attacked as do other victims. At the moment, there is a review of the court process and its availability to people with handicaps being done by a member of the Ontario judiciary.

658. McPherson, C. (1984, February 6). Metro defense courses teach disabled to survive. *Toronto Star,* p. B3.

This newspaper article indicates that many self-protection and education courses are specifically tailored to teach people with disabilities how to fend for themselves. Within Metro Toronto, a number of courses are offered. The article details the programs offered by different agencies representing people with handicaps.

659. McPherson, C. (1990). Concerns around the gaps in legislation re: The assault and sexual assault of people with disabilities. *Victims of Violence Report, 1*(2), 40-42.

This author offers several recommendations for filling the gaps in the legislation regarding the assault and sexual assault of people with disabilities: extend provisions of C-15 to all vulnerable victims, not just children; remove the requirement for understanding an oath; provide interpreters for all victims who require them; establish clearer guidelines for the misuse of authority under § 265 (3) (d) of the criminal code, which establishes that teachers, health service providers, or other caregivers of people with disabilities are misusing authority when they have sex with a service consumer unless the care provider can clearly demonstrate unprejudiced, informed consent on the part of the service consumer; mandate reporting of abuse of people with disabilities; provide whistle-blower protection measures; allow hearsay when it is the best available source; require complete abuse protocols for all agencies serving vulnerable populations; screen all employees before hiring to agencies serving vulnerable populations; provide an emergency substitute guardian who can consent to examination when current guardian is suspected of abuse; provide independent advocates for all people living in institutions; provide emergency placement for vulnerable adults in danger of abuse; provide money through criminal injuries compensation boards to fund victim treatment services or special accommodations required to make these services accessible and appropriate; use civil proceedings to direct compensation to victims in order to fund treatment; lengthen the time for suing for damages related to incest, sexual abuse, and sexual assault; strengthen professional standards and regulations exercised by professional associations; provide a medicare diagnostic classification of child abuse and wife assault in order to assist in gathering more data; provide mandatory testing for sexually transmitted diseases in alleged abusers; reduce the length of time before cases are heard since delay may reduce the chances of the victim with a disability remembering or testifying; ensure that the best forensic evidence possible is available in cases with victims with disabilities since challenges to their testimony may make this evidence more vital to successful prosecution; and enact mandatory arrest laws that require the police to charge suspected abusers.

660. McRae, K. N., Cameron, A., Ferguson, C. A., Loadman, E., Rongstaf, S., & Snyder, R. (1984). The forensic pediatrician as a child advocate. *Journal of Developmental and Behavioral Pediatrics, 5*(5), 259-262.

This article examines the medico-legal activities of six pediatricians from a Canadian children's hospital who made 93 court appearances during a 12-month period in cases involving neglect, sexual abuse, physical abuse, and divorce. It describes the categories in which physicians appeared as court witnesses, and it suggests that children of undervalued ethnic and cultural groups (e.g., Native North Americans), children of divorce, and children of parents with mental handicaps need advocacy in court. The authors conclude that pediatricians are best equipped to act as child advocates because of their skills in the areas of physical, intellectual, and emotional development of children.

661. MD guilty on sex charge. (1987, October 25). *The Province.*

A local pediatrician was convicted of sexually assaulting a girl with mental retardation. Based on the testimony of a nurse who saw him fondle the girl while in bed, he was acquitted on one charge that did not have a corroborating witness but convicted on another charge because of the nurses corroboration.

662. Meddin, B. J. (1985). The assessment of risk in child abuse and neglect case investigations. *Child Abuse & Neglect, 9*, 57-62.

In the process of investigating reports of abuse and neglect, child protective service workers are called upon to make numerous case decisions. Critical to much of this decision-making is the assessment by the worker of the potential risk for harm that exists to the child regarding further abuse or neglect. This paper, based on two separate research studies, identifies the criteria that child protective service workers use to assess this potential risk for harm to the child: 1) the age of the child, 2) the functioning of the child (physical and mental abilities), 3) the cooperation of the prime caregiver, 4) functioning of the prime caregiver, 5) the intent of the perpetrator, 6) the current access that the perpetrator has to the child, 7) the severity of the current incident, and 8) the existence of previous incidents.

663. Meier, J. H. (1978). *A multifactorial model of child abuse dynamics* [Monograph No. 3:4/83]. Beaumont, CA: Research Division, CHILD-HELP USA/INTERNATIONAL.

A model of child abuse is discussed that includes parental, child, and ecological factors. Some factors discussed that may have special significance for people with disabilities are abuse of the parent as a child, parental demoralization, chronic parental anxiety, parental alcohol and/or drug dependency, family stress, mental or physical illness of the child, child behavior problems, lack of communication behavior by the child, disturbance of relationship between parents, social isolation, and lack of relevant family education.

664. Meier, J. H., & Nelson, W. P. (no date). *Relationship between child abuse and neglect and developmental disabilities.* Beaumont, CA: Children's Village, USA.

Based on program findings from a residential treatment facility for children who have experienced severe abuse or neglect and have extreme behavioral or developmental problems, this article discusses the relationship of child abuse and neglect to developmental disabilities. Intellectual functioning and behavior in the abused child are described as part of a preliminary report on a larger study yet to be completed. The larger study is aimed at testing techniques for use with any child who has been abused or neglected. The role of causality between abuse and neglect is discussed. Degree and type of developmental delay is described as well as typical behavioral and emotional sequelae.

665. Meier, J. H., & Sloan, M. P. (1982). *Acts of God or rites of families: Accidental versus inflicted child disabilities.* **Beaumont, CA: Children's Village, USA. (ERIC Document Reproduction Service No. ED 234 891)**

In this document, child abuse is studied in terms of a multifactorial model in which neglect dynamics play a central role. Particular attention is paid to the operation of these dynamics between parents and a child with handicaps. The role of reproductive pay-off in the neglect of a weaker or less fit child is discussed. The effects of removing a child are considered as a factor in the dissolution of the family or the begetting of a new infant. The authors suggest interdisciplinary family-oriented intervention and that parents will need support regarding the resolution of conflicts surrounding the damaged parent-child relationship.

666. Meier, J. H., & Sloan, M. P. (1984). The severely handicapped and child abuse. In J. Blacher (Ed.), *Severely handicapped young children and their families* **(pp. 247-274). Orlando, FL: Academic Press.**

These authors point out the uncertainty of the relationship between the contribution of abuse to developmental delays and the contribution of developmental delays to abuse. This chapter's primary focus is on physical abuse, not sexual abuse, but many of the issues raised appear to generalize across these two forms of abuse. The authors point out that the majority of children who are victims of physical abuse have developmental handicaps.

667. Melberg, K. (1984). Mentally retarded easy prey. *Spokesman, 17*(19), 5-6, 14.

This short article discusses how myths commonly held about women are applied to people with mental retardation (i.e., people with mental retardation are devalued in the same way that women are devalued).

668. Melberg, K. (1984). The tangled web of red tape. *Spokesman, 17*(16), 11-12.

This article discusses the use of interpreters in assisting people with mental retardation who are victims of sexual crimes to bring their assailants to court.

669. Melberg, K. (1984, April). The silent epidemic. *SAMR Dialect,* **p. 8.**

This author discusses changes to the Criminal Code which now offer protection for all persons, including

people with mental handicaps. Abuse must be brought out into the open, or laws will be useless. As well, prevention and treatment programs cannot be developed unless the problem is acknowledged. Advocates for people with mental handicaps must ensure exploitation does not occur, but they must also recognize the rights of individuals to choose how they live (e.g., not to be overprotected).

670. Melberg, K. (1984, June). The silent epidemic. *SAMR Dialect,* **pp. 11-12.**

In the second part of her series, this author addresses the issue of assault victims with mental handicaps whose court cases have resulted in acquittal or dismissal due to the court's position that the victims are not reliable witnesses. Advocates of people with mental handicaps believe that responsibility lies with advocates and members of the justice system to ensure that the rights of people with mental handicaps are upheld. In particular, interpreters could be used in court to overcome communication problems. To achieve the goal of successful prosecution of these crimes, lawyers need to familiarize themselves with people with mental handicaps, and professionals working with this population need to acquaint themselves with the workings of the legal system.

671. Melberg, K. (1984, August). The silent epidemic. *SAMR Dialect,* **p. 10.**

This author discusses the options available when a person with mental handicaps is sexually assaulted. An alternative to a criminal charge is a complaint of sexual harassment under the Human Rights Code. In such a case, the burden of proof is not as severe since no jail term is involved. In court cases, spending time with the victim with mental handicaps can help assure the victim; however, the prosecutor's case is only as strong as the witness. Since the evidence given by people with mental handicaps usually is not given much weight, education of police, lawyers, and judges must occur before changes in attitude will take place.

672. Melberg, K. (1985, December). The silent epidemic. *SAMR Dialect,* **p. 6**

Greater awareness among police, social workers, prosecutors, and judges is needed to deal with abuse of people with handicaps. Although these professionals have a mandate to work with the abused child, many are not comfortable with children and this type of crime, whether the child is handicapped or not. Because of believability, it is very difficult to have evidence given by children under 10 admitted in court. Preparing children for the courtroom experience ahead of time has been helpful in obtaining strong evidence from them. The author recommends that the use of interpreters for people with handicaps must at the least be tried.

673. Melling, L. (1984). Wife abuse in the deaf community. *Response to Violence in the Family and Sexual Assault, 7*(1), 1-2, 12.

This article focuses on wife abuse in the deaf

community. Violence against women who are deaf is inflicted by men who are deaf as well as by hearing men. For the woman who is hearing impaired, all the problems facing battered women are exacerbated by communicating with those who do not speak her language and the critical lack of information and services available to her. The woman who is deaf has special problems in that there is an information gap between herself and others. There is also the community factor. The deaf community is extremely close, strong, and insular. The wife has a greater dependence on this community and is afraid of threatening this support system. Professionals are beginning to develop responses to the problem. Their approach is operating on three levels: 1) to educate those working with domestic abuse victims about the special needs of women who are deaf, 2) to educate people with hearing impairments about the problem of domestic violence, and 3) to train those working with people who are deaf to identify and assist battered women.

674. **Melton, G. B. (1987). Special legal problems in protection of handicapped children from parental maltreatment. In J. Garbarino, P. E. Brookhouser, & K. J. Authier (Eds.), *Special children-special risks: The maltreatment of children with disabilities* (pp. 179-193). New York: Aldine de Gruyter.**
Parents have a legal duty to care for their children. When the child is handicapped, the state requires that the child receives a free, appropriate education, including whatever related services are needed. Currently in the United States, the legislative trend is toward expanding jurisdiction for state intervention to protect children from maltreatment. The primary purpose of state intervention is prevention. The question then arises of whether child protective services can be used to prevent handicapping conditions. Primary and secondary prevention of handicaps are prone to substantial practical, ethical, and legal problems. Problems such as competency to testify, proof of harm, dispositional planning, and termination of parental rights are discussed.

675. **Menolascino, F. J., & Stark, J. A. (Eds.). (1984). *Handbook of mental illness in the mentally retarded*. New York: Plenum.**
This is a general text on the treatment and management of people with the combined symptoms of mental retardation and mental illness. The book is comprised of articles written by various authors and is broken into five sections: nature of the dual diagnosis, treatment and management interventions, challenges in training health personnel, research and future directions, and special service systems, such as in-patient programs, day treatment programs, home intervention programs, and services for people with multiple handicaps. Sexuality is only briefly mentioned.

676. **Ment, L. R., Duncan, C. C., & Rowe, D. S. (1982). Central nervous system manifestations**

of child abuse. *Connecticut Medicine, 46*(6), 315-318.
This article addresses the need for physicians to perform numerous diagnostic evaluations such as CAT scans (computerized tomography) and physical, ophthalmalogic, and radiologic tests when presented with children with central nervous system (CNS) trauma of unknown etiology. Common abuse-related CNS injuries include subarachnoid hemorrhage, subdural hematoma, intracerebral hematoma, cerebrovascular insult (e.g., stroke), and encephalomalacia, all of which result in serious neurodevelopmental handicaps. Failure to make the diagnosis of child abuse may leave the infant at risk for further injury. (Note: The availability of advanced technology for detecting signs of child abuse has resulted in a need to revise upward our estimate of child abuse's contribution to disability.)

677. **Mental and physical incompetency. (1985). *Mental and Physical Disability Law Reporter, 9*(6), 412-413.**
This article describes five cases in which incompetency to stand trial claims were reviewed for a person who was deaf, could not speak, and had mild mental retardation (Louisiana v. Smith, 471 So.2d. 954 [La. Ct. App. 1985]), a former drug user (Ohio v. Pruitt, 480 N.E.2d. 499 [Ohio Ct. App. 1984]), a person who had a seizure in the jury's presence (Washington v. Hicks, 704 P.2d. 1206 [Wash. Ct. App. 1985]), a man with amnesia about the day of the offense (Illinois v. Schwartz, 482 N.E.2d. 104 [Ill. App. Ct. 1985]), and an individual's multiple suicide attempts, repeated head injuries, bizarre behavior, and alcoholism (Boag v. Raines, 769 F.2d. 1341 [9th Cir. 1985]).

678. **Mental capacity of witnesses reviewed. (1985). *Mental and Physical Disability Law Reporter, 9*(1), 31-32.**
This discussion describes two criminal cases where psychiatric examinations for witnesses in a sexual abuse case and admissibility of a petition seeking to have the victim of a burglary declared mentally ill were reviewed: Massachusetts v. Widrick, 467 N.E.2d. 1353 (Mass. S. Jud. Ct. 1984) and Gratton v. Alabama, 456 So.2d. 865 (Ala. Crim. App. 1984). It discusses a civil case, Johnston v. Brown, 468 N.E.2d. 597 (Ind. Ct. App. 1984), where an Indiana court of appeals found a boy with mental retardation, who was struck by a moving truck, guilty of contributory negligence and denied his petition for damages; and it discusses a case, South Carolina Department of Social Services v. Forrester, 320 S.E.2d. 39 (S.C. Ct. App. 1984), where an appeals court upheld an order to compel a man to undergo a psychiatric examination after a family court action against him for alleged child sexual abuse.

679. **Mentally disabled man convicted of murder. (1984). *Mental and Physical Disability Law Reporter, 8*(5), 452.**
This article describes a case, New York v. Williams, 465 N.E.2d. 327 (N.Y. Ct. App. 1984), where the New York

Court of Appeals upheld the murder and rape conviction of a 20-year-old with functional illiteracy and borderline mental retardation who suffered from organic brain damage.

680. Mentally disabled offenders. (1985). *Mental and Physical Disability Law Reporter, 9*(1), 20-21.

This article describes a case, Cates v. Indiana, 468 N.E.2d. 522 (Ind. S. Ct. 1984), where the Indiana Supreme Court upheld an attempted murder conviction, finding that failure to introduce evidence of the defendant's mental and physical health did not amount to ineffective counsel. It describes a case, Illinois v. Redmon, 468 N.E.2d. 1310 (Ill. App. Ct. 1984), where an Illinois appeals court reversed and remanded a murder and attempted armed robbery conviction because the defendant with borderline mental retardation had not made a knowing, intelligent, and voluntary waiver of his rights before confessing. It describes Johnston v. Alabama, 455 So.2d. 152 (Ala. Crim. App. 1984), a case where an Alabama criminal appeals court reversed a trial court's finding that a defendant's confession was involuntary due to his subnormal intelligence. It also describes Wiggins v. Georgia, 319 S.E.2d. 5228 (Ga. Ct. App. 1984), a case where a defendant with mental illness, charged with aggravated assault and making a terrorist threat, successfully appealed her conviction because the lower court had not considered her mental condition properly in finding criminal intent beyond a reasonable doubt.

681. Mentally disabled persons in criminal cases. (1985). *Mental and Physical Disability Law Reporter, 9*(2), 111.

This article describes Hameed v. Jones, 750 F.2d. 154 (2d Cir. 1984), a case where the Second Circuit held that a New York statute providing that a trial court must replace a discharged juror with an alternate did not limit a trial court's discretion to declare a mistrial and did not require the trial court to substitute an alternate when one of the deliberating jurors experienced a psychiatric episode, and Minnesota v. Hitch, 356 N.W.2d. 820 (Minn. Ct. App. 1984), a case where a Minnesota appeals court upheld a conviction of criminal sexual assault because the evidence showed that the victim was mentally defective, the defendant knew or should have known of the victim's incapacity, and the incident occurred without the victim's consent.

682. Mentally retarded persons in criminal cases. (1986). *Mental and Physical Disability Law Reporter, 10*(5), 367-368.

This article describes three court cases which addressed the participation of defendants with mental disabilities and a witness in criminal cases: Rhode Island v. Perry, 508 A.2d. 683 (R.I. S. Ct. 1986); Massengale v. Texas, 710 S.W.2d. 594 (Tex. Crim. App. 1986); and California v. Taylor, 225 Cal. Rptr. 733 (Cal. Ct. App. 1986). No consistent approach has yet been established by the courts.

683. Mercer, J., Andrews, H., & Mercer, A. (1983). The effects of physical attractiveness and disability on client ratings by helping professionals. *Journal of Applied Rehabilitation Counseling, 14*(4), 41-45.

Graduate and undergraduate students in personal and guidance counseling, rehabilitation counseling, or social work rated a client on 22 bipolar adjectives which were later factored into six orthogonal factors: social attractiveness, prognosis, physical attractiveness, personal evaluation, severity of presenting problem, and adjustment. Students rated the same female confederate in one of four conditions: attractive with physical disability, attractive without physical disability, unattractive with physical disability, and unattractive without physical disability. A multiple analysis of variance procedure indicated that the attractive confederate was rated more favorably. The client with a disability received higher ratings on all six factors, with the exception of the severity of the presenting problem. These findings indicate that a positive stereotype for a female with a disability exists.

684. Merson, R. M. (1987). Sexuality in communication disorders. *Asha, 29*(12), 27-28.

This author points out that effective sex therapy and counseling are often complicated by communication disorders. The author makes a plea for greater involvement of speech, hearing, and language professionals in research and intervention programs that focus on sexual rehabilitation.

685. Mertz, A. W. (1986). Sexual abuse of anesthetized patients. In A. W. Burgess & C. R. Hartman (Eds.), *Sexual exploitation of patients by health care professionals* **(pp. 61-65). New York: Praeger.**

This chapter provides a brief but explicit description of a particular case of sexual abuse of an anesthetized patient. It focuses on hospital and community reaction, including initial disbelief by hospital staff, administration, the community, the victims' families, and the victims themselves.

686. Mesibov, G. B., & Schopler, E. (1983). The development of community-based programs for autistic adolescents. *Children's Health Care, 12*(1), 20-24.

This article discusses the development of community-based programs for adolescents with autism in North Carolina. It describes the materials and programs, including diagnostic and comprehensive assessment instruments, appropriate day programs, and a range of residential options. The article examines some new approaches to the problems of sex education and crisis intervention and describes the development of specialized approaches to deal with these situations. The authors stress appropriate and individualized instruction for developing necessary skills and for seeing parents as an integral part of the treatment process, and they emphasize close parent-professional cooperation.

687. Messier, C. (1984). Les abus sexuels d'enfants [The sexual abuse of children]. *Relations, July-August,* 190-194.

This article indicates that there is a steady rise in the sexual abuse of children. For every four girls abused, one boy is abused. The author delineates the profile of the abuser and finds the following: In 92% of cases, the abuser is known to the victim. The average victim age is 12.1 years, with 7% having an intellectual deficit and 6% having a physical handicap. Intervention is discussed in terms of judiciary action and treatment at the psychosocial level. This article places an equal accent on prevention, largely in terms of sex education. (This article is available in French only.)

688. Michael, A. (1987). A trip to Boys Town: A focus on midwest programs. *Behavior in Our Schools, 1*(1), 2-7.

In this article, Boys Town programs for homeless, disadvantaged, or high-risk children in Omaha, Nebraska are described. Also described is the Center for Abused Handicapped Children.

689. Miller, T. W., Veltkamp, L. J., & Janson, D. (1987). Projective measures in the clinical evaluation of sexually abused children. *Child Psychiatry and Human Development, 18*(1), 47-57.

This article discusses the use of human figure drawings in the assessment of children who have been sexually abused.

690. Miller, W. L., Kaplan, S. L., & Grumbach, M. M. (1980). Child abuse as a cause of post-traumatic hypopituitarism. *New England Journal of Medicine, 302*(13), 724-728.

This study describes three cases of child battery resulting in subdural hematoma, brain injury, anterior hypopituitarism, and impaired growth. The injuries were not related directly to disturbances of the hypothalamic-pituitary axis; rather, they reflect the severity of the head trauma experienced. The authors recommend that all children with serious head injuries, regardless of cause, require long-term observation for signs of impaired growth and hypopituitarism.

691. Ministry of Social Services and Housing, Government of British Columbia. (1988). *Inter-ministry child abuse handbook: An integrated approach to child abuse and neglect* (3rd ed.). Victoria, BC: Queen's Printer for British Columbia.

This is the third edition of this handbook, and it is intended for anyone who works with children. The handbook was prepared by the British Columbia Ministries of Social Services and Housing, the Attorney General, Health, the Solicitor General, and Education. Two major goals of the project were to ensure uniformity of practice throughout the province by providing information about the policies and procedures of these ministries and, secondly, to ensure that an integrated approach to child abuse is adopted by professionals and others who provide services to children. The handbook is divided into three parts: overview, the specific roles of the five Ministries, and protocols for specific situations, including abuse and neglect in licensed facilities. The appendices offer valuable guidelines regarding interviewing children, recognizing signs of abuse, and the role of the physician. The appendix on interviewing children includes a discussion on videotaping and audiotaping, with the recommendation that videotaping be used in cases in which the child has a handicap affecting his or her ability to communicate. Failing this, an alternative method is to have a skilled observer present at the interview so that validity of disclosure does not rest on the interviewer's credibility alone.

692. Minnesota Program for Victims of Sexual Assault. (1983). *Are children with disabilities vulnerable to sexual abuse?* St. Paul: Author.

This 5-page pamphlet is designed to acquaint parents of children with disabilities with the problem of sexual abuse. The pamphlet focuses on prevention.

693. Mitchell, D. R. (1987). Parents' interactions with their developmentally disabled or at-risk infants: A focus for intervention. *Australia and New Zealand Journal of Developmental Disabilities, 13*(2), 73-81.

This article reviews comparative studies of infants with developmental disabilities or who are at-risk and normal infants in dyadic interaction with their mothers. The findings are discussed in terms of the literature on optimal parent-child interaction. Implications for early intervention programs are discussed.

694. Modzeleski, W. (1987). Abused handicapped children in the criminal justice system. In J. Garbarino, P. E. Brookhouser, & K. J. Authier (Eds.), *Special children-special risks: The maltreatment of children with disabilities* (pp. 195-209). New York: Aldine de Gruyter.

The criminal justice system traditionally held that issues relating to child maltreatment were best dealt with by social service agencies. Only serious abuse cases, such as those resulting in death, were considered matters for the criminal court. Only since 1980 has child abuse been viewed as a crime to be dealt with by the criminal justice community. The author discusses the events that led to the changes in the perception of and the attitude toward child maltreatment. As a consequence of these events, the criminal justice system has come to the forefront in child abuse cases. Law enforcement officers must make decisions in child abuse cases about whether arrest and prosecution should occur. Often, the circumstances are not clear as to whether abuse has taken place. The author also discusses problems that children with handicaps and children in general have with the criminal justice system.

695. Moglia, R. (1986, March). Sexual abuse and disability. *SIECUS Report,* pp. 9-10.

This author tells the true story of a girl with disabilities who was sexually assaulted by her stepfather. The story is only one of numerous cases. A review of the statistics available on sexual assault of people with disabilities is given. A general overview of the problem is briefly discussed.

696. Monast, S., & Burke, D. (1985). Sexuality of the adolescent with neurogenic communicative disorders. *International Journal of Adolescent Medicine and Health, 1*(3/4), 315-323.

This article describes the problems concerning sexuality of adolescents with neurogenic communicative disorders, which include damaged body image, loss of independence, fears of rejection, and inability to communicate. The authors offer recommendations to assist professionals when providing these adolescents with counseling and appropriate referrals, and they emphasize that sexual health care should be an integral component of these adolescents' rehabilitation programs.

697. Monat, R. K. (1982). *Sexuality and the mentally retarded: A clinical and therapeutic guidebook.* **San Diego, CA: College-Hill Press.**

This book provides an overview of sexuality in the lives of people with mental retardation. It groups people with mental retardation according to severity and the concurrent presence of physical handicaps. Sexual needs in all groups appear to be similar and not typically different from anyone else. Problems in social integration and communication skills, however, often complicate sexuality for people with more than mild mental retardation. Sexual abuse is discussed in regard to the offender with mental retardation but not in regard to the victimization of people with mental handicap. (An updated and revised edition of this book is in press at Paul H. Brookes Publishing Co., and is scheduled for release in the summer of 1991.)

698. Monat-Haller, R. K. (1987). Speech-language pathologists as counselors and sexuality educators. *Asha, 29*(12), 35-36.

This guest editorial discusses the relationship between communication skills, sex education, and sexual adjustment. The author suggests that speech-language pathologists can be particularly effective in enhancing the social and sexual interactions of their clients. She also suggests that communication disorder therapists may play an important role as co-counselors in individual and group therapy. She suggests that traditional speech therapy has contributed to the asexualization of clients in many ways, for example, by omitting the genitalia when teaching body parts. The need for assisting people to develop the communication skills that will allow useful testimony regarding sexual abuse is particularly stressed. She suggests a number of skills and concepts that should be taught. These include making and expressing personal decisions and effectively asserting personal rights (e.g., the right to privacy, the right to control one's own body).

699. Money, J. (1982). Child abuse: Growth, IQ deficit, and learning disability. *Journal of Learning Disability, 15*(10), 579-582.

Behavior that has been criminalized makes criminals not only of those who practice it but also of professionals who fail to report their knowledge of it. Professionals have invented the "bastard science" of victimology, in which, by focusing on the victims and handing the offenders over to the law, they miss the scientific opportunity to discover the cause and prevention of the offense. Evidence of child abuse and neglect as a primary cause of permanent IQ impairment and learning disability, though long-known, has been largely disregarded in favor of hereditary and quasineurological theories of etiology. There is a syndrome, namely abuse dwarfism (also known as psychosocial dwarfism), in which growth in stature and pubertal physique, growth in intelligence, and growth and maturation of behavior all are retarded and even permanently impaired in response to child abuse and neglect. Early rescue into a nonabusive environment permits catch-up growth; whereas, delayed rescue hinders it, with consequent persistent IQ impairment and learning disability.

700. Moore, T., & Thompson, V. (1987). Elder abuse: A review of research, programmes and policy. *The Social Worker, 55*(3), 115-122.

This article provides a good general review of elder abuse in Canada. It discusses major theories of abuse: 1) learning theory and the abused-abuser cycle, 2) dependency and learned helplessness, 3) caregiver stress leading to abuse, 4) social attitudes that dehumanize the elderly, and 5) family isolation. Each of these might be considered as constructs for explaining abuse of all populations of people with disabilities.

701. More abuse found in disabled. (1987, March 31). *Winnipeg Free Press.*

This newspaper article discusses a report done in Ontario on the abuse of women with disabilities as compared to nondisabled women. The article discusses the findings of the survey on 62 women with and without disabilities. The author of the report was in Winnipeg for a weekend conference with members of a group called the DisAbled Women's Network (DAWN) Canada.

702. Morgan, S. R. (1987). *Abuse and neglect of handicapped children.* **San Diego, CA: College-Hill Press.**

Children with disabilities are victims of abuse at least as often as other children. Some children acquire handicapping conditions as a result of abuse. Premature infants are abused and neglected significantly more than others. Infants with birth defects are more likely to be victims of gross life-threatening neglect. Alcohol is noted as a factor in child sexual abuse and other forms of abuse. Chapters include societal attitudes toward people with handicaps, the definition of child abuse and neglect, the question of cause and effect between disabilities and abuse, the characteristics of parents who abuse, and abuse by professionals.

703. Morris, A. (1982). *A curriculum guide: Social and self-protection skills for the severely handicapped.* Washington, DC: Molly Roeseler Anderson.

This is an appropriate guide for teaching nonverbal students about self-protection skills in order to prevent abuse. The guide can be used independently of other written material or audiovisuals.

704. Morse, C. W., Sahler, O. Z., & Friedman, S. B. (1970). A three-year follow-up study of abused and neglected children. *American Journal of Diseases of Children, 120,* 439-446.

These authors studied 25 abused children. Of these, 42% had IQ scores below 80, and all but one of those had been diagnosed as having a mental handicap prior to the onset of abuse.

705. Moss, S. R. (1986). Women in prison: A case of pervasive neglect [Special issue: The dynamics of feminist therapy]. *Women and Therapy, 5*(2/3), 177-185.

This article discusses the neglect suffered by women in prison. It finds that the neglect of women in prison is partly due to the fact that only 4% of state and 6.5% of federal prisoners in the United States are women, and it uses data from the Colorado Department of Corrections and the Colorado Women's Correctional Facility to illustrate these problems and to indicate areas for intervention. The author concludes that as an abused and neglected population whose needs and problems are not adequately addressed female inmates are likely to perpetuate their problems, from criminal behavior to patterns of abuse, through their children.

706. Mowbray, C. T. (1987, May). *Research on out-of-home child sexual abuse: Public and legal attention.* Paper presented at the biennial meetings of the Society for Research in Child Development, Baltimore, MD. (ERIC Document Reproduction Service No. ED 285 659)

This paper describes the difficulties encountered by a group of researchers studying the effects of long-term sexual abuse in a day care operating in a small conservative American town. Problems included the community's doubts as to the credibility of the sexual abuse allegations, civil suits launched against the day care center and/or personnel, and the resulting legal obstructions to gaining access to data. To alleviate these research problems, a community advisory panel was created and a federal Confidentiality Certificate to protect research data from subpoena was obtained. The practical value as well as the methodological procedures and ethical implications of these strategies are briefly discussed.

707. Mrazek, P. B. (1981). The nature of incest: A review of contributing factors. In P. B. Mrazek & C. H. Kempe (Eds.), *Sexually abused children and their families* (pp. 97-107).

Elmsford, NY: Pergamon.

This author reviews known and suspected factors of incest. Several factors may have particular relevance to populations of people with developmental disabilities. Social isolation (which has been identified as a factor) has been identified as a problem for many families with children with handicaps. Stress is another factor that exists as a constant reality for many families with children with handicaps. Alcoholism has also been noted as a significant factor of incest. Alcoholism within the family has also been identified as a major cause of handicapping conditions for children. Mental subnormality has also been identified as a factor in both the adult and the child.

708. Mrazek, P. B., & Mrazek, D. A. (1981). Effects of child sexual abuse. In P. B. Mrazek & C. H. Kempe (Eds.), *Sexually abused children and their families* (pp. 225-245). Elmsford, NY: Pergamon.

These authors point to three studies that suggest that impaired educational performance and intellectual retardation may result from sexual abuse of the child.

709. Mueser, K. T., Valenti, H., & Yarnold, P. R. (1987). Dating skills groups for the developmentally disabled: Social skills and problem solving versus relaxation training. *Behavior Modification, 11*(2), 200-228.

In this study, three group treatment strategies for teaching dating skills to 41 adult out-patients with mild to moderate mental retardation are compared. The strategies include traditional problem-solving training, flexible problem-solving training, and relaxation training. Role-play assessments were done at pre-treatment, post-treatment, and one month after the completion of the 12-session program. Traditional problem-solving correlated with significant increases in physical attractiveness, represented by changes in the pleasantness of facial expression and in higher rates of social interaction with opposite-sex peers during mid-session breaks. In terms of social skills, the relaxation training group and the drop-out group were rated lower than the other two strategy groups.

710. Mullen, C. (1988, September 13). Disabled more likely targets of sexual assault, study finds. *The Edmonton Journal,* p. B8.

This article summarizes some of the results of the University of Alberta—Health and Welfare Canada study on sexual abuse and the disabled. Some major points include the following: many victims with disabilities experience repeated attacks; many victims are afraid or unable to report attacks; when charges are laid, few convictions follow; and personal care attendants and other service providers should be carefully screened to prevent known sexual offenders from securing these positions.

711. Mullen, C. (1988, September 15). Centre agrees disabled people face higher risk of sexual

attack. *The Edmonton Journal*, p. B5.

This article presents community reaction in Edmonton to a University of Alberta study reporting increased risk of sexual abuse among people with disabilities. The directors of the Edmonton Sexual Assault Centre and the Alberta Committee of Disabled Citizens acknowledge the problem and discuss some efforts being made to improve the situation. An Edmonton City Police spokesman indicated that police in Edmonton will make the best possible effort to investigate and charge anyone committing sexual abuse of or assault on an individual with a disability.

712. **Muller, N. D. (1984). The law: A point of view.** *Australia and New Zealand Journal of Developmental Disabilities, 10*(3), 179-181.

This article investigates how the principles of normalization, the least restrictive alternative, and deinstitutionalization apply to human relationships and sexuality for the intellectually handicapped in Australia. It examines the current law, originally introduced to prevent the sexual exploitation of intellectually handicapped females (stemming from 1899) and finds the definition of handicap questionable and derogatory. The author suggests that agreeing that the terms "idiot" and "imbecile" are demeaning is the first step in establishing a common ground for discussion between people from various ethical and moral perspectives.

713. **Mullins, J. B. (1986). The relationship between child abuse and handicapping conditions.** *Journal of School Health, 56*(4), 134-136.

In this article, the impact of child abuse, including sexual abuse and neglect, on the development of physical and psychological disabilities is discussed. The author posits that child abuse is a cause of disability in children who otherwise would not be disabled. Also, the presence of disabilities in children as a cue to abuse is addressed as well as the exacerbation of handicaps through abuse. Specific recommendations are made to school personnel regarding the detection and reporting of abuse. Recommendations include the following: recognizing the problem; addressing the need for teachers, school nurses, and doctors to share abuse detection skills; promoting accurate knowledge of the law and mandatory reporting; developing community programs to alleviate parental stress; and developing a curriculum that emphasizes what constitutes good parenting skills.

714. **Murphy, D. M. (1986). The prevalence of handicapping conditions among juvenile delinquents.** *RASE Remedial and Special Education, 7*(3), 7-17.

In this study, the literature is reviewed in order to compare the rate of incidence of handicapping conditions seen in juvenile delinquents with rates seen in nondelinquent populations. Despite inconsistencies between studies in the definition of key concepts, the overall findings suggest that a far greater number of juveniles living in correctional facilities have handicapping conditions than is seen in juveniles who are not delinquent. The specific incidence of emotional disturbance, mental retardation, learning disability, and neurological perceptual deficits are described. Recommendations include the development of standardized definitions and the establishment of more uniform and reliable methods in assessment and record-keeping within the criminal justice system.

715. **Murphy, G. J. (1981). The institutionalized adolescent and the ethics of desexualization. In D. A. Shore & H. L. Gochros (Eds.), *Sexual problems of adolescents in institutions* (pp. 27-35). Springfield, IL: Charles C Thomas.**

This chapter examines the concept of desexualization of adolescents in institutions. Sexual segregation, lack of privacy and access to appropriate social and sexual interaction, a taboo on the discussion of sexuality, and a number of other factors interfere with normal sexual development. These factors operationalize the myth that these adolescent inmates are asexual and that any sexuality is deviant and immoral, which in turn contributes to self-devaluation of the individual. Although vulnerability to sexual abuse, assault, or exploitation is not directly discussed, desexualization and the subsequent personal devaluation may be important factors contributing to the vulnerability of these adolescents.

716. **Murphy, L., & Della, S. (1987). Abuse and the special child.** *Special Parent/Special Child, 3*(1). (ERIC Document Reproduction Service No. ED 288 323)

The major focus of this 8-page presentation is on education and increasing adult awareness of the problem of abuse of children with handicaps. The vulnerability of these children to abuse is emphasized. Guidelines are given on how to collect information when a child discloses and on how to evaluate changes in the child that suggest abuse. Report procedures are outlined as well as signs of physical and sexual abuse. Also included is a list of things for parents to do and not to do in order to reduce the chances of abuse and increase the chances for detection.

717. **Murphy, W. D., Coleman, E. M., & Abel, G. G. (1983). Human sexuality in the mentally retarded. In J. L. Matson & F. Andrasik (Eds.), *Treatment issues and innovations in mental retardation* (pp. 581-643). New York: Plenum.**

This 1983 review is organized into six sections: the physical development, sexual behavior, and sex role development of people with mental retardation; a summary of the results of a survey the authors conducted on the sexual attitudes and education policies seen in residential institutions for people with mental retardation; attitudes toward sexuality and people with mental retardation; sex education; sterilization; and a discussion of a case presentation of a sex offender with mental retardation.

718. Murphy, W. D., Coleman, M. A., & Haynes, M. R. (1983). **Treatment and evaluation issues with the mentally retarded sex offender.** In J. G. Greer & I. R. Stuart (Eds.), *The sexual aggressor* (pp. 22-41). New York: VanNostrand Reinhold.

This book chapter examines the prevalence of sex offenses among the population of people with mental handicaps, reviews treatment studies, and suggests possible treatment methods. The authors found that there is only a slightly higher percentage of people with mental retardation among sex offenders than would be expected by population statistics alone. The authors discuss arousal, social skills, sex education, and cognitive factors in terms of assessment and treatment methods.

719. Musick, J. L. (1984). **Patterns of institutional sexual assault.** *Response to Violence in the Family and Sexual Assault, 7*(3), 1-2, 10-11.

This article describes an analysis of sexual assaults in psychiatric settings. The assault accounts were provided by 26 former patients with mental illness and 39 facility staff members. From these accounts, several common institutional practices emerged: allowing male staff to care for and escort female patients; inadequate supervision and control of male patients in coed spaces; inadequate supervision of heavily medicated, restrained, or isolated female patients; and inadequate supervision and absence of security in isolated spaces. Factors that increase patient vulnerability include incapacitation by chemical or physical restraints, social powerlessness, social isolation, and objectification by staff. When abuse is detected, the supervisory staff often allow the "staff-assailants" to resign with no notation on their records; therefore, the employee can seek work at another institution. This method of dealing with the problem also fails to provide a strong deterrent to others. A number of patient-perpetrator assaults were committed by men known to be violent but who had nevertheless been admitted to general and coed psychiatric units. Reports of assault/abuse are often not taken seriously by staff, who believe most complaints are false. When police are called in, they often take the attitude that the problem is an internal one that the institution should deal with itself. However, unless patient reports are treated as criminal complaints, the acts cannot be treated as crimes, and assailants cannot be deterred or punished.

720. Myers, J. E. (1982). **Legal issues surrounding psychotherapy with minor clients.** *Clinical Social Work Journal, 10*(4), 303-314.

This article examines the legal issues surrounding psychotherapy with clients who are minors. It describes exceptions to the parental consent requirement, which include the case of the minor who is legally emancipated, emergency treatment, and the "mature minor" who is capable of understanding the nature and consequences of the proposed treatment. It discusses issues of confidentiality that arise when parents demand to know of any communications between the therapist and minor client because of the legal requirement that the therapist report suspected cases of abuse and neglect and because of the duty to disclose confidential information to protect a third person from harm threatened by the client. The author stresses the need for constructive communication between legal and therapeutic professionals in order to reach workable solutions to the legal implications of psychotherapy.

721. Myre, J. G. (1986). *Les enfants mal aimés: On en retrouve dans votre quartier et chez vous...Réagissons [Children in need: They are in your neighbourhood and in your home...Do something about it].* Québec: Comité de protection de la protection de la jeunesse.

This report states that sexual abuse is a reality for one girl out of two and for one boy out of three. Of the children studied, three out of five were threatened or physically forced by their abusers. For the most part, the offenders were known to the victim and held a position of trust. In this article, the author places equal emphasis on both the consequences for the child and on intervention. A directory of resources in Québec is included. (This report is available in French only.)

•N•

722. Nanaimo Rape/Assault Centre. (1984). *Realities of child sexual abuse.* Nanaimo, British Columbia: Author.

This book provides a good summary of basic information and issues related to child sexual abuse. The text is generally well written and free of technical jargon. Helpful lists of references and resources are included. Special issues related to disabilities are not discussed.

723. National Center on Child Abuse and Neglect (DHEW). (1980). *Child abuse and developmental disabilities: Essays.* Washington, DC: Author.

This document presents expert opinion and research on the relationship between developmental disabilities and child abuse. One focus of the presentation is to facilitate cooperation between professionals working in these two areas. Other topics include parental reactions to developmental disabilities in their children, advocacy, the identification of high-risk infants, the use of community resources, efforts by Parents Anonymous, and the development of counseling and referral skills.

724. National Center on Educational Media and Materials for the Handicapped. (1978). *Mildly handicapped: Sex education, secondary level.* Columbus, OH: Author.

This bibliography contains 66 abstracts of sex education materials (e.g., films, books, filmstrips) that are considered suitable for junior or senior high school students with mild handicaps. Each abstract contains evaluation information (if available), type of media, and full descriptions and states of the group for whom the material would be suitable.

725. **National Committee for the Prevention of Child Abuse. (1986).** *Guidelines for child sexual abuse prevention programs.* **Chicago: Author. (Exceptional Child Education Resources Clearinghouse accession number EC 19 1439)**
In this document, an ad hoc committee appointed by the National Committee for the Prevention of Child Abuse offers guidelines for child sexual abuse prevention programs. Among specific target groups discussed are children with developmental or physical disabilities. (Copies of this document are available from the National Committee for the Prevention of Child Abuse.)

726. **Neff, J. (1983). Sexual well being: A goal for young blind women.** *Journal of Visual Impairment and Blindness, 77*(6), 296-297.
This article discusses obstacles to the development of sexuality and sexual awareness in young adults, particularly young girls who are blind. The conscious process of goal setting in sexual development is discussed as well as the need for a sense of identity in young people.

727. **Neistadt, M. E. (1986). Occupational therapy treatment goals for adults with developmental disabilities.** *American Journal of Occupational Therapy, 40*(10), 672-678.
In this study, occupational therapy evaluations for 54 adults with developmental disabilities are reviewed. Findings indicate that remedial goals significantly outnumbered adaptive goals, sexuality being among the group of adaptive goals that received little or no attention.

728. **Neistadt, M. E. (1986). Sexuality counseling for adults with disabilities: A module for an occupational therapy curriculum.** *American Journal of Occupational Therapy, 40*(8), 542-545.
This article describes the development, philosophy, goals, objectives, and format of a program on sexuality and disability offered to occupational therapy students. It discusses evaluations from 288 students who participated in the two 3-hour module sessions over a 6-year period and finds that all the students considered the module a pertinent part of their academic program.

729. **Neistadt, M. E., & Freda, M. (1987).** *Choices: A guide to sex counseling with physically disabled adults.* **Malabar, FL: Robert E. Krieger Publishing Co.**
This 117-page book provides useful basic information for occupational therapists and other health care profes-

sionals who may provide occasional counseling on sexuality to adults with physical disabilities. It stresses positive attitudes toward sexuality and flexibility in finding appropriate expressions of sexuality and intimacy for people with disabilities.

730. **Nelson, M., & Clark, K. (1986).** *The educator's guide to preventing child sexual abuse.* **Santa Cruz, CA: Network Publications.**
This 209-page book is a useful tool for teachers. It includes 19 short chapters, descriptions of 19 programs, and seven useful appendices (i.e., an overview of reporting, a description of how reports are treated, a glossary, a concise but thorough list of abuse indicators, a bibliography, information about contributors, and a directory of programs). In addition to Shaman's chapter on "Prevention of abuse for children with disabilities," many chapters include information related to special needs.

731. **Nesbit, W. C., & Karagianis, L. D. (1982). Child abuse: Exceptionality as a risk factor.** *The Alberta Journal of Educational Research, 28*(1), 69-76.
Child abuse and neglect is defined as including physical or mental injury, sexual abuse, and negligent treatment or maltreatment. It is clear that abuse can cause a handicapping condition, but it is not clear whether handicap antedates abuse or results from it. To unravel the matrix and assign a weighting to a specific handicap as a causal factor presents extreme difficulties. This article reviews the literature on a handicapping condition as a causal factor for abuse. The article also reviews literature on how the community, school, and teacher can help prevent child abuse associated with exceptionality.

732. **Newberger, C. M., & Newberger, E. H. (1986). When the pediatrician is a pedophile. In A. W. Burgess & C. R. Hartman (Eds.),** *Sexual exploitation of patients by health care professionals* **(pp. 99-106). New York: Praeger.**
This chapter uses a case history as a basis for discussion of pediatricians' sexual offenses against children and society's response to these cases. Difficulty in proving allegations and the treatment of a physician as a special case are seen as major problems in protecting children against this form of abuse.

733. **Newbern, V. B. (1989). Sexual victimization of child and adolescent patients.** *Image: The Journal of Nursing Scholarship, 21*(1), 10-13.
The Patient Abuse Questionnaire, developed by the author, was administered to 272 respondents working in acute care institutions, nursing homes, state institutions for people with mental illness or mental retardation, public health or home health agencies, and military hospitals or mental health centers. Respondents included registered nurses, licensed practical nurses, nursing aides, psychologists, social workers, physiotherapists, and occupational therapists. The author studied three categories of abuse: physical, psychological, and socially acceptable. The author found that all three forms

were reported as occurring as often as three times a week or more. Eight percent of the sample reported sexual abuse where sexual abuse was narrowly defined as "forcible rape, whether completed or attempted." Respondents reported the sexual abuse of children and adolescents in many health care settings, including emergency rooms, drug rehabilitation programs, pediatric hospitals, physicians offices, mental health centers, and state institutions for people with mental illness or mental retardation. Case reports supplement the study. The methodological limitations of the study are discussed. The author recommends that research be done in the area of sexual abuse of children and adolescents in health care settings.

734. New York State Commission on Quality of Care for the Mentally Disabled. (1987). *Child abuse and neglect in New York mental hygiene facilities.* **Albany, NY: Author. (ERIC Document Reproduction Service No. ED 301 990)**

This study by the New York State Commission on Quality of Care for the Mentally Disabled looks at child abuse and neglect reports taken from mental health and mental retardation residential facilities. The annual report rate of abuse and neglect in the New York City facilities was found to be more than twice the annual rate for the State of New York. The Commission identified trends in the characteristics of children most at risk and defined terms of highest risk in an effort to better offer specific recommendations for improved reporting, investigation, and prevention of abuse and neglect in these facilities. Included in the appendices are tabular statistics of abuse occurrence as well as the response of state offices to the report.

735. New York State Education Department, Office for the Education of Children with Handicapping Conditions. (1987). *Children with handicapping conditions: Regulations of the Commissioner of Education* **(Subchapter P., Part 200). Albany, NY: Author. (ERIC Document Reproduction Service No. ED 290 244)**

Besides including a discussion of the New York State Regulations, this document provides a description of procedures for the prevention of abuse, maltreatment, or neglect of children with disabilities living in residential facilities.

736. Nicholson, E. B., Horowitz, R. M., & Parry, J. (1986). Model procedures for child protective service agencies responding to reports of withholding medically indicated treatment from disabled infants with life threatening conditions. *Mental and Physical Disability Law Reporter, 10*(3), 221-249.

In response to the American Child Abuse Amendments of 1984, the American Bar Association's National Resource Center of Child Advocacy and Protection and Commission on the Mentally Disabled have developed model procedures to assist American states in the development of written policies to respond to reports of the withholding of medically needed treatment from infants with a disability who have a life-threatening condition. The model addresses definition of terms, planning by child protection agencies, intake procedure, preliminary investigation, on-site investigation, the decision process, and follow-up.

737. Nigro, G. (1976). Some observations on personal relationships and sexual relationships among lifelong disabled Americans. *Rehabilitation Literature, 37*(11), 328-330, 334.

This author discusses his experience of working with people with physical and mental handicaps in the area of sex education. It is often the case that these persons have little understanding in the area since they have been very dependent on others most of their lives and have reduced contact with other children in peer-oriented situations. The author states that there is a four-fold task for professionals working in this area: 1) improve the attitude of the public, the professionals who work with people with disabilities, their families, and people with disabilities themselves; 2) provide knowledge about human sexuality; 3) promote opportunities for sexual experiences for any person with handicaps who chooses to indulge in sex; and 4) improve the ability to establish meaningful personal relationships that may then become sexual.

738. Noble, B. (1987). Sexual concepts and the visually impaired. *Child Sexual Abuse Newsletter, 6,* 9.

This author states that children who are visually impaired have to be taught sex education differently than sighted children. Their sexual experience is limited by their sight. It is necessary to modify existing programs of sex education so that verbal dialogue makes up for the visual images presented in the program.

739. No private right of action under CRIPA. (1989). *Mental and Physical Disability Law Reporter, 13*(5), 471.

An American Fifth Circuit court affirmed a decision denying relief to a social worker fired by a Louisiana institution for the criminally insane when he reported crimes allegedly occurring in the institution directly to police rather than limiting himself to reporting to the institution. Previously, the social worker had been reprimanded by his employers for reporting a sex for drugs staff-patient exchange directly to the police. When other numerous illegal activities came to the attention of the social worker, including other drug-related activities and beatings of residents by security staff, he claimed having reported these activities to his superiors but that no action was taken. He then reported these activities to the FBI. Later, upon learning that the Justice Department was investigating the facility, he assisted residents in reporting their assaults to the Justice Department. His employers then suspended and fired him for spreading rumors and breaching confidentiality. The appeals court explained that employees are not part of that group of people for whom the CRIPA private right of action applies. The employers' authority to discipline employees for making disruptive statements was upheld.

740. **Norton, W. A. (1985). Mentally and developmentally handicapped offenders: Evolution of concepts and terminology. In M. H. Ben-Aron, S. J. Hucker, & C. D. Webster (Eds.), *Clinical criminology: The assessment and treatment of criminal behaviour* (pp. 255-279). Toronto: Clarke Institute of Psychiatry, University of Toronto.**
This chapter provides an overview of the legal system as it relates to people with differing degrees of mental retardation in the United Kingdom, Canada, and the United States. The author stresses the importance of adapting criminological approaches to the offender.

741. **Nucci, M., & Reiss, S. (1987). Mental retardation and emotional disorders: A test for increased vulnerability to stress. *Australia and New Zealand Journal of Developmental Disabilities, 13*(3), 161-166.**
This study investigates the widely held belief that people with mental retardation are particularly vulnerable to stress. Using a 2 x 3 factorial design, an experiment was undertaken in which participants waited to perform a counting task under conditions designed to induce stress, no particular emotional state, or a state of relaxation. The control group and the experimental group made up of people with mental retardation both showed similar amounts of improvement after having waited under conditions of stress. These authors found no support for the belief that people with mental retardation have special difficulties managing stress.

742. **Nuehring, E. M., Abrams, H., & Zuckerman, M. (1984). *Preventing abuse and neglect, Vol. 3: A model system covering developmentally disabled persons in residential facilities.* Miami Shores: Barry University, Abuse and Neglect Prevention Research Project.**
The focus of this document is on the protection of people with disabilities living in state and private residential facilities from abuse and neglect. A model system of American state legislation and staff training was developed from an analysis of the laws and administrative procedures in 50 American states. The model addresses expeditious reporting and investigations of suspected incidences, the provision of protective services consonant with individual rights, the establishment of a central abuse and neglect register, and penalties for failure to report and for breaches of confidentiality protecting reporters, victims, and abusers.

743. **Nunno, M. A., & Motz, J. K. (1988). The development of an effective response to the abuse of children in out-of-home care. *Child Abuse & Neglect, 12*(4), 521-528.**

This article discusses differences in the investigation of maltreatment in the familial situation and in the out-of-home care situation. Investigation is discussed in terms of the essential components of an investigation, identification, reporting, assessing risk factors in the initial report, the gathering of evidence, levels of culpability, and approaches to corrective actions. The authors point out that the protection of children in out-of-home care falls almost exclusively in the hands of child protective agencies. They suggest that specialized investigation units may better suit these cases.

•O•

744. **Oates, K., & Peacock, A. (1984). Intellectual development of battered children. *Australia and New Zealand Journal of Developmental Disabilities, 10*(1), 27-29.**
In this study, 38 children who had been admitted to the hospital due to battering on an average of 5 1/2 years earlier were compared to a matched control group on current test scores achieved on the WISC-R and the WPPSI. Although the severity of the injuries initially leading to hospitalization could not account for the lower scores, the battered group had significantly lower scores. The authors conclude that long-term treatment is necessary in view of the long-term effects of child battering.

745. **O'Connor, A. (1987). Female sex offenders. *British Journal of Psychiatry, 150,* 615-620.**
This article explores information on 19 women (average age 35.9 years) convicted of indecency and 62 women convicted of two other groups of sex offenses. It reveals that those convicted of indecency offenses had poor social skills and a high incidence of mental illness, mental handicap, and alcoholism. It also found that in 39 (63%) of the sex offenses with individual victims, the victims were children, and in nine cases, the offender was the mother or stepmother. The author also found that 48% of those convicted of indecent assault on persons under 16 years of age and of gross indecency with children had a previous history of psychiatric disorder.

746. **O'Day, B. (1983). *Preventing sexual abuse of persons with disabilities.* St. Paul: Minnesota Department of Corrections, Program for Victims of Sexual Assault.**
Sexual abuse prevention curricula are given for students with hearing impairments, physical disabilities, blindness, or mental retardation. Each curriculum contains lessons that basically cover the following: vocabulary, types of touching, myths and facts about sexual abuse, acquaintance rape, what to do if you are

victimized, reactions and feelings of victims, personal safety, and assertiveness. Some variations are made, depending on the group being addressed. Accompanying each lesson, information is provided in terms of objectives, materials to be used, and presentation instructions. This 181-page manual also contains a parent's guide, a teacher's guide, exercises, and 20 posters illustrating aspects of the lessons.

747. O'Day, B. (1983). *A resource guide for signs of sexual assault: A supplement to: Preventing sexual abuse of persons with disabilities: A curriculum for hearing impaired, physically disabled, blind and mentally retarded students.* **St. Paul: Minnesota State Department of Corrections. (ERIC Document Reproduction Service No. ED 277 213)**

This manual is part of a curriculum on preventing sexual abuse of people with disabilities and is intended to assist instructors presenting material to people with hearing impairments. Illustrations of signs in sign language for legal terms and terms for sexual offenses are presented.

748. Oliver, J. E. (1975). Microcephaly following baby battering and shaking. *British Medical Journal, 2*(5965), 262-264.

This article discusses three cases of microcephaly, which resulted in severe retardation in previously normal children. Because detailed social and psychiatric information was taken, the diagnosis of child abuse could be made. Otherwise, the three children would have become part of the large group of institutionalized individuals whose deficits are of unknown origin.

749. Oliver, J. E. (1985). Successive generations of child maltreatment: Social and medical disorders in the parents. *British Journal of Psychiatry, 147,* **484-490.**

This article examines 147 families in which there was a pattern of two or more generations of child maltreatment and multi-agency involvement and where there were two or more children maltreated in the current generation (born between 1960 and 1980). It studies data obtained from 34 service agencies, from child abuse case conferences, from direct personal clinical involvement with family members, and from previous research by the author and colleagues. In examining the behavior disorders of the parents of the 1960-1980 children, the author discovered that very high levels of disturbance were common in this population and that characteristics common in the parents and antecedents include the following: mental and personality disorders; suicidal attempts; mental handicap; dependence on drugs, particularly among the mothers, or on alcohol, particularly among the fathers; epilepsy; and criminality.

750. Ombudsman of British Columbia. (1987). *The use of criminal record checks to screen individuals working with vulnerable people* **(Public Report No. 5). Victoria: Queen's Printer for British Columbia.**

The Ombudsman of British Columbia proposed several guidelines for screening individuals who work with vulnerable people: all employees whose work assignments bring them into contact with vulnerable people must authorize disclosure of police records; positions of trust to be monitored must be clearly defined and monitored; vulnerable people must be clearly defined; criminal record screening must be performed on every employee meeting the definition; criminal record screening must be performed on prospective employees prior to employment; criminal record screening must be mandated for private as well as public employees; there must be a mechanism for checking agency and individual compliance; information must be released to both employee and employer; past conduct confirmed by conviction or admission of guilt in diversions or discharges must be included, and offenses for which pardons have been granted shall not be released; rules must be established for who bears the cost of criminal record screening; information received must be assessed on the basis of relevancy; the agency must consider that if the behavior is repeated will there be a threat to client safety or welfare, interfere with duties, or pose other specific threats; they must consider the circumstances of the charge (e.g., offender's age); they must consider the recency of the charge; they must allow the employee to provide supplemental information related to the area of concern; decisions must be made consistently; the privacy of the individual who is being checked must be maintained; information obtained should not be available for other purposes; permanent records of information disclosed must not be maintained except in exceptional cases and by mutual agreement; appeal procedures must be developed, available, and explained to employees asked to make disclosures; and data should be maintained to monitor complaints of abuses of criminal record checks as well as the benefits of policy. As criminal records may be incomplete because of errors, exclusion of juvenile offenders (58% of all pedophiles commit first offense as adolescent), and so forth, the Ombudsman made several recommendations: caution must be exercised so that checks do not perpetuate racial or class bias; because Canadian provinces have varying policies, training and certification agencies should incorporate these procedures or inform individuals seeking training that they will be required to undergo checks later on; those administering the process must be trained; consent forms should specify the information sought, how it will be used, how the information will be available to the prospective employee, and assure confidentiality; adverse decisions based on these records should be communicated in writing to the individual affected, explaining the reasons and outlining the appeal process; these procedures must be recognized as limited and not be expected to replace other safeguards, including other screening procedures; and no information should be released that cannot be verified. (Note: Police checks can only eliminate those with previous convictions or current charges pending for related charges, but the elimination of a few chronic offenders may reduce the number of victims by hundreds.)

751. Ontario Hospital Association. (1983). *The treatment of persons who have been sexually assaulted: Guidelines for hospitals.* **Toronto: Author.**

This document outlines a treatment services package for use by hospitals in Ontario in the treatment of people who have been sexually assaulted. The goals of the package include prompt emergency service, privacy, attending to emotional needs, follow-up procedures, and cooperation between the agencies and institutions that may be brought into action. Sample topics include the following: role of the administration; medical procedure in the documentation of evidence of assault; role of physicians, nursing staff, and social workers in the community; rape crisis centers; the police and crown; the designation of specific hospitals for the treatment of sexual assault victims; and treatment. Also, the document describes a sexual assault evidence kit developed by the Provincial Secretariat for Justice in Ontario.

752. Oreskes, M. (1984, August 8). State inquiry set in child abuse at Bronx Center. *The New York Times,* **pp. A1, B4.**

This article discusses sexual abuse at the Bronx, New York, Praca Day Care Center. Three employees were arrested for sexually abusing children; 30 of 135 children reported abuse. The District Attorney also charged that officials of the Human Resources Administration impeded the investigation of abuse. Documents were withheld by this agency during the investigation. The interagency dispute illustrates the bureaucratic conflicts that often hinder action against institutional child abuse.

753. O'Sullivan, C.M. (1989). Alcoholism and abuse: The twin family secrets. In G. W Lawson & A. W. Lawson (Eds.), *Alcoholism & substance abuse in special populations* **(pp. 273-303). Rockville, MD: Aspen Systems.**

This chapter addresses the relationship between alcoholism and family violence. The author points to high rates of wife and child battering among alcoholics. Some of these children have been born with disabilities due to Fetal Alcohol syndrome (FAS). The author also points to high rates of sexual abuse in alcoholic homes, suggesting that 4 million children in the United States are growing up with the combined problems of alcoholism and sexual abuse. The author also cites research that indicates 26% of children living in alcoholic homes have been incest victims. (Note: Alcohol's role in wife and child battering also increase the likelihood of organic damage to the child before birth or in childhood which may result in physical, sensory, or mental disability. Thus, chronic familial use of alcohol may be be an important, but often hidden, factor linking disability to both physical and sexual abuse)

754. Oswin, M. (1979). The neglect of children in long-stay hospitals. *Child Abuse & Neglect,* **3(1), 89-92.**

This article discusses the institutional abuse of children in terms of emotional deprivation, deprivation of normal childhood experiences, and physical neglect, including lack of therapy for their disabilities and lack of warm nurturing contact.

•P•

755. Page, F. (1986). The therapeutic use of puppetry with mentally handicapped people. *British Journal of Occupational Therapy,* **49(4), 122-125.**

This article describes a student project that investigated the therapeutic application of puppetry with residents with mental handicaps in a hospital. It discusses the use of puppets to facilitate group interaction in sex education and in assertion training. The reactions of the residents to the sessions and the author's evaluations of the sessions are also discussed.

756. Page, R. C., Cheng, H. P., Pate, T. C., Mathus, B., et al. (1987). The perceptions of spinal cord injured persons toward sex. *Sexuality and Disability,* **8(2), 112-132.**

In this study, a marital adjustment checklist was administered to 25 males and 13 females who were either quadruplegic, paraplegic, or severely disabled. Results indicate the following: Although the respondents were permissive in the sex options they considered, many of them reported experiencing problems in their sexual relationships.

757. Paiement, J., & Pilon, J. (1985). *Les agressions sexuelles faites aux enfants: Parlons-en pour mieux les prévenir [Sexual abuse of children: Talk about it and help prevent it].* **Montréal: Parents anonymes du Québec, Inc.**

Examples of sexual abuse are presented in the form of a lexicon that includes such terms as rape, incest, pedophilia, and so forth. Topics discussed include the effects of abuse on children and the factors likely to influence the degree of trauma. These factors are the relationship between the child and the abuser, the nature and frequency of the abuse, the personality and the age of the child, and reactions from the outside. A distinction is made between long- and short-term effects. A profile of the abuser is presented as well as a discussion of attitudes to adopt and rules to follow when helping a child who has been sexually abused. Attitudes and reactions to avoid are also discussed. (This book is available in French only.)

758. Painsky, A., Katz, S., & Kravetz, S. (1986). The impact of institutionalization on the sex

identity and sexual behavior of mildly handicapped young persons. *International Journal of Adolescent Medicine and Health, 2*(2), 145-151.

This article investigates the effect of the length of institutionalization on sex identity and heterosexual behavior patterns of 60 people with mild mental retardation, half of whom had spent 75% of their lives in institutions and half of whom had spent 25% of their lives in institutions. For men with mental handicaps, this study found that the length of institutionalization negatively affected sexual identity. The study also found that although heterosexual behavior was related to sexual identity it did not appear related to the length of institutionalization and sex of the subjects.

759. Painsky, A., Katz, S., & Kravetz, S. (1986). Sexual behavior patterns of institutionalized mentally handicapped persons. *International Journal of Rehabilitation Research, 9*(3), 276-279.

This article describes a study that investigated whether the length of institutionalization and sex of residents had an effect on the sexual behavior of 30 male and 30 female 18-30 years old subjects (IQ range 56-64). The study found that although the frequency of sexual behaviors of the subjects was less than that of nonhandicapped persons the quality of their behavior indicates that they had adopted sexual norms similar to those of the normal population.

760. Paniagua, C., & De-Fazio, A. (1983). Psychodynamics of the mildly retarded and borderline intelligence adult. *Psychiatric Quarterly, 55*(4), 242-252.

This article discusses the special problems of development and adjustment to the community experienced by adults with mild mental retardation and borderline intelligence and provides four case studies with psychodynamic formulations.

761. Paradis, D. M., Wagner, D., & Lucas, B. M. (1985). Model program: Michigan. In V. L. Vivian (Ed.), *Child abuse and neglect: A medical community response* (pp. 195-208). Chicago: American Medical Association.

These authors outline several reasons why physicians fail to respond to child abuse and neglect: most physicians do not know the signs of child abuse and neglect; most physicians do not understand the implications of failing to report abuse; physicians have little confidence in the courts and protective services; most physicians are unfamiliar with the court system and will avoid any court proceedings whenever possible; court proceedings are too time-consuming to permit participation by practicing physicians; most physicians feel isolated in regard to child abuse concerns; physicians do not view themselves as reporters of abuse and are concerned that reporting may interfere with their relationships with patients; physicians generally have no protocol for detecting and reporting abuse; physicians are reluctant

to admit that their patients are abusers or victims; and physicians sometimes justify their failure to report by claiming that social services and courts cannot really help.

762. Parish, R. A., Myers, P. A., Brandner, A., & Templin, K. H. (1985). Developmental milestones in abused children, and their improvement with a family-oriented approach to the treatment of child abuse. *Child Abuse & Neglect, 9*(2), 245-250.

This paper examines the effect of the Family Development Center Program on preschool children who have been abused and their parents. While in the program, children attend a therapeutically oriented playschool on a daily basis. Their parents participate in group therapy and anger management technique training. Using the Learning Assessment Technique Profile, the authors found that 79% of the 53 children tested demonstrated improved developmental skills. The greatest improvement was seen in fine motor and language skills, areas that were initially significantly delayed for the group as a whole. The authors also plan to follow the children tested over a 5-year period.

763. Parmelee, A. H., Howard, J., & Beckwith, L. (1984). Infant mental health and biological risk [Special issue: Infant mental health—from theory to intervention]. *Child Abuse & Neglect, 8*(2), 219-226.

This article examines three common types of problems and appropriate methods for ensuring special recognition and effective handling by the physician of psychological problems in infants and the promotion of their mental health: 1) infants seen with defined medical conditions that generally have associated psychosocial problems, including child abuse; 2) infants seen who have fully recovered from critical illnesses but are considered at risk for later developmental disability; and 3) infants seen with normal variations of behavior that are misinterpreted by their parents or physicians.

764. Participation by victims, witnesses, and defendants. (1986). *Mental and Physical Disability Law Reporter, 10*(1), 28-29.

This paper describes four competency court cases that review the courtroom participation of victims with mental retardation, a victim with an alleged mental illness, and a defendant with mental retardation: 1) the conviction of a father who engaged in sexual relations with his 20-year-old daughter with mental retardation, Michigan v. Karelse, 373 N.W.2d. 200 (Mich. Ct. App. 1985); 2) a defendant's conviction for the rape of a female with mental retardation, Hawaii v. Gonsalves, 706 P.2d. 1333 (Hawaii Ct. App. 1985); 3) a defendant, convicted of kidnapping, was not deprived of his right to conduct a vigorous cross-examination of a witness with an alleged mental disability, New York v. Chan, 493 N.Y.S.2d. 778 (N.Y. App. Div. 2nd Dept. 1985); and 4) a defendant's below average intelligence and previous psychological problems did not compel suppression of his incriminating statements to the police regarding the kidnapping, assault, and sexual offense against a 6-year-old child, North Carolina v. Simpson, 334 S.E.2d. 53 (N.C. S. Ct. 1985).

765. Pasamanick, B. (1975). Ill-health and child abuse [Letter to the editor]. *Lancet, 2*(7934), 550.

Maternal tension was found to be associated with a child with neurological impairments, whether premature or full-term. Prematurity in children without neurological impairments was not found to be associated with maternal tension. The relationship of maternal tension to child abuse is discussed.

766. Passer, A., Rauh, J., Chamberlain, A., McGrath, M., & Burket, R. (1984). Issues in fertility control for mentally retarded female adolescents: Parental attitudes toward sterilization. *Pediatrics, 73*(4), 451-454.

This article reports on a study of parental attitudes concerning sterilization of daughters with mental retardation. Sixty-nine parents were interviewed. Forty-six percent had considered sterilization. Thirteen of 32 parents who had considered sterilization decided against it. Eighteen parents were still seeking sterilization, and the remaining parent had obtained the procedure for her daughter. Fifty-two percent of parents of daughters with mild mental retardation thought their children should give informed consent. Nineteen percent and 10% of parents of daughters with moderate and severe mental retardation, respectively, thought their daughters could give consent. When asked about attitudes concerning sterilization legislation, 67 parents responded. Eighty-five percent favored a statute enabling sterilization of people with mental retardation. Twelve percent did not favor such a statute, and 3% of respondents answered that they did not know.

767. Payne, A.T. (1978). The law and the problem parent: Custody and parental rights of homosexual, mentally retarded, mentally ill and incarcerated parents. *Journal of Family Law, 16*(4), 797-818.

This article examines the determination of child custody cases where the parents are either homosexual, in prison, mentally ill, or mentally retarded. Regarding people with mental retardation, the author found that there is a widespread fear of allowing people with mental retardation to parent despite the fact that the determination of the degree of mental retardation is often based on the parent's articulation skills and economic status. Further, people with mental illness are given more opportunity to benefit from more objective assessment than are people with mental retardation. From the case histories studied, the author found that imprisoned parents suffered the least discrimination of the four groups. (Note: While intellectual impairment and its possible relationship to inadequate parenting has often been used as a rationale for sterilization and even apprehension of children from parents with disabilities,

society has been more reluctant to intrude on other parents relationships with their children suggesting a double standard.)

768. Penfold, P. S. (1982). Children of battered women. *International Journal of Mental Health, 11*(1/2), 108-114.

This article examines 16 children with multihandicaps (ages 2-11) of abused mothers who were referred to a child psychiatry center (1 subject had an abused father). The article identifies several problems, including behavior and learning problems, hyperactivity, overdependence, anxiety, bizarre behavior, and asthma. The author concludes that the effects on children of mothers who are abused and the detection of woman battering when children are referred as patients are hampered by stereotypical attitudes that preserve male prerogatives and veil violence toward women and by pervasive beliefs that mothers are to blame for their children's problems.

769. Penny, R. E., & Chataway, J. E. (1982). Sex education for mentally retarded persons. *Australia and New Zealand Journal of Developmental Disabilities, 8*(4), 204-212.

This article discusses a sex education program for people with mild to moderate mental retardation. The results of post-tests at 1 week and 2 months after the completion of the program reveal that the program is effective, and since sex knowledge continued to increase after the completion of the program, these results suggest that the small-group teaching situation may have facilitated the sharing of sex information among group members.

770. Per-Lee, M. S. (1981). *Victim witness project for the handicapped: Victim justice for disabled persons: A resource manual.* Washington, DC: Gallaudet College.

This author discusses a number of factors related to service accessibility for victims with disabilities. The author states that service accessibility for persons with disabilities is limited. Factors related to accessibility include degree of architectural and programmatic suitability, willingness to individualize to client's needs, and the client's awareness of service accessibility.

771. Pervin-Dixon, L. (1988). Sexuality and the spinal cord injured. *Journal of Psychosocial Nursing and Mental Health Services, 26*(4), 31-34.

In this article, the author argues that sexuality needs to be accorded the same importance as other aspects of the rehabilitation of people with spinal cord injuries. Programs designed to deal with the sexual rehabilitation of this population of clients are described.

772. Petchesky, R. P. (1979). Reproduction, ethics and public policy: The federal sterilization regulations. *Hastings Center Reports, 9*, 29-41.

This article contains a comprehensive discussion of

ethical and social issues involved in sterilization and its misuse. Regarding sterilization of people with mental handicaps, one argument in its favor is that it is a means of protecting this population from sexual exploitation and abuse. The author disagrees, however, stating that sterilization is not a remedy because, while it does prevent pregnancy, it does not prevent abuse. In fact, by eliminating the most obvious evidence of sexual abuse, it may increase vulnerability. Sterilization, when used to dispose of problems of sexuality, sex education, and birth control, becomes a rationalization for neglecting the basic needs and services required by people with mental handicaps.

773. **Peterson, Y. (1979). The impact of physical disability on marital adjustment: A literature review.** *Family Coordinator, 28*(1), 47-51.
This literature review addresses marital adjustment among couples where physical disability exists. Disability-associated stress is explored. Role flexibility is identified as a major variable and differs between men and women. The response of nonhandicapped spouses to a spouse with severe handicaps is discussed.

774. **Pettis, K. W., & Hughes, R. D. (1985). Sexual victimization of children: Implications for educators.** *Behavioral Disorders, 10*(3), 175-182.
These authors provide information to educators who may come into contact with sexual abuse. Several articles are cited in which the authors found higher risk of abuse in populations with mental or physical handicaps or emotional disorders.

775. **Phaneuf, J. (1987). Considerations on deafness and homosexuality.** *American Annals of the Deaf, 132*(1), 52-55.
This article examines the emotions, attitudes, and general reactions toward homosexuality in individuals who are deaf and in the deaf community. It reviews the literature on sexuality and deafness to provide a background, and it discusses, along with related social, familial, and personal implications, the social and emotional context in which a person who is deaf deals with homosexual identity and behavior and the coming-out process. The author also considers counselling, other forms of intervention, sex education, and research implications.

776. **Phillips, L. R. (1983). Elder abuse: What is it? Who says so?** *Geriatric Nursing, 4*(3), 167-170.
This article discusses obstacles hindering nurses in the identification and reporting of elder abuse. Discussion includes difficulties in the formulation of an operational definition of elder abuse, unacknowledged variables affecting identification of the problem, and some important unanswered questions (e.g., the role of intention as justification on the part of the abuser and the development of rights of ownership). Professional and social-political concerns for the nursing profession are discussed.

777. **Phillips, L. R. (1988). The fit of elder abuse with the family violence paradigm, and the implications of a paradigm shift for clinical practice.** *Public Health Nursing, 5*(4), 222-229.
This article provides a discussion of some of the complex issues in elder abuse. The author concludes that it is more useful for public health nurses to view elder abuse in terms of the met and unmet needs of the elder than in terms of identified violence.

778. **Phillips, L. R., & Rempusheski, V. F. (1985). A decision-making model for diagnosing and intervening in elder abuse and neglect.** *Nursing Research, 34*(3), 134-139.
In view of the absence of an empirically based operational definition of elder abuse among health professionals, the authors present a four-stage decision-making model for identifying poor quality care of elders in the home. The model is based on a grounded theory technique and addresses intervention. Audiotaped interviews with 16 nurses and 13 social workers were coded and analyzed. Hypotheses were generated as a result and are offered as guidelines for future research geared toward assisting health professionals in the decision to intervene in home-care situations.

779. **Phillips, L. R., & Rempusheski, V. F. (1986). Caring for the frail elderly at home: Toward a theoretical explanation of the dynamics of poor quality family caregiving.** *Advances in Nursing Science, 8*(4), 62-84.
In order to determine perceptions of quality of care toward frail elderly family members in the home, 39 families were studied. The data collected were used to generate a model consisting of five constructs staged within the framework provided by symbolic interactionism and social exchange theory. The model addresses the dynamics of good and poor quality family caregiving, the relationship among contextual and perceptual variables and behavior between elders and caregivers, and at what points intervention by nurses is most effective.

780. **Phillips, L. R., & Rempusheski, V. F. (1986). Making decisions about elder abuse.** *Social Casework, 67*(3), 131-140.
This article discusses factors influencing health care providers in the identification of elder abuse and in decisions to intervene. A grounded theory methodology was used in interviews held with 16 nurses and 13 social workers. A common detection problem identified was deciding whether a given situation was serious enough to constitute abuse of the elder. Intentionality on the part of the abuser was taken into account. Whether a situation was seen as abusive also depended upon the relationship between the caregiver and the professional. Determining appropriate intervention was seen as a complex and difficult task.. Concerns with self-protection on the part of health care providers were also identified. The need for detection and intervention guidelines is discussed.

781. **Pillai, V., Collins, A., & Morgan, R. (1982). Family Walk-In Centre-Eaton Socon: Evaluation of a project on preventive intervention based in the community.** *Child Abuse & Neglect, 6*(1), 71-79.

This article discusses an intervention program designed to encourage parents to visit a family walk-in center. The program includes informal and formal group work, family casework, and education in social and physical skills. Findings of an evaluation of 100 families who used the center indicate a significant reduction in the registration of new cases of child abuse, self-referrals significantly exceeded other modes of referral, and loneliness and parenting difficulties are the major characteristics of families seeking help.

782. **Pillemer, K. (1985). The dangers of dependency: New findings on domestic violence against the elderly.** *Social Problems, 33,* 146-158.

This article reviews research related to dependency as a factor in elder abuse. The author concludes that dependency of the elder victim on the abuser is not adequate to explain the abuse. Mutual dependency, typically physical dependency of the victim on the abuser and financial dependency of the abuser on the victim, appears to be a critical factor in elder abuse. This finding might be applied to caregiver abuse since paid caregivers depend on their victims for their income.

783. **Pillemer, K. A. (1988). Maltreatment of patients in nursing homes: Overview and research agenda.** *Journal of Health and Social Behavior, 29*(3), 227-238.

This article reviews the social science literature on the maltreatment of patients in nursing homes. Problems in defining maltreatment are discussed as well as a rationale for the sociological study of the problem. A theoretical model of potential causes of patient maltreatment is proposed. Factors include the nursing home environment and staff and patient characteristics. Research implications are discussed.

784. **Pillemer, K., & Finkelhor, D. (1988). The prevalence of elder abuse: A random sample survey.** *Gerontologist, 28*(1), 51-57.

In this study, 2,020 elderly persons age 65 years or older and living in the community were interviewed regarding their experience of physical abuse, verbal aggression, and neglect. Per 1,000 participants, 32 reported having been maltreated, with physical violence being reported most frequently. Abusers were most likely to be spouses. Victims were about equally likely to be male or female, though women suffered more serious abuse. The authors conclude that service providers and the elderly need to be educated regarding spouse abuse.

785. **Pillemer, K., & Finkelhor, D. (1989). Causes of elder abuse: Caregiver stress versus problem relatives.** *American Journal of Orthopsychiatry, 59,* 179-187.

This article reports research results from a study designed to determine the relative importance of caregiver stress and caregiver personality problems for predicting elder abuse. The study found that problem caregivers accounted for abuse to a much larger extent than dependency of the victim or family stress.

786. **Pincus, S. (1988). Sexuality in the mentally retarded patient.** *American Family Physician, 37*(2), 319-323.

This article examines the difficulty experienced by physicians who provide care for patients with mental disabilities when making decisions involving sexuality, contraception, and marriage.

787. **Pitceathly, A. S., & Chapman, J. W. (1985). Sexuality, marriage and parenthood of mentally retarded people.** *International Journal for the Advancement of Counselling, 8*(3), 173-181.

These authors discuss the sexuality of people with mental handicaps, pointing out that these individuals require knowledge about the physical and emotional aspects of development. As well, with increasing normalization and integration into the community, there is greater risk that people with mental handicaps will be abused and exploited. The authors present suggestions for counselors who are involved in providing sex education and marriage counseling to people with mental handicaps.

788. **Pope, K. S. (1986). Research and laws regarding therapist-patient sexual involvement: Implications for therapists.** *American Journal of Psychotherapy, 40*(4), 564-571.

Legal and ethical prohibitions regarding therapist-patient sexual intimacy are discussed as well as research results regarding the prevalence and consequences of this phenomenon. Treatment issues for therapists working with clients who have had sexual intimacy with a previous therapist are also discussed.

789. **Pope, K. S. (1987). Preventing therapist-patient sexual intimacy: Therapy for a therapist at risk.** *Professional Psychology Research and Practice, 18*(6), 624-628.

This article summarizes research findings in the area of therapist-patient intimacy. Indications are that this phenomenon is a major problem for the profession. Research findings suggest that many male and female therapists feel sexually attracted to some of their clients and are uncomfortable with it. Most therapists will not act on their feelings, but some become sexually intimate with their patients. The author emphasizes the need for the development of various intervention models enabling therapists to accept and understand this attraction and so avoid acting it out. Using a fictional case study, the author suggests a preliminary approach to developing an intervention model. The model addresses such issues as confidentiality, the use of contracts, education, covert modeling, and cognitive-behavioral techniques.

790. **Pope, K. S. (1988). How clients are harmed by sexual contact with mental health professionals: The syndrome and its prevalence.** *Journal of Counseling and Development, 67*(4), 222-226.

This article discusses therapist-patient sexual intimacy in terms of its prevalence, types, consequences, and contributing factors. The potential for the phenomenon to form into a distinct syndrome is discussed. Symptoms in the therapist include the following: guilt; feelings of emptiness and isolation; sexual confusion; impaired ability to trust; identity, boundary, and role confusion; emotional lability; suppressed rage; increased risk for suicide; and difficulties in concentration and attention.

791. **Pope, K. S., & Bouhoutsos, J. C. (1986).** *Sexual intimacy between therapists and patients.* **New York: Praeger.**

This book explores the common, but unacceptable phenomenon of sexual intimacy between psychotherapists and their patients. It includes information on the nature and extent of occurrences, characteristics of offenders and patients likely to become involved, legal and ethical concerns and procedures, and recommendations for prevention. The section on vulnerabilities of certain varieties of patients is of particular interest. Often, these victims have a history of incest or other abuse as children and feel powerless to resist authority figures. The book includes extensive discussion of the harm often done to the patients as a result of these relationships, citing a number of studies and published reports. Although therapists are always solely responsible for preventing sexual contact with patients, legal remedies are often complicated by the questionable competency of the victim. The authors suggest education as an important method of prevention in addition to legal and administrative controls to combat the problem.

792. **Pope, K. S., Keith-Spiegel, P., & Tabachnick, B. G. (1986). Sexual attraction to clients: The human therapist and the (sometimes) inhuman training system.** *American Psychologist, 41,* 147-158.

This article addresses the issue of psychologist-client sexual attraction and interaction. The authors suggest that 95% of male therapists and 76% of female therapists had experienced some sexual attraction to a client on at least one occasion. About 5%-10% of male therapists and 1%-2% of female therapists admitted to actually having a sexual relationship with one or more clients. The authors also discuss the traumatic effects on the clients who become angry, distrustful, and fearful as a result of these sexual contacts.

793. **Pope, K. S., Tabachnick, B. G., & Keith-Spiegel, P. (1987). Ethics of practice: The beliefs and behaviors of psychologists as therapists.** *American Psychologist, 42*(11), 993-1006.

This article addresses the need for the systematic and comprehensive collection of data regarding psychologists' beliefs about and compliance with ethical principles. Survey data were collected from 456 APA Division 29 members regarding ethical behavior. Twelve of the 83 behaviors studied were judged by the respondents to be very difficult to evaluate on the basis of ethics. Respondents also rated resources in terms of their helpfulness in guiding behavior. The most helpful sources were found to be colleagues, the APA Ethical Principles, and internship training. Least helpful were state and federal law, published research, and local ethics committees.

794. **Port Angeles lawyer charged with rape. (1989, March).** *Washington Coalition of Sexual Assault Programs Newsletter,* **pp. 2-3.**

This article describes the charges against a lawyer who received national recognition as a humanitarian for being the adoptive father of a number of children from underdeveloped countries. He was charged with sexual abuse of his 12-year-old, adopted Guatemalan daughter who was blind. A 30-year-old adopted son was also charged with sexual assaults against the same child. Three other girls and one other boy in the home also indicated that they had been sexually abused by their adoptive father.

795. **Poteat, G. M., Pope, J. G., Choate, C., & Grossnickle, W. F. (1989). Wife abuse as it affects work behavior in a center for mentally retarded persons.** *Journal of Clinical Psychology, 45*(2), 324-330.

This article reports the results of research on the relationship between the potential for child abuse by abused women and by nonabused women. The Child Abuse Potential (CAP) Inventory was filled out by 377 female employees of a residential institution along with questions regarding their own history of abuse. While no significant relationship existed between history of being abused and work performance appraisal ratings or absenteeism, a strong relationship existed between history of being abused and potential for abusing others as measured by the CAP Inventory. While the mean CAP score for women who had been physically abused was above that for women who had been emotionally abused, there was no significant difference. Some caution should be used in interpreting the results since elevated CAP scores were also associated with socio-economic factors.

796. **Priegert, P. (1989, March 30). Easy targets: People with disabilities easily victimized.** *The Edmonton Sun,* **p. 30. (Canadian Press wire service story)**

This article describes sexual abuse of people with disabilities and related problems, and it states that "experts agree that people with disabilities are more likely to be victims of sexual assaults." It discusses the University of Alberta research program and the Canadian conference on sexual assault and abuse of people with disabilities.

797. **Protective services for disabled children. (1986).** *Mental and Physical Disability Law Reporter, 10*(4), 303-304.

This document discusses two court case rulings regarding the abuse and neglect of children with mental and physical handicaps.

798. *Public welfare of juveniles.* (1984, June). **Hearing before the Subcommittee on the Constitution of the Committee on the Judiciary. United States Senate, 98th Congress, Second Session on S.520, A bill to promote the public welfare by protecting dependent children and others from institutional abuse, and S. 552, A bill to promote the public welfare by removing juveniles from adult jails. (ERIC Document Reproduction Service No. ED 260 318)**
This document presents testimony in favor of the proposed bills and testimony in opposition. The text of the two bills is included.

799. Pueschel, S. M. (1986). **The impact on the family: Living with the handicapped child.** *Issues in Law and Medicine, 2*(3), 171-187.
In this article, the effect of family grief over the presence of a disability in a child is discussed. The stages of adaptation to the arrival of a child with a disability into the family is described as well as the role of professional assistance and support resources. Chronic grief is addressed. (Note: The stages of adaptation of parents to the birth or diagnosis of a child with a disability are controversial. Others suggest that these stages do not exist, exist for only some parents, or do not exist in a fixed sequence)

800. Pueschel, S. M., & Scola, P. S. (1988). **Parents' perception of social and sexual functions in adolescents with Down's syndrome.** *Journal of Mental Deficiency Research, 32*(3), 215-220.
The parents of 36 males and 37 females with Down syndrome, ages 13 to 20, were queried on their perceptions of their children's socio-sexual knowledge and development. About half of the parents felt that their children should be sterilized or use birth control. More parents of girls feared their child might be sexually exploited. More than half of the young people showed interest in the opposite sex and were attending social gatherings. Although few had an interest in sexual relationships, many wanted to marry, and few had had sex education.

801. Purnick, J. (1984, August 8). **Head of city's department for child welfare resigns.** *The New York Times,* p. B4.
This article recounts the resignation of the head of New York City's Office of Special Services amid charges that the agency was seriously negligent in investigations of child abuse. This followed a 2-year investigation of the agency, which culminated in a highly critical report. The investigation began two years after a city social worker brought the deaths of some children to the attention of supervisors. (Note: The allegations reported in this case appear similar to those reported in many others suggesting officials often fail to act against abuse.)

•Q•

802. Qualey, T. L., Jr. (1989). **Sexual victimization of child and adolescent patients [Letter to the editor].** *Image: Journal of Nursing Scholarship, 21*(2), 116.
In this letter, the author, a Director of Nursing, responds to V. B. Newbern's article "Sexual victimization of child and adolescent patients" (*Image: Journal of Nursing Scholarship, 21*[1], 10-13). The author comments on the portrayal of staff in nursing homes as well as on methodological issues in this area of study.

803. Quinn, K. M. (1986). **Competency to be a witness: A major child forensic issue [Special issue: Child forensic psychiatry].** *Bulletin of the American Academy of Psychiatry and the Law, 14*(4), 311-321.
This article discusses the legal and psychiatric issues surrounding the competency of child witnesses to testify in criminal cases. It describes the criteria used to establish testimonial capacity of children, and it presents guidelines for conducting forensic examinations to determine competency of child witnesses. It describes five case examples in order to illustrate the major issues encountered by forensic psychiatrists during competency evaluations, and it highlights the roles of mental retardation and mental disturbances in competency determinations and the distinction between competency and credibility.

•R•

804. Rabb, J., & Rindfleisch, N. A. (1985). **Study to define and assess severity of institutional abuse/neglect.** *Child Abuse & Neglect, 9*(2), 285-294.
This empirical study addresses the need for the development of operational definitions of institutional abuse and neglect. Six-hundred-and-thirty respondents rated 24 instances of child maltreatment in institutions in terms of their degree of harmfulness. The respondents included direct caregivers, managers in institutions, public child welfare workers, foster-parents, board members of caregiving facilities, and children in care. Situations were judged to be harmful more often than they were judged to be instances of abuse or neglect. Generally, judgments about out-of-home care were not different from judgments about in-home care. Different negative sequelae for the child resulted in different harm ratings and judgments of abuse or neglect.

805. Raboch, J. (1986). Sexual development and life of psychiatric female patients. *Archives of Sexual Behavior, 15*(4), 341-353.

This article examines a study that investigated the sexual development and sex lives of 51 schizophrenic, 50 manic-depressive, 50 neurotic, 30 hysterical, and 20 anorexic female psychiatric in-patients (ages 20-50 years old) and 101 same-aged gynecological patients in aftercare. Findings indicate that the sexual development of schizophrenics was retarded, that of anorexics was accelerated in the initial stages, and that of hysterics was disharmonious. The study found no differences between people with manic-depressiveness and controls regarding sex life in adulthood; however, all of the other groups of psychiatric patients showed decreased sexual activity and/or reactivity. The author concludes that sexual dysfunctions in the female psychiatric population are frequent, especially among women with schizophrenia, anorexia, or hysterical reactions.

806. Ramteke, B. S., & Mrinal, N. R. (1984). Defense mechanisms in orthopaedically handicapped. *Indian Journal of Clinical Psychology, 11*(1), 53-59.

Forty participants with an orthopedic handicap and 40 controls responded to the Defense Mechanism Inventory. Each group contained equal numbers of males and females. Males from the control group used the cluster defense "Turning Against Object" more than both handicap groups and the females in the control group. Males from the handicap group used the defense clusters "Turning Against Self and Reversal" more often. Other defense clusters studied include "Projection" and "Principalization."

807. Rawicki, H., & Lording, D. W. (1988). Assisted fertility in complete paraplegia: Case report. *Paraplegia, 26*(6), 401-404.

This study documents the use of electroejaculation in obtaining semen from a man with spinal cord injury below the thoracic segment. Artificial insemination resulted in a successful pregnancy. Guidelines for a comprehensive fertility program are briefly discussed.

808. Ray, C., & West, J. (1983). Spinal cord injury: The nature of its implications and ways of coping. *International Journal of Rehabilitation Research, 6*(3), 364-365.

This article examines the social stigma, sexual difficulties, self-esteem, and emotional adjustment of 11 male and 11 female paraplegics. It found that most of the subjects experienced sexual difficulties and some frustration or depression. The authors discuss strategies for dealing with the pity of others, and they review the implications for counselors.

809. Ray, C., & West, J. (1984). Coping with spinal cord injury, II. *Paraplegia, 22*(4), 249-259.

This article investigates the social, sexual, and emotional problems and their effects on 22 male and female paraplegics. The study found that paraplegics use

a number of coping strategies for dealing with other people and their attitudes and for readjusting sexually, including suppression, denial and repression, resignation and acceptance, positive thinking, and independence and assertiveness. The authors conclude that counselling should recognize the range of coping strategies that are available and be able to guide the individual toward those that best match their needs and the demands of the situation.

810. Re B (1987) 2 All ER 206 (HL).

This case report is about a local authority who had care of a 17-year-old girl with mental handicaps and epilepsy who had a mental age of 5 or 6. She had no understanding of the connection between sexual intercourse and pregnancy and birth, and she would not be able to cope with birth nor care for a child of her own. She was not capable of consenting to marriage. She was, however, exhibiting the normal sexual drive and inclinations for someone of her chronological age. There was expert evidence that it was vital that she should not be permitted to become pregnant and that certain contraceptive drugs would react with drugs administered to control her instability and epilepsy. There was further evidence that it would be difficult, if not impossible, to place her on a course of oral contraceptive pills. The local authority, which had no wish to institutionalize her, applied to the court for her to be made a ward of the court and for leave to be given for her to undergo a sterilization operation. The application was supported by the minor's mother. The judge granted the application, and an appeal to the Court of Appeal was dismissed. The final appeal to the House of Lords was also dismissed. The court held that the paramount consideration for the exercise of the wardship jurisdiction was the welfare and best interests of the ward in question, and accordingly, where it was for the welfare and in the best interests of the ward that he or she be sterilized, the court had jurisdiction to authorize the operation. Given the facts, sterilization was for the welfare and in the best interests of the minor and therefore the appeal would be dismissed. There is express disagreement in the case with the view taken by the Supreme Court of Canada on the limits of the *parens patriae* jurisdiction. The court states that the issue is not whether the sterilization is therapeutic or non-therapeutic, but whether it is in the best interests of the person whom the court is asked to protect. Lord Templeman expresses the opinion that the decision should be made by a Superior Court rather than left to a parent or guardian. (This is a 1987 British House of Lords decision of the case Re B reported in Vol. 2 of the *England Report*, p. 206.)

811. Reed, J., & Clements, J. (1989). Assessing the understanding of emotional states in a population of adolescents and young adults with mental handicaps. *Journal of Mental Deficiency Research, 33*, 229-233.

This article investigates emotional awareness and the recognition and understanding of various emotional states in a nonclinical population of adolescents and young adults with mental handicaps. Though a high correlation was found between emotional awareness and language comprehension, findings suggest that many participants had specific emotional awareness deficits that do not correlate with their language comprehension abilities. The authors conclude that the assessment of emotional awareness is an important step in the choice of self-report measures assessing emotional state.

812. Re Eve (1986) 2 S. C. R. 388 (SCC).
This law report concerns the court case involving an adult with mental retardation, Eve, and her mother's request for permission to consent to the sterilization of Eve. The mother feared that Eve might innocently become pregnant and consequently force Mrs E., who was widowed and approaching 60, to assume responsibility for the child. The application sought the following: a) a declaration that Eve was mentally incompetent pursuant to the Mental Health Act, b) the appointment of Mrs E. as committee of Eve, and c) authorization for Eve's undergoing a tubal legation. The application for authorization for sterilization was denied and an appeal to the Supreme Court of Prince Edward Island was launched. The appeal was allowed. An appeal was made to the Supreme Court of Canada to reverse the decision. The court found that permission for Eve's mother to consent to the sterilization could not be given. The court based its finding on the following rationale: First, the court found that there was no relevant provincial legislation that gives a court jurisdiction to appoint a committee vested with the power to consent to or authorize surgical procedures for contraceptive purposes on an adult who is mentally incompetent; and second, the court's *parens patriae* jurisdiction is only available if the purpose of the sterilization is therapeutic. To reach its conclusion on jurisdiction, the court engaged in an extensive examination of the origins, scope, and limits of *parens patriae* jurisdiction. This finding of the court means two things: First, it excludes nontherapeutic sterilization from the *parens patriae* jurisdiction; and second, a nontherapeutic sterilization can never safely be determined to be in the best interest of a person who is mentally incompetent. The court also found that the onus of proof lies upon the person seeking the authority for sterilization, and the burden, although a civil one, must be commensurate with the seriousness of the measure proposed. The court did not address the issue as to whether the Canadian Charter of Rights and Freedoms protects an individual against a nontherapeutic sterilization without that individual's consent. The court stated that the legislatures may legislate for nontherapeutic sterilization, but the legislation must be able to withstand the scrutiny of the courts under the Charter. (This is a 1986 Supreme Court of Canada decision of the case Re Eve reported in Vol. 2 of *The Supreme Court of Canada*, p. 388.)

813. Reinhart, M. A. (1987). Sexually abused boys. *Child Abuse & Neglect, 11,* 229-235.
This article presents data from a review of reports of 189 sexually abused boys evaluated between 1983 and 1985 and compares results with a sample of sexually abused girls matched for age and race. This study found about 16.4% of sexually abused children to be boys and lists other studies finding 95%, 13%, 14%, 18%, and 25%. Only 4% of these boys were abused by females. In most respects, patterns of abuse for boys were similar to the patterns of abuse for girls; however, these boys tended to be abused by younger offenders, and sodomy was more frequent in older boys.

814. Reiter, R. S. (1987). Romance, sexuality, and hearing loss. *Asha, 29*(12), 29-30.
Through a series of brief examples, this article discusses the relationship between sexuality and hearing disorders. It suggests that in some cases therapy for people with hearing disorders has resulted in better sexual adjustment.

815. Reivich, J. S., & Fraley, Y. L. (1983). *The parent education curriculum of family school.* **Yeadon, PA: Family Support Center.**
This curriculum was developed for professionals working with groups of parents of preschool children. It covers 75 hours of instruction and is designed to help families overcome factors leading to child abuse. Special units address issues for children with handicaps and exceptional children. Family Support Center policies are described in the appendix.

816. Renvoize, J. (1982). *Incest: A family pattern.* **London: Routledge & Kegan Paul.**
This book provides a good general discussion of incest. Of particular interest is a chapter on the "pro-incest lobby" and the effects of incest. It points out that there are still elements of society that see incest as socially acceptable and deny the damaging effects to its victims and their families.

817. Resource Access Project Network. (no date). *Preventing maltreatment of children with handicaps.* **Washington, DC: Author.**
This training manual was developed for the Head Start program staff and focuses on the prevention of family dysfunction and child abuse and neglect. The identification of families in need and methods for working with these families are discussed. The stresses of parenting children with disabilities and general parenting skills are discussed. Workshops include the development of child abuse policies and the building of healthy families. Also included is a self-assessment procedure for determining to what extent a given program conforms to U.S. government guidelines as well as suggestions for program modifications. The manual includes a section on interagency agreements, a discussion of referral procedures and the role of the witness in child abuse cases, and an extensive chronological bibliography.

818. Ricci, L. R. (1988). Medical forensic photography of the sexually abused child. *Child Abuse & Neglect, 12,* 305-310.

This article indicates the need for using forensic photography in suspected cases of child sexual abuse and suggests specific methods for photographing lesions that may be evidence of sexual abuse. Even when thorough and careful notes are kept by the physician, issues that arise in court at a later date may cast doubt on the evidence or its interpretation. Good quality photographs of the lesions may be critical in preserving evidence and ensuring its best use.

819. Richards, D. (1986). Sterilization: Can parents decide. *Exceptional Parent, 16*(2), 40-41.

In this article, the mother of a young adult with Down syndrome discusses her decision to have her daughter sterilized.

820. Richman, G. S., Ponticas, Y., Page, T. J., & Epps, S. (1986). Simulation procedures for teaching independent menstrual care to mentally retarded persons. *Applied Research in Mental Retardation, 7*(1), 21-35.

Independent menstrual care skills were taught to four adolescent females with mental retardation. A multiple baseline analysis showed that participants demonstrated fewer correct responses during baseline probes but that consistent improvements corresponded with training. Generalization to untrained skills was seen in all four participants.

821. Rideau, W., & Sinclair, B. (1983). The mentally retarded offender. *Journal of Prison and Jail Health, 3*(2), 101-111.

There is a general consensus that a significant number of people with mental retardation are in prisons. They are often victims of abuse or manipulation. Experts in the field agree that offenders with mental retardation confess more easily, are more open to intimidation, and plead guilty more often. Their sentences may be longer because they do not know how to plea bargain. Offenders with mental retardation are less likely to receive probation. They are more likely to be non-White. Identification of mental retardation among offenders is a large problem. If not identified, the offender with mental retardation becomes "lost" in the prison system. Few special programs exist for these offenders. The authors discuss the question of whether offenders with mental retardation should remain in prison or be placed in other institutions for treatment.

822. Ridington, J. (1989, March). *Beating the "odds": Violence and women with disabilities* **(Position paper 2). Vancouver: DAWN (DisAbled Women's Network) Canada.**

This 45-page position paper reports results from a survey of women with disabilities with 245 respondents. The author reports that 40% (i.e., 99/245) had experienced some form of abuse, about 12% had been raped, and 15% had been assaulted. For 56%, sexual or physical abuse began after the onset of their disability, and for another 26%, abuse occurred both before and after the onset of disability. For 19%, abuse had occurred

before but not after the onset of disability. Some form of violence or sexual assault was experienced by women in all disability categories, and there was some evidence that multiple disabilities increased risk. Perpetrators of abuse, rape, or assault included spouses and exspouses (37%), parents (15%), strangers (28%), service providers (10%), boyfriends or dates (7%), and the remainder by other relatives, neighbors, or their own children. Reports were made to police, social service agencies, parents, teachers, or spouses in 43% of the cases, and the author points out that this rate may be high because more than half of the respondents in their sample were members of consumer groups with disabilities, and more than 40% were members of women's advocacy groups. The most common reasons cited for not reporting were fear and dependency. Only about 10% of the sample had used shelters or other services, about 15% reported that no services were available or that they tried unsuccessfully to obtain services, and 55% did not attempt to obtain services at all. The report also includes much more information on the DAWN Canada study and several others.

823. Rieve, J. E. (1989). Sexuality and the adult with acquired physical disability. *Nursing Clinics of North America, 24*(1), 265-276.

In this article, the role of nurses in fostering healthy sexuality in patients with acquired physical disabilities is discussed. Topics include the professional's attitudes about sexuality, assessment issues, and intervention.

824. Rindfleisch, N., & Bean, G. J. (1988). Willingness to report abuse and neglect in residential facilities. *Child Abuse & Neglect, 12*, 509-520.

This article reports the results of research that is related to the willingness of staff involved in residential care to report abuse. Situations that included potentially reportable abuse were presented to 598 respondents who were asked to indicate their willingness to report. Based on these responses, a model delineating factors that influence reporting was developed. The model accounts for about 45% of variance in willingness to report. The type of incident and the respondent's commitment to the residents were particularly powerful factors. Staff position, vignette characteristics (e.g., number of observers, child's age, child's sex), deviance or severity assessment of incident, organizational support for reporting, and the nature of the respondents' affiliation with residential care also contributed to willingness to report abuse and neglect.

825. Rindfleisch, N., & Hicho, D. (1987). Institutional child protection: Issues in program development and implementation. *Child Welfare, 66*(4), 329-342.

Forty-eight American states and the District of Columbia were surveyed regarding procedures for handling complaints of abuse and neglect of children in institutions. This article summarizes findings on statutes and policies, prevention programs, reporting, investigation, and efforts to reduce conflicts of interest. The authors suggest that a checklist could serve as a tentative framework for viewing child protection services in the different American states. Site visits to four states were conducted to verify survey information.

826. Rindfleisch, N., & Rabb, J. (1984). How much of a problem is resident mistreatment in child welfare institutions? *Child Abuse & Neglect, 8*, 33-40.

The purpose of this article is to provide information developed since 1980 by the Institutional Children Protection Project regarding the size and significance of the problem of mistreatment in child welfare residential institutions. In the 1,700 facilities surveyed, there are about 69,000 children and youths. Maltreatment in the survey meant abuse and neglect. The definition of abuse and neglect used in the survey was the respondent's own subjective view. As a result, the authors believe the data represent incidents of a generally more serious nature, but the survey does not give a breakdown of the specific type of abuse. Rates of utilization vary among Health and Human Services (H.H.S.) regions from 8 reports per 10,000 to 19 per 10,000 children and youths in the population. The average rate is 12 per 10,000. The survey also included visits to sites to confirm the results. Observations of site visitors suggest that only one out of five complainable situations may be reported to child protection agencies. A list of complainable occurrences that come to the attention of site visitors is included to document the problem. The list includes incidents of sexual abuse. The authors believe residential complaint rates may be twice as large as intrafamilial complaint rates.

827. Rinear, E. E. (1985). Sexual assault and the handicapped victim. In A. W. Burgess (Ed.), *Rape and sexual assault* (pp. 139-145). New York: Garland Publishing.

This chapter discusses the problem of sexual assault of people with handicaps. A person with handicaps is more vulnerable to sexual assault and may also face a number of additional problems. Individuals with communication disorders may have difficulty telling others what has happened to them. Individuals with emotional handicaps may find that others fail to believe that they were actually assaulted or victimized. Individuals with physical and perceptual handicaps may also be targeted as victims of sexual offenders because of their restricted abilities. People with handicaps are also limited in the type and amount of resistance that they are able to mount against their assailants. Individuals with handicaps who are dependent on others may be exploited by offenders who manipulate the victim's dependence. The article discusses the coping behaviors used by rape victims. These can be viewed as comprising three distinct phases: 1) the threat of attack, 2) the attack itself, and 3) the period immediately after the attack. The article also discusses possible methods of prevention of the victimization of people with handicaps. Possible preventative methods include self-defense classes for people with handicaps, crisis centers and support group availability, education of the public and prosecutors, and educational programs implemented in institutions.

828. Rioux, M., & Yarmol, K. (1987). The right to control one's own body: A look at "Eve" decision. *Entourage, 2*(1), 26-31.

This article describes the controversy around the Canadian 1986 Supreme Court "Eve" ruling that the courts have no power to approve sterilization for contraceptive purposes of any person who does not give her or his consent.

829. Risin, L. I., & Koss, M. P. (1987). The sexual abuse of boys: Prevalence and descriptive characteristics of childhood victimizations. *Journal of Interpersonal Violence, 2*(3), 309-323.

This article focuses on determining the frequency of childhood sexual abuse experiences among a sample of 2,972 male students in higher education in the United States. In this sample, 7.3% of the participants met at least one of the three following criteria proposed by the authors as defining sexual abuse: the abuser was a caregiver or authority figure, coercion was used, and/or there was an age discrepancy between the abuser and the child. Three levels of abuse were identified and include exhibition, fondling, and penetration. Characteristics differentiating these levels are presented.

830. Ritvo, E. R., Brothers, A. M., Freeman, B. J., & Pingree, C. (1988). Eleven possible autistic parents. *Journal of Autism & Developmental Disabilities, 18*(1), 139-143.

This article reviews data that suggest that there is a mild form of autism that is compatible in adulthood with marriage, parenting, a satisfying sex life, and gainful employment.

831. Robertson, G. (1988). A problem of sexual behaviour presenting in an adult training centre [Special issue: Giving away the behavioural approach]. *Behavioural Psychotherapy, 16*(2), 95-101.

This article describes the reduction of sexually inappropriate behavior in a 29-year-old man with mild mental retardation. The approach combined behavioral modification through the use of a token system and counseling. During a 3-year follow-up, the behavior change remained intact.

832. Robinault, I. P. (1978). *Sex, society, and the disabled: A developmental inquiry into roles, reactions, and responsibilities.* New York: Harper & Row.

A rapidly interacting and poorly understood variety of cultural forces have concurrently produced a sexual revolution that expresses itself haphazardly in literature, in the entertainment media, and in some overt behavior of youths and adults. It is the premise of this book that a developmental perspective, discussed in easily understood terms, may prove to be a connecting thread though this confusion. Therefore, the sexuality of individuals with chronic disability (congenital or acquired) is presented in the sequence of the life cycle from infancy through older ages. The challenges at each stage are pointed out from the perspective of how individuals and their advocates in the helping professions balance innate and acquired capabilities, realistic, interpersonal experiences, confusing social cues, and the limitations of present-day knowledge and technologies. Samples are chosen from real life experience and research reports to illustrate, at each stage, what people with disabilities share with their able-bodied contemporaries, where adjustments have to be considered, and what realistic options exist. The book's purpose is to stimulate productive inquiry among professionals who concern themselves with the sexuality of people with disabilities and to relate existing professional resources to the needs of people with disabilities. A comprehensive bibliography on the sexuality of people with disabilities is also included.

833. Robinson, L. D. (1979). Sexuality and the deaf culture. *Sexuality and Disability, 2*(3), 161-168.
This article discusses the psychosexual development of people who are deaf. The author discusses the results of a questionnaire administered to professionals in 1976 regarding sexual issues and people who are deaf. The findings suggest the following: People who are deaf have the same kinds of sexual behaviors and problems as hearing people, but they do not have the same resources for addressing their sexuality. The need for training professionals is discussed.

834. Robinson, S. (1984). Effects of a sex education program on intellectually handicapped adults. *Australia and New Zealand Journal of Developmental Disabilities, 10*(1), 21-26.
This article discusses the effect of a 10-week sex education program on the socio-sexual knowledge and attitudes of 41 subjects with mild intellectual handicaps (16.5-52 years old) (Raven Standard Progressive Matrices IQ 50-80). The program included anatomy of sexual organs, typical sexual development (male and female), varieties of sexual behavior, conception, gestation and birth, contraception and venereal disease, interpersonal relationships, sexual values and decision-making, and relationships between self-concept and sexuality. The findings of this study indicate that community-based subjects knew more initially than did institutionalized subjects and that all subjects showed improved knowledge and attitude scores after participating in the program.

835. Rockney, R. M., Fritz, G. F., & Caldamone, A. (1989). Enuresis following masturbation in a mentally retarded adolescent. *Journal of Adolescent Health Care, 10*(2), 165-167.
These authors discuss a multidisciplinary approach to the problem of enuresis following masturbation in an adolescent with mental retardation. The approach resulted in the identification of the circumstances of the symptom and its successful treatment.

836. *Roettger v. United Hospitals of St. Paul,* 380 N.W.2d. 856 (Minn. App. 1986).
A female patient in the hospital suffered serious physical and emotional harm as a result of an assault by a trespasser. The hospital was held negligent because they did not provide a reasonable level of security to prevent such attacks.

837. Rogers, R. G. (1990). *Reaching for solutions: The report of the Special Advisor to the Minister of National Health and Welfare on Child Sexual Abuse in Canada.* Ottawa: Health and Welfare Canada, National Clearinghouse on Family Violence. (Department of Supply and Services Catalogue No. H.74-28/1990E)
This author offers recommendations for reaching solutions for child sexual abuse in Canada: A Children's Bureau should be established within Health and Welfare Canada with a mandate for a broad range of children's interests, including combatting child abuse, day care concerns, and many other functions; a National Resource Centre on Child Abuse should be established within the Children's Bureau; five to seven Regional Resource Centres for the Prevention of Child Abuse should be established across Canada; each province should develop an interministerial mechanism to coordinate efforts of various Provincial Departments relevant to child abuse; the Canadian Medical Association should assume an increased role in prevention, detection, and treatment of child abuse; each local community should develop interdisciplinary and interjurisdictional protocols for prevention and treatment; each province should develop and maintain a mechanism for monitoring child protection and other relevant services; appropriate audiovisual materials should be developed or obtained and distributed to increase public awareness; federal and provincial governments should continue to support public education as community-based primary prevention; the Minister of Justice should review legislation that will address the protection of children from the harmful effects of pornography; the Canadian Radio and Television Commission should assume a more active role in regulating the amount of violence and sexually exploitive material broadcast; all relevant professional associations should develop policies related to the role of their members in prevention, detection, and treatment; all organizations (including churches) and agencies within Canada should further develop their efforts to prevent child abuse within their agencies; policies should set out guidelines on selection, screening, and training of leaders and staff as well as investigation and reporting of any reports of abuse; each law enforcement jurisdiction should develop a clear policy for charging and prosecuting offenders; local protocols should not delay treatment of the offender pending resolution of criminal proceedings.

All police officers should receive multidisciplinary training; the federal government should fund and assess model programs and collect and disseminate information; the federal Department of Justice should monitor and defend Bill C-15; further reforms should be made to the legislation governing child sexual abuse prosecutions in order to permit qualified experts to testify on the reliability of testimony, to permit witnesses to testify about out of court statements made by a child, to permit judges to require accused individuals to vacate the premises as a condition of bail, to permit an adult to accompany a child in the witness stand, and to permit the use of videotaped statements by any child witness in a child abuse prosecution; the appointment of counsel to protect the needs of child victim witnesses should be considered; provincial governments should take steps to effectively implement the provisions of Bill C-15; those responsible should ensure that policies on expert witnesses show sensitivity to the needs of those professionals; scheduling priority should be given to child sexual abuse cases; a commission should be developed to study the development of architectural designs for courthouses sensitive to the needs of children and other vulnerable witnesses.

The national Judicial Education Centre and provincial organizations should ensure that education programs include child sexual abuse and capabilities of child witnesses; a model ethics code should be developed for dealing with children and other vulnerable witnesses; victim impact statements and information about the long-term effects of child sexual abuse should be imparted to sentencing judges and included as part of judicial education programs; departments of corrections should make treatment available to convicted child abusers; federal legislation should be amended to allow judges to order treatment services to be made available; post-charge programs for offenders should be established on an experimental basis and carefully evaluated; the criminal code should be revised to allow extended probation (up to life terms) for those convicted of child sexual offenses; parole legislation should be amended to allow longer periods of supervision; provincial and territorial governments should amend legislation to facilitate evidence given by children in civil cases at least to the extent currently provided under Bill C-15; police and child protection investigators should have special training in the dynamics of abuse allegations in the context of parental custody disputes; provincial and territorial legislation should be amended to permit civil damages to adult survivors of child sexual abuse.

Criminal Injury Compensation Boards should develop legislation and policy that supports compensation of victims of sexual abuse; compensation as restitution should be considered as part of the offender's sentence; Health and Welfare Canada should support programs that assist voluntary organizations in reducing the risk for abuse, including guidelines for supervision and screening of volunteers, and that all such agencies should have clear policies and procedures regarding the prevention, detection, and reporting of abuse; federal and provincial government agencies should ensure that policy and procedure make possible the release of records of criminal offenses of individuals applying for and

working in paid or voluntary positions with children; government and private agencies should develop and implement appropriate staff screening procedures; provincial and territorial governments should establish mechanisms for identifying and registering abusers; addressing the needs of adult survivors of sexual abuse should be an important priority for provinces and territories; provincial and territorial governments should address the current gaps in services; federal, provincial, and territorial governments should study the special needs of rural and isolated communities and develop initiatives for meeting those needs; nonoffending members of families should be considered and included in treating victims; the federal government should fund research and evaluation of treatment for victims, families, and offenders; the Expert Advisory Committee on Healing and Treatment should develop a long-range plan for effective offender treatment; in order to ensure that frontline specialists are available, the Canadian Association of Chiefs of Police and the Royal Canadian Mounted Police (RCMP) should review policy and practice related to investigation and the expertise and resources needed to support policies.

The Canadian Police College should require senior police officials to take an orientation program on child abuse; Canadian law schools should ensure that all students acquire a basic understanding of family violence and child sexual abuse and that interested students should have the opportunity to take more advanced classes; provincial Attorney Generals should offer a week-long training program for Crown Attorneys on child victim witness preparation and related matters; probation and parole officers should receive specialized training in child sexual abuse; Health and Welfare Canada should ensure that appropriate training regarding identification and treatment of victims is available and encouraged; professional schools and colleges should ensure that those who work with children can recognize child sexual abuse and respond appropriately; federally funded projects in child abuse should include research and evaluation components; Health and Welfare Canada should maintain an ongoing dialogue with scholars, researchers, clinicians, and other stakeholders; the proposed Children's Bureau of Health and Welfare Canada should develop common definitions so that a national statistical database can be established; the federal government should establish an Aboriginal Expert Advisory Committee; the proposed Children's Bureau of Health and Welfare Canada should establish a special task force to examine the issues of child abuse for very young children, children in institutional settings, children with disabilities and disturbances, and new Canadians; the proposed Children's Bureau of Health and Welfare Canada should establish a special task force to examine the issues of child abuse in rural and remote settings; and the federal government should publish an annual report that describes progress in combatting child abuse. (Note: During the Fall of 1990, Canada's Prime Minister, Brian Mulroney, announced the establishment of a Children's Bureau during United Nations meetings on the rights of children.)

838. Rose, E., & Hardman, M. L. (1981). **The abused mentally retarded child.** *Education and Training of the Mentally Retarded Child, 16*(2), 114-118.

These authors review research in the area of child abuse and mental handicaps. The literature reveals a higher incidence of mental handicaps in children who have been abused, the handicaps being a result of abuse or neglect. The authors point out that a problem with interpreting the research is that definitions of mental retardation and child abuse are not standardized across studies. A discussion of ways of breaking the abused child-abusing parent cycle and treatment is included.

839. Rotegard, L. L., Hill, B. K., & Lakin, K. C. (1983). **Sex as a bona fide occupational qualification for direct care staff in residences for mentally retarded people.** *Mental Retardation, 21*(4), 150-152.

This article discusses Title VII of the American Civil Rights Act of 1964 that strictly prohibits sex discrimination in employment. Many courts have ruled that the need for privacy from observation by members of the opposite sex during the care of intimate bodily functions constitutes a legitimate limitation on the original position.

840. Rousso, M. (1982). **Special considerations in counseling clients with cerebral palsy.** *Sexuality and Disability, 5*(2), 78-88.

Addressed to clinicians, this article discusses the social and sexual issues faced by people with cerebral palsy. Topics include people with disabilities, the asexual role, the demystification of sexuality, the development of a positive body image, mastering essential social skills, understanding sexual functioning, and the effect of the clinician's attitudes and stereotypes. Much of the article can be generalized to include people with other types of disabilities.

841. Rousso, M. (1986). **Positive female images at last!** *Exceptional Parent, 16*(2), 10-12,14.

This article discusses the Networking Project for Disabled Women and Girls. The aim of the project is to provide role models of successful women with disabilities in the community for adolescent girls. Promoting healthy sexuality is one aspect of the project.

842. Rowe, W. S., & Savage, S. (1987). *Sexuality and the developmentally handicapped: A guidebook for health care professionals.* **Queenston, Ontario: The Edwin Mellen Press.**

This volume provides a substantial review of the literature as well as useful information and interesting recommendations and suggestions for health care and other professionals working with people with developmental handicaps. Chapter topics include human sexuality, knowledge (i.e., background information), attitudes, skills for professionals, policy and law (United States and Canadian), masturbation, homosexuality, assaultive and offensive sexual behavior, and

sexual variations. There is much helpful resource and reference information. Much more emphasis is placed on the role of people with disabilities as offenders than as victims of sexual assault, but the general information is very useful.

843. Rowe, W., Savage, S., & Dennis-Delaney, J. (1987, September). *The effects of training in human sexuality for individuals working with developmentally disabled persons.* **Paper presented at the annual meeting of the American Association of Mental Deficiency, Region IV, Edmonton, Alberta.**

A study was conducted to explore: a) whether a course in human sexuality and developmental disabilities results in more accepting attitudes toward the sexuality of people with developmental disabilities, and b) whether the course participants would have greater skills in dealing with sexual issues in counseling. The participants attended a 2 1/2 day workshop that focused on three aspects of clinical training in human sexuality knowledge, attitudes, and skill. Results show that the training positively influenced participants' attitudes toward sexuality and people with developmental disabilities but that skill development did not significantly improve after training. It is suggested that skill development may require ongoing consultation and training.

844 Rowitz, L. (1988). **The forgotten ones: Adolescence and mental retardation.** *Mental Retardation, 26*(3), 115-117.

This article examines the need for more research on the biological and social developmental problems faced by adolescents with mental retardation. Issues discussed include social stigma and self-concept, conflicts with parents, teenage pregnancy, substance abuse, health care, and sex education.

845. Rowitz, L. (Ed.). (1989). **Developmental disabilities and HIV Infection: A symposium on issues and public policy** [Special issue]. *Mental Retardation, 27*, 197-262.

This issue of *Mental Retardation* is devoted to the growing concern regarding HIV infections of people with developmental disabilities. HIV infections that have been acquired prenatally are emerging as a major infectious cause of intellectual impairment. Acquired immuno deficiency syndrome (AIDS) is also a concern for children and young adults with developmental disabilities. This issue contains a number of articles on related issues of incidence, clinical course, precautions against transmission, preventive education, and several other topics.

846. Rozovsky, L. E., & Rozovsky, F. A. (1990). **Mental health: Rights of property and person.** In CCH Canadian Limited (Ed.), *Canadian health facilities law guide* (pp. 6071-6074). **Don Mills, Ontario: CCH Canadian Limited.**

Codified rights of patients in mental health facilities

generally include the right not to be detained without consent or cause. Additional rights sometimes include the right to be informed of one's rights and the right to communicate with others.

847. **Rozovsky, L. E., & Rozovsky, F. A. (1990). Patients' rights. In CCH Canadian Limited (Ed.),** *Canadian health facilities law guide* **(pp. 4001-4016). Don Mills, Ontario: CCH Canadian Limited.**
This article discusses patient's bills of rights. Generally, they do not carry force of law and are viewed as philosophy statements since they are often too vague to be enforceable and lack enforcement provisions. The authors advise the following: If facilities adopt a bill of rights as standards of care, these may become a basis for litigation; but if the bill of rights is adopted as philosophy, it is unlikely to serve as a basis for litigation.

848. **Ruff, K. (1986). Hospital Riviere-des-Prairies: Not a place to call home.** *Entourage, 1*(1), 6-13.
This article describes a controversial Quebec hospital for children with psychiatric disabilities and catalogs the abuses and neglect suffered by the in-patients and the struggle to change conditions. The author also discusses the effects of the conflict on a parent advocacy group, professional authorities, and the government of Quebec.

849. **Rusch, R. G., Hall, J. C., & Griffin, H. C. (1986). Abuse-provoking characteristics of institutionalized mentally retarded individuals.** *American Journal of Mental Deficiency, 90*(6), 618-624.
This article examines the abuse-provoking characteristics of institutionalized individuals with mental retardation. It discusses possible explanations for higher rates of abuse directed against certain types of patients and suggests recommendations for reducing abuse of patients with mental retardation through improved staff training, reconsideration of the practice of grouping aggressive residents together, and the provision of incentives to staff members working with aggressive clients.

850. **Rutledge, H., & Haines, A. (1983). Law and the intellectually disabled defendant.** *Australia and New Zealand Journal of Developmental Disabilities, 9*(1), 23-29.
This article investigates the problems encountered by the defendant with intellectual disabilities when dealing with the legal system, and it discusses the issues of competence and admissibility. The authors propose a model to correct some of the problems, and they stress the importance of educating the community, especially the legal system, about people with intellectual disabilities and of educating people with disabilities about the law.

851. *R. v. Ogg-Moss* **(1984), 54 N. R. 81.**
A counselor for people with mental retardation struck an adult with mental handicaps under his supervision five times in the forehead with a large metal spoon. When charged with assault, he attempted to use the defense of §43 of the Criminal Code of Canada: "Every schoolteacher, parent or person standing in the place of a parent is justified in using force by way of correction toward a pupil or child as the case may be who is under his care, if the force does not exceed what is reasonable under the circumstances." The counselor was originally acquitted on the basis of this defense, but he was later convicted by the Ontario Court of Appeal since the victim was not a child and the individual committing the assault was not a parent, school teacher, or person serving in place of a parent. This appeal to the Supreme Court was made on the same basis as the original defense, but the court ruled that §43 was not applicable and upheld the conviction for assault.

852. **Ryerson, E. (1981). Sexual abuse of disabled persons and prevention alternatives. In D. G. Bullard & S. E. Knight (Eds.),** *Sexuality and physical disability: Personal perspectives* **(pp. 235-242). St. Louis: C.V. Mosby.**
This chapter was instrumental in raising the public awareness about the nature and extent of the problem of sexual abuse of people with disabilities. It also describes the Seattle Rape Relief Crisis Center's work with people with disabilities. This program was one of the first to attempt to recognize and meet the unique challenges of this group and has become a model for programs internationally.

853. **Ryerson, E. (1984). Sexual abuse and self-protection education for developmentally disabled youth: A priority need.** *SIECUS Report, 13*(1), 1-3.
This author states that the reporting rate of sexual abuse among people with developmental disabilities is lower than that of the general population. The explanation given is that 99% of the abusers are relatives or care workers, and therefore, the victim is either unaware that he or she is being exploited or is very confused about the sexual activity and the intent of the offender. The offender often leads the victim to believe that theirs is a "special" relationship or convinces the victim to keep the activity a secret. The Developmental Disabilities Project's curriculum for preventing sexual exploitation is available to schools, but due to economic issues and the sensitivity of the subject matter, it is not being used by many schools. The author stresses that self-protection education is of critical importance and should be a priority, overriding economic concerns and embarrassment.

854. **Ryerson, E., & Sundem, J. M. (1981). Development of a curriculum on sexual exploitation and self-protection for handicapped students.** *Education Unlimited, 3*(4), 26-31.
Given the overwhelming statistics concerning the psychological as well as the physical consequences for victims, the national trend toward greater independence

for individuals with handicaps, the lack of programs designed to assist people with handicaps to prevent sexual exploitation, and the need for such material expressed by special educators, The Curriculum for Developing an Awareness of Sexual Exploitation and Teaching Self-Protection Techniques was developed by the Seattle Rape Relief Developmental Disabilities Project. This article explains the curriculum. It was tested by thirteen teachers who taught this pilot curriculum and completed as part of the pilot program test a Field Test Questionnaire on each lesson they completed. The suggestions from these questionnaires were that students needed some basic background prior to being taught the program and the teachers needed support from parents, school district administration, and additional personnel in order for the program to work. Information was also collected regarding critical incidents that may have occurred since the beginning of the curriculum in February, 1980.

•S•

855. Sanders, G. L. (1984). Relationships of the handicapped: Issues of sexuality and marriage. *Family Therapy Collections, 11,* 63-74.
This article describes a treatment model for therapists and counselors working with sexual and/or marital issues in couples in which one or both partners has a handicap. The model emphasizes a hierarchy of interventions: permission, limited information, specific suggestion, and intensive therapy. The author also discusses three useful basic assumptions: symptoms can have multiple messages and meanings; the same depth of treatment is not required to treat all problems; and the goal of therapy is to provide clients with the opportunity to expand their options as they wish. Clinical assessment is also addressed.

856. Sanders, G. L. (1984). Relationships of the handicapped: Issues of sex and marriage. In E. I. Coppersmith (Ed.), *Families with handicapped members* (pp. 63-64). Rockville, MD: Aspen Systems.
Following a general discussion of evaluation and treatment issues, this article presents Annon's PLISSIT model as applied to people with physical handicaps. The model allows for the organization of a hierarchy of therapeutic intervention needs. An illustrative case study is discussed in which one partner has multiple sclerosis.

857. Sandgrund, A., Gaines, R. W., & Green, A. H. (1974). Child abuse and mental retardation: A
problem of cause and effect. *American Journal of Mental Deficiency, 79*(3), 327-330.
This article reports on a study of abused children using control groups that was undertaken in order to determine the psychological effects of abuse on the victim. Sixty abused and 60 nonabused children were interviewed and tested by a psychiatrist and a psychologist. The results indicate that 25% of the abused sample, 20% of the neglected sample, and 3% of the nonabused sample have intellectual retardation. The authors conclude that the cause-effect relationship between retardation and abuse cannot be determined from their study.

858. Santamour, M., & West, B. (1977). *The mentally retarded offender and corrections.* Washington, DC: National Institute of Law Enforcement and Criminal Justice, Law Enforcement Assistance Administration, U. S. Department of Justice.
This 55-page monograph contains a great deal of information regarding offenders with intellectual impairment who are incarcerated in prison. It includes a review of studies on the representation of people with intellectual impairment in the prison population, a discussion of legal issues, and suggestions for treatment. The authors recommend that sex education and appropriate social-sexual behavior be included among rehabilitation training components.

859. Sarkadi, L. (1990, February 14). Psychiatrist accused of sexual harassment. *Edmonton Journal,* p. A3.
This article describes the case of a psychiatrist who voluntarily resigned from Alberta Hospital (a psychiatric facility) and relinquished his standing with the Alberta College of Physicians and Surgeons after coming under investigation for professional misconduct. He subsequently moved to Yellowknife in the Northwest Territories, and at the time of the writing of the article, he was involved in a court battle to stop the Stanton Yellowknife Hospital Board from suspending his hospital privileges after being accused by female patients of sexual harassment and misconduct.

860. Saunders, S., Anderson, A. M., Hart, C. A., & Rubenstein, G. M. (1984). *Violent individuals and families: A handbook for practitioners.* Springfield, IL: Charles C Thomas.
This article examines the developmental and family origins of violence and vengeance as well as guidelines for treatment, including the limitation of catharsis and the expression of hostility. While the article does not focus on people with disabilities, the behavioral treatment of aggression in institutions for people with mental retardation or who are emotionally disturbed is discussed. Drug intervention and staff training procedures are examined.

861. Savells, J. (1983). Child abuse in residential institutions and community programs for

intervention and prevention. *Child Abuse & Neglect, 7*(4), 473-475.

In this article, specific problems areas are identified in regard to the approach taken by residential care facilities toward child care. Examples include the alienation of community officials, staff shortages, overcrowding leading to abuse or objectionable means of control, the repression of spontaneity, and few alternatives to institutionalization. Possible solutions are discussed (e.g., change in priorities, community involvement).

862. Schaefer, G. (1987, July 5). Molester "sorry." *The Province*. (Vancouver, British Columbia)

This newspaper article is a report of a sentencing hearing of a 53-year old former Surrey, British Columbia school trustee who had pleaded guilty to 10 counts of molesting eight foster-children. The man now states that he is sorry for his actions. Some of his victims were children with mental retardation placed in his care by the British Columbia government. (Note: Foster care placements have frequently been identified as settings in which abuse takes place. However, little information is available that allows valid comparison of this risk to risks associated with natural homes or other residential alternatives.)

863. Scharfetter, C. (1984). Ein Anliegen der Menschheitserziehung: Delegierte Destruktivatat [An objective of education of mankind: Delegated destructiveness]. *Schweizer Archiv fur Neurologie, Neurochirurgie und et Psychiatrie, 134*(2), 279-293.

This article, which is in German only, discusses the extermination of 100,000 mental hospital in-patients and 5,000 children with mental retardation in Nazi Germany under the Hitler regime between 1939 and 1941. It traces the ideological precursors of these actions and describes the ethological and anthropological aspects of inner-species destruction in human phylogenesis. It examines the psychological and social conditions of social destructiveness under normal and exceptional conditions and discusses the consequences for education.

864. Schetky, D. H. (1988). The child as witness. In D. H. Schetky & A. H. Green (Eds.), *Child sexual abuse: A handbook for health care professionals* (pp. 166-180). New York: Brunner/ Mazel.

This chapter discusses issues and practices related to the role of sexually abused children appearing as witnesses in court. There is a brief discussion of the legal history of children as witnesses in the United States, a discussion of the evaluation of competency (including the consideration of "mental disease or defect"), a discussion of consideration of whether it is in the child's interest to testify, and a number of recommended changes in the relationship between the child-witness and the legal system. Most of the discussion is relevant to all children, including those with disabilities. The application of some of the principles to some adults

with developmental disabilities might be useful if care is taken to recognize the distinct needs of this group and the individual needs of its members.

865. Schetky, D. H., & Green, D. H. (1988). *Child sexual abuse: A handbook for health care professionals*. New York: Brunner/ Mazel.

This 248-page book provides useful information on a number of topics related to child sexual abuse. Chapters on special issues in child sexual abuse and the child as witness may be of particular relevance to people working with victims of abuse with disabilities. An appendix lists a number of generic training materials for prevention and professional development along with addresses for distributors.

866. Schilit, J. (1979). The retarded offender and criminal justice personnel. *Exceptional Children, 46*, 16-22.

This article discusses people with mental handicaps who are accused of a crime. One of the findings, however, is also important for victims with disabilities. Schilit found that 90% of police officers, judges, and lawyers involved in criminal cases had no training or expertise in mental retardation.

867. Schilling, R. F., Kirkham, M. A., & Schinke, S. P. (1985). *Coping, social support, and the prevention of maltreatment of handicapped children: Final report*. Seattle: Washington University, Child Development and Mental Retardation Center.

This study compares nonabusing families with low-income and single-parent families. All families in the study had a child with a handicap or developmental disability. Questionnaire and interview data were collected. The authors found that socio-economic status differentiated families on measures of stress, that the child's specific disability and level of functioning were not predictive of parent's coping style or appraisal of stress, and that, in general, no relationship existed between marital status, age of the parent or the child, and stress, coping, or social support. For both groups, economic worries were general in nature and did not revolve around the child with a disability. However, parents with more effective personal coping responses reported greater use of social supports. Also, compared to mothers, fathers showed less optimism about the future, used a narrower range of coping devices, and had fewer social supports.

868. Schilling, R. F., Kirkham, M. A., & Schinke, S. P. (1986). Do child protection services neglect developmentally disabled children? *Education and Training of the Mentally Retarded, 21*, 21-26.

These authors consider the relationship between child protection services and children with developmental disabilities. In spite of data suggesting that children with developmental disabilities are more likely to be abused, they are underrepresented in the caseloads of child protection workers. The authors point out that child protection agencies may consider children with handicaps to be outside their mandate and assume they are served by other agencies. In their survey of Child Protection Service workers, the authors found that although 82% believed that developmental disability increased risk of abuse 84% had never served a client with developmental disability (12% had only served one, and 4% had only served two).

869. **Schilling, R. F., Kirkham, M. A., Snow, W. H., & Schinke, S. P. (1986). Single mothers with handicapped children: Different from their married counterparts? [Special issue: The single parent family].** *Family Relations Journal of Applied Family and Child Studies, 35*(1), 69-77.

Thirty-three single and forty-eight married mothers of children with handicaps responded to questionnaires measuring stress, life satisfaction, and perceptions of their child. Findings are discussed in terms of economic and social supports, intervention, and the contribution of the father to child-rearing. Most differences between the two groups were in relation to family life in general and not in relation to parenting a child with a handicap.

870. **Schilling, R. F., & Schinke, S. P. (1984). Maltreatment and mental retardation. In J. M. Berg & J. M. de Jong (Eds.),** *Perspectives and progress in mental retardation: Social, psychological, and educational aspects* (Vol. 1, pp. 11-22). **Baltimore: University Park Press.**

These authors state that children with mental retardation are at greater risk for abuse and neglect since ordinary care standards are inadequate for this group. Children with mental retardation may have unique requirements for feeding, clothing, prosthetics, and attention to safety. There is also a higher risk of emotional neglect by parents who are unable to accept their child's limitations. Some children with mental retardation have behavioral characteristics, such as tantrums, aggressiveness, and noncompliance, that negatively affect the parents. In general, the physical, emotional, and financial burden of raising a child with a handicap causes family stress and increases the risk of abuse. In regard to intervention, parents can be taught coping skills and how to enhance their social supports. The authors conducted pilot studies of group training for families. The results show more self-control, calmness, positive self-talk, and self-praise among the participants. In their discussion of people with mental retardation in the community, the authors state that as people with mental retardation gain greater freedom they will be at greater risk for exploitation since their relative dependency puts them in a vulnerable position. People with mental handicaps may have difficulty grasping community standards of sexuality (e.g., conversation, touching, and public masturbation) and therefore may find themselves in exploitive situations. Prevention of sexual abuse includes training in appropriate sexual behavior, meaning both rights and responsibilities.

871. **Schilling, R. F., & Schinke, S. P. (1984). Personal coping and social support for parents of handicapped children.** *Children and Youth Services Review, 6*(3), 195-206.

This article discusses the stress in families with children with developmental disabilities and the daily coping strategies of parents of children with special needs. It presents an overview of existing research and suggests a prescription for future research on parental stress, personal coping styles, and social support for families.

872. **Schilling, R. F., Schinke, S. P., Blythe, B. J., & Barth, R. P. (1982). Child maltreatment and mentally retarded parents: Is there a relationship?** *Mental Retardation, 20*(5), 201-209.

This article reviews the child protection and mental retardation literature and suggests a relationship between parents' intelligence and maltreatment of children. It discusses the findings and deficiencies in studies of parents with mental retardation and maltreating parents and suggests further research examining the relationship between parents with mental retardation and child maltreatment, how parents with mental retardation care for children, and approaches to helping such parents.

873. **Schilling, R. F., Schinke, S. P., & Kirkham, M. A. (1985). Coping with a handicapped child: Differences between mothers and fathers.** *Social Science and Medicine, 21*(8), 857-863.

In this article, research on the differences in coping styles between mothers and fathers of children with developmental disabilities is reviewed. Mothers were found to turn to both internal and external coping sources. Fathers relied primarily on internal means of coping. Gender-related coping differences may function in a complementary or a conflicting manner in the family where there is a child with a handicap.

874. **Schinke, S. P., Blythe, B. J., Schilling, R. F., & Barth, R. (1981). Neglect of mentally retarded persons.** *Education and Training of the Mentally Retarded, 16*(4), 299-303.

This paper addresses the need for professionals working with people with mental retardation to address these people's emotional needs. In an effort to facilitate data collection in treatment environments, the authors present a framework for defining the physical and emotional neglect of people with handicaps. Primary caregivers should have social, educational, and health services made available to them in order to remediate and prevent neglect. Early assessment and intervention are presented as being critical in upgrading the skills of parents, siblings, group home staff, and institutional attendants. The natural environment is seen as the preferred teaching environment for instructing caregivers, and relying completely upon lecture-style professional education sessions is seen as a weaker approach. Human service workers must redefine neglect in relation to their target population. In the case of mental retardation, workers must regularly re-evaluate rehabilitation programs.

875. **Schinke, S. P., & Schilling, R. F. (1987).** *Developmental neglect: Testing a social support intervention.* **Seattle: Washington University, School of Social Work, National Center on Child Abuse and Neglect.**

The aim of this study was to test the efficiency of social support enhancement groups for parents of neglected children who have handicaps. The study used a generalized, randomized block design. Participants were blocked on professional assessment of the child's developmental status and randomly assigned to one of three conditions: social support groups, social support groups with boosters, or a control condition. In the control condition, participants received standard professionally accepted interventions from community agencies. Data were collected using questionnaires completed by all parents. The developmental status of the children involved was assessed by teachers and specialists. The design included pre-test, post-test, and 6-month follow-up data. The follow-up data were collected using an additional set of batteries and inventories. Outcome analyses examined contributing and dependent variables. Follow-up data were analyzed with repeated measures analysis of variance.

876. **Schinke, S. P., Schilling, R. F., Kirkham, M. A., Gilchrist, L. D., Barth, R. P., & Blythe, B. J. (1986). Stress management skills for parents.** *Journal of Child and Adolescent Psychotherapy, 3*(4), 293-298.

This article evaluates a stress management skills intervention program conducted with 13 mothers and 10 fathers (mean age 30.21 years) of children with developmental disabilities (mean age 3.69 years). This program used group training to increase the parents' self-control, interpersonal communication, and child discipline skills and to expand their social support networks. A post-test and a 6-month follow-up revealed that parents who had participated in the intervention program had better attitudes toward their children, improved ability to manage anger and cope with stress, and more positive observed interactions with a misbehaving child when compared to parents in a no-intervention control group.

877. **Schirmer, B. R. (1986, April).** *Child abuse and neglect: Prevalence, programs and prevention with the hearing impaired.* **Paper presented at the 70th Annual Meeting of the American Educational Research Association, San Francisco, CA. (ERIC Document Reproduction Service No. ED 270 954)**

This document reviews literature related to abuse and neglect of children who are hearing impaired and the services available to them. Findings indicate that while children with preexisting handicapping conditions seem to be at higher risk for child abuse and neglect, no particular group of children with handicaps was found

to be more at risk than others. The author suggests, however, that the communication deficits of children with hearing impairments may increase the child's vulnerability to be abused and neglected. Effective prevention program components identified include parent education, parent support groups, and periodic respite care. A nationwide survey of the United States did not uncover any existing prevention programs for this group.

878. **Schlesinger, B. (Ed.). (1986).** *Sexual abuse of children in the 1980s: An annotated bibliography.* **Toronto: University of Toronto Press.**

This book contains 10 essays on different aspects of child sexual abuse as well as an annotated bibliography of 310 articles dated from 1980-1985. The annotated bibliography is divided into different subject areas. One of the subject areas is titled "Mentally Retarded and Sexual Abuse," and it contains one reference.

879. **Schmideberg, M. (1980). Criminals and their victims.** *International Journal of Offender Therapy and Comparative Criminology, 24*(2), 128-133.

This article discusses the social, situational, and physical factors of crime victimization. Common everyday offenses largely affect people who are poor and people with handicaps. Victimization engenders acceptance of exploitation, low self-image, and fear. Violence in the family is discussed in terms of early victimization, the inability to find escape routes, and misplaced loyalty.

880. **Scholz, J. P., & Meier, J. H. (1983). Competency of abused children in a residential treatment program. In J. E. Leavitt (Ed.),** *Child abuse and neglect: Research and innovation* **(NATO Advanced Sciences Series, pp. 211-234). The Hague, Netherlands: Nijhoff.**

This study and review found that more than half of the child abuse victims tested suffered significant developmental delays.

881. **School for the disabled loses federal support. (1989, March).** *Washington Coalition of Sexual Assault Programs Newsletter,* **pp. 1-2.**

This article discusses the withdrawal of federal aid from Fircrest, an institution for 500 people with developmental disabilities in the state of Washington, over concerns of negligence, physical abuse, and sexual assault of residents of the institution. Sexual assaults reported at Fircrest were committed by residents against residents, but the lack of protection provided became a central issue in the loss of funding.

882. **Schopler, E. (1986). Treatment abuse and its reduction.** *Journal of Autism and Developmental Disorders, 16*(2), 99-104.

This article discusses ways in which oversimplification

leads to confusion between the merit of a therapeutic technique for the treatment of children with handicaps and factors affecting the vulnerability of parents to unsubstantiated claims for cure or relief. It notes the following: For cases of crisis with incompletely understood illness or behavior, certain experimental therapy techniques that are easily abused may offer the best intervention. The author suggests that the risks of abuse can be significantly reduced by early intervention and family support, examining other treatment options, and improving legislative protection against abuse and malpractice.

883. Schor, D. P. (1987). Sex and sexual abuse of developmentally disabled adolescents. *Seminars in Adolescent Medicine, 3*(1), 1-7.
This author discusses aspects of sexuality and sexual abuse of adolescents who are developmentally disabled. These adolescents have difficulty achieving maturation and independence, partly due to being dependent on others for physical care. As well, caregivers and school personnel may be overprotective and inhibit these children's learning of self-care and social skills. The author uses Finkelhor's (1984) Four Preconditions of Sexual Abuse model to explain the victimization of adolescents with handicaps. The model suggests the presence within the potential offender of a motivation to sexually abuse a child which acts to overcome internal and external inhibitions against acting on this motivation as well as helping to overcome the child's resistance. In applying the model, the author points to motivational factors of the perpetrator, such as attraction to the child-like behavior of certain adolescents with mental retardation and satisfaction in engaging in an adult relationship without an adult emotional interaction. It may be easier for the perpetrator to overcome internal (societal) inhibitions to abuse in a society that devalues people with mental handicaps. Since people with mental handicaps are often stereotyped as having abnormal sex drives, prohibitions may be further weakened. Overcoming external (situational) inhibitions may be easier because adolescents with mental handicaps have fewer situational safeguards to protect them from sexual exploitation. These adolescents lead more isolated lives and are often cared for by surrogates who can restrict access to outsiders. Typically, the child is unaware of how to obtain help if a problem arises. Characteristics of people with mental handicaps can contribute to the perpetrator overcoming the child's resistance. They are often more easily led and have a greater need to please others. Often, they are lacking attention and affection. They may have no sex education. In addition, they may face being disbelieved or may lack communication skills to report abuse. The author discusses prevention, noting that programs to prevent sexual abuse of adolescents with developmental disabilities are rare. However, information on this group is readily available for caregivers. There has also been an increased awareness of stresses placed on families with children with disabilities, and many physicians recognize that some children are at greater risk for abuse due

to their individual behavior. Activities or programs to assist in attaining independence and social competency can reduce vulnerability. Sex education, including abuse prevention, can serve to protect many adolescents with developmental disabilities.

884. Schor, D. P., & Holmes, C. S. (1983). Partial recovery from severe child neglect and abuse. *Journal of Developmental and Behavioral Pediatrics, 4*(1), 70-74.
This article describes the case of a 3-year-old boy and his 9-month-old sister in order to illustrate partial recovery from severe child neglect and abuse. After spending 5 months together in a foster care setting, significant impairments in growth, cognition, adaptive skills, and language noted in the children during the initial assessment were not as severe at follow-up.

885. Schover, L. R., & Jensen, S. B. (1988). *Sexuality and chronic illness: A comprehensive approach.* **New York: Guilford Press.**
This book provides information on a wide range of chronic illnesses and their relationship to sexuality. It stresses the need for all members of the health care team to understand and address sexuality issues. There is a brief section on "Prevention of sexual abuse by clinicians" that points out that patient-therapist sexual contact is a frequent occurrence, that they often result in significant harm to the patient, and that these contacts have been clearly designated as unethical by some major professional associations. The authors point out that sexual exploitation by technicians and caregivers in institutions is reported to be even more common than sexual exploitation by health care professionals. They recommend that training programs address sexuality and abuse prevention. In a second brief section, "Coping with the seductive or acting-out patient," the authors suggest some guidelines for therapists.

886. Schover, L. R., & von Eschenbach, A. C. (1985). Sex therapy and the penile prosthesis: A synthesis. *Journal of Sex and Marital Therapy, 11*(1), 57-66.
This article addresses the need for urologists and sex therapists to coordinate their efforts in the establishment of a comprehensive treatment plan for candidates requiring a penile prosthesis. A model for the use of sex therapy techniques in the evaluation and treatment of candidates seeking penile prostheses is described. Components include preoperative assessment regarding sexual repercussions, offering presurgical sex therapy to men at high risk for a negative diagnosis following surgery, the use of follow-up visits during post-operative recovery and again at 2 to 3 months following surgery, and the initiation of sex therapy if needed. A case example of a 70-year-old man who experienced erectile dysfunction following surgery for cancer and subsequently became a candidate for a prosthesis is described.

887. Schuler, M. (1982). Sexual counseling for the spinal cord injured: A review of five pro-

grams. *Journal of Sex and Marital Therapy, 8*(3), 241-252.

This article investigates five sexual counseling programs for people with spinal cord injuries and compares them to guidelines proposed for the treatment of sexual dysfunction in people with nonphysical disabilities. Findings reveal that programs for people with spinal cord injuries devote the most attention to education and information, attitude change, and prescribing changes in behavior and that there are four features that vary among the programs: length of the program, whether the programs are group- or individual-focused, amount of time after injury of program participation, and participants. The author concludes that one of the major goals for people with spinal cord injuries is to redefine sexuality; consequently, sex must be differentiated from procreation and redefined as sexual relations, regardless of the ability to obtain an erection.

888. **Schultz, G. L. (1981). Sexual contact between staff and residents. In D. A. Shore & H. L. Gochros (Eds.),** *Sexual problems of adolescents in institutions* **(pp. 90-103). Springfield, IL: Charles C Thomas.**

This chapter discusses sexual contact that occurs between staff and adolescent residents of institutions. The questions of abuse and exploitation in these contacts is not fully addressed, and the focus is on the development of appropriate sexual and social relationships. While the failure to address exploitative relationships is a serious omission, this chapter is worth reading. The described desexualization and enforced celibacy of adolescents in institutions may be important factors in increasing their vulnerability to sexual exploitation.

889. **Schultz, J. B., & Adams, D. U. (1987). Family life education needs of mentally disabled adolescents.** *Adolescence, 22*(85), 221-230.

These authors investigate the family life education needs of adolescents with minimal and mild mental disabilities in order to develop curriculum. Using responses from 134 students from 11 school districts in a midwestern state, the authors identified six clusters or groups of family life education needs: basic nutrition, teenage pregnancy, sex education, developmental tasks of adolescents, marriage and parenthood, and planning and decision-making. They also found that females had a greater need for information on nutrition, teenage pregnancy, and marriage and parenthood.

890. **Schuster, C. S. (1986). Sex education of the visually impaired child: The role of parents.** *Journal of Visual Impairment and Blindness, 80*(4), 675-680.

This author describes strategies that parents can use to cultivate positive sexual attitudes in their children with visual impairments. The author maintains that parents can educate their children by allowing them to touch themselves and other family members as well as bathing and toileting together, keeping in mind that such behavior satisfies the child's learning needs, not the adult's

needs. Appropriate learning experiences are outlined for each stage of the child's life.

891. **Schuster, C. S. (1987). "Sex education of blind children re-examined:" Dr. Schuster responds.** *Journal of Visual Impairment and Blindness, 81*(3), 98-99.

In this article, the author responds to critiques involving negative stereotyping made by J. Vaughan and C. E. Vaughan in the article, "Sex education of blind children re-examined" *(Journal of Visual Impairment and Blindness, 81*[3], 95-98). The author argues that there is a need for alternative approaches in providing sex education to children with visual handicaps.

892. **Schwier, K. M. (1989, October). Parents must take first step to recognize sexual abuse as reality.** *Dialect: Newsmagazine of the Saskatchewan Association for Community Living,* **p. 11.**

This article discusses Charlene Senn's book, *Vulnerable,* but it goes beyond a review to discuss underlying issues related to sexual abuse of people with intellectual impairments. Parents are urged to recognize the risks and work toward controlling the risk by ensuring that their children receive appropriate social, sexual, and assertiveness skills training.

893. **Scott, M. L., Cole, J. K., McKay, S. E., Golden, C. U., & Liggett, K. R. (1984). Neuropsychological performance of sexual assaulters and pedophiles.** *Journal of Forensic Sciences, 29*(4), 1114-1118.

This article describes a study that administered the Luria-Nebraska Neuropsychological Battery to persons arrested for either the forcible sexual assault of a post-pubescent child or for nonviolent sexual assault of a post-pubescent child. The results were compared to those of a group of controls. Both groups of sexual assaulters performed significantly worse on 7 of the 14 scales of the battery. The data were then broken down into three groups: 1) participants who had forcibly assaulted post-pubescent victims, 2) participants who had sexually molested a prepubescent child, and 3) participants who served as controls. A discriminant analysis correctly classified 68% of the subjects on the basis of their neuropsychological performance alone.

894. **Seagull, E. A. W., & Scheurer, S. L. (1986). Neglected and abused children of mentally retarded parents.** *Child Abuse & Neglect, 10*(4), 493-500.

This article examines the placement outcomes of 64 neglected and abused children with a parent with mental retardation. Findings include the following: 11 of 64 children remained with their parents with low-functioning abilities, 40 were adopted, 9 were in foster care, 2 had been awarded to their nonretarded parent following divorce, and 2 had died. The authors conclude that there is the need for a mechanism whereby the retarded adult's right to parent and the child's right to nurturance and protection may both be preserved. Because of their cognitive limitations, most of the parents with mental retardation were unable to benefit from community services that would enable them to adequately parent their children. Until these goals can be guaranteed, the authors recommend that the decision to terminate parental rights be made more quickly.

895. Seattle Rape Relief Developmental Disabilities Project. (1982). *Special education curriculum on sexual exploitation: Level I kit (ages 6-11).* **Seattle: Comprehensive Health Education Foundation.**

This special education curriculum on sexual exploitation consists of four filmstrips, a teacher's guide with written narrative, six pamphlets, and a body map. It is designed for students ages 6-11 years old who have physical disabilities, learning disabilities, or whose learning difficulties place them in the slow learner to educably retarded range. The focus of the curriculum is on awareness of the problem, how to avoid or prevent different kinds of sexual exploitation, and on where and how to report incidents.The teacher's guide includes specific lesson plans, pre- and post-tests, and resource lists. The written narrative is made up of stories, role-play situations, and scripts for the filmstrips. A body map includes overlays. Three pamphlets provide information on sexual exploitation to parents and others involved with students who are handicapped. The other three pamphlets describe the elementary level curriculum to parents.

896. Seattle Rape Relief Developmental Disabilities Project. (1982). *Special education curriculum on sexual exploitation: Level II Kit (Ages 12-19).* **Seattle: Comprehensive Health Education Foundation.**

This special education curriculum on sexual exploitation consists of 20 filmstrips, a teacher's guide with written narrative, six pamphlets, and a body map. It is designed for students ages 12-19 years old who have physical disabilities, learning disabilities, or whose learning difficulties place them in the slow learner to educably retarded range. The focus of the curriculum is on awareness of the problem, how to avoid or prevent different kinds of sexual exploitation, and on where and how to report incidents. The teacher's guide includes specific lesson plans, pre- and post-tests, and resource lists. The written narrative is made up of stories, role-play situations, and scripts for the filmstrips. A body map includes overlays. Three pamphlets provide information on sexual exploitation to parents and others involved with students who are handicapped. The other three pamphlets describe the secondary level curriculum to parents.

897. Seattle Rape Relief Developmental Disabilities Project. (no date). *Sexual exploitation: What parents of handicapped persons should know.* **Seattle: Author.**

This brochure provides practical and background information for parents. It is also useful for caregivers, educators, and other professionals and paraprofessionals working with children with disabilities.

898. Seemanova, E. (1971). A study of the children of incestuous matings. *Human Heredity, 21,* **108-128.**

Mental retardation was found in 14% of mothers of children born as a result of incestuous relationships, about 460 times the number expected by chance. The author does not control for any increased expectation of women with mental handicaps being more likely to conceive children as a result of incest or for differences in case finding in populations with and without handicaps.

899. Semmler, C. J. (1983). The therapist, an expert witness in a custody case: A case study. *Physical and Occupational Therapy in Pediatrics, 3*(2), 61-68.**

This article examines the case study of an occupational therapist called as an expert witness in a custody hearing of a 3-month-old abused child. It describes the court process and offers suggestions for the appropriate preparation for therapists who may be asked for court testimony.

900. Sengstock, W. L., & Vergason, G. A. (1970). Issues in sex education for the retarded. *Education and Training of the Mentally Retarded, 5*(3), 99-103.**

These authors state that youths with handicaps should be expected and encouraged to have the same kinds of relationships and positive attitudes toward sex as we expect for all children. The topics taught in sex education should be related to the students' chronological age, while instructional methods should be adjusted to mental age. More visual aids and suitable materials should be used. Also, rather than reinforcing "cute" behavior in children with mental handicaps, age appropriate behavior should be encouraged at all times. Although nonhandicapped children gain much of their sexual knowledge incidentally, children with handicaps must be taught in a systematic way in the classroom. Educators must face the fact that students with handicaps have the same sex drives as nonhandicapped students but that they have little opportunity to reduce them. It is reasonable to assume that youths with handicaps can learn about sex in the same way they learn about other behavior. The authors recommend involving parents in their children's education. Informing parents in advance about how the topic will be presented and obtaining parental support, if possible, should prove helpful.

901. Senn, C. Y. (1988). *Vulnerable: Sexual abuse and people with an intellectual handicap* **[Monograph]. Downsview, Ontario: G. Allan Roeher Institute. (ERIC Document Reproduction Service No. ED 302 975)**

This 95-page monograph prepared for the Family

Violence Prevention Division of Health and Welfare Canada provides a thorough treatment of its topic. The author summarizes a number of studies that appear to show increased risk of sexual abuse for people with intellectual impairments, though indicating caution in interpretation because estimates by researchers of this and the nondisabled population vary widely. The author points out difficulties in obtaining data from institutional settings, but she presents indirect evidence of sexual abuse problems in institutions and explores developmental disabilities as a risk factor. She concludes that people with intellectual impairment experience at least equal risk for sexual abuse. Finkelhor's model of risk factors is used as a conceptual basis for explaining increased risk among children with intellectual impairments. Symptoms of child sexual abuse are discussed in relation to children with intellectual impairment. The author summarizes information on sexual offenders with disabilities, pointing out that many of these offenders had been victims of sexual abuse as children. Legal issues related to consent, ability to testify in court, and Charter implications are explored. Detailed recommendations for prevention and treatment are included. The report includes a long list of references, including many unpublished papers and difficult-to-find documents.

902. Sex abuse of child more common than is realized. (1975). *Pediatric News, 9*(3), 3, 76.
Incest is identified as the most common form of sexual abuse. Brother-sister incest was found to be the most common form of incest and to be less traumatic than father-daughter incest. Sterilization is discussed as a means of treatment for girls with mental retardation who turn to sex in order to compensate for deficient childhoods.

903. Sex on CT sparks call for screening. (1988, August 30). *Calgary Herald*, p. A1.
This newspaper article discusses incidents of sexual harassment and improper advances occurring on city buses. Reference is also made to past incidents of sexual harassment of passengers with handicaps on Calgary's Handi-bus system. The Handi-bus system is funded by city social services, but it is run by a separate organization. It is not known if charges were laid in the incidents involving passengers with handicaps, but counseling was made available to ensure that these passengers would know how to recognize sexual harassment.

904. Sexual assault: A case history. (1988, January). *The Spokesman, XVI*, pp. 6-7.
This article presents a personal account of sexual assault as told by a man with disabilities who was sexually assaulted. It provides a realistic, but emotional picture of the frustrations encountered in reporting the sexual assault, only to find that the justice system failed to convict the offender and that threats from the social service system to discontinue vital services followed attempts to achieve justice.

905. Sexual exploitation and abuse of people with disabilities. (1984). *Response to Violence in the Family, 7*(2), 7-8.
This article addresses the prevalence of sexual abuse among people with disabilities or special vulnerabilities. Also, it addresses the need for services for people with disabilities who are victims of rape and other forms of sexual abuse.

906. Sgroi, S. M. (Ed.). (1982). *Handbook of clinical intervention in child sexual abuse.* Lexington, MA: Lexington Books.
This book provides many chapters on the treatment of victims of child sexual abuse. There is virtually no discussion, however, of special needs of victims with disabilities. The methods discussed generally depend heavily on the verbal skills of the victim, which has serious implications for victims with little receptive or productive language.

907. Sgroi, S. M. (1982). Introduction: The state of the art in child-sexual-abuse intervention. In S. M. Sgroi (Ed.), *Handbook of clinical intervention in child sexual abuse* (pp. 1-8). Lexington, MA: Lexington Books.
In discussing child sexual abuse, the author refers to information that suggests that child sexual abuse is characterized by power inequalities and that the abusive act is motivated by power, aggression, and the perceived power disadvantage of the victim. This suggests a conceptual framework for understanding why people with disabilities are at greater risk. They are perceived as defenseless (and in many cases are more vulnerable) by their abusers and become more attractive victims.

908. Sgroi, S. (1986). *L'agression sexuelle et l'enfant: Approche et thérapies [Sexual aggression and the child: Approaches and therapies].* Québec: Editions du Trécarré.
This 427-page book addresses the issue of child exploitation both in terms of diagnosis and treatment. An overview of their exploitation reveals that incest is a common phenomenon in cases involving sexual exploitation. Among possible treatment choices, group therapy for victims is given particular emphasis. Treatment is also recommended for the mothers and the family. Current programs are evaluated, and suggestions are presented regarding both prevention and intervention. In this volume, no mention is made of victims of sexual abuse who also have a handicap. (This book is available in French only.)

909. Sgroi, S. (1987). Les agressions sexuelles contre les enfants: Le point de vue d'une spécialiste américaine [Sexual aggression against children: One American's professional opinion]. *Justice, September*, 10-11.
This article reports on a conference given by an American in Montreal. The presenter addresses the topic of sexual abuse from many angles and recommends adopting an integrated approach (e.g., medical, social,

judicial) in order to combat it. In the presenter's opinion, the ideal way to stop sexual aggression is to impose therapy on the aggressor. Treatment should last at least 5 years, with the ideal treatment modality being group therapy. As well, the aggressor should help defray the cost of therapy, as is done in the United States. (This article is available in French only.)

910. Shah, C. P., Holloway, C. P., & Valkil, D. V. (1982). Sexual abuse of children. *Annals of Emergency Medicine, 11*(1), 18-23.

This article reviews the characteristics of 843 cases of sexual abuse seen at the emergency department of the Hospital for Sick Children (HSC) in Toronto in 1962, 1967, and from 1977 to 1978. The children ranged in age from 23 days old to 18 years of age, with a mean age of 9.8 years. Most were girls (89.4%). The 174 cases seen from 1977 to 1978 were analyzed in detail. Among these, intercourse was the form of abuse in 70 cases (40%), molestation in 41 (24%), and exhibitionism in 36 (20%). Almost half (49%) of the offenses occurred in the child's or assailant's home. Of the 174 cases, there were seven children who were diagnosed previously as having mental retardation. The age range for those seven with mental retardation was from 12 to 17 years, with a mean age of 14.3 years. All but one were girls. The assailant was unknown in three cases, an acquaintance in three other cases, and a relative in one case.

911. Sha'ked, A. (1978). *Human sexuality in physical and mental disabilities: An annotated bibliography.* Bloomington: Indiana University Press.

This 303-page book is a comprehensive bibliography containing references to books and articles related to sexuality. Categories include physical disabilities, blindness, deafness and hearing impairment, mental retardation and learning disability, cerebral palsy, and spinal cord injury, in addition to 18 other medical or psychiatric conditions.

912. Shaman, E. (1985). *Choices: A sexual assault prevention workbook for persons who are deaf and hard of hearing.* Seattle: Seattle Rape Relief Crisis Center.

The primary goal of this workbook is to reduce the risk of sexual assault for persons who are deaf and hard of hearing by providing information about sexual assault and prevention strategies. The workbook discusses what sexual assault is, the facts on sexual assault, the law on sexual assault, the offenders, sexual assault prevention skills, safety recommendations, and available resources. The workbook provides exercises for the student to complete, along with questions and theoretical situations that a deaf or hard of hearing student might encounter.

913. Shaman, E. (1985). *Choices: A sexual assault prevention workbook for persons with physical disabilities.* Seattle : Seattle Rape Relief Crisis Center.

The primary goal of this workbook is to reduce the risk

of sexual assault for persons who are physically disabled by providing information about sexual assault and prevention strategies. The workbook discusses what sexual assault is, the facts on sexual assault, the law on sexual assault, the offenders, sexual assault prevention skills, safety recommendations, and available resources. The workbook provides exercises for the student to complete, along with questions and theoretical situations that a student with physical disabilities might encounter.

914. Shaman, E. (1985). *Choices: A sexual assault prevention workbook for persons with visual impairments.* Seattle: Seattle Rape Relief Crisis Center.

The primary goal of this workbook is to reduce the risk of sexual assault for persons with visual impairments by providing information about sexual assault and prevention strategies. This workbook has large print, which makes it easy reading for those with visual impairments. The workbook discusses what sexual assault is, the facts on sexual assault, the law on sexual assault, the offenders, sexual assault prevention skills, safety recommendations, and available resources. The workbook provides exercises for the student to complete, along with questions and theoretical situations that a student with visual impairments might encounter.

915. Shaman, E. J. (1986). Prevention programs for children with disabilities. In M. Nelson & K. Clark (Eds.), *The educator's guide to preventing child sexual abuse* (pp. 122-125). Santa Cruz, CA: Network Publications.

This short chapter describes the resources, services, and staff training activities that were provided by the Disabilities Project of the Seattle Rape Relief Crisis Center. It also makes recommendations relevant to prevention programs and includes some data (e.g., compared to 65%-85% when victims do not have disabilities, people with disabilities that experience sexual assault know the offender in 99% of cases). Problems with overemphasis on teaching children to obey authority, isolation, and the myth of the asexuality of people with disabilities are discussed. There is a brief description of training programs. The author stresses the importance of clarifying the values and perceptions of those who will provide sex education, the necessity of a team approach, the recognition and accommodation of differences across individuals and cultures, and the cooperation and coordination of parents. A four-paragraph description of the Disabilities Project is also included on pages 160-161 of this book.

916. Shane, J. F. (1988). *Abuse against children with developmental handicaps: An annotated bibliography.* Toronto: Ontario Association for Community Living.

This annotated bibliography lists 32 items and is organized into five sections: causal factors, parents with developmental handicaps, legal issues, general information, and educational material. The focus is on the causal relationship between child abuse and developmental disabilities. Research articles are included.

917. **Shapiro, E. S., & Sheridan, C. A. (1985). Systematic assessment and training of sex education for a mentally retarded woman. *Applied Research in Mental Retardation, 6*(3), 307-317.**
This article describes a systematic sex education program used to teach a 30-year-old woman with mental retardation to label basic reproductive body parts and describe and demonstrate a breast examination, pap test, and pelvic examination. The training program was conducted on 3 days over a 2-week period, and it consisted of a multiple-probe design across skill areas that provided factual information, required the subject to repeat factual information, used concrete teaching aids, demonstrated examination procedures, required the subject to demonstrate the specified examinations, and provided praise for correct responses. The results reveal dramatic increases in sexual knowledge and indicate that the increase in sexual knowledge was maintained over 3 weeks.

918. **Shapiro, E. T. (1987). Sex in the MD's office. *Hastings Center Report, 17*(3), 11-12.**
In this article, a professor of psychiatry argues for the need for the unambiguous prohibition of consensual sex between a patient and physician in the context of a professional relationship. At present, and through the APA code of ethics, only psychiatrists are specifically prohibited from engaging in sexual relations with patients. The lack of consensus regarding sanctions and appropriate interventions is discussed.

919. **Shaughnessy, M. F. (1984). Institutional child abuse. *Children and Youth Services Review, 6,* 311-318.**
This paper examines institutional child abuse and its causes. A major factor that is identified is the child's inability to deal with bureaucracy. Abuse stems from human, bureaucratic, and fiscal problems. Specific problems include organizational roadblocks to proper treatment (e.g., poor staff-administration relations, little accountability in large institutions, lack of cooperation between departments, policies that require specialized staff, heavy paperwork duties for therapists). Other problems include incompetent staff, staff turnover, a remote location that isolates children from parents, inappropriate placement of children as a stopgap measure, the use of medication as a form of social control, premature discharge, and inadequate follow-up. Inadequate follow-up is discussed as a form of abuse.

920. **Shevin, M., & Klein, N. K. (1984). The importance of choice-making skills for students with severe disabilities. *Journal of The Association for Persons with Severe Handicaps, 9,* 159-166.**
These authors point out the limited decision-making

skills and high degree of cue dependency of people with severe handicaps. The authors indicate that this may result more from inappropriate training than from the disability. They urge decision-making training and claim such training may be essential to the development of meaningful prevention programs.

921. **Shore, D. A. (1982). Sexual abuse and sexual education in child caring institutions. In J. R. Conte & D. A. Shore (Eds.), *Social work and child sexual abuse* (pp. 171-184). New York: Haworth Press.**
The author of this chapter suggests that although sexual neglect and sexual abuse are problems in institutional care of children and youths, this topic has not been the subject of any research. Sexual neglect is discussed as the failure to provide appropriate role models, adequate sex education, or opportunities for appropriate sexual expression. Sexual neglect, in addition to being directly harmful, is viewed as contributing to the risk of sexual abuse.

922. **Shore, D. A., & Gochros, H. L. (Eds.). (1981). *Sexual problems of adolescents in institutions.* Springfield, IL: Charles C Thomas.**
This edited book addresses some of the issues raised about the care of adolescents in various types of institutional care. It includes sections on historical and social perspectives, administrative concerns, legal issues, sex education staff training, sexual contact between staff and residents, clinical approaches, and various special population groups. Many issues are discussed, with particular focus on the desexualization of adolescents by the institutions that serve them. There is almost no mention of the sexual assault and abuse problems that so often affect the lives of these adolescents before, during, and after their institutionalization, but much of the material that is included in the book has direct or indirect bearing on the prevention and treatment of these problems.

923. **Shrey, D. E. (1979). Sexual adjustment counseling for persons with severe disabilities: A skill-based approach for rehabilitation professionals. *Journal of Rehabilitation, 45*(2), 28-33.**
This article takes a step-by-step approach to the facilitation of sexual adjustment in people with severe disabilities. Issues include physiological deficits and assets, adjustment counseling as a process, psycho-social deficits and assets, sexual values, and the focus that assessment takes as the counseling process unfolds.

924. **Shuger, N. B. (1980). Procreation, marriage, and raising children. In R. L. Burgdorf, Jr. (Ed.), *The legal rights of handicapped persons: Cases, materials, and text* (pp. 857-992). Baltimore: Paul H. Brookes Publishing Co.**
This chapter discusses the laws in the United States concerning people with disabilities and procreation, marriage, and raising children. The author traces the

historical sources of deprivation of the right to pro-create for people with disabilities. In the 1920s, a eu-genics movement spurred the belief that the prevalence of mental and physical disabilities was the root of all social problems and that mental retardation was heredi-tary in all cases. The result was a number of statutes that required sterilization of all criminals, idiots, imbe-ciles, or rapists. The statutes were tested in court on the ground of being unconstitutional. Some cases were successful on this basis, and others were not. (The author has reproduced these cases.) Gradually, the unconstitu-tionality of the legislation and the realization that not all mental retardation is hereditary led to a movement away from sterilization. The modern legal approach has been to accept legislation that permits sterilization when it is in the best interest of the person with mental retardation, when it is in the best interest of the public, and when it is likely that the person with mental retardation would procreate a child with mental retar-dation. This approach permits sterilization in rare cases. In the absence of a statute, there is not any authority for a guardian to have a person with mental retardation sterilized. The author also sets out cases dealing with marriage of people with handicaps. There have been and still are a large number of statutes restricting people with handicaps from the right to marry. Some of the laws have been struck down, but others have not, de-pending upon whether the statute satisfies procedural due process, substantive due process, and equal protec-tion. The issue of capacity to marry and presumption of validity is also discussed. The right of a parent to raise children, although constitutionally ingrained, has not been applied in all cases to parents with mental retarda-tion and their children. The author gives cases where a child can be taken from his or her parent with mental retardation on the basis that there is the superior right of the state to take custody when the parent is mentally or morally unfit, is incapable of caring for the child, or the welfare of the child requires it. Cases are cited that test the constitutional validity of such an action.

925. **Sigelman, C. K. (1981). Asking questions of retarded persons: A comparison of yes-no and either-or formats.** *Applied Research in Mental Retardation, 2*(4), 347-357.

This study addresses the frequent tendency of people with mental retardation to respond in the positive to yes-no questions, and it compares the use of the yes-no format with the either-or format.

926. **Sigelman, C. K. (1981). When in doubt, say yes: Acquiescence in interview with mentally retarded persons.** *Mental Retardation, 19*(2), 53-58.

This study investigates the rates of acquiescence by people with mental retardation living in institutions or in the community to questions, regardless of their con-tent. Participants with lower IQ scores tended to ac-quiesce more than participants with higher IQ scores. The author discusses the danger of relying on yes-no questions when working with this population.

927. **Sigelman, C. K. (1982). Evaluating alternative techniques of questioning mentally retarded persons.** *American Journal of Mental Deficien-cy, 86*(5), 511-518.

This article examines the use of questions in interview-ing people with mental retardation and discusses impli-cations for question design. Question types were tested with preteens, teens, and adults with mild to severe mental retardation. Open-ended questions were found to be unanswerable by many of the participants. Further-more, the interviewers found that trying to clarify or enlarge upon such a question only resulted in increased response bias. Questions with a yes-no format yielded higher response rates, but they also introduced a serious acquiescence bias. However, multiple choice questions, particularly if used in conjunction with pictures, yielded valid answers from many of the participants.

928. **Sigelman, C. K. (1982). The responsiveness of mentally retarded persons to questions.** *Education and Training of the Mentally Retarded, 17*(2), 120-124.

In this study, responsiveness to questions was measured using an interview format in two groups of children and one group of adults with mental retardation. Questions with a yes-no format and questions requiring partici-pants to choose among pictures consistently resulted in increased responsiveness as compared to questions with an either-or format. Verbal, multiple choice questions and open-ended questions resulted in the lowest levels of responsiveness.

929. **Silva, J. A., Leong, G. B., & Weinstock, R. (1989). An HIV-infected psychiatric patient: Some clinicolegal dilemmas.** *Bulletin of the American Academy of Psychiatry and the Law, 17*(1), 33-43.

In this article, the case of an HIV seropositive psychiatric patient who participates in unsafe sex is discussed for the purpose of illustrating clinicolegal dilemmas. The patient has a bipolar disorder and uses drugs intravenously.

930. **Silverman, R. A. (1974). Victim typologies: Overview, critique, and reformulation. In I. Drapkin & E. Viano (Eds.),** *Victimology* **(pp. 55-65). Lexington, MA: Lexington Books.**

This author critically reviews major victim typologies. He examines victim classifications undertaken by von Hentig, Mendelsohn, Abdel-Fattah, and Sellin and Wolfgang. Von Hentig's classification is based on social, psychological, and biological factors, one of which is people with mental defectiveness and another of which is the person who is mentally deranged. Mendelsohn's classification is characterized by the amount of guilt a victim contributes to the event. One classification is the "completely innocent" victim, and an example of this class is all children. Abdel-Fattah's classification is based on the participation of the victim in the crime. One classification is latent or predisposed victims who are more liable than others to be victims of certain types of offenses because of peculiar predispositions or traits of character. Sellin's and Wolfgang's classification is based on relatedness of the victim to the crime. For example, primary and secondary victims are two classifications. The author makes a recommendation as to the best typology.

931. Silverton, R. (1982). Social work perspective on psychosocial dwarfism. *Social Work in Health Care, 7*(3), 1-14.

This article describes the social work perspective on psychosocial dwarfism. It suggests that emotional trauma from the social environment contributes to retarded growth pattern, and it shows a striking similarity in the pattern of disturbance in parent-child interaction between cases of growth retardation and cases of child abuse and maltreatment. It also discusses the difficulties encountered by social workers in the assessment and treatment of these families.

932. Simpson, K. M. (1988). Teaching about AIDS: Youth with sensory or physical disabilities. In M. Quackenbush & M. Nelson (Eds.), *The AIDS challenge: Prevention education for young people* **(pp. 419-428). Santa Cruz, CA: Network Publications.**

This chapter provides brief suggestions for adapting AIDS prevention training to youths with physical and sensory disabilities. The author points out several special concerns for youths with disabilities: 1) often there is an implicit social assumption that they are asexual, 2) specific disabilities may require specific adaptations of materials, 3) often they are deprived of sex education, and 4) these problems may damage self-esteem, which aggravates the situation.

933. Sinason, V. (1988). Smiling, swallowing, sickening and stupefying: The effect of sexual abuse on the child. *Psychoanalytic Psychotherapy, 3*(2), 97-111.

By examining the process of small everyday abuse in a loving home, this article discusses the meaning of child sexual abuse and its effect on the child. This is done by means of extracts from a baby observation and by tracing in the twice weekly psychoanalytical psychotherapy of two children (a preadolescent boy and a 5-year-old girl) the infantile processes of smiling, swallowing, being sick, and "becoming stupid." The study found that the trauma of sexual abuse played a part in the mental handicap of the boy, who is seen moving from being a tragic victim of abuse to being an adolescent struggling against abusing, and that sexual abuse produced emotional and learning difficulties in the girl.

934. Sinason, V. (1989). Uncovering and responding to sexual abuse in psychotherapeutic settings. In H. Brown & A. Craft (Eds.), *Thinking the unthinkable: Papers on sexual abuse and people with learning difficulties*

(pp. 39-50). London: FPA Education Unit.

This chapter discusses the interpretation of indirect disclosures made by people with intellectual impairments who have been sexually abused. The author uses two case studies to illustrate the complexity of interpretation and other relevant points.

935. Siskind, A. B. (1986). Issues in institutional child sexual abuse: The abused, the abuser, and the system. *Residential Treatment for Children and Youth, 4*(2), 9-30.

This article reviews sexual abuse in residential institutions for children. Profiles of the abuser and the victim are described. The author suggests that the abuser and the victim must be understood outside of the residential institute before they can be understood within it. Recommendations for treatment and prevention are discussed.

936. Sisson, L. A., Hasselt, V. B. V., & Michael, H. (1987). Psychological approaches with deaf-blind persons: Strategies and issues in research and treatment. *Clinical Psychology Review, 7*(3), 303-328.

This article reviews the literature on the psychological assessment of people who are both blind and deaf. A description of the cognitive development and behavioral characteristics of this group of clients is presented. Other topics include assessing basic skill levels, managing inappropriate behavior (e.g., self-injury, aggression), self-help and social skill learning, adaptation to vocational situations, and research issues. The authors suggest that early research lays the groundwork for later efforts in encouraging productivity and independence.

937. Sjogren, K., & Egberg, K. (1983). The sexual experience in younger males with complete spinal cord injury. *Scandinavian Journal of Rehabilitation Medicine: Recent Advances in Rehabilitation Medicine, 9,* 189-194.

This article examines the sexual experience of younger males with complete spinal cord injuries. The authors found the following: In spite of severe genital-sexual dysfunctions experienced by this group, the majority continued having intercourse and about half felt orgasmic; sexuality maintained its preinjury significance for nearly all subjects; most characterized their sexual lives as at least to some extent satisfactory; loco-motor impairment and autonomous dysreflexia were more frequently given as causes of reduced sexual pleasure than were sexual dysfunctions; and high spinal cord severance and lack of a regular partner were negative factors for continuation of satisfying sexual experiences. The authors conclude that as many younger tetra- and paraplegics appear to be able to identify new and gratifying ways of sexual fulfillment and that genital sexual dysfunction is but one factor determining level of sexual satisfaction after a spinal cord trauma.

938. Sjogren, K., & Fugl-Meyer, A. R. (1982). Adjustment to life after stroke with special reference to sexual intercourse and leisure. *Journal of Psychosomatic Research, 26*(4), 409-417.

This article investigated three groups of single-stroke hemiplegics to assess whether they maintained or decreased their sexual activity after the stroke. Findings indicate that daily dependence, degree of motor disability, and impaired cutaneous sensitivity were the major negative factors affecting intercourse and leisure. This investigation suggests that the marked changes in sexual and leisure activities are due to unsuccessful coping with the stroke and its sequelae.

939. Skinner, B. F. (1953). *Science and human behavior.* New York: Macmillan.

Skinner explores the notion of counter-control, and he presents a model in which power and authority must be restrained by individual or social counter-controls to prevent abuse. This model is consistent with the notion that people with disabilities are victimized because they lack counter-control and that "absolute power corrupts absolutely."

940. Sloan, I. J. (1983). *Child abuse: Governing law and legislation.* New York: Oceana Publications.

This book deals generally with child abuse laws and legislation in the United States. Chapter 2 surveys key elements of the statutes dealing with the reporting of suspected or known cases of child abuse and neglect. The key elements of these statutes include the following: a) the purpose of the state reporting law, b) reportable circumstances, c) the definition of abuse and neglect, d) age limits of children, e) the required state of mind of the reporter, and f) who must and may report. Also discussed are immunity for reporting and other acts, abrogation of privileges, special exemptions, and the criminal and civil sanctions imposed for failure to report. In terms of the sexual abuse of children with handicaps, the purpose of any reporting statute is threefold: 1) to identify the child in peril as quickly as possible, whether handicapped or not; 2) to designate an agency to receive and investigate reports of suspected child abuse; and 3) to offer, where appropriate, services and treatment. The definition of child abuse and neglect is often different from state to state. Most definitions include sexual abuse, and there are some states, such as Florida, which broaden it to include sexual exploitation. The age limit federally for child abuse is any child under 18 or the age specified by the state. Several states include in their age limit definition people with mental retardation, regardless of age. Ohio sets the age at 18 years, with the inclusion of any child with physical or mental handicaps under 21. Washington's law applies to adults with developmental disabilities, and Nebraska extends protection to people who are incompetent or disabled. Most states require physicians and teachers to report. Only 19 jurisdictions mandate "any person" or "any other person" to report, but 32 require care workers to report. Where the agency responsible for the investigation of the abuse is related administratively to the institution in which the alleged abuse took place, a number of states incorporate clauses into their legislation ensuring independence in the investigation. Forty-eight states specifically include "sexual abuse" in their reporting law definitions. The trend is to make sexual abuse by a parent or caregiver a form of child abuse that must be reported if suspected; however, some states' reporting law definitions of sexual abuse include abuse caused by any person. Chapter 5 deals with the legal issue of sexual abuse of children. All states have established statutory standards, criteria, and procedures for bringing a civil child protective proceeding in juvenile or family court based on an allegation of abuse by a parent or caregiver. Like other types of child abuse, sexual abuse may be the grounds for the proceeding even if sexual abuse is not explicitly mentioned in the state's statutory definition. The threshold question in all child abuse cases relates to the competency of the child victim/witness. Most jurisdictions no longer set an age below which a child is incompetent to testify; instead, the court has discretion to allow a child to testify if he or she is capable of accurately observing and communicating past events and understands the necessity of telling the truth. Although the article does not comment on this fact, people with handicaps are particularly affected by this law. Furthermore, the use of children (and people with mental handicaps, although not discussed in this article) as witnesses raises evidentiary issues in most courts. Most evidence of sexual abuse is only circumstantial, requiring corroboration, and the child's testimony may change or be forgotten by the time of trial.

941. Sluyter, G. V., & Cleland, C. C. (1979). Resident abuse: A continuing dilemma. *American Corrective Therapy Journal, 33*(4), 99-102.

These authors propose a system for dealing with physical abuse in residential settings. A standardized process for investigating reports of abuse must be developed. A decision paradigm for administrators to use in determining what action should be taken is presented. The decision paradigm takes into account whether there are demonstrable injuries or not, whether the client can or cannot testify on his or her own behalf, whether witnesses (if any) are reliable, and whether the suspect admits or denies guilt. The recommended action for the given circumstances is included. As a step toward prevention, clients could be physically examined on admission; consequently, any scars or lesions brought to light could be evaluated in terms of the client's initial examination. Another preventive measure is informing new employees of the unacceptability of abuse and the consequences to be expected if it occurs. Keeping routine records of accidental injuries before an abuse situation arises may provide clues as to the perpetrator by checking frequency of injuries across dormitories and shifts when a complaint is registered.

942. Smigielski, P., & Steinmann, M. (1981). Teaching sex education to multiply handicapped adolescents. *Journal of School Health*, *51*(4), 238-241.

This article presents principles for health educators in providing sex education to individuals with cognitive and visual handicaps. The principles are applied to the case study of David, a 19-year-old man with moderate mental retardation and blindness. The experience in providing sex education for David reinforced that sex education for students with multiple handicaps must involve a coordinated effort between school administrators, teachers, school nurses, and parents. In developing a sex education program for an adolescent with mental retardation and blindness, the program must emphasize concrete teaching, visual compensators, resource persons, repetition of content, and opportunities for social learning. Nurses and special educators can serve as consultants to health educators in planning a sex education program. They may reduce parental discomfort by stressing sexuality as an indicator of normalcy. They also may serve as resources to parents by providing listings of sex education materials as well as offering guidance and support in dealing with the emerging sexuality of their child. The combined efforts of these persons can help to protect the rights of every child to have access to adequate sex education despite the limitations of a handicap.

943. Smith, J. T., & Bisbing, S. B. (1988). *Sexual exploitation by health care and other professionals* (2nd ed.). Potomac, MD: Legal Medicine Press.

This monograph provides considerable information regarding the legal aspects of sexual exploitation by physicians, psychiatrists, psychologists, and a number of other professionals. The issues of abuse of power and violation of trust are explored. Abstracts of many civil and criminal cases are provided. Many of the cases involve patients with minor or major psychiatric diagnoses, and some of the victims had other types of disabilities. Most cases cited involve victims who were women, but some victims were male, and some were children. An interesting issue running through many of the court cases is the responsibility of hospitals and other institutions. The argument has frequently been made and sometimes been accepted that institutions do not carry responsibility for their employees since sexual misconduct is outside the scope of their practice.

944. Smith, S. (1983). The link between sexual maturation and "adolescent grieving" in parents of the dependent disabled. *Sexuality and Disability*, *6*(3/4), 150-154.

This article investigates the grieving process experienced by many parents of adolescents with disabilities when their children begin to display visible signs of sexual maturation and/or overt sexual behavior. The author concludes that parents of people with disabilities need to address wider issues having to do with the grieving process as many parents have not responded positively to issue-centered approaches. The author offers suggestions for professionals who are working with these families.

945. Smith, S. L. (1984). Significant research findings in the etiology of child abuse. *Social Casework*, *65*(6), 337-346.

This article examines the use of three variables—sociological-environmental factors, the role of the child, and the psychological-personality factors of the parent—for analyzing the current findings on physical abuse of children. The author found that environmental factors contributing to abuse include social class, cultural values and norms, environmental stress (e.g., marital conflict), social isolation, and lack of environmental support. The author also states that factors that may affect a child's chances of being abused include mental or physical handicaps, attachment or bonding difficulties, and provocative behavior by the child. Characteristics prevalent among abusive parents include low sense of self-worth, dependence frustration, emotional deprivation, impulsivity, feelings of isolation, and rigidity.

946. Smith, S. M. (1983). 134 battered children: A medical and psychological study. In R. J. Gelles & C. P. Cornell (Eds.), *International perspectives on family violence* (pp. 83-96). Lexington, MA: D. C. Heath.

Battering was studied in 134 Canadian children. Fifty-three children admitted to emergency care with injuries not due to accident or trauma served as a control group. Battered children were found to be younger than children in the control group and tended to have multiple injuries in various stages of healing. Over one-third of the battered children had intracranial hemorrhage due to violent whiplash shaking. In general, battering was often found to result in permanent neurological damage.

947. Smith, S. M., & Kunjukrishnan, R. (1986). Medicolegal aspects of mental retardation. *Psychiatric Clinics of North America*, *9*(4), 699-712.

This article uses the description of legal cases to demonstrate that improved treatment of people with mental retardation had to be either legislated by government, as occurred in Europe, or decided through case law, as occurred in Canada and the United States. The article also includes a discussion on the improvements seen in the treatment of people with mental retardation in legal proceedings and on the lack of appropriate treatment services for people with mental retardation who are committed to an institution.

948. Sobsey, D. (1988). Research on sexual abuse: Are we asking the right questions? *News and notes: Quarterly newsletter of the American Association on Mental Retardation*, *1*(4), pp. 2-3.

This article discusses some of the problems facing researchers of sexual abuse of victims with disabilities and attempts to establish a research agenda. It suggests that research should move away from questions of incidence and prevalence of abuse in special populations since adequate, although not very precise, answers are currently available. It suggests that researchers move to more applied problems of prevention of sexual abuse and treatment of survivors.

949. Sobsey, D. (1988). Sexual offenses and disabled victims: Research and implications. *Vis-a-Vis: A national newsletter on family violence, 6*(4), 2-3.

This article reports the results of a study that indicates that people with a wide range of disabilities are more likely to experience sexual abuse or assault, are less likely to find appropriate treatment, and are less likely to see the offender convicted. The perceived vulnerability of people with disabilities is viewed as an important factor in increasing the person's with disabilities risk for sexual abuse. Exposure to large numbers of caregivers and isolated programs are also seen as contributing factors. (This article is also available in French.)

950. Sobsey, D. (1988). Sexual victimization of people with disabilities: Professional & social responsibilities. *Alberta Psychology, 17*(6), 8-9.

This article discusses the psychologist's role in preventing, identifying, and treating sexual abuse and sexual assault of victims with disabilities. It emphasizes current service inadequacies and makes suggestions for improving future services.

951. Sobsey, D. (1989). Whiplash Shaking syndrome. *News and notes: Quarterly newsletter of the American Association on Mental Retardation, 2*(6), pp. 2, 8.

This article discusses the possible relationship between brain damage due to violent shaking of children and a significant percentage of cases of mental retardation. It points out some of the problems of poor detection and how this may contribute to the "unexplained" relationship between abuse and developmental disabilities.

952. Sobsey, D. (1990). Too much stress on stress? Abuse & the family stress factor. *News and notes: Quarterly newsletter of the American Association on Mental Retardation, 3*(1), pp. 2, 8.

This article reviews research on the three-stage model of disability that claims disability creates family stress and family stress leads to abuse of the family member with disabilities. Several studies are cited which suggest that this model is incorrect or at least overemphasized in explaining abuse of people with disabilities.

953. Sobsey, D., & Varnhagen, C. (1988). *Sexual abuse, assault, and exploitation of people with disabilities.* Ottawa, Ontario: Health and Welfare Canada.

This document contains a 13-page report and an earlier version of the annotated bibliography that you are now reading. The study, commissioned by National Health Research and Development Program, includes a litera-

ture review, a survey of agencies serving Canadian survivors of sexual abuse and assault, and a survey of Canadian victims of sexual assault or abuse who are disabled. The authors conclude that people with a wide range of disabilities are at increased risk for sexual assault and sexual abuse and that current prevention and treatment programs do not respond adequately to the needs of people with disabilities.

954. Sobsey, D., & Varnhagen, C. (1989). Sexual abuse of people with disabilities. In M. Csapo & L. Gougen (Eds.), *Special education across Canada: Challenges for the 90's* (pp. 199-218). Vancouver: Centre for Human Development & Research.

This chapter reports and analyzes some data from a Canadian study on the sexual abuse and assault of people with disabilities. It goes beyond the data to discuss possible factors that result in the high rate of assault and abuse in special populations and suggests steps to reduce risks and provide more appropriate services for victims.

955. Sobsey, D., & Varnhagen, C. (in press). Sexual abuse, assault, and exploitation of Canadians with disabilities. In C. Bagley (Ed.), *Preventing child sexual abuse.* Toronto: Wall and Emerson.

This chapter presents the results of an analysis of Canadian cases of sexual abuse of people with disabilities and makes recommendations for prevention, detection, and treatment.

956. Sobsey, D., Wells, D., & Gray, S. (1989). *Sexual assault and abuse of people with disabilities: Networking directory.* Edmonton: University of Alberta, Department of Educational Psychology, Severe Disabilities Program.

This 46-page directory includes information about more than 100 people and organizations concerned about prevention and treatment of sexual abuse of people with disabilities. In addition to names, addresses, and phone numbers, the directory includes information on services provided and specific interest areas. Entries are listed alphabetically by name, with an interest area index and a professional discipline index to help readers locate information. Many entries are from Alberta, but some are included from across Canada and the United States.

957. Soeffing, M. (1975). Abused children are exceptional children. *Exceptional Children, 42,* 126-133.

Research in the area of abused children and handicaps is reviewed in this article. Several studies found that many abused children do have intellectual or physical handicaps. Research on handicaps as a result of abuse has reported a high incidence of mental, emotional, and physical handicaps. Implications for educators are discussed in terms of signs of abuse and school policy on reporting. A summary of federal programs in the United States is also given.

958. Sohn, H. A. (1983, October). *Child abuse prevention and the mentally handicapped.* **Paper presented at a conference on "The Mentally Handicapped Parent," Chatham, Ontario.**

This author addresses the question of whether children of parents with mental retardation are at greater risk for abuse. Literature reviews by other authors are cited. The overall conclusion is that people with mental handicaps make unacceptable parents; however, the research reviewed is considered to be methodologically weak. The author concludes that more research is necessary since there is sufficient reason to be concerned about the relationship between child abuse and mental handicaps.

959. Solnit, A. (1984). Keynote address: Theoretical and practical aspects of risks and vulnerabilities in infancy. *Child Abuse & Neglect,* *8*(2), 133-144.

This paper explores the relationship between two classes of variables that may lead to child abuse. The first category addresses the vulnerability of children and infants and discusses the effects of a child's weaknesses, deficits, defects, or unattractiveness on parental response. The second category includes environmental risk factors such as low income families, disruption or illness in the family, single parent families, and teenage pregnancy.

960. Solomons, G. (1978). Developmental disabilities and child abuse. *Medical Newsletter,* *30*(3), 12-17.

This article uses incidence studies to alert physicians to issues concerning abuse of children with developmental disabilities. Low birth weight infants and children with handicaps are particularly vulnerable to abuse. The author signals the high vulnerability of the infantile head, brain, and eyes and cites the following finding by Nelson and Ellenberg: In a sample of 38,533 children with cerebral palsy, intracranial infection and head injury were the most common causes of acquired motor handicap. This article also discusses the following: heavy parenting duties; parental guilt, anger, and denial; and parents' negative self-image. Recommendations are made to assist the physician in the detection of the potential for abuse in caregivers, including parents and professionals.

961. Solomons, G. (1979). Child abuse and developmental disabilities. *Developmental Medicine and Child Neurology,* *21*(1), 101-108.

This author reviews literature in the area of child abuse and developmental disabilities. Handicaps are found to be both contributing to and resulting from abuse. As a member of the medical profession, this author stresses the importance of recognizing abuse in patients and offering assistance to families when abuse is discovered.

962. Solomons, G., Abel, C. M., & Epley, S. A. (1981). Community development approach to the prevention of institutional and societal child maltreatment. *Child Abuse & Neglect,* *5*(2), 135-140.

This article describes a Community-Institutional Development (CID) system aimed at primary prevention of child maltreatment in institutions. The system emphasizes collaboration between the institution and the community. The CID team is comprised of 20 to 30 people, half of whom are lay volunteers, and half of whom represent various disciplines related to the rights and care of residents in institutions. The team works with the institution to improve child treatment and performs periodic reviews assessing conditions contributing to institutional and societal maltreatment.

963. Somers, M. N. (1987). Parenting in the 1980s: Programming perspectives and issues. *Volta Review,* *89*(5), 68-77.

This article addresses changes needed in parenting programs for the parents of children with a hearing impairment. Sample topics include the effects of societal change on parenting and a discussion of the special programming needs of working parents, single parents, and low-income families.

964. Somerville, M. A. (1982). Birth technology, parenting and "deviance." *International Journal of Law and Psychiatry,* *5*(2), 123-153.

This article examines access to birth technology and custody decisions affecting access to a group of individuals described as "deviant" parents, that is, parents outside the traditional, married, self-supporting, heterosexual relationship. It discusses the following: the right to reproduce; birth technology and homosexual, lesbian, transsexual, single, and unmarried parents; people with mental retardation as parents; and the rights of "deviant" parents to custody of and access to their children. The author suggests careful analysis before denying or regulating claims of persons who are labeled deviant either to reproduce children or to have custody of or access to children.

965. Souther, M. D. (1984). Developmentally disabled, abused and neglected children. In Department of Health and Human Services (Ed.), *Perspectives on child maltreatment in the mid 80's* **(pp. 33-35). Washington, DC: Human Development Services.**

Abused and neglected children are frequently at risk for developmental disabilities. Studies show that children who have been abused and neglected can become handicapped because of their maltreatment.

966. Sovner, R. (1988). Five myths about psychotropic drug therapy and mentally retarded persons. *Psychiatric Aspects of Mental Retardation Reviews,* *7*(5), 29-33.

This article suggests that negative experiences arising from the use of drug therapy with people with mental retardation have resulted in myths about drug therapy that have decreased the quality of mental services to this population of clients. Myths concern the effects of drugs on behavior, the relationship between drug therapy and psychosocial therapy, the suitability of drug therapy for specific conditions, the need for withdrawal programs, and the effects of drugs on cognitive functioning and prosocial behavior.

967. **Sovner, R., & Hurley, A. D. (1982). Diagnosing depression in the mentally retarded.** *Psychiatric Aspects of Mental Retardation Newsletter, 1*(1), 1-4.
Based upon the Diagnostic and Statistical Manual (DSM-III), this article discusses the clinical diagnosis of major depression in people with mental retardation. Sample topics include psychotic depression, interpretation of the dexamethasone suppression test, and antidepressant drug therapy.

968. **Sovner, R., & Hurley, A. D. (1982). Diagnosing mania in the mentally retarded.** *Psychiatric Aspects of Mental Retardation Newsletter, 1*(3), 10-12.
This article addresses the diagnosis of mania in people with mental retardation and presents a discussion of the features associated with mania in this population. The failure to recognize that manics can be irritable and psychotic can result in a misdiagnosis of schizophrenia. The role of hyperactivity in mania is discussed. Diagnostic and Statistical Manual (DSM-III) criteria are presented and discussed.

969. **Sovner, R., & Hurley, A. D. (1982). Psychotropic drug side effects presenting as behavior disorders.** *Psychiatric Aspects of Mental Retardation Newsletter, 1*(12), 45-48.
This article discusses the need for regular surveillance of the prescription of psychotropic drugs to people with mental retardation. Behavioral reactions to psychotropic drugs may be mistaken for signs of psychological disturbance, particularly in people lacking good communication skills. Possible side-effects of benzodiazepines, antipsychotic drugs, tricyclic antidepressants, MAO inhibitors, and lithium carbonate are discussed as well as the management of side-effects, including mania, tardive dyskinesia, aggressiveness, and impaired sexual function. The authors conclude that any change in behavior following the initiation of treatment with psychotropic drugs should be evaluated as a possible drug side-effect.

970. **Sovner, R., & Hurley, A. D. (1982). Suicidal behavior in mentally retarded persons.** *Psychiatric Aspects of Mental Retardation Newsletter, 1*(10), 37-40.
This article briefly reviews the literature dealing with suicide among persons with mental retardation and offers recommendations for mental health professionals in identifying and working with suicidal behavior in this population. Sample topics include differentiating suicidal behavior from self-injurious behavior and the increased risk for suicide following the initiation of treatment for suicidal depression.

971. **Sovner, R., & Hurley, A. D. (1983). Anorexia nervosa.** *Psychiatric Aspects of Mental Retardation Newsletter, 2*(1), 1-4.
This article discusses the clinical diagnosis and treatment of anorexia nervosa in people with mental retardation. Because of impaired communication skills, these clients may not directly express their fear of obesity or the self-perception of being overweight. Hoarding, crumbling, or concealing food may be indicative of this disorder as well as such symptoms as vomiting and binging. When the condition is associated with depression, antidepressants are commonly used. Behavioral treatment techniques are discussed. A modified version of the Diagnostic and Statistical Manual (DSM-III) criteria for diagnosing this condition in people with mental retardation is presented.

972. **Sovner, R., & Hurley, A. D. (1983). Do the mentally retarded suffer from affective illness?** *Archives of General Psychiatry, 40*(1), 61-67.
This article reviews 25 published reports on the incidence of depression and mania in over 3,000 persons with mental retardation. Diagnoses were made using Diagnostic and Statistical Manual (DSM-III) criteria. The full range of affective disorders was seen in the sample population. While clinical presentation was influenced by impairments in intellectual and social functioning, the development of affective symptomatology was not. In people with mild or moderate mental retardation, standard DSM-III criteria may be used. In people with severe and profound mental retardation, the basis for a clinically useful diagnosis may be found by considering changes in behavioral and vegetative functioning and the history of affective illness in the family. The authors contend that people with mental retardation who display psychiatric symptoms should be evaluated for affective symptomatology regardless of the severity of their mental retardation. Also, the full range of treatments should be considered, including psychotherapy and pharmacotherapy. The Thematic Apperception Test (TAT) and the Rorschach Test may be useful in diagnosing these clients.

973. **Sovner, R., & Hurley, A. D. (1983). The mental status examination: I. Behavior, speech, and thought.** *Psychiatric Aspects of Mental Retardation Newsletter, 2*(2), 5-8.
In this first article of a two-part series describing the use of the mental status examination in adults with mental retardation, the authors discuss four useful evaluation procedures. These are the use of objects or tasks to elicit responses, ask concrete questions, do not ask questions that can be answered by "yes" or "no," and the use of pictures to elicit verbal responses. The tendency for concrete thinking in this population is emphasized. For example, the grandiosity of manics with mental retardation might revolve around daily life skills rather than for plans for conquering the world. Other topics include the assessment of appearance, behavior, speech, and thought processes. Also included is an outline for the Mental Status Exam.

974. Sovner, R., & Hurley, A. D. (1983). The mental status examination: II. *Psychiatric Aspects of Mental Retardation Newsletter, 2*(3), 9-12.

In this second article of a two-part series describing the use of the mental status examination in adults with mental retardation, the authors discuss the evaluation of mood and affect, psychotic symptoms, cognitive functioning, and various psychiatric symptoms, such as phobias and avoidance behaviors.

975. Sovner, R., & Hurley, A. D. (1983). Preparing for a mental health consultation. *Psychiatric Aspects of Mental Retardation Newsletter, 2*(10), 39-40.

This article describes the quality and type of information needed to assess mental health in persons with mental retardation. Assessment components include reason for referral, duration of the problem, presence of precipitants, information regarding the client's mental retardation, psychosocial status, primary contact person, current medical condition, current drug therapy, previous behavioral and/or psychosocial problems, family history of mental retardation, and changes in vegetative functioning and behavior.

976. Sovner, R., & Hurley, A. D. (1983). Schizophrenia. *Psychiatric Aspects of Mental Retardation Newsletter, 2*(7), 25-28.

This article discusses the clinical diagnosis and treatment of schizophrenia in people with mental retardation. Due to the client's impaired communication skills and decreased conceptual ability, a diagnosis based on the client's self-report of psychotic experiences is difficult. In clients with an IQ below 45, it may be nearly impossible. The authors caution against making a diagnosis of schizophrenia based only upon psychotic or disorganized behavior. To receive this diagnosis, clients must manifest clear diagnostic signs. Care must be taken to not label clients simply on the basis of their grossly impaired or disruptive behavior.

977. Sovner, R., & Hurley, A. D. (1983). The subjective experience of mentally retarded persons. *Psychiatric Aspects of Mental Retardation Newsletter, 2*(11), 41-42.

This article outlines the need for clinicians to be sensitized to the importance of considering the subjective feelings and perceptions of clients with mental retardation when assessing a client and establishing a treatment program. The client's impairment in communication and abstract thinking should not preclude consideration of this important aspect of psychological functioning.

978. Sovner, R., & Hurley, A. D. (1986). Four factors affecting the diagnosis of psychiatric disorders in mentally retarded persons. *Psychiatric Aspects of Mental Retardation Reviews, 5*(9), 45-49.

This article addresses the limitations of the use of the Diagnostic and Statistical Manual (DSM-III) in the psychiatric diagnosis of people with mental retardation. Problems arise due to the presence of nonspecific effects of developmental disorders, such as impaired communication skills. The term pathoplastic is introduced to designate the distorting effects of personality and intelligence on the presentation of psychiatric disorders. Four pathoplastic factors significantly affecting diagnosis are discussed: intellectual distortion, psychosocial masking, cognitive disintegration, and baseline exaggeration. The authors contend that clinical interviews are of limited use with these clients and that they must be supplemented by information gathered from caregivers, family members, and treatment records. Furthermore, the DSM-III diagnosis of these clients may have to be inferred from global presentation rather than on the basis of specific criteria.

979. Sovner, R., & Hurley, A. D. (1987). Guidelines for the treatment of mentally retarded persons on psychiatric inpatient units. *Psychiatric Aspects of Mental Retardation Reviews, 6*(2/3), 7-14.

This article discusses client factors that complicate treatment, such as psychotic-like presentation, the honeymoon effect, poor adaptive functioning, and susceptibility to social reinforcement of symptomatic behavior. Staff factors complicating treatment include acute care orientation, lack of knowledge regarding mental retardation, and lack of familiarity with behavioral data collection. Indications for hospitalization are presented as well as nine guidelines for treatment.

980. Sovner, R., & Hurley, A. D. (1987). Objective behavioral monitoring of psychotropic drug therapy. *Psychiatric Aspects of Mental Retardation Reviews, 6*(10), 47-51.

This article presents reasons why traditional drug monitoring techniques do not work with people with mental retardation. The authors suggest that behavioral monitoring of treatment is the most effective method of evaluating response to psychotropic drug therapy. The components of a behavioral monitoring system are presented.

981. Sovner, R., & Hurley, A. D. (1989). Ten diagnostic principles for recognizing psychiatric disorders in mentally retarded persons. *Psychiatric Aspects of Mental Retardation Reviews, 8*(2), 9-16.

In this article, the importance of mental health clinicians "seeing past" the disability when evaluating people with developmental disabilities is discussed. Also, clinicians must have an appreciation of normal stress responses in people with all degrees of mental retardation. It is only when the individual's adaptive responses are identified that psychiatric symptoms, of often treatable mental disorders, become clear. Ten diagnostic principles are discussed: 1) people with mental retardation suffer the full range of psychiatric disorders, 2) psychiatric disorders usually present as maladaptive behavior, 3) the origin of psychopathology is multi-determined (the article discusses six distinct types of psychopathology that may present alone or in combination), 4) an acute psychiatric disorder may present as an exaggeration of long-standing maladaptive behavior, 5) maladaptive behavior rarely occurs alone, 6) the severity of the problem symptom is not necessarily diagnostically relevant, 7) the clinical interview alone is rarely diagnostic, 8) it is virtually impossible to diagnose psychotic disorders in patients with moderate or greater handicaps (pseudopsychotic features are discussed), 9) maladaptive behavior can be organized into a behavior hierarchy (first, second, and third order behaviors, as conceived of by the authors, are discussed), and 10) state and trait psychopathology frequently coexist. State psychopathology refers to symptoms that remit once the disorder is treated. Trait psychopathology refers to symptoms that are due to long-standing personality disturbances. In most cases, treatment raises the threshold for the expression of these traits rather than resulting in remission.

982. **Sovner, R., Hurley, A. D., & LaBrie, R. (1985). Is mania incompatible with Down's syndrome?** *British Journal of Psychiatry, 146,* **319-320.**
This article investigates all published cases of psychiatric illness in people with Down syndrome from three computerized databases. These cases were assessed for mood disorder diagnoses using Diagnostic and Statistical Manual (DSM-III) criteria, and each case (i.e., 28 major depressive, 3 depressive neurosis, and 21 possible major depressive) was given a diagnostic validity rating of definite, probable, or possible. The authors suggest that the findings are consistent with the hypothesis that Down syndrome precludes the development of mania.

983. **Sparks, S., & Caster, J. A. (1989). Human sexuality & sex education. In G.A. Robinson, J. R. Patton, E. A. Polloway, & L. R. Sargent (Eds.),** *Best practices in mild mental disabilities* **(pp. 289-313). Reston, VA: Council for Exceptional Children, Division on Mental Retardation.**
This chapter discusses sex education for people with mild to moderate mental disabilities. It includes a rationale, a discussion of issues, and the basic framework for a curriculum. The curriculum includes a stand on self-protection in addition to biological information, health and hygiene, emotions and feelings, and social skills.

984. **Spica, M. M. (1989). Sexual counseling standards for the spinal cord-injured.** *Journal of Neuroscience Nursing, 21*(1), **56-60.**
This article outlines proposed standards of care for sexuality counselling with people with a spinal cord injury. Topics include theoretical approaches, counseling objectives, and the preparation and role of the nurse in providing sexuality counseling. (Note: There remains a strong need for counselors knowledgeable about disability.)

985. **Staff report on the institutionalized mentally disabled and a response from the Justice Department. (1985).** *Mental and Physical Disability Law Reporter, 9*(2), **154-157.**
This article describes selected parts of a report covering conditions in mental institutions, a review of the Justice Department's enforcement of the Civil Rights of Institutionalized Persons Act, and a response from former Assistant Attorney General W. B. Reynolds. The staff contends that abuse and neglect exist and that care and treatment must be provided in an atmosphere of dignity and respect and that the Justice Department activities suggest that the Department is engaged in a concerted attempt to narrow the rights of the institutionalized people with mental disabilities. In spite of these contentions, Reynolds states that the Department is proud of its record of enforcement.

986. **Starr, R., Dietrich, K. N., Fischhoff, J., Ceresnie, S., & Zweier, D. (1984). The contribution of handicapping conditions to child abuse.** *Topics in Early Childhood Special Education, 4*(1), **55-69.**
The literature on the contribution of low birth weight, prenatal problems, congenital disorders, and mental retardation to child abuse is reviewed. While existing transactional and ecological theories suggest such child factors should contribute to abuse, a careful analysis of studies indicates handicapping conditions are not major causal factors. Results of prospective, longitudinal research suggest that minor deviations in child behavior rather than major handicaps are related to the occurrence of abuse. Efforts to help families adjust to having a handicapped child, while helpful in alleviating the stresses in such families, will not have a major impact on the incidence of abuse.

987. **Stavis, P., & Tarantino, L. (1986). Sexual activity in the mentally disabled population: Some standards of the criminal and civil law.** *Quality of Care, October-November,* **2-3.**
This article discusses American law in relation to sexuality and people with mental disabilities. Topics include basic rights, consent issues, prosecution of offenders whose victims have mental disabilities, the right to marry, investigation of sexual abuse occurring in developmental or psychiatric centers, and non-criminal sexual activity.

988. **Stavrakaki, C., & Vargo, B. (1986). 1986 and beyond: A look into the future.** *Psychiatric Clinics of North America, 9*(4), **797-803.**
This paper discusses future directions in the field of mental retardation. Sample topics include legislation, offenders with mental retardation, legal issues, marriage, parental rights, and research.

989. **Steele, B. F., & Alexander, H. (1981). Long-term effects of sexual abuse in childhood. In P. B. Mrazek & C. H. Kempe (Eds.),** *Sexually abused children and their families* **(pp. 223-234).**

Elmsford, NY: Pergamon.
In reviewing the prognosis for victims of child sexual abuse, the authors point out that children with intellectual deficits or emotional disorders have a worse prognosis for long-term adjustment than nonhandicapped victims.

990. **Steele, S. (1986). Assessment of functional wellness behaviors in adolescents who are mentally retarded.** *Issues in Comprehensive Pediatric Nursing, 9*(5), 331-340.
This article discusses a questionnaire administered to 46 community-based adolescents with mild mental retardation enrolled in an educational and vocational training program to determine their skills in the area of functional wellness. The data were pertinent to self-sufficiency in wellness monitoring and in treatment of minor illness, substance abuse, sexual history, exercise and relaxation, and the use of dental floss and seat belts. The study revealed that very few of the subjects with mental retardation had attained full competence in the assessed areas, and the author suggests that greater attention should be given to these areas in developmental programs for people with mental retardation.

991. **Sterling-Honig, A. (1980). Parent involvement and the development of children with special needs.** *Early Child Development and Care, 6*(3), 179-199.
This paper examines the ways in which parents may be helped and supported in the task of providing stimulating environments for young children with handicaps and in the development of their skills as therapists and educators. Parents have a special relationship with the child and are well-placed to help him or her. They require support, however, in coming to terms with the handicap. Children with handicaps have been found to be at risk for child abuse and neglect by parents or caregivers; therefore, primary prevention means that parents have to be the focus of therapeutic efforts to help families nurture their young. When neglect or abuse has occurred, treatment must include the family or recurrence may be inevitable. Furthermore, an effort should be made to prevent child abuse by educating parents before the abuse occurs. Therefore, help for the child with handicaps must be considered in light of help for the family.

992. **Stewart v. Extendacare Ltd., 4. W. W. R. (Sask. Q. B. 1986).**
The husband of a nursing home resident sued the nursing home for damages on her behalf after she suffered a broken hip as a result of an assault by a resident with intellectual impairments. Damages were awarded because the staff were aware of the resident's violent behavior and failed to exercise reasonable caution and diligence. The nursing home was held to owe a duty for keeping the residence reasonably safe. (Note: The responsibility of institutions and agencies to maintain reasonable safety is a key issue in prevention of assaults by residents against other residents.)

993. **Stiggall, L. (1988). AIDS education for individuals with developmental, learning or mental disabilities.** In M. Quackenbush & M. Nelson (Eds.), *The AIDS challenge: Prevention education for young people* (pp. 405-418). Santa Cruz, CA: Network Publications.
This chapter provides brief suggestions for adapting AIDS prevention training for youths with physical and sensory disabilities. The author points out that sexual abuse and exploitation is a common phenomenon among this population and that it may be responsible for a high rate of transmission of sexually transmitted diseases, including AIDS. She points out that caregivers are often the perpetrators and urges education and control of these service providers as an essential factor in AIDS prevention. She includes references to a number of specific programs and training materials.

994. **Stoneman, Z., & Brady, G. H. (1984). Research with families of severely handicapped children: Theoretical and methodological considerations.** In J. Blacher (Ed.), *Severely handicapped young children and their families: Research in review* (pp. 179-214). Orlando, FL: Academic Press.
Methods for studying families are reviewed. The authors suggest that a child with severe handicaps places great stress on the mental and physical resources of family members. The authors also stress the fact that little is really known about the family dynamics of families with children with severe handicaps. They point out that spousal relationships may be altered by the demands of the child with severe handicaps.

995. **Streissguth, A. P., Barr, H. M., & Martin, D. C. (1983). Maternal alcohol use and neonatal habituation assessed with the Brazelton Scale.** *Child Development, 54*, 1109-1118.
This article describes some of the research that helped document the nature and extent of mental retardation that is associated with maternal alcohol use during pregnancy. The evidence suggests that maternal alcohol use is a major causal factor in mental retardation.

996. **Striar, S. L., & Ensor, P. G. (1986). Therapeutic responses to adolescent psychiatric patients' sexual expression: Beyond a restriction/ permission stance [Special issue: Adolescent sexualities: Overviews and principles of intervention].** *Journal of Social Work and Human Sexuality, 5*(1), 51-69.
This article discusses institutional policies regarding sexual expression among adolescent psychiatric in-patients in treatment or group residential facilities. The development of these policies should be based on clinical and legal concerns rather than on strictly moral ones. Policies must be clear and formally establish a humanistic, consistent, and individualized approach to the adolescent and his or her socio-sexual development. The role of sex education and sex counseling is also discussed.

997. Strongman, K. T. (1985). Emotion in mentally retarded people. *Australia and New Zealand Journal of Developmental Disabilities, 10*(4), 201-213.

This article focuses on the nature of emotions in people with mental retardation. Often, emotion in these groups has been equated with psychiatric disorder. In an effort to gain a new perspective, the author reviews recent research and theory. Three avenues of research warrant further investigation: the behavioral tradition, the investigation of emotional expression and recognition, and the study of emotional development in nonhandicapped human infants. The last type of research involves naturalistic observation, primarily of mother-child interaction.

998. Stuart, C. K. (1986). Helping physically disabled victims of sexual assault. *Medical Aspects of Human Sexuality, 20*(11), 101-102.

This article explains the approach a physician should take when dealing with a victim of sexual assault with physical disabilities. The physician must be aware of the two myths about sexual assault of victims with disabilities: people with disabilities are immune to sexual assault and only women are raped. There are four stages of recovery: 1) shock, 2) anger, 3) understanding and acceptance, and 4) integration into life experience. For victims with physical disabilities, there may be more difficulty in negotiating these stages than for an able-bodied victim. The physician's role is to provide for the physical and emotional needs of the victim and to gather medical evidence for possible prosecution of the perpetrator. It is important to remember that people with disabilities have an additional need, which is to be allowed to make decisions for themselves. The decision to be made involves the crime itself and how the victim will deal with it.

999. Stuart, C. K., & Stuart, V. W. (1981). Sexual assault: Disabled perspective. *Sexuality and Disability, 4*(4), 246-253.

This article discusses sexual assault against people with disabilities with regard to common myths about sexual assault, defense against assault, rape, recovery from assault, and suggestions for assisting sexual assault victims with disabilities.

1000. Stuart, C. K., & Stuart, V. W. (1983). *Sexuality and sexual assault: Disabled perspectives.* **Minnesota: Learning Resources.**

These authors share their concept of a model workshop whose general goals are to improve sexual awareness of persons with disabilities and to introduce such persons to issues relating to sexual assault, its prevention, and emergency care and recovery. It is structured for 10 3-hour sessions.

1001. Sullivan, P. M., & Scanlan, J. M. (1987). Therapeutic issues. In J. Garbarino, P.E. Brookhouser, & K. J. Authier (Eds.), *Special children-special risks: The maltreatment of children with disabilities* (pp. 127-159). New York: Aldine de Gruyter.

Available treatment programs for children with disabilities and the staff to serve them are lacking. Research on the effects of abuse and outcome studies on efficacy of therapeutic methods are also lacking for the population of people with handicaps. Studies of long-term effects of sexual abuse on nonhandicapped children have had conflicting results. The authors' own study of 67 victims of childhood sexual abuse show that all the children have more than one behavior problem as measured by the Child Behavior Checklist. Considerations that are crucial to the provision of adequate psychotherapy services to abused children with handicaps include the issue of involuntary patients, authoritative intervention, ancillary patients, the site of therapy, accessibility of the site of therapy, and characteristics of the therapist. Therapeutic methods and techniques are described briefly, and 13 treatment goals included in psychotherapy treatment plans at the Center for Abused Handicapped Children are explained.

1002. Sullivan, P. M., Vernon, M., & Scanlan, J. M. (1987). Sexual abuse of deaf youth. *American Annals of the Deaf, 132*(4), 256-262.

These authors cite four studies of sexual abuse of children who are deaf which indicate that 54% of boys who are deaf and 50% of girls who are deaf have been sexually abused, compared with 10% of hearing boys and 25% of hearing girls. Children who are deaf are especially unlikely to discuss sexual abuse unless asked. In addition to fear of rejection, loss of love, punishment, or blame, children who are deaf face another problem: The parent, teacher, or other caregiver may not know enough sexual signs to understand when the child reports sexual abuse. As with other children with handicaps, children who are deaf are taught to comply with authority and, therefore, are more susceptible to bribes and threats. They tend to be not only curious but also naive about sexual norms. In terms of reporting abuse, schools have historically handled the problem internally. The authors believe this is a serious error, leading to "ethical compromises of the worst sort." Often, the perpetrator is asked to resign and is promised a good recommendation if he or she does so. Thus, the abuser finds another position in a school where he or she can abuse more children. Lecturing the abuser "not to do it again" is another unacceptable approach and is not a solution for such a serious problem as sexual abuse. The authors describe the legal, ethical, and professional statutes and standards to be followed when dealing with child abuse.

1003. Sumarah, J., Maksym, D., & Goudge, J. (1988). The effects of a staff training program on attitudes and knowledge of staff toward the sexuality of persons with intellectual handicaps. *Canadian Journal of Rehabilitation, 1*(3), 169-175.

This study assesses the effect of a comprehensive

sexuality education program on the attitudes and knowledge of staff working in institutional and community residences for adults with mental retardation. The first two levels of training are described in terms of goals and content. A qualitative evaluation of Level one training involving 275 participants indicates significant enhancement of staff attitudes and knowledge. Data from a 1-year follow-up questionnaire found changes to be intact. The authors also discuss the implications for the content and design of staff sexuality education programs.

1004. Sundram, C. J. (1984). Obstacles to reducing patient abuse in public institutions. *Hospital and Community Psychiatry, 35*(3), 238-243.
This article examines the problems that hinder the reporting, investigation, and prevention of patient abuse in public facilities. The author claims that the reporting of minor abusive conduct is influenced by working conditions and that the reporting of major abusive conduct is influenced by powerful factors in the administrative and disciplinary structures of state institutions. The author suggests measures designed to decrease the incidence of abuse and to ensure the reporting of any such incidents.

1005. Sundram, C. J. (1986). Strategies to prevent patient abuse in public institutions. *New England Journal of Human Services, 6*(2), 20-25.
Although United States law requires an advocacy system and prosecutor in every state, this author suggests that advocacy systems must be independent of all service providers. The author claims that institutions have chosen to neglect abuse problems, and abuse problems have not been high priorities for institutional administrations. Consequently, this author offers several recommendations: Eliminating abuse must be placed as the highest priority for institutional administrations; staff screening and staff training is critical; administrative and professional staff must be actively present in all institutional venues; staff and residents must be impressed with the importance of reporting; the code of silence must be broken; reporting staff and employees must be protected from retribution through "whistleblower" legislation and/or administrative policy; and reporting and investigation policy and procedures must differentiate between more and less serious complaints.

1006. Swanson, C. K., & Garwick, G. B. (1990). Treatment for low-functioning sex offenders: Group therapy and interagency coordination. *Mental Retardation, 28*(3), 155-161.
This article reviews possible historical reasons for the lack of specialized therapy for sex offenders with mental retardation or who are in the borderline-normal range of intelligence. Inconsistent and often abusive societal responses to these offenders are identified. A group-based therapy system for adult sex offenders with IQs ranging from 55 to 85 is presented. Rates of goal attainment and recidivism are discussed.

1007. Swedish Institute for the Handicapped. (1986). *Sexuality and disability: A matter that concerns all of us.* **Broma, Sweden: Author. (ERIC Document Reproduction Service No. ED 281 334)**
This document is a training manual for medical, educational, and institutional staff who work with adolescents and adults with disabilities. It provides basic information and dispels common myths concerning sexuality and disability: the distinction between disability and handicap, the reactions of able-bodied persons to questions and problems concerning sexuality, staff evasiveness in dealing with sexual problems, the role of self-esteem in establishing personal relationships, attitude change, providing information supporting the positive sexual identity of people with disabilities, developing alternatives to compensate for a disability, providing realistic information to the mass media, sexual rights, changing or improving sexual interactions, sexual aids, sexual rehabilitation, adolescent liberation and sexual knowledge, staff attitudes and responsibilities, sexuality in rehabilitation, and starting study groups and discussion groups for the staff, people with disabilities, and their families.

1008. Swick, K. J. (1984). Understanding special needs families. *Journal of Instructional Psychology, 11*(1), 37-47.
This article defines special needs families as those involved in child abuse, families with children with handicaps, families experiencing the various stages of a divorce, families in which there is a critical illness or death, and single parent families. It describes characteristics of special needs families and the unique situations they face. It also discusses the role of the helping professional (e.g., child care workers and teachers) and offers specific strategies for working with special needs families.

1009. Szasz, G., Paty, D. W., Lawton-Speert, S., & Eisen, K. (1984). A Sexual Functioning Scale in multiple sclerosis. International Federation of Multiple Sclerosis Societies: Symposium on a minimal record of disability for multiple sclerosis (1983, Vancouver, Canada). *Acta Neurologica Scandinavica, 70* (Suppl. 101), 37-43.
This article describes an evaluation of 73 patients with multiple sclerosis (MS) that used a 5-point scale (SFS) to assess the degree of sexual activity pre- and post-onset and the subjects' attitudes toward changes in sexual activity. The authors analyze the demographic features, impairment, disability, and handicap profile of subjects in the various SFS categories, and the results indicate that the sexually less active or inactive subjects were different from the active-as-before subjects in various ways, such as in their difficulties with toilet transfer and bladder functioning. The authors also discuss implications for programs and services that address the sexual concerns of patients with MS.

1010. Szasz, G., Paty, D., & Maurice, W. L. (1984). Sexual dysfunctions in multiple sclerosis: Conference of the New York Academy of Sciences. Multiple sclerosis: Theory and practice (1983, New York). *Annals of the New York Academy of Sciences, 436*, 443-452.

This article discusses the epidemiology, diagnosis, and management of the sexual dysfunction associated with multiple sclerosis (MS). It describes treatment strategies, which include relevant information, education, physical rehabilitation, and supportive therapy in combination with medical intervention and, when indicated, surgical treatment or sex therapy. The authors use four case histories to illustrate sexual problems or dysfunctions that are and are not related to MS.

1011. Szymanski, L. S., & Biederman, J. (1984). Depression and anorexia nervosa of persons with Down's syndrome. *American Journal of Mental Deficiency, 89*(3), 246-251.

This article describes symptoms of major depression in three adults with Down syndrome, one of whom was also anorexic. Symptomatology depended on developmental level, particularly on verbal skills. In higher-functioning clients, affective symptoms were more easily identified, while in clients with more severe mental retardation, behavioral and vegetative symptoms were predominant. Major depression in people with Down syndrome may be more frequent than previously assumed. Standard Diagnostic and Statistical Manual (DSM-III) criteria may be used if modified in accordance with the client's developmental level.

1012. Szymanski, L. S., & Jansen, P. E. (1980). Assessment of sexuality and sexual vulnerability of retarded persons. In L. S. Szymanski & P. E. Tanguay (Eds.), *Emotional disorders of mentally retarded persons* (pp. 111-128). Baltimore: University Park Press.

These authors note that most often sexual abuse is perpetrated not by delinquent individuals, but by society and its laws. There are references given to the studies and laws which deny the right of sexual expression to people with mental retardation. The authors discuss: a) sexuality of people with mental retardation as a genetic threat to society, b) sexuality of institutionalized people with mental retardation, c) unconstitutionality of laws restricting sexuality of people with mental retardation, d) prevention and management of sexual abuse of people with mental retardation, e) treatment of sexual abuse, and f) prevention of sexual abuse.

1013. Szymanski, L. S., & Kiernan, W. E. (1983). Multiple family group therapy with developmentally disabled adolescents and young adults. *International Journal of Group Psychotherapy, 33*(4), 521-534.

This article describes the multiple family therapy groups that have been conducted since 1974 in the Developmental Evaluation Clinic of the Children's Hospital Medical Center in Boston. The psychotherapy groups are part of the Prevocational/Vocational Work Experience Program. Optimum group size was found to consist of four to six families. Example topics addressed by therapy include independence, the presence and nature of the handicap, and sexuality and peer relationships.

1014. Szymanski, L. S., & Tanguay, P. E. (Eds.). (1980). *Emotional disorders of mentally retarded persons: Assessment, treatment and consultation.* Baltimore, MD: University Park Press.

This book is comprised of articles written by various authors discussing such topics as professional roles and training, assessment, treatment (including psychotherapy, psychopharmacology, and behavior therapy), and consultation to education programs and residential facilities. One article addresses the assessment of sexuality and sexual vulnerability of people with mental retardation (see also Szymanski & Jansen, 1980).

•T•

1015. Taitz, L. S. (1981). Follow-up of children "at risk" of child abuse: Effect of support on emotional and intellectual development. *Child Abuse & Neglect, 5*(3), 231-239.

This article describes a follow-up study of 57 children who had been identified 3 years earlier as at risk for child abuse. Findings suggest that in families with childrearing practices that produce emotional and developmental impairment the usual social work support and other conventional methods are not effective in reversing the harm or in preventing further deterioration. Of 10 children who had been originally rated as "unsatisfactory" in terms of their development and vulnerability to abuse within their family of origin and had subsequently been placed in foster homes, 4 were found to be normal, and 5 had improved.

1016. Talbot, Y., & Shaul, R. (1987). Medical students learn about attitudes and handicaps. *Entourage, 2*(3), 6-11.

This article discusses the lack of training of medical professionals to understand the needs of people with developmental disabilities. The authors suggest that professional training for physicians should include components related to people with mental handicaps and their families.

1017. Tasch, V. (1988). Parenting the mentally retarded adolescent: A framework for helping families. *Journal of Community Health Nursing, 5*(2), 97-108.

This author applies systems theory, crisis theory,

developmental theory, and Orem's nursing theory of self-care to programs for families in which there is an adolescent with mental retardation. The author suggests that nurses working in schools, in the community, and in health care settings are strategically placed to assist these families.

1018. Taylor, M. E. (1985). Qualitative and quantitative strategies for exploring the progress of sex education for the handicapped. *Health Education, 16*(3), 16-19.
The objectives of this study are three-fold: to determine the types of sex education programs available through agencies serving people with handicaps, to interview college students with handicaps regarding experiences of and attitudes toward sex education programs, and to review current sexuality textbooks regarding sexual issues as they relate to people with handicaps.

1019. Taylor, M. E., & Wolford, C. A. (1985). Sexuality and the disabled: Apathy on the campus. *Journal of American College Health, 34*(1), 34-36.
This article describes a study of 9 college students with physical disabilities and 262 nondisabled college students concerning the issue of sex education, sexuality in relation to campus life, and sexuality in relation to other students and parents. Study findings reveal that it was difficult for the college students with physical disabilities to obtain information about sexual activity, that sex education for these students with disabilities is opposed from a variety of sources, and that there was a high level of apathy about socio-sexual relations among students with disabilities. The authors also summarize the attitudes of the nondisabled students toward the perceived proper sources of sex education.

1020. Taylor, M. O. (1989). Teaching parents about their impaired adolescent's sexuality. *MCN: American Journal of Maternal Child Nursing, 14*(2), 109-112.
In this article, the author describes how the parents of an adolescent with mental retardation or a developmental disability can be brought to accept their child's sexuality. The article examines seven working assumptions about the nature of caregiving and also discusses the formalization of a care plan and how to gauge success in teaching parents.

1021. Tegtmeier, W. (1977). Sex education with retarded adults. *Special Children, 3*(3), 19, 21-36.
This article is a transcript of one meeting of a sex education group of women with mental retardation at the AHRC Training Center and Workshop in New York City. This particular session is not meant to be a model of sex education or of counseling for people with mental retardation, but it is meant to illustrate the kind of discussion that can occur when an atmosphere of openness is fostered. It also illustrates some of the ways in which clients react to sexual material. A real attempt

is made in these groups and throughout the shop to relate directly and acceptingly to trainees' sexual feelings. The program tries to help them overcome the fear, guilt, confusion, and frustration that sexuality causes many adults with mental retardation.

1022. Termination of parental rights. (1986). *Mental and Physical Disability Law Reporter, 10*(5), 368-370.
This article discusses decisions by eight state appeals courts regarding termination of parental rights due to mental illness, mental retardation, and alcohol abuse: Michigan v. Kreft, 384 N.W.2d. 843 (Mich. Ct. App. 1986); Colorado v. R.B.S., 717 P.2d. 1004 (Colo. Ct. App. 1986); New York v. Keon Lee M., 502 N.Y.S.2d. 784 (N.Y. App. Div. 1986); Mississippi v. M.R.I., 488 So.2d. 788 (Miss. S. Ct. 1986); North Dakota v. V.J.R., 387 N.W.2d. 499 (N.D. S. Ct. 1986); Rhode Island v. Lori D., 510 A.2d. 421 (R.I. S. Ct. 1986); Massachusetts v. Petition of Department of Social Services, 493 N.E.2d. 197 (Mass. S. Jud. Ct. 1986); and Minnesota v. Welfare of P.L.C., 384 N.W.2d. 222 (Minn. Ct. App. 1986).

1023. Thies, A. P. (1976). The facts of life: Child advocacy and children's rights in residential treatment. In G. P. Koocher (Ed.), *Children's rights and the mental health professions* **(pp. 85-96). New York: John Wiley and Sons.**
In this chapter, the author asserts that children's needs will become legal rights only when they are accepted as enforceable claims against other persons or institutions. Protection is not enough. Also, children rely on adult advocates no matter what the system, rules, or laws. Anyone involved with the welfare of children must be aware of any conflict between their own interests and the child's interests.

1024. Thomas, A., Bax, M., Coombes, K., Goldson, E., Smythe, D., & Whitmore, K. (1985). The health and social needs of physically handicapped young adults: Are they being met by the statutory services? *Developmental Medicine and Child Neurology, 27*(4, Suppl. 50), i-iv, 1-20.
This article examines the difficulties encountered by young adults who are physically handicapped with cerebral palsy, spina bifida, and muscular dystrophy. It discusses health care issues, including housing adaptations, provision and repair of aids and equipment, physiotherapy and speech therapy, incontinence, dental health, sex education and sexual and genetic counseling, and maladjustment and psychiatric problems. The authors also review the support provided by local authorities and social services departments, factors contributing to financial hardship in families caring for a dependent with a handicap, and the education, training, employment, and social life of people with handicaps.

1025. Thomas, G. (no date). *Residential child maltreatment: An unrecognized problem in the United States.* **Athens, GA: Regional Insti-**

tute of Social Welfare Research, Inc.
This document discusses the role of American state
governments in the protection of children in foster
homes and child care institutions. Only a small proportion of state governments mandate reporting institutional abuse and neglect or license nongovernmental
child placement facilities. The author suggests that the
emphasis on placement over protection needs to be
addressed and that reform efforts must focus on legal
actions to limit and alter the presumptive powers of
state, judicial, and professional authorities related to
child placement and protection. Also, the establishment
of clearer standards for professionals' and judges'
conduct will provide the necessary base for the definition of the problem and its national recognition.

1026. Thomas, G. (1973). *Social justice: The*
cornerstone for treatment in children's
institutions. **Athens, GA: Regional Institute**
of Social Welfare Research, Inc.
This document focuses on the personal rights of children
in institutions. Social justice is necessary to the child's
growth and development. Three steps should be taken in
implementing these rights: review of structural
arrangements so as to identify and change impediments
to social justice; instruments and measurements should
be developed for the recruitment and evaluation of staff;
and the child must be evaluated in terms of his or her
increasing understanding of social justice.

1027. Thorn-Gray, B. E., & Kern, L. H. (1983).
Sexual dysfunction associated with physical
disability: A treatment guide for the
rehabilitation practitioner. *Rehabilitation*
Literature, 44(5/6), 138-144.
This article addresses psychological factors associated
with the treatment of sexual problems in people who
have become disabled. The underlying premise of the
article is that post-disability sexual adjustment hinges
upon predisability adjustment, sexual and otherwise.
Selected topics include the need for practitioners to
examine their own sexual adjustment and knowledge, a
step-by-step discussion of intervention strategies, and
when referral to a specialist is needed.

1028. Three states review trial competency
standards. (1986). *Mental and Physical*
Disability Law Reporter, 10(1), 12-13.
This article describes six cases that involve the
defendants' competency to stand trial and/or fitness to
waive important rights, such as, the insanity defense and
the right to counsel: New Hampshire v. Faragi, 498
A.2d. 723 (N.H. S. Ct. 1985); New Hampshire v.
Champagne, 497 A.2d. 1242 (N.H. S. Ct. 1985); New
Hampshire v. Spargue, 497 A.2d. 1212 (N.H. S. Ct.
1985); Washington v. Ortiz, 706 P.2d. 1069 (Wash. S.
Ct. 1985); Washington v. Hahn, 707 P.2d. 699 (Wash.
Ct. App. 1985); and Louisiana v. Braud, 475 So. 2d. 29
(La. Ct. App. 1985). The defendants included a person
with paranoid schizophrenia with delusions, an
individual with mild mental retardation, and a person

with paranoid schizophrenia who was floridly psychotic. The decisions found that both trial competency
and competency to waive the insanity defense are
governed by the same standards, while a higher level of
competency is necessary to waive the right to counsel.

1029. Thurer, S. L. (1982). Women and rehabil-
itation. *Rehabilitation Literature, 43*(7/8),
194-197.
This article examines the basic issues involved in the
rehabilitation of women with disabilities and identifies
areas of need. It discusses the employment of women
with disabilities, benefits, psychological concerns, sexual exploitation, and problems of mothers of individuals
with disabilities, and it raises major questions about the
current structure of rehabilitation services. The author
advocates a number of changes in social policy.

1030. Tilelli, J. A., Turek, D., & Jaffe, A. C. (1980).
Sexual abuse of children: Clinical findings and
implications for management. *New England*
Journal of Medicine, 302, 319-323.
This article reports on a number of factors in child
sexual abuse. The authors report that the adults with the
greatest contact with the victims are most likely to be
the offenders. This is consistent with the finding that
service providers are likely to be the abusers of children
with disabilities and become more likely with the
severity of disability. The authors suggest that reducing
the number of adults to whom children have isolated
exposure may be a means of reducing risk.

1031. Torres, E. R. (1987). From the analysis of a
perversion. *International Journal of Psycho-*
analysis, 68(3), 353-370.
The material for this article is drawn from the early
months of the psychoanalysis of a male homosexual
with a physical disability. The author's hypothesis is
that the mother and the son entered into a pact wherein
the son attributed a phallus to his mother who in return
disavowed his handicap. This hypothesis is elucidated
through a discussion of the Freudian concepts of narcissism, disavowal, and splitting of the ego. The fusion
of mother and son is addressed as well as separation
difficulties. The function of the father is also discussed.

1032. Tower, C. C. (1989). *Understanding child*
abuse and neglect. **Newton, MA: Allyn and**
Bacon.
This book provides a clear general discussion of child
abuse and neglect. There are a total of 18 chapters, which
include chapters on physical abuse, neglect, sexual abuse,
incest, extrafamilial sexual abuse, case management,
sexual abuse treatment, prevention, and adults abused as
children. There are occasional references to the increased
risk associated with chronic illness or disability and
some discussion of institutional abuse.

1033. Towns, F., & Feldman, M. A. (1987). Services
for parents with a developmental handicap.
Entourage, 2(1), 40-41.

This article describes how with proper training and support potentially abusive parents, including people with disabilities, can learn good parenting skills. The Parent Education Project at Surrey Place in Toronto is described as well as a number of other resources available to parents with developmental disabilities.

1034. Traustadottir, R. (1990). Women, disability and caring. *TASH Newsletter, 16*(3), 6-7.
This article is based on a 2-year qualitative study undertaken by the author to study families of children with disabilities and the services that provide support to these families in the United States. The research involved a case study of one family support program, in-depth interviews with families and service providers, and participant observations in a parent support group and at training events for parents of children with disabilities. A major focus of the study was to explore how stereotypical sex roles influence child care in the family and how traditional roles and values about sex roles influence the delivery of family support services. The author suggests that people working in the disability field must become sensitized to women's issues if the rights of people with disabilities are to be fully recognized.

1035. Traynard, J., Fournel, G., & Dumas, J. (1982). Avatars et limites de l'information sexuelle donnee dans une institution pour adolescents intellectuellement peu doues [Avatars and limits of sexual education given in an institution for intellectually impaired adolescents]. *Genitif, 4*(8), 8-16.
This article describes a sex education program in a training institute and how it was modified to meet the needs of a changing group of 240 adolescents with mild to moderate mental retardation, ages 12-20 years old. The authors detail the program according to how much information is presented, by whom the information is presented, means of presentation of information, and classification of information according to its appropriateness for specific age groups. The authors also describe student reactions to the program's informational content.

1036. Trevelyn, J. (1988). When it's difficult to say no. *Nursing Times, 84*(32), 16-17.
This article describes how *Kidscape* was adapted for use by children with learning disabilities. *Kidscape* was initially developed by M. Elliot and W. Titman to help children recognize and cope with potentially dangerous situations, including the possibility of sexual abuse. In *Kidscape* and its adaptation, sexual safety is seen in the broader context of personal safety. In the adapted version, lessons are learned through stories, discussion, role-play, writing, and drawing. However, most students with severe learning difficulties could not cope with having trusted adults role-playing hurtful characters in the simulation exercises. The author suggests that puppets will be tested as an alternative to role-playing.

1037. Tripp, A. W., & Kahn, J. V. (1986). Comparison of the sexual knowledge of hearing impaired and hearing adults. *Journal of Rehabilitation of the Deaf, 19*(3/4), 15-18.
This article compares the sexual knowledge of 11 men with hearing impairments and 19 women with hearing impairments (ages 25-81 years old) with that of 12 hearing men and 18 hearing women (ages 19-74 years old) using a sexual knowledge survey covering physiology, slang, general, pregnancy and fetal development, contraceptives, and male and female anatomy. The findings indicate that the adult deaf community is in need of sex education.

1038. Turner, T. S. (1988, February). Human rights concerns in health care institutions. *Spokesman,* pp. 17-18.
This article discusses the effect of institutionalization on the social, emotional, and legal status of those who enter them. The author points out that institutionalization is characterized by choicelessness, powerlessness, and vulnerability. People typically adapt by becoming increasingly passive, dependent, and compliant, and although the author does not directly address abuse issues, such an individual as previously described is likely to be at risk for abuse and exploitation.

•U•

1039. Ufford Dickerson, M. (1982). New challenges for parents of the mentally retarded in the 1980s. *The Exceptional Child, 29*(1), 5-12.
The person who has mental retardation is the primary client for professionals, and his or her family system is an important but secondary concern. Since the adult person who has mental retardation must be viewed as the primary client, all discussion and plans that concern him or her must be formulated with him or her and not on his or her behalf. Although considerable attention has been given to securing lifetime financial support and educational opportunities for people with mental retardation, there has been less attention given to meeting the general health needs of these people. In the 1980s, parents of people with mental retardation will have to meet the following challenges with respect to the general health of these people: a) dare to raise adults, not children; b) resist limiting individuals because of labels that result from evaluation; c) discuss the child's retardation openly with him or her; d) celebrate the child's emerging sexuality; e) discuss the child's sexuality in relation to mental retardation; f) use respite services to promote growth and development; g) accept recommendations for treatment; h) anticipate

the child's separation from home; i) resist the temptation to provide unnecessary guardianship; and j) confirm the child's right to maturity. Each of these challenges is discussed in the article.

1040. Ultman, M. H., Belman, A. L., Ruff, H. A., Novick, B. E., Cone-Wesson, B., Cohen, H. J., & Rubinstein, A. (1985). Developmental abnormalities in infants and children with acquired immune deficiency syndrome (AIDS) and AIDS-related complex. *Developmental Medicine and Child Neurology, 27*, 563-571.

These authors investigated seven children with AIDS and nine children with ARC (AIDS Related Complex). The children ranged in age from less than 1 year to 6 years, 2 months. In all children in the AIDS group, developmental disabilities and objective signs of neurological dysfunction were present. In the ARC group, delays and neurological deficits were sometimes present, but findings were highly variable. The authors point out that these findings may be related to the maternal status of intravenous drug user or other maternal social and health factors and not necessarily as a direct result of the child's infection.

1041. Underwood, N. (1989). The abuse of children. *Maclean's, 102*, 56-59.

This article discusses the growing recognition of child sexual abuse in Canadian society. The author discusses examples and suggests that many Canadian children experience damage that affects them adversely throughout their lives.

1042. Underwood, N. (1989). Sex and scandal: An inquiry hears graphic allegations of abuse. *Maclean's, 102*, 84.

This article reviews the work of the Hughes inquiry into sexual and physical abuse of children at Mt. Cashel Orphanage run by the Christian Brothers, a Roman Catholic lay order in St. John's, Newfoundland. Although the boys abused at Mt. Cashel were not disabled, this episode is a classic example of institutional abuse. Widespread and documented physical and sexual abuse can be traced through at least two decades at Mt. Cashel. The offenders were authority figures with little counter-control to limit their power over their victims. At least 25 reports of the abuse reached law enforcement and social service authorities on several occasions, but investigations were suppressed, and the institution was considered by external authorities to be responsible for and capable of solving the abuse problems. When any action was taken against offenders, it generally consisted of encouraging them to leave Mt. Cashel without any formal action or charges against them. These offenders typically moved to other residential care facilities where they were in a position to continue abusing children. Many of the boys who experienced abuse modeled the abusive behavior and went on to abuse other boys in the orphanage. These features of residential abuse have been observed in institutions for people with hearing impairment,

developmental disabilities, and other populations with and without disabilities. The pattern suggests that institutional care may contribute to the risk of abuse more directly than disability and that the high rate of abuse among people with disabilities may at least in part be a reflection of their increased likelihood of being placed in institutional care.

1043. University of Minnesota Medical School, Program in Human Sexuality. (1975). *Resources for rehabilitation practitioners: Sexuality and disability*. Minneapolis: Author.

This compilation of articles, brochures, and readings covers a wide range of related topics. Sections include fantasy, masturbation, church/law resources, same sex, sex roles, anatomy and physiology, sexual dysfunction, selected readings, and seven sections on specific disabilities and their effects on sexuality.

1044. Unkovic, C. M., & Klingman, J. A. (1980). The continued neglect of the mentally retarded offender. *Corrections Today, 42*, 38-39.

The most crucial issue involved in the status of the offender with mental retardation is that of identification. If mental retardation is not identified at time of intake, it will be too late to offer diversion. The criminal justice system sees the offender with mental retardation as being the responsibility of someone else, and the mental retardation system sees him or her as being the responsibility of the criminal justice system. This means many offenders with mental retardation are not receiving any help at all. A few states have made progress in improving the status of offenders with mental retardation. Brief descriptions of four state programs for offenders with mental retardation are given.

1045. U. S. Senate Subcommittee on the Handicapped. (1984). Staff report on conditions in intermediate care facilities for the mentally retarded. *Joint Hearings on Services for Mentally Retarded Persons*. Washington, DC: U.S. Government Printing Office.

As a result of evidence of neglect, abuse, and other conditions of substandard care in federally funded institutions for people with mental handicaps, Senate staff conducted on-site visits to gather information about conditions in these facilities. Rape, unexplained pregnancy, other sexual and physical abuse, and the housing of vulnerable residents with mental handicaps with violent sex offenders with mental handicaps were some of the abuses uncovered by the investigators. In response, the Department of Health and Human Services decided it would increase the number of random inspections of institutions. If deficiencies were found, the state would be given a set time period in which to put forth a plan of correction. Efforts to comply with the plan of correction would then be monitored. If deficiencies were not corrected within the specified time period, the facility would be decertified and its funding revoked. (Note: See abstract 881 for example of funding withdrawal.)

1046. U. S. Senate Subcommittee on the Handicapped. (1985). Staff report on the institutionalized mentally disabled. *Joint Hearings of the Subcommittee on the Handicapped.* Washington, DC: U.S. Government Printing Office.

As a follow-up to a previous review of conditions in facilities for people with mental disabilities, Senate staff visited 31 facilities to examine conditions and monitor abuse and neglect. The investigators found cases of rape, residents afflicted with venereal disease, staff-to-patient and patient-to-patient sexual contact (including prostitution), and sexual harassment. Many other types of physical abuse and neglect were also reported. Hospital administrators expressed frustration with union grievance procedures that prohibit employee termination or allow employees to be reinstated after they have been fired. Another complaint was that in many jurisdictions it is almost impossible to have charges filed if either the victim or suspect has a mental disability.

•V•

1047. Vadasy, P. F., Fewell, R. R., Greenberg, M. T., Dermond, N. L., & Meyer, D. J. (1986). Follow-up evaluation of the effects of involvement in the Fathers Program. *Topics in Early Childhood Special Education, 6*(2), 16-31.

This article describes a follow-up study aimed at determining the longitudinal effects of an innovative program for fathers of children with handicaps. Forty-five fathers participated in the program and completed six measures of stress, depression, social support, family environment, grief, and information needs, both 1 year before taking part in the program and 1 or more years after participation. Mothers completed the measures as well. Differences and similarities between the fathers and the mothers are discussed. The authors conclude that the family is an important unit of analysis in research on the outcomes of interventions for the parents of children with handicaps.

1048. Vadasy, P. F., Fewell, R. R., Meyer, D. J., & Greenberg, M. T. (1985). Supporting fathers of handicapped young children: Preliminary findings of program effects [Special issue: Early intervention]. *Analysis and Intervention in Developmental Disabilities, 5*(1/2), 151-163.

In this study, the Supporting Extended Family Members (SEFAM) Father's Program was evaluated. Both parents of participating families responded to the Beck Depression Inventory, the Family Environment Scale, the Questionnaire on Resources and Stress, and an inventory of parents' experiences. In addition, a parent-needs inventory was administered to the fathers. Two groups of parents were compared: parents who had been enrolled in the pilot program for a period of 1-3 years and a group of newly enrolled parents who served as controls. Parents who had participated in the pilot program showed evidence of lower levels of stress and depression and higher levels of satisfaction with social support.

1049. Valentich, M., & Gripton, J. (1984-86). Facilitating the sexual integration of the head-injured person in the community. *Sexuality and Disability, 7*(1/2), 28-42.

This article describes a psychosocial framework for assessing the sexual functioning of people with head injuries and applicable intervention techniques. Factors found to influence the sexual adjustment of a subject with disabilities include the impairment, medical treatment, developmental stage, social environment and the effects of these factors on physical sexual performance, psychosexual development, sexual self-image, and social interaction. The case of a 29-year-old man presenting inappropriate sexual behavior and attempting to achieve independent living in the community is used to illustrate the framework and the process of helping. The authors outline intervention techniques, including cognitive restructuring, assertiveness training, social skills training, and behavioral assignments.

1050. Valles, G. (1982). Attitude des parents face a la sexualité et l'education sexuelle des débiles mentaux [Parental attitudes toward sexual activity and education for the mentally deficient]. *Genitif, 4*(9), 24-32.

This article describes a survey of 170 parents of people with moderate to profound mental retardation (ages 6-18 year olds) and 165 parents of normal children to determine their attitudes toward sexual activity and education for people with mental handicaps. The survey addressed four areas: sexual behavior, premarital sex, marriage and reproduction, and sexual education. The findings show no significant difference in the responses of the two groups, and although the parents seemed willing to accept normalization of sex lives of people with mental handicaps, they were uncertain as to how to implement sex education and facilitate sexual adjustment. The results of this survey are also compared to those reported by Trembly and Dupras among a French Canadian population.

1051. Vander-Kolk, C. J. (1982). Physiological arousal of beginning counselors in relation to disabled and non-disabled clients. *Journal of Applied Rehabilitation Counseling, 13*, 37-39.

This article examines physiological stress reactions in 42 graduate student counselors in training to verbally presented situations involving work with clients with and without disabilities presenting various problems. The findings suggest that beginning counselors experience a high stress level in relation to working with any type of client and that the level of physiological reaction to clients will vary across individual counselors.

1052. Vander Mey, B. J. (1988). The sexual victimization of male children: A review of previous research. *Child Abuse & Neglect, 12,* 61-72.

This article reviews research on the sexual abuse of boys. Evidence suggests that extrafamilial sexual abuse is more common than intrafamilial sexual abuse. Residing in a neglectful home or with a mother but no father seems to be associated with increased risk. Familial sexual abuse appears to be more common when the father was a victim of sexual abuse as a child. Effects on adjustment are variable but often severe and long-lasting. Abused male children appear to be at greater risk for becoming abusers as adults.

1053. VanDusen, L. (1987). "We just want the truth." *Maclean's, 100*(44), 56, 58.

In 1986, Montréal police laid 250 charges against 14 people after investigating sexual abuse in a group home. Charges were all dropped 1 year later after determination that the witnesses, between 8 and 12 years old, would not provide reliable testimony. Québec officials indicated that in spite of the high number of charges, the case has not produced wide-scale public interest because it is outside the mainstream of regular schools and day cares.

1054. Vanier, J. (1982). La quete sous jacente de la sexualité humaine [The quest for human sexuality]. *Genitif, 4*(8), 2-7.

This article discusses affective and sexual fulfilment in people with mental handicaps. Topics include the fragility of self-concept, acting-out, and distrust in human relationships.

1055. Vanier, J. (1984). *Man and woman He made them.* **Toronto: Anglican Book Centre.**

This book discusses the concept of "normalization" as applied to the domain of sexuality for people with mental handicaps. The book applies the model of l'Arche Communities for people with mental disabilities and the underlying ethic of Christian fellowship. The normalization of sexuality is seen as a key component in eliminating isolation and attaining meaningful social integration.

1056. van Staden, J. T. (1979). The mental development of abused children in South Africa. *Child Abuse & Neglect, 3*(3/4), 997-1000.

Using the Griffith's Mental Development Scale, the scores of 30 abused white South African children, ranging in age from 6 months to 6 years, were compared with these of a control group of 20 nonabused children. Although the locomotor skills of abused children did not differ significantly from those of the control group, abused children were found to suffer severe

interpersonal and practical deficits due to stunting of all other areas of mental development.

1057. Varley, C. K. (1984). Schizophreniform psychoses in mentally retarded adolescent girls following sexual assault. *American Journal of Psychiatry, 141*(4), 593-595.

This article examines the cases of three females with mild mental retardation (ages 14-17 years old) who developed schizophreniform psychoses following sexual assault. The author uses these cases to illustrate how female adolescents with mental retardation are particularly vulnerable to sexual exploitation and how their response to sexual assault may be qualitatively different from that of victims without mental retardation. As the assault was not identified in any of the cases until the psychosis had been resolved through neuroleptic treatment and family therapy, the author states that psychiatrists should be aware that sexual assaults can contribute to a psychotic condition in adolescents with mental retardation and that there is a need for the development of prophylactic services through sex education for people with developmental disabilities.

1058. Varnet, T. (1984). Sex education and the disabled: Teaching adult responsibilities. *The Exceptional Parent, 14*(4), 43-46.

The parent of a young girl with developmental disabilities explains the necessity of parents ensuring adequate sex education for their child. This paper is a parent's personal account of the problems encountered when attempting to get sex education as part of her child's regular curriculum.

1059. Vaughan, J., & Vaughan, C. E. (1987). Sex education of blind children re-examined. *Journal of Visual Impairment and Blindness, 81*(3), 95-98.

This article critiques an article by C. S. Schuster (1986) on sex education for children with visual impairments. The issue of negative stereotyping is raised in reference to assumptions made regarding the determinants of gender in early adulthood and the imagery used to describe children who are blind.

1060. Verkunen, M. (1974). Incest offenders and alcoholism. *Medicine, Science and the Law, 14,* 124-128.

This article presents data suggesting a strong relationship between the use of alcohol and other drugs that reduce inhibition and incest offenses. This relationship may be due to disinhibition in the offender.

1061. Viossat, P., & Desbrus, L. (1982). Réflexion sur la sexualité des adultes handicapés [A reflection on the sexuality of handicapped adults]. *Genitif, 4*(9), 15.

This article explores the structure of object relationships in the sexual psychology of people with mental handicaps. It considers the attitudes toward the sexuality of people with mental handicaps and notes the relation of sexuality to the structure of the person's with handicaps personality and to the expressions of parents and educators.

1062. Vizard, E. (1989). **Child sexual abuse and mental handicap: A child psychiatrist's perspective.** In H. Brown & A. Craft (Eds.), *Thinking the unthinkable: Papers on sexual abuse and people with learning difficulties* (pp. 18-28). London: FPA Education Unit.

This chapter includes general information on child sexual abuse as viewed by a child psychiatrist and a discussion of some of these issues as they specifically relate to children with intellectual disabilities. Some of the issues addressed are the increased vulnerability of children with disabilities, the sexualized behavior of child victims that may expose them to further sexual abuse and reinforce the false impression that they are to blame for their own abuse, the possibility that behavioral changes that result from sexual abuse may simulate or aggravate intellectual impairment, and the perception of children with disabilities as potential victims.

1063. Vocational & Rehabilitation Research Institute. (1986). *Sexual assault manual: Information and procedures following a sexual assault.* Calgary: Author.

This manual provides practical procedures and information for parents, teachers, and other caregivers regarding what to do after a sexual assault has occurred that involves a victim with disabilities. It includes useful guidelines for interacting with medical and law enforcement services. It explores special issues regarding the recognition of physical and emotional trauma in victims with disabilities and suggests supportive measures. Many forms are provided for reporting the assault and documenting post-assault services. Some content is specific to Alberta or Calgary, but much of the information can be easily generalized to other locations.

1064. Vockell, E., & Vockell, K. (1977). **Social perception: Implications for sex education of the mentally retarded.** *Special Children, 3*(2), 5-8.

Sex education programs have typically focused on two main concerns: 1) imparting information about sexual matters to students and 2) developing healthy attitudes toward sexuality. Such programs have bypassed the possibility that sexual behavior might be closely related to students' levels of social and emotional perception and that assessment of functional levels in this area might be an important factor in the success of sex education programs. Whenever possible, such perception training should be provided as a normal part of a child's education rather than as a part of a "crash" sex education program. The student could engage in intensive practice for specific social situations, such as dating.

1065. Vogel, P. (1987). **The right to parent.** *Entourage, 2*(1), 33-39.

This article addresses legal issues regarding the right of people with developmental disabilities to parent. The role of the Canadian Charter of Rights and Freedoms and of Canadian law in general are discussed.

1066. Vogel, P. A. (1982). **Treating lower-functioning institutionalized mentally handicapped with severe behavior problems: An emphasis on language.** *Tidsskrift-for-Norsk-Psychologforening, 19*(12), 601-608.

Written in English, this Norwegian paper is a guide for psychologists working with institutionalized people with mental retardation. The guide emphasizes the role of language in working with this population and the importance of good communication between staff and residents. The model discussed is largely based on social learning theory, with some reference to developmental psychology and the improvement of communication in the family therapy setting. Guidelines for the use of differential reinforcement in replacing problem sexual behaviors with acceptable behaviors are described.

1067. Volunteers of Finex House. (1989). *Escape! A handbook for battered women who have disabilities.* Jamaica Plain, MA: Finex House.

This 65-page book provides a variety of potentially useful information for battered women who have disabilities and those who provide service or support to them. It includes information on the nature of abuse experienced by women, specific information about what can be done to escape from abuse, information and suggestions for service providers, and a list of resources that includes names and addresses. Although the information is very specific (some is specific to Massachusetts or the Boston area), much of the information and the model that this document provides could be useful anywhere.

1068. von Hentig, H. (1967). *The criminal and his victims.* Hamden, CT: Archon Books.

This book examines the characteristics of criminals and their victims. It notes that certain studies suggest a relationship between physical disability and crime. The studies cannot be conclusive since the size of the population of people with disabilities is unknown and other social factors affect this figure, for example, the second world war produced a number of people with disabilities and past criminal activity was punished by disfigurement of a person. The author also notes that the superstition that mental deficiency is a direct cause of crime has been done away with but that studies show that those with lower intelligence populate the prison system. This fact may arise because crimes committed by those with higher intellects go undetected. The author recognizes four general classes of victims: the young, the female, the old, and people with mental defects. These classes are more likely to be a victim of an attack because of their weakness or vulnerability. The author has classified victims by "general classes" and by "psychological" types. The author bases his criteria on social, psychological, and biological factors that offer indications for classification. The author also has seven more specific classes: 1) the immigrants, minorities, and dull normals; 2) the depressed; 3) the acquisitive; 4) the wanton; 5) the lonesome and heart broken; 6) the tormentor; and 7) the blocked, exempted, and fighting victim.

•W•

1069. Wagner, G. N. (1986). Crime scene investigation in child-abuse cases. *American Journal of Forensic Medicine and Pathology, 7(2),* **94-99.**

This article addresses the need for adequate documentation in the investigation of child abuse and neglect. Child abuse cases submitted for consultation to the Armed Forces Institute of Pathology show consistent deficits in scene investigation and documentation. The author asserts that the time delays often seen between an incident and its subsequent discovery do not preclude adequate investigation.

1070. Walbroehl, G. S. (1987). Sexuality in the handicapped. *American Family Physician, 36(1),* **129-133.**

This author claims sexuality is often overlooked in rehabilitation of patients with handicaps and that these patients need a family physician who can offer constructive help without being embarrassed or awkward. The author also states that the awareness that sexuality encompasses more than physical attractiveness and penile-vaginal intercourse, and the use of sexual imagery and concentration on body areas that retain sensation are essential in the sexual rehabilitation of patients with handicaps. The author concludes that rehabilitation is more likely to succeed when the patient has a supportive sexual partner.

1071. Walmsley, S. (1989). The need for safeguards. In H. Brown & A. Craft (Eds.), *Thinking the unthinkable: Papers on sexual abuse and people with learning difficulties* **(pp. 5-15). London: FPA Education Unit.**

This chapter provides a discussion of the need to establish safeguards against sexual abuse for people with learning difficulties. It begins with a general discussion of vulnerability factors and proceeds to a more specific discussion of risks for both children and adults. The role of total institutions in dehumanizing residents is considered as a factor. The author goes on to provide specific recommendations for controlling risks based on her own experience with service delivery systems.

1072. Walter, E. (1982). Continuity of sexuality education in programs serving people with mental handicaps. *Sexuality and Disability, 5(1),* **9-13.**

In order for sex education programs for people with mental handicaps to be successful, three factors are of major importance. First, the sex education program must be seen as a priority rather than a 1-time event. Second, a local source of training, consultation, and teaching materials is necessary for agencies to draw upon. Third, the needs of the clients, agencies, parents, and the public must be recognized at the program's outset.

1073. Ward, S. (1990, February 14). Boy's tale of sex abuse questioned. *Edmonton Journal,* **p. A12.**

This article discusses testimony at the Hughes Inquiry on sexual abuse at the Mount Cashel Orphanage in Newfoundland. It centers on earlier Social Services investigations of reports of abuse. In spite of repeated reports of sexual abuse that social workers described as believable, no action was taken because the institution had a good reputation and record of service. Shirley White, a social worker who interviewed boys who had run away from the institution after being sexually abused, is quoted as saying, "Basically, I was questioning my own judgment....The perceived image, I guess, of Mount Cashel at that time was that they had a good reputation of providing a valuable service." That year, Social Services received complaints of sexual abuse involving 21 boys, and numerous complaints had been lodged since 1975. Apparently, these frequent and long-standing complaints were not adequate reason to question the reputation of the institution.

1074. Ward-McKinlay, T., Botvinn-Madorsky, J. G., & Ward-McKinlay, C. (1983). Sexuality and disability. *Family Therapy Collections, 5,* **129-152.**

This article discusses the effect of spinal cord injury, heart disease, and other disorders on sexuality. It examines the positive effects on the sexuality of people with handicaps due to increases in sexual information for this population, increases in the training of professionals, and changes in the attitudes of people with handicaps. It states that treatment considerations for people with disabilities should include the time of onset of the disability (i.e., before or after puberty), whether it is stable or progressive in nature, and the sex of the person with the disability. The authors suggest that the initial interview with a client with a disability should elicit information on physiological functioning, the patient's psychosocial assets and deficits, and the individual's sexual attitudes and beliefs. They claim that intervention must emphasize the patient expressing his or her concerns and acting on them and that a systematic treatment program should include feedback from the patient and his or her significant other.

1075. Washington State Department of Social and Health Services. (1983). *Sexual exploitation:*

What parents of handicapped persons should know. Olympia: Author. (ERIC Document Reproduction Service No. ED 258 408)

This brochure defines the major areas of sexual exploitation under Washington state law. Changes in child behavior that may indicate victimization are discussed as well as immediate and long-term action that parents can take. Also described are services offered by the Seattle Rape Relief Developmental Disabilities Project.

1076. Wasserman, G. A., & Allen, R. (1985). Maternal withdrawal from handicapped toddlers. *Journal of Child Psychology and Psychiatry and Allied Disciplines, 26*(3), 381-387.

This study supports clinical reports of maternal withdrawal from young children with handicaps. Standardized observations were made of mother-toddler interactions both with children having a handicap and children having no handicap. At 24 months, toddlers with handicaps were more likely to be ignored by their mothers as compared to controls. Moreover, while there was no difference in Bayley scores obtained from the two groups at age 12 months, the ignored toddlers had lower concurrent IQ scores at 24 months, dropping an average of 30 points between the two test times.

1077. Watson, J. D. (1984). Talking about the best kept secret: Sexual abuse and children with disabilities. *The Exceptional Parent, 14*(6), 15, 16, 18-20.

Children with disabilities are more vulnerable to sexual abuse as they are likely to be more dependent, physically and psychologically, on adults. Poor social judgment and lack of experience about appropriate sexual behavior can leave a child unable to recognize deviant behavior. Although children with disabilities may be physically or psychologically unable to report sexual abuse, they may display symptoms that parents and teachers should recognize. Responses to abuse and preventive measures are also discussed.

1078. Way, I. I. O. (1987). *Sexual assault manual: Information and procedures following a sexual assault: A manual for the mentally and physically challenged and their support persons*. Calgary, Alberta: Author.

This 45-page document is designed to be a comprehensive working manual for staff, advocates, parents, guardians, and others assisting a person with a mental handicap through the procedures following an alleged sexual assault. Specific topics include emergency measures, legal information, practical approaches to assessing the services required, procedures following an alleged sexual assault, the police interview, stress indicators, and survivor rights and guardianship. Appendices include a short glossary and examples of various forms and documents.

1079. Wayment, H. A., & Zetlin, A. G. (1989). Coping responses of adolescents with and without mild learning handicaps. *Mental Retardation, 27*, 311-316.

This article reports research on the responses that adolescents use to cope with stressful situations. Nondisabled adolescents were more likely to use active strategies to deal with stressful situations, and adolescents with mild intellectual impairments were more likely to react passively. The authors point out that these "differences were especially noticeable in response to items that placed them in the position of hypothetical victim." The passive responses of these research subjects may provide a clue to the vulnerability to abuse of some people with disabilities. Caution must be exercised in reporting this finding since the passivity found in this group is not necessarily associated with the disability itself. This passivity may result from the compliance-based educational experiences of many people with disabilities.

1080. Waynberg, J. (1981). *Handicap et sexualité [Handicap and sexuality]*. Paris: Masson.

In this monograph, the first topic addressed is that of the sexuality of people with physical handicaps. Next, several subchapters address the sexuality of people with psychiatric impairments. The author decries the repression of the sexuality of this group of patients, particularly in institutions. An opinion poll on the sexuality of people with mental retardation was undertaken and reveals the belief that this group of people should not be permitted to reproduce. Lastly, it is to be noted that one of the chapters presents a critique of publications dealing with the sexual abuse of people with mental retardation. (This monograph is available in French only.)

1081. Weicker, L. (1987). Federal response to institutional abuse and neglect: The Protection and Advocacy for Mentally Ill Individuals Act. *American Psychologist, 42*(11), 1027-1028.

This article suggests that state institutions for people with mental disabilities are often filled with abuse, neglect, and tragedy. It discusses factors that thwart efforts aimed at providing quality mental health services to individuals in need. It describes the U.S. Federal Government's response to these conditions, that is, the Protection and Advocacy for Mentally Ill Individuals Act (PL 99-319), which established a nationwide system of protection and advocacy for individuals with mental illness in residential facilities.

1082. Weiner, B., Perry, R. P., & Magnusson, J. (1988). An attributional analysis of reactions to stigmas. *Journal of Personality and Social Psychology, 55*(5), 738-748.

This article presents the results of two experiments examining the perceived controllability and stability of the causes of ten stigmas. Drawing upon attribution theory, the authors investigated the affective reactions of pity and anger, judgments to help, and the efficacy of five intervention techniques. Physically-based stigmas were found to be perceived as onset-uncontrollable and irreversible, elicited pity and no anger, and resulted in judgments to help. Mental-behavioral stigmas were perceived as onset-controllable and reversible, elicited anger and no pity, and resulted in judgments to neglect. In the second experiment, the authors manipulated perceptions of causal controllability for the stigmas. Although changes in attribution were not equally possible for all stigmas, these manipulations resulted in attributional shifts.

1083. **Welbourne, A., Lifschitz, S., Selvin, H., & Green, R. (1983). A comparison of the sexual learning experiences of visually impaired and sighted women.** *Journal of Visual Impairment and Blindness, 77*(6), 256-259.
This article discusses a comparison of the sexual learning experiences of women with visual impairments and sighted women. It reveals that a group of 39 women with visual impairments (mean age 30.4 years) had significantly lower sex knowledge scores and obtained their information at a somewhat later age than a matched group of 39 sighted women. Factors influencing the sexual experiences of the women with visual impairments included difficulty in meeting dating partners, attitudes of sighted people toward blindness, and a lack of awareness of social cues. The authors also present the subjects' recommendations for improving sex education for people with visual impairments.

1084. **West Contra Costa Rape Crisis Center. (1986).** *Disabled children's prevention program.* San Pablo, CA: Author.
This center offers a program for children with various disabilities for sex assault prevention. The program has the following components: a) a disability awareness training program for child abuse prevention program staff members who will be working with children with disabilities in the schools, b) training for special education teachers in an abuse prevention curriculum they can use with their students in the classroom, c) parent and teacher workshops with a disability focus, and d) assault prevention workshops for children in special classes.

1085. **West Virginia University, University Affiliated Center for Developmental Disabilities. (1985).** *Diagnosis and referral of developmentally disabled, abused, and neglected children: A training manual.* Morgantown, WV: Author.
This training manual discusses the diagnosis and referral of abused and neglected children with developmental disabilities. The first section describes the initial development of a screening instrument. The second section describes changes made in the screening instrument after having been tested on a statewide basis.

1086. **West Virginia University, University Affiliated Center for Developmental Disabilities. (1985).** *Diagnosis and referral of develop-*

mentally disabled, abused, and neglected children. Final report. Morgantown, WV: Author.
This report describes a project aimed at developing a screening methodology for use by West Virginia's Human Services Child Protective Workers in the detection of developmental disabilities in abused and neglected children 0-18 years of age. The project mandate also involved the development of a tracking referral approach to assure appropriate and timely service delivery. This report is a summary of the first two years of the project and discusses third-year project activities, conclusions, and recommendations.

1087. **Weymar, W. (1989). Psychiatrische einrichtung und AIDS [The psychiatric facility and AIDS].** *Psychiatrische Praxis, 16*(3), 97-100.
This article discusses the need for recognition of the risk of HIV infection for people who suffer from chronic mental illness or mental retardation and live in large institutions. Ethical, legal, and practical implications are discussed. (This article is available in German only.)

1088. **White, R., Benedict, M. I., Wulff, L., & Kelley, M. (1987). Physical disabilities as risk factors for child maltreatment: A selected review.** *American Journal of Orthopsychiatry, 57*(1), 93-101.
This article reviews the literature on child abuse and suggests that children with physical disabilities may be at increased risk for maltreatment or neglect. It evaluates theoretical, definitional, and methodological concerns and discusses research issues. The authors conclude that the reviewed literature supports, but does not confirm, linkages between children with disabilities and the risk of maltreatment.

1089. **Whittaker, J. K. (1987). The role of residential institutions. In J. Garbarino, P. E. Brookhouser, & K. J. Authier (Eds.),** *Special children-special risks: The maltreatment of children with disabilities* (pp. 83-100). New York: Aldine de Gruyter.
This chapter first examines what is known about the incidence of maltreatment in residential institutions. Next, internal and external factors relating to child maltreatment in institutional environments are discussed. In regard to internal factors influencing maltreatment, references are made to various sources that outline institutional policies that ensure residents' rights, appropriate treatment plans, and family involvement. The author points out the following: While good programs for institutions are available, they are useless without proper staff training. Evaluation of programs and providing staff support are also of great importance. External factors that can help to prevent maltreatment in institutions are family involvement, strategies for community liaison, and citizen review.

1090. **Wickens, B. (1989). Multiple personalities: Some victims develop a separate personality.**

Maclean's, 102, 60-61.
This article discusses the emerging relationship between sexual abuse and multiple personality disorders. Once believed to be an extremely rare phenomenon, multiple personality disorders are being diagnosed with increasing frequency. Patients typically exhibit about 15 personalities, and some develop as many as 1,000 distinct personalities. Current evidence suggests an incidence of about 1 in 1,000. Ninety percent of patients with multiple personality disorders have experienced extreme abuse as children, often sexual abuse (Blatt & Brown, 1986). This contribution of abuse to psychiatric disability provides one link that helps explain the relationship between disability and abuse.

1091. **Widerstrom, A. H., & Dudley-Marling, C. (1986). Living with a handicapped child: Myth and reality.** *Childhood Education, 62*(5), 359-367.
Myths dealing with familial response to the presence of a child with a handicap in the family are addressed in view of research findings. These include increased difficulty in daily living, higher divorce rates, more marital discord, and increased difficulty in the fathers accepting a child who is handicapped. Recent research indicates that the degree of marriage stability seen in the family before the arrival of the child with special needs determines later marital harmony. Also, while fathers do appear to have difficulty in accepting a child with a handicap, acceptance may be fostered through increased involvement with the child's care, informal support, and acceptance of the child by the father's parents.

1092. **Williams, R., Singh, T. H., Naish, J., Bentovim, A., Addy, D. P., Gillon, R., & Dyer, C. (1987). Medical confidentiality and multidisciplinary work: Child sexual abuse and mental handicap registers.** *British Medical Journal, 295*(6609), 1315-1319.
In this article, a general practitioner, a consultant psychiatrist, a consultant pediatrician, an expert in medical ethics, and a solicitor comment on the issue of medical confidentiality in child sexual abuse. In a separate discussion, the same experts comment on the issue of medical confidentiality in releasing information for inclusion in a mental handicap register.

1093. **Williamson-Ige, D. K., & McKitric, E. J. (1985). An analysis of sex differences in educating the handicapped.** *Journal of Research and Development in Education, 18*(4), 72-78.
This article uses research findings to examine gender similarity and difference characteristics among students with handicaps. Areas in which gender differences are reported include emotional versus physical problems, structured versus unstructured learning, communication, mathematical skills, self-concepts, judgments of speech variations and physical beauty, behavior, and the long-term effects of no sex education. Similarities include medical problems, dependency, stereotyped reactions, role model exposure, and economic and career choice disadvantages.

1094. **Willmuth, M. E. (1987). Sexuality after spinal cord injury: A critical review.** *Clinical Psychology Review, 7*(4), 389-412.
This article reviews the literature on sexuality after spinal cord injury. Four major areas are reviewed: the sexual response cycle, reproductive functioning, sexual behavior and adjustment, and sexual counseling and rehabilitation. Sex differences are addressed. The author notes that recent literature in particular addresses the psychosocial aspects of sexual adjustment. Methodological problems and areas for future research are discussed.

1095. **Winett, R. W., & Winkler, R. C. (1972). Current behavior modification in the classroom: Be still, be quiet, be docile.** *Journal of Applied Behavior Analysis, 5,* 499-504.
This article provides an early but articulate indictment of the way in which behavior modification has been applied to students (especially those in special education) in the classroom. The authors review the definitions of appropriate and inappropriate behavior used by others in published studies and find that passive and docile behavior was consistently defined as good and active and assertive behavior was consistently defined as bad. The authors report being able to find only one study that did not reinforce "silence and lack of movement." Although the authors suggest that these problems have almost universally been associated with behavior modification programs, they do not view them as necessary characteristics of behavior modification. They suggest the following: If used properly, behavior modification could be a valuable tool for increasing active participation and the exercise of personal choice.

1096. **Winkler, W. H. (1987). Sexuality in trauma. In J. J. Gerhardt, E. S. Reiner, B. Schwaiger, & P. King (Eds.),** *Interdisciplinary rehabilitation in trauma* **(pp. 234-235). Baltimore: Williams & Wilkins.**
This article outlines the importance of sexual adjustment as a goal for people who have suffered physical trauma (e.g., spinal cord injury, amputation, head injury). General guidelines are suggested for the rehabilitation practitioner. The role of sex therapy is discussed.

1097. **Wolf, L., & Zarfas, D. E. (1982). Parents' attitudes toward sterilization of their mentally retarded children.** *American Journal of Mental Deficiency, 87*(2), 122-129.
A survey of parents of children with mental retardation revealed that 71% agreed with involuntary sterilization, and 67% agreed with voluntary sterilization. Forty-four percent felt that consent should be legally regulated, 49% did not, and 6% did not know. Sixty-four percent of parents did not feel a need for a legally authorized third person or committee to be involved in sterilization decisions. Twenty-five percent did desire external input,

and 11% did not know. The authors conclude that a number of issues must be addressed when discussing sterilization. Questions to be answered include the following: a) Can parenting ability be predicted by tests? b) Are children of parents with mental retardation at a disadvantage? c) How successful are marriages of people with mental retardation? d) What stresses are involved for people with mental retardation who marry and parent and is support available? and e) How do people with mental retardation adjust to sterilization?

1098. Wolf, R. S., Godkin, M. A., & Pillemer, K. A. (1986). Maltreatment of the elderly: A comparative analysis. *Pride Institute Journal of Long Term Home Health Care, 5*(4), 10-17.

In this article, factors are discussed that were identified as differentiating among various types of maltreatment in 328 cases of elder abuse and neglect seen between 1981 and 1983 in the context of three model projects. The elders lived at home. Abusers were family members, neighbors, or others. Cases of neglect were characterized by the victim being a very elderly female with disabilities who depended totally on an adult child. Physical, psychological, and material abuse were characterized by interdependence between the victims and the perpetrators.

1099. Wolfe, D. A., St. Lawrence, J., Graves, K., Brehony, K., Bradlyn, D., & Kelly, J. A. (1982). Intensive behavioral parent training for a child abusive mother. *Behavior Therapy, 13*(4), 438-451.

This article examines an intensive behavioral parent training program for a child abusive mother. It describes a direct parent training technique used to reduce abuse-related behaviors in a 29-year-old mother with low-functioning (WAIS IQ 78) abilities and epilepsy who displayed high rates of abusive behavior toward her 2-year-old girl and 9-year-old twin boys with epilepsy and mental retardation. The authors also discuss the importance of assessing parenting skills and including intensive training in child management with supportive agency services for abusive parents.

1100. Wong, C.B. (1978). Parent involvement in a public school program. *The Exceptional Parent, 8*(5), 15-19.

This author describes a sex education program for students with mental handicaps at her daughter's school. The three goals of the program were as follows: 1) to develop in the students an awareness of themselves as sexual beings, 2) to help students understand that sexual feelings exist and are not shameful, and 3) to teach students about the attitudes and expectations of society. The underlying aims of the program were to prevent unacceptable social behavior and to reduce the likelihood of exploitation.

1101. Wood, M. H. (1985). Learning disabilities and human sexuality. *Academic Therapy, 20*(5), 543-547.

This article describes a survey that investigated learning disabilities and human sexuality. The results of a questionnaire on human sexuality administered to 124 students with learning disabilities (ages 13-17 years old) and to 220 adults with learning disabilities (ages 18-53 years old) in 16 states indicate that adults had more difficulty than youths interpreting gestures, facial expressions, the meaning of the tone of another's voice, and making and keeping friends. Findings reveal that females in both groups often felt the need to touch or hug others when talking to them, were comfortable when someone touched them, could not interpret the tone of another's voice, had difficulty making and keeping friends, and did not know when they were leading someone on. The author suggests that the education of students with learning disabilities should focus more on social cues.

1102. Wooden, K. (1976). *Weeping in the playtime of others: America's incarcerated children.* **New York: McGraw-Hill.**

This book, which is an exposé of institutions for children in the United States during the 1970s, contains a chapter on facilities for people with mental retardation. The author visited hospitals and institutions as well as correctional facilities. He found that the institutions that are rarely visited— forgotten by society in general— were the ones in which the worst abuses occurred, including physical and sexual abuse by staff and inmates and suspicious deaths. However, facilities more "visible" to the public, such as juvenile penal facilities where children with mental retardation can be found by the "hundreds," were also rife with these abuses.

1103. Woodhead, J. C., & Murph, J. R. (1985). Influence of chronic illness and disability on adolescent sexual development. *Seminars in Adolescent Medicine, 1*(3), 171-176.

This article addresses the need for physicians who treat children and adolescents with chronic illnesses to recognize the importance of sexuality to overall development and to become familiar with effects disease can have on sexuality, including the physical, psychoemotional, and social aspects. The article addresses the following developmental segments: birth to 5 years, preadolescence, early adolescence, middle adolescence, and late adolescence.

1104. Worthington, G. M. (1984). Sexual exploitation and abuse of people with disabilities. *Response to Victimization of Women & Children, 7*(2), 7-8.

This article discusses vulnerability as an important determinant in the selection of sexual assault victims. Vulnerability traits addressed include presence of a disability, dependency of people with disabilities on caregivers, and the lack of education regarding sexuality, sexual abuse, and helping agencies. The need for helping agencies with specialized services for sexual assault victims with disabilities is addressed. The Coalition of

Sexuality and Disability, New York City, is briefly described as well as the efforts by the Minnesota Program for Victims of Sexual Assault in establishing a task force to examine sexual abuse of people with disabilities.

1105. Wright, E. C. (1982). The presentation of mental illness in mentally retarded adults. *British Journal of Psychiatry, 141,* 496-502.
This study discusses the signs and prevalence of affective disorders and schizophrenic conditions in adults living in large long-term hospitals for people with mental handicaps. Of 1,507 patients, three-quarters of whom had severe intellectual deficits, 2.8% were identified as having a current typical affective illness, 1.8% were diagnosed as having schizophrenia, and 2.7% were identified as having an atypical affective illness superimposed on an early childhood psychosis. Diagnosis was made difficult by the fact that half of these patients were preverbal. Schizophrenia could be diagnosed only on verbally expressed symptoms.

•Y•

1106. Yates, A., Beutler, L. E., & Crago, M. (1983). Characteristics of young, violent offenders. *Journal of Psychiatry and Law, 11*(2), 137-149.
In this study, the results of semi-structured interviews conducted with three groups of young, violent, incarcerated male offenders are contrasted. The person-offender group was found to be relatively similar to the murder group. Compared to these two groups, the members of the property offender group had histories of more severely impaired relationships and were more often labeled as emotionally disturbed and learning disabled in schools. The authors emphasize the need to consider ethnicity when studying violent young offenders and the need for the inclusion of a property contrast group in this type of study.

1107. Yoshida, L., Wasilewski, D. L., & Friedman, D. L. (1990). Recent newspaper coverage about persons with disabilities. *Exceptional Children, 56*(5), 418-423.
This article addresses the power of newspapers as a medium for developing public opinion regarding people with disabilities. Using a sample of five American metropolitan-area newspapers, the authors found three issues to be most recurrent: budget, expenditures, or taxes; housing or normalization; and treatment in institutions. The authors indicate that they found the press interested in issues regarding people with

disabilities and that developing a strong relationship with the press can go a long way toward educating the public.

1108. Yuille, J. C., King, M. A., & MacDougall, D. (1988). *Child victims and witnesses: The social science and legal literatures.* **Ottawa: Department of Justice Canada. (Department of Supply and Services Catalogue No. J23-4/1-1988)**
These authors state that there is a long history of labeling children as untrustworthy witnesses. Although difficult to determine, researchers believe that false allegations of child sexual abuse exist in about 7.8% of cases. The great majority of these appear to be custody cases, but also, these may occur in some delusional psychiatric disorders. Although medical evidence corroborating sexual abuse is available in about 15% of cases, explicit detail, child's eye view perspective, and idiosyncratic details may be indicators of truthful allegations. Anatomically detailed dolls may be of some benefit, but such behavior as exploring the orifices of the dolls or avoiding them also occur in about half of nonabused children; consequently, they should be used with caution. Play and drawing may also provide some useful information. Checklists have limited utility, and no standards for interpretation have been developed. These authors suggest several interview components: begin with irrelevant, unthreatening questions to get a baseline measure of the child's abilities, style, and so forth; seek a free account without asking specific or leading questions; ask specific but nonleading questions; check extent with which child is susceptible to suggestion; and analyse interview according to specific criteria (Note: Research is currently being done to validate this protocol.) The authors suggest that questioning may need to be more specific, depending less on free recall, and that suggestibility and fabrication may occur outside the realm of the individuals lived experience but be very accurate within it. Although the courts have been inconsistent about allowing experts to testify regarding interpretation of a child's evidence, they have been asked to do so in regard to four issues: diagnosis (e.g., child's statement or behavior is characteristic of a child who has been abused; courts divided on acceptance); credibility (e.g., child's statement appears truthful on the basis of expert analysis; generally rejected by courts); explanation (e.g., explaining why child changed story; courts have generally accepted); and capacity to give testimony (e.g., child is capable of giving accurate evidence; courts response not yet clear). The authors suggest that the courts should probably decide based on relevance, necessity, qualifications, and so forth. They also include a list of books, brochures, videos, and films that are available to help prepare children for court. (Note: Many of the issues related to children as witnesses also may be relevant to adults with cognitive or communication impairment. However, when courts have made accommodations, they have been made solely on the basis of age and not on the basis of disability or capacity.)

•Z•

1109. Zadnik, D. (1973). Social and medical aspects of the battered child with vision impairment. *New Outlook for the Blind, 67*(6), 241-250.

The article does not discuss sexual abuse specifically but deals with abuse generally. The author relates a personal experience of an abused child who was blind. Many children may be visually handicapped or blind due to child abuse, or their handicap may make them susceptible to abuse. Often, the problem is unrecognized by agencies who work with children who are blind. The article suggests that certain eye disorders are indicators of child abuse. Furthermore, the general characteristics of the parents may also be a factor in indicating abuse. It is important for agency and school personnel to offer immediate, consistent, and continuing emotional support to the family. Some experiences in an agency for people who are blind illustrate the possible tragedy of inadequate awareness of child abuse as well as some practical suggestions for serving the suspected battered child and his or her family.

1110. Zakarewsky, M. S. S. (1979). Patterns of support among gay and lesbian deaf persons. *Sexuality and Disability, 2*(3), 178-191.

Following a period of informal study of the patterns of support among gay men who are deaf and lesbian women who are deaf, formal interviews were conducted with the men and women and their families. Survey questionnaires were also sent to professionals and agencies serving these populations. Findings indicate that these client populations are in need of social services currently not available to them.

1111. Zantal-Weiner, K. (1987). *Child abuse and the handicapped child.* **Reston, VA: ERIC Clearinghouse on Handicapped & Gifted Children Digest No. 446. (ERIC Document Reproduction Service No. ED 287 262)**

This 3-page summary reviews research on child abuse and disability. It suggests that children with disabilities may be more likely to be abused because of impaired ability to physically defend themselves, impaired ability to report abuse, impaired judgment regarding inappropriate or appropriate treatment, greater dependency (producing passivity and compliance), fear of losing services (which may create reluctance to report), and because they are treated as less credible when reports are made. The author cites a number of studies showing increased risk for abuse or increased incidence of abuse among children with mental, behavioral, and physical disabilities.

1112. Zeller, C. (1987). *Des enfants maltraités au Québec [Maltreated children in Québec].* **Québec: Les publications du Québec, Comité de protection de la jeunesse.**

In this monograph, the author discusses child abuse in Quebec. Of the abused children studied, 28% were found to have one or more handicaps, most commonly in the areas of language dysfunction or in the area of mental retardation. Half of the children studied have problems with social adaptation. In the case of sexual abuse, one victim in five was found to have a handicap, while 11% had more than one handicap. Fifty-seven percent were seen to have problems with social adaptation. One chapter focuses on incest and another on the sexuality of youths. The author places an emphasis on the importance of the protection of victims of sexual abuse and on the treatment of incest in particular. (This monograph is available in French only.)

1113. Zelman, D. B., & Tyser, K. M. (1979). *Essential adult sex education for the mentally retarded (EASE).* **Santa Monica, CA: James Stanfield Film Associates.**

This curriculum is designed for adolescents and adults with mental handicaps. Pretests and diagnostic profile forms are included to provide the instructor with information on which topics need the most attention. The instructional content is presented in a what, who, why, when, and where format. Information that would not lend itself to this format is included in the clarifications section. Suggested teaching steps are given, as are relevant comments and responsibilities of the student. The material covered includes body parts, stages of human development, pubertal changes, menstruation, erection, orgasm, adolescent feelings, masturbation, sexual intercourse, birth control, sterilization, conception, pregnancy, abortion, childbirth, venereal disease, dating, and marriage. The only reference made to exploitation is in the section on illegal sexual behavior, which includes definitions of rape, child molestation, and incest. As well, very basic precautions to take in order to avoid being a victim are given (e.g., do not hitchhike or accept rides from strangers). Instructions on reporting a crime are outlined briefly. Materials included in the kit are curriculum guide, diagnostic profile forms, two filmstrips, two audiotapes, one menstrual hygiene kit, one birth control device kit, and 12 teaching pictures.

1114. Zetlin, A. G., & Turner, J. L. (1985). Transition from adolescence to adulthood: Perspectives of mentally retarded individuals and their families. *American Journal of Mental Deficiency, 89*(6), 570-579.

This article describes a study of 46 subjects with mild mental retardation, ages 23-60 years old, over an 18-month period that used observations during intensive interactions at home, in relatives' homes, and in social and work locations. The study identified two areas that affected emotional adjustment during adolescence: parent-child relations and identity issues. It also found that parent imposed restrictions often resulted either in inhibiting sexual development or creating defiance of parental controls.

1115. Ziff, S. F. (1984-1986). Symbolic sexual vocabulary for the severely speech impaired. *Sexuality and Disability, 7*(1/2), 3-14.

This article examines the development of the symbolic sexual vocabulary (SSV) for nonverbal clients (e.g., those with severe cerebral palsy) that used symbolic vocabularies and a language board. The author concludes that the SSV facilitates the ability of people with severe physical handicaps and mild to moderate mental retardation to talk about sexuality and that it has the potential for many other uses. The author also includes some symbols to illustrate the vocabulary.

1116. Zigler, E., & Balla, D. (1981). Issues in personality and motivation in mentally retarded persons. In M. J. Begab, H. C. Haywood, & H. L. Garber (Eds.), *Psychosocial influences in retarded performance* (pp. 197-218). Baltimore: University Park Press.

These authors cite their research findings in regard to personality characteristics of individuals with mental handicaps living in institutions. Several characteristics have been found to be typical in people with mental handicaps. Social deprivation tends to increase the child's with handicaps motivation to interact with adults for social reinforcement. Overdependency on peers, teachers, and other nonfamily socializing agents increases as the child with mental handicaps grows older. These children also tend to make choices that increase their chances of receiving reinforcement when given problem-solving tasks, which indicates an expectancy of failure. Imitativeness and outerdirectedness, meaning a great reliance on external cues to guide behavior, are also common character traits. The potential effects of the characteristics noted regarding sexual abuse are that people with mental handicaps may be easily coerced into exploitive situations because of the attention and affection the victim perceives he or she is getting. As well, the reliance on cues from external sources and dependence on others decreases the chances of the victim resisting the abuser. In situations where the child does object to the abuse, the expectation of failure may inhibit him or her from trying to stop the abuse or from asking for help.

1117. Zimlich, N. et al. (1985). *Preventing sexual abuse in day care programs: National program inspection.* Seattle: Department of Health and Human Services. (ERIC Document Reproduction Service No. ED 260 836)

Professionals working in 49 American states and the parents of children in day care participated in a 1984 national study on preventing child abuse in day care programs. The article summarizes major findings and offers recommendations for research, screening procedures, and education. Employee screening is discussed in terms of Public Law and the FBI criminal record system, current practice in the United States, and the effectiveness and potential scope of screening.

1118. Zirpoli, T. J. (1986). Child abuse and children with handicaps. *Remedial and Special Education, 7*(2), 39-48.

This article reviews factors contributing to parental physical abuse of children with handicaps. Abuse was found to be a response to an interaction of variables within the parent, the child, and the environment. These variables were found to be associated with many characteristics of families who had children with handicaps. Characteristics of abused children were found to be similar to characteristics of many children with handicaps. As well, children with handicaps were found to be at considerable risk for abuse and, in fact, were disproportionately represented in child abuse samples. Intervention and the role of educators is also discussed.

1119. Zirpoli, T. J., & Bell, R. Q. (1987). Unresponsiveness in children with severe disabilities: Potential effects on parent-child interactions. *The Exceptional Child, 34*(1), 31-40.

This article presents a model to explain why parents and/or caregivers perceive a child with severe mental and physical impairments to be responsive or unresponsive in interpersonal interactions. The authors discuss the role of extinction effects on caregivers' behavior as well as proposing that perceived unresponsiveness in these infants may be more critical than the disability.

1120. Zirpoli, T. J., Snell, M. E., & Loyd, B. H. (1987). Characteristics of persons with mental retardation who have been abused by caregivers. *Journal of Special Education, 21*(2), 31-41.

The relationship between specific characteristics of individuals with mental retardation, as rated by their teachers, and their abuse by residential caregivers is investigated in this article. Teacher ratings of 91 abuse victims from five state training centers in Virginia for individuals with mental retardation were compared to 91 randomly selected control subjects from the same facilities. Discriminant analysis results indicate a significant relationship ($p<.001$) between abuse status and a linear combination of subject characteristics. In addition, the Pearson Chi Square Test of independence was used to test the relationship between individual characteristics and behaviors of subjects and abuse status. Results indicate a significant relationship ($p<.05$) between abuse status and teacher ratings of level of functioning and frequency of maladaptive behaviors. Implications for caregivers and educators are discussed.

1121. Zitzow, D. (1983). *Human sexuality for the mentally retarded.* Ridfield: SD: South Dakota State Division of Elementary and Secondary Education, Pierre. (ERIC Document Reproduction Service No. ED 232 350)

This document describes the program Human Sexuality for the Mentally Retarded. This program is designed to train educable clients with mental retardation in cognitive awareness of sexuality. The program also trains inservice staff regarding attitudes and in recognizing cognitive awareness changes. Client training addresses sexual discrimination, body parts, puberty changes, social behaviors, and appropriate behavior. Nine residents demonstrating inappropriate behaviors were given behavior modification therapy. Inservice training was provided to 456 staff members. The outcome of staff training was measured through climate observation and the use of questionnaires. Outcomes were good for clients and staff alike. The author suggests that the program may generalize well to other institutions.

1122. **Zuckerman, M., Abrams, H. A., & Nuehring, E. M. (1986). Protection and advocacy agencies: National survey of efforts to prevent residential abuse and neglect.** *Mental Retardation, 24*(4), 197-201.

This article describes a survey that investigated the involvement of protection and advocacy agencies in 43 states in investigations of abuse and neglect of persons with developmental disabilities in residential facilities. It examines strategies used by protection and advocacy agencies in the investigation and remediation of abuse and neglect and identifies barriers that limited their involvement in abuse and neglect cases, including the following: laws that restrict agencies from conducting investigations unless responding to specific complaints and upon request by clients or guardians, and the percep-

tion of having too few staff dollars to stretch across large states with too many clients.

1123. **Zwerner, J. (1982). A study of issues in sexuality counseling for women with spinal cord injuries [Special issue: Current feminist issues in psychotherapy].** *Women and Therapy, 1*(3), 91-100.

This article describes a study of issues in sexuality counseling for women with spinal cord injuries. It discusses sexuality issues for a group of 68 women with spinal cord injuries in terms of previous research and physiological and psychosocial considerations. The results of this study indicate that only 30 subjects had received some type of sexuality counseling and that all the subjects needed more information. It identifies several topics that should be included in sexuality counseling: sexual complications related to disability, sexual positions, birth control methods and their side-effects, and orgasm. The author concludes that counselling should become an integral part of the rehabilitation process for women with spinal cord injuries.

Name Index

All numbers in this index refer to abstract numbers.

A

Abbott, D. A., 1
Abel, C. M., 962
Abel, G. G., 2, 63, 717
Abrams, H., 3, 742
Abrams, H. A., 1122
Abramson, P. R., 4
Ackerman, L. J., 511
Adam, H., 6
Adams, D. U., 889
Adams, G. L., 7
Adams, K., 8
Addy, D. P., 1092
Adelson, L., 9
Adler, R., 10
Agathonos, H., 12
Aiello, D., 13, 14
Akuffo, E. O., 15
Albee, G. W., 170
Alcorn, D. A., 7
Alexander, H., 989
Allen, R., 1076
Allen, W. A., 480
Alpert, J. J., 60
Althof, S. E., 587
Altman, K., 188
Amary, I. B., 16
Ames, T. R. H., 19
Ammerman, R. T., 20, 21, 22, 23, 24, 25
Anderson, A. M., 860
Anderson, C., 26
Anderson, J., 27
Anderson, S., 28
Andrasik, F., 717
Andre, C. E., 29
Andrews, H., 683
Andron, L., 30, 205
Anton-Culver, H., 650
Appelbaum, M., 400
Ashman, A. F., 144

B

Askwith, J., 32
Asrael, W., 33
Atwell, A. A., 34
Authier, K. J., 113, 358, 359, 360, 674, 694, 1001, 1089
Ayrault, E. W., 35
Azar, S., 305

Badgley, R. F., 36
Bagley, C., 955
Bain, J., 485
Baird, P. A., 37
Bajt, T. R., 38
Baker, L. B., 39
Baladerian, N. J., 40, 41
Balch, T. J., 91
Balla, D., 1116
Bancroft, J., 42
Banning, A., 43
Barker, D., 44
Barlow, M. M., 45
Barnes, K., 46, 47
Barnett, B., 48
Barnhill, L. R., 284
Baron, L., 317
Baron, R. B., 49
Barowsky, E. I., 50, 51
Barr, H. M., 995
Barrett, M., 52
Barrett, R. P., 526, 636
Barrett, T. R., 53
Barrmann, B. C., 54
Bartel, N. B., 55
Barth, R. P., 872, 874, 876
Barthell, C. N., 56
Baruth, L. G., 57
Barzansky, B. M., 65
Bauer, H., 58

Baugh, R. J., 59
Baum, E., 60
Bax, M., 61, 1024
Bean, G. J., 824
Beck, C. M., 62
Beck, F. W., 189
Becker, J. V., 2, 63
Beckham, K., 64
Beckmann, C. A., 65
Beckmann, C. R., 65
Beckwith, L., 763
Beezley, P., 627
Begab, M. J., 1116
Behrns, C., 323
Bell, R. Q., 66, 1119
Bellamy, G., 67
Bellehumeur, D., 529
Bellett, G., 68
Belman, A. L., 1040
Belsky, J., 69
Ben-Aron, M. H., 740
Benedict, M. I., 1088
Benefield, L., 70
Bensberg, G. J., 96
Benson, B. A., 71
Bentovim, A., 383, 1092
Berg, J. M., 871
Bergdahl, M., 363
Bergman, R., 395
Berkman, A., 72
Bernstein, N. R., 73, 74
Besharov, D. J., 53, 75
Beutler, L. E., 1106
Bianconi, S., 162
Bibb, T., 138
Biederman, J., 1011
Billick, S. B., 76
Bills, G. F., 649
Birrell, J., 77
Birrell, R., 77
Bisbing, S. B., 943
Bittle, R. G., 341

Blacher, J., 78, 79, 107, 666, 994
Blanc, P. M., 80
Blatt, B., 81, 82
Blatt, E. R., 83
Blaylock, M., 188
Blum, R. W., 84
Blumberg, M. L., 85
Blyden, A. E., 86
Blythe, B. J., 872, 874, 876
Boat, B. W., 87, 88
Boatman, B., 117
Bobek, B., 89
Boersma, F. J., 207
Bolea, A. S., 90
Bonney, W. C., 442
Bonvillian, J. D., 203
Bopp, J., Jr., 91
Boriskin, J. A., 347, 348
Borthick, W., 320
Botvinn-Madorsky, J. G., 1074
Bouhoutsos, J. C., 791
Bourgeois, M., 92
Bourland, G., 607
Bowden, M. L., 93
Bowles, R. T., 201
Boyle, G., 94
Boyle, P. S., 19
Bradlyn, D., 1099
Brady, G. H., 994
Brandner, A., 762
Brandwein, H., 95
Brannan, A. C., 96
Brantlinger, E. A., 97, 98, 99
Brashear, D. B., 100
Brauner, A., 101
Brauner, F., 101
Bregman, S., 102, 103, 569
Brehony, K., 1099
Brenner, S., 571
Briar, K. H., 104
Bright, R. W., 105
Bristol, M. M., 106, 107
Britt, J. H., 108
Brodyagg, L., 109
Broggini, M., 110
Bronfenbrenner, U., 111
Brookhouser, P. E., 112, 113, 114, 358,
    359, 360, 674, 694, 1001, 1089
Bross, D. C., 115
Brothers, A. M., 830
Brown, G., 300
Brown, H., 116, 200, 426, 934, 1071
Brown, S. W., 83
Browne, S., 421
Browning, D. H., 117
Bruininks, R. H., 579
Bryant, G., 118
Buchanan, A., 119
Buchanan, D. C., 538
Buchanan, S., 120
Bullard, D. G., 121, 122, 314, 852

Bullough, V. L., 123
Burgdorf, R. L., Jr., 124, 924
Burgess, A. W., 125, 126, 344, 365,
    685, 732, 827
Burgess, R. L., 595
Burggraf, M. Z., 57
Burke, D., 696
Burket, R., 147, 766
Burnstein, D., 126
Bussel, B., 149
Bustow, S., 232
Buttler, J. T., 145
Byer, J. C., 299

C

Caffey, J., 129, 130
Caldamone, A., 835
Camblin, L. D., Jr., 132
Cameron, A., 660
Canty-Lemke, J., 262
Caparulo, F., 134
Capkin, L., 14
Caplan, P., 135
Carelli, L., 547
Carr, J., 137
Carrick, M. M., 138
Carter, U. E., 139
Carty, E. A., 140
Cash, T., 141
Cassisi, J. E., 20
Caster, J. A., 142, 983
Catania, H., 14
Caton, D. J., 143
Cavanagh, J., 144
Ceresnie, S., 986
Chacko, M. R., 145
Chadwick, D. L., 278
Chakraborti, D., 146
Chamberlain, A., 147, 766
Champagne, M. P., 148
Chapelle, P. A., 149
Chapman, J. W., 150, 787
Chataway, J. E., 769
Chellson, J. A., 151
Cheng, H. P., 756
Chess, S., 152
Chipouras, S., 192, 212
Choate, C., 795
Christian, R., 414
Chubon, R. A., 159
Chwalisz, K., 160
Cicchinelli, L. F., 537
Cirrin, F. M., 161
Citterio, C., 162
Clark, G. M., 67

Clark, J. F., 164
Clark, K., 163, 730, 915
Clark, M. W., 532
Clark, R. E., 164
Clarke, D. J., 165
Cleland, C. C., 941
Clements, J., 811
Clowers, M. R., 175
Cohen, D. S., 349
Cohen, H. J., 1040
Cohen, S., 166, 167
Cohn, A. H., 168
Cole, L. K., 893
Cole, S. S., 169, 170, 171, 172, 173,
    174, 175
Cole, T. M., 173, 174, 175
Coleman, E. M., 176, 717
Coleman, M. A., 718
Collacott, R. A., 177
Collier, B., 594
Collins, A., 781
Collins, C., 178
Comarr, A. E., 180
Comfort, A., 181
Comfort, M. B., 181
Comfort, R. L., 182
Cone-Wesson, B., 1040
Conine, T., 304
Conine, T. A., 140, 184
Conney, M. H., 190
Connors, D., 421
Conoley, C. W., 345
Conrath, T. B., 299
Conte, J. R., 921
Conway, A., 187
Conway, E. F., 627
Cook, J. V., 201
Cook, J. W., 188
Coombes, K., 1024
Coon, K. B., 189
Coon, R. C., 189
Cope, J. G., 143
Coppersmith, E. I., 856
Corin, L., 191
Cornelius, D., 192, 212
Cornell, C. P., 946
Corrigan, J. P., 193
Cozzolino, J. P., 197
Craft, A., 116, 197, 199, 200, 426, 934,
    1071
Craft, M., 197, 199
Crago, M., 1106
Crain, L. S., 201
Cressy, J. M., 180
Crittenden, P. M., 203
Crossmaker, M., 204
Cruz, V. K., 205
Csapo, M., 954
Csesko, P. A., 206
Cullin, J. L., 207
Cunningham-Rathner, J., 2

D

Dale, F., 208
Daley, M. R., 209
Daniel, A. E., 210
Daniels, S. M., 192, 211, 212
Danley, W. E., 280
Darty, T. E., 213
D'Aubin, A., 214
Daugherty, W. E., 215
Dave, A. B., 216
Dave, P. B., 216
Davidson, H. A., 115
Davies, M., 217
Davies, R., 219
Davies, R. K., 218
Davis, L., 220, 221
De Champlain, J., 223
De-Fazio, A., 760
DeHaan, C. B., 224
de Jong, J. M., 871
Della, S., 716
De Lotto, P., 528
Delseries, J., 225
Demarest, D. S., 413
Demetral, G. D., 226
Denkowski, G. C., 227, 228
Denkowski, K. M., 227, 228
Denmark, J. C., 229
Dennis-Delaney, J., 843
Dermond, N. L., 1047
Desbrus, L., 1061
Desserprit, A., 231
Deutsch, H., 232
DeVault, S., 233
Devereux, S. A., 566
Dewis, M. E., 238
de Young, M., 239
Diamond, L. J., 240, 515, 516
DiBrezzo, R., 486
Dickens, B. M., 241
Dickin, K. L., 242
Dickman, I. R., 243
Diener, E., 160
Dietrich, K. N., 986
Distad, L., 247
Dixon, H., 249
Docherty, J., 250, 251
Donovan, A. M., 252
Dorner, S., 253
Doucette, J., 254, 255
Downes, M., 256
Drakes, O., 257
Drapkin, I., 930
Dreyer, L., 258
Driessen, J., 226
Droegemueller, W., 541
Drouet, M., 259
Drummond, H. P., 260
Dubé, R., 261
Dudley-Marling, C., 1091
Dumas, J., 1035

Duncan, C. C., 676
Duncan, D., 262
Duncan, D. F., 458
Dunivant, N., 535
Dunn, M., 263
Dupras, A., 264, 265, 266, 267
Dupre la Tour, M., 268
Dutton, D. G., 653
Dyer, C., 1092
Dykes, L. J., 269

E

Eaton, M. W., 649
Edmonson, B., 270
Edwards, J. P., 271, 272, 273
Egberg, K., 937
Egeland, B., 274
Egley, L. C., 275
Eisen, K., 1009
Eisen, P., 276
Elder, B. P., 277
Eldredge, E., 278
Elgar, S., 279
Elias, S. F., 280
Elias-Burger, S. F., 281
Elkins, T. E., 272, 282, 283
Ellerstein, N. S., 557, 626
Elliott, F. A., 284
Elliott, M., 285
Ellis, J. W., 286, 287
Ellis, M., 288
Ellison, P. H., 289
Elmer, E., 290
Elonen, A. S., 291
Embry, L. H., 292
Emery, R. E., 456
Ende, A., 293
Endicott, O., 294, 295, 296
Englehardt, B., 452
Engman, K., 297, 298
Enos, W. F., 299
Ensor, P. G., 996
Epley, S. A., 962
Eppler, M., 300
Epps, S., 820
Evans, A. L., 301, 302
Evans, J., 303, 304
Everson, M. D., 87, 88

F

Fachting, D. D., 431
Fantuzzo, J. W., 305
Farber, J., 530
Feinmann, J., 309
Feinstein, C., 526
Feldman, M. A., 1033
Felske, A. W., 94
Felton, D. K., 602
Fenlon, S., 341
Ferguson, C. A., 660
Fernandez, P., 152
Feutl, R., 310
Fewell, R. R., 346, 1047, 1048
Fidone, G. S., 311
Fifield, B. B., 312
Fine, M. J., 313
Finkel, P., 314
Finkelhor, D., 315, 316, 317, 318, 784, 785
Fischer, H. L., 319, 320
Fischer, J., 386, 450, 548, 561
Fischhoff, J., 986
Fisher, G., 323
Fisher, N. W., 322
Fishwick, M., 314
Fitz-Gerald, D. R., 324, 325, 326
Fitz-Gerald, M., 324, 325, 326
Fletcher, D., 327, 328
Flinn, S., 329
Floor, L., 330
Floorian, V., 331
Flor, H., 332
Flynn, M. C., 333, 334
Flynn, R. J., 335
Flynt, S. W., 336
Foon, D., 337
Forchuk, C., 628, 629
Ford, A., 443
Forget, C. A., 338
Forrester, R. G., 339
Fournel, G., 1035
Foxx, R. M., 340, 341, 342
Fraley, Y. L., 815
Frankish, P., 343
Franklin, A. W., 436, 613
Freda, M., 729
Frederick, C. J., 344
Freeman, B. J., 830
Freeman, S. T., 345
Frey, K. S., 346
Friedman, D. L., 1107
Friedman, P. R., 623
Friedman, S. B., 704
Friedrich, W. N., 347, 348, 349
Frisch, L. E., 350
Fritz, G. F., 835
Frodi, A. M., 351
Fryer, G. E., 352, 353
Fugl-Meyer, A. R., 354, 938
Fujii, K., 355

G

Gabinet, L., 356
Gafford, L. S., 282
Gaines, R. W., 406, 407, 857
Gallagher, D., 160
Gallagher, J. J., 106
Galler, K. C., 521
Gallo, L. G., 357
Garbarino, J., 113, 114, 358, 359, 360, 361, 399, 674, 694, 1001, 1089
Garber, H. L., 1116
Gardner, D. M., 537
Gardner, N. E. S., 362
Garfinkel, L., 363
Garmise, R., 364
Gartell, N. K., 365
Garwick, G. B., 1006
Gates, M., 109
Gath, A., 366
Geist, C. S., 367
Geist, R. F., 368
Gelles, R. J., 946
Gerbner, G., 81
Gerhardt, J. J., 1096
Gerring, J. P., 369
Giami, A., 370, 371, 372
Gibbens, T. C., 373
Gibson, D. E., 374
Gigeroff, A. K., 375
Gil, E., 376, 377
Gilbert, T., 378, 379
Gilchrist, L. D., 876
Giles, K., 380
Gillan, P., 381
Gillberg, C., 382
Gillon, R., 1092
Gioia-Hasick, D., 605
Giordano, J. A., 64
Gittler, M., 65
Glantz, L., 60
Glaser, D., 383
Glass, D. C., 530
Glisson, C. A., 384
Glueckauf, R. L., 385
Gochenor, C., 601
Gochros, H. L., 100, 339, 384, 386, 450, 519, 524, 542, 547, 548, 561, 574, 596, 634, 715, 888, 922
Gochros, J. S., 386, 450, 542, 548, 561
Godkin, M. A., 1098
Goerdt, A., 387
Goff, G. A., 226
Goins, C., 305
Goldberg, B., 388
Goldberg, M., 363
Goldberg, P. F., 363
Golden, C. U., 893
Golden, G., 282
Golden, J. S., 605
Goldman, B. D., 400
Goldson, E., 1024

Goldstein, H., 389
Gomes-Schwartz, B., 390
Goodman, L., 391
Goodman, R. E., 392
Goodwin, J., 393, 395
Goodwin, L. R., 394
Goodwin, O., 395
Gordon, N. H., 514
Gordon, S., 170, 396
Gorka, C., 363
Gostason, R., 397
Gothard, T. W., 398
Gottlieb, B. H., 399
Goudge, J., 1003
Gougen, L., 954
Gowen, J. W., 400
Graff, D., 401
Grant, L. J., 402
Grant, S. T., 93
Gravel, S., 403
Graves, K., 1099
Gray, S., 956
Green, A. H., 404, 405, 406, 407, 857, 864, 865
Green, B., 408
Green, D. T., 409
Green, F. C., 410
Green, R., 434, 1083
Greenberg, M. T., 1047, 1048
Greenberg, S., 363
Greengross, W., 411
Greenland, C., 412
Greer, J. G., 718
Gregg, G. S., 290
Greydanus, D. E., 413
Griffin, H. C., 849
Griffiths, D., 414, 415, 471
Gripton, J., 416, 1049
Grob, G. N., 417
Grodin, M. A., 60
Gross, M., 418
Grossman, R., 419
Grossnickle, W. F., 143, 795
Groth, N., 420
Grothaus, R. S., 421
Grumbach, M., 690
Gruson, L., 422
Gualdi, G., 162
Guarnaschelli, D., 423
Gudalefsky, A. B., 6
Gudjonsson, G. H., 424
Guess, D., 425
Guggenheim, P. D., 364
Gunn, M., 424, 426
Gunner, A., 427
Gural, M., 640

H

Haavik, S. F., 428, 429

Haddock, M. D., 430
Hadler, J. L., 398
Haight, S. L., 431
Haines, A., 432, 850
Hakim-Elahi, E., 433
Hall, J. C., 849
Hall, J. E., 434, 435
Hall, M. H., 436
Hall, R., 305
Halliday, S., 437
Halliechuk, R., 438
Hallingby, L., 439
Halpern, R., 440
Halstead, K., 441
Halstead, L. O., 441
Hammond, D. B., 442
Hamre-Nietupski, S., 67, 443, 444
Handy, L., 485
Hanke, G. C., 445
Hansen, C., 446
Hansen, J. C., 284
Hanson, R., 377, 447, 473
Hardman, M. L., 838
Harrell, S. A., 448
Harrington, A., 363
Harris, V. S., 449
Harrison, D. F., 450
Harry, B., 451
Hart, C. A., 860
Hartman, C., 452
Hartman, C. R., 125, 126, 344, 365, 685, 732
Harvey, M. A., 453
Harvey, W., 454
Haseltine, B., 258
Hasselt, V. B. V., 936
Hastings, M. M., 455
Haugaard, J. J., 456, 457
Hawkins, W. E., 458
Haynes, M. R., 718
Haywood, H. C., 1116
Head, D. W., 70
Hébert, M., 261
Hebert, P., 459
Heger, B., 261
Helfen, C. S., 604
Helfer, R. E., 460, 461, 462, 565, 624
Helmstetter, E., 425
Hensy, O., 463
Herman, J., 464
Herman, J. L., 365
Herold, E. S., 615
Herrenkohl, E. C., 465
Herrenkohl, R. C., 465
Hersen, M., 20, 21, 22, 23, 24, 25
Heshusius, L., 466
Hewitt, S. E., 467
Hicho, D., 825
Hickman, M. L., 529
Hill, B. K., 839
Hill, G., 468

Hingsburger, D., 414, 415, 469, 470, 471
Hirayama, H., 472
Hirschbach, E., 473
Hitching, M., 200
Hobbs, C. J., 474
Hochstadt, N. J., 475
Hoffman, N. D., 476
Hohenshil, T. H., 477, 489
Holbrook, T., 478
Holder, V., 479
Hollingsworth, D. K., 483
Holloway, C. P., 910
Holmes, C. S., 884
Holmes, G. E., 394
Hopper, C. E., 480
Hopper, D., 481
Horowitz, J. M., 390
Horowitz, R. M., 482, 736
Hosie, T. W., 483
Howard, J., 763
Hoxter, S., 484
Hucker, S., 485, 740
Huggins, J., 339
Hughes, H. M., 486
Hughes, R. C., 487
Hughes, R. D., 774
Hulnick, H. R., 488
Hulnick, M. R., 488
Humbert-Viveret, C., 372
Humes, C. W., 489
Hunter, R. S., 490
Hurley, A. D., 491, 492, 493, 494, 495, 496, 497, 967, 968, 969, 970, 971, 972, 973, 974, 975, 976, 977, 978, 979, 980, 981, 982
Hurley, F. J., 491, 492

I

Ilett, S. J., 463
Irvine, A. C., 506

J

Jabaley, T., 584
Jacobson, A., 508, 509, 510
Jacobson, J. W., 511, 514
Jaffe, A. C., 1030
James, B., 513
Jamison, C. B., 34
Janicki, M. P., 514
Jansen, P. E., 1012
Janson, D., 689
Jaudes, P. K., 240, 475, 515, 516
Jensen, S. B., 885

Jerrell, J. M., 517
Johnson, D. G., 639
Johnson, E., 261
Johnson, G. S., 518
Johnson, J. D., 519
Johnson, W. R., 520
Johnson-Martin, N., 400
Johnston, P. R., 219
Jones, C. O., 521
Jones, D. P. H., 522
Jones, T. R., 523
Jones-Brown, C., 509
Joseph, B., 524

K

Kaeser, F., 525
Kahn, J. V., 582, 583, 1037
Kaminer, Y., 526
Kaplan, S. J., 527
Kaplan, S. L., 690
Karagianis, L. D., 731
Kastner, T. A., 528, 529
Katz, I., 530
Katz, M., 563, 564
Katz, S., 758, 759
Kaufman, B., 644
Kazak, A. E., 531, 532
Keall, B., 533
Kearns, A., 534
Keilitz, I., 535
Keith-Spiegel, P., 792, 793
Kelleher, M. E., 536
Keller, R. A., 537
Keller, S., 538
Kelley, M., 1088
Kelley, S. J., 539
Kellogg, R. C., 540
Kelly, J. A., 1099
Kempe, C. H., 541, 624, 627, 707, 708, 989
Kempe, R. S., 460, 461, 462, 522, 565
Kempton, W., 542, 543, 544, 545, 546, 547, 548
Kennedy, M., 549
Kent, D., 550
Kern, L. H., 1027
Kerns, D. L., 278
Kerr, D. L., 552
Kester, B. L., 553
Kiernan, K. E., 554
Kiernan, W. E., 1013
Kilstrom, N., 490
King, M. A., 1108
King, P., 1096
Kirkham, M. A., 555, 556, 867, 868, 869, 873, 876
Kirkland, R. T., 145

Klein, D. M., 557
Klein, N. K., 920
Kline, D. F., 558, 559
Klingman, J. A., 1044
Knappett, K., 560
Knight, S. E., 121, 122, 314, 561, 852
Knopp, F. H., 562
Knudsen, C., 367
Koehler, J. E., 509
Koller, H., 563, 564
Korbin, J. E., 565
Koss, M. P., 829
Kraizer, S. K., 352, 353
Krajicek, M. J., 319, 320
Kratochvil, M. S., 566
Krausz, S., 567, 568
Kravetz, S., 758, 759
Kreigsman, K. S., 569
Krenk, C. J., 570
Krents, E., 571
Krug, R. S., 572
Krugman, R. D., 573
Kubie, U., 407
Kunkel, D., 472
Kunkel, O. D., 574
Kurland, J. A., 595
Kurtz, P. D., 575
Kusinitz, M., 576

L

LaBarre, A., 577
LaBrie, R., 982
Lafrance, G., 578
Lakin, K. C., 579, 839
Laman, D. S., 71
Lamond, D. A. P., 580
Lane, M. E., 581
Lang, R. E., 582, 583
Langevin, R., 485
Largent, J. A., 289
Larsen, J. K., 517
Laszlo, K., 584
Laval, D., 372
Lawson, A. W., 753
Lawson, G. W., 753
Lawton-Speert, S., 1009
Leavitt, J. E., 541, 880
Lee, U., 423
LeGrand, C., 585
Lehne, G. K., 586
Leitenberg, H., 170
Leong, G. B., 929
Letch, M., 180
Levine, S. B., 587
Levitt, C. J., 588
Lévy, J. J., 265, 266, 267
Levy, J. M., 589
Levy, P. H., 589

Lewark, C. A., 590
Lewis, K. C., 591
Liebow, P. R., 593
Lifschitz, S., 1083
Liggett, K. R., 893
Light, J., 594
Lightcap, J. L., 595
Linafelter, G. T., 363
Lister, L., 596
Livneh, H., 597
Llewellyn, M. H., 598
Lloyd-Bostock, S., 599
Loadman, E., 660
Lobato, D., 553
Loda, F., 490
Lombana, J. H., 600
Long, T. E., 143
Longo, R. E., 601
Lorber, R., 602
Lording, D. W., 807
Love, E., 603
Loyd, B. H., 1120
Lubetsky, M. J., 21, 22, 25
Lucas, B. M., 761
Lucido, D. J., 530
Luckasson, R. A., 287
Luiselli, J. K., 604
Lukoff, D., 605
Lund, J., 606
Lundervold, D., 607
Luterman, D., 608
Lutzer, V. D., 609

M

Mabli, J., 228
MacDonald, A., 610
MacDonald, J. M., 611
MacDougall, D., 1108
MacEachron, A. E., 612
MacIntosh, B., 452
MacKeith, R., 613
Macleod, S., 614
Magnusson, J., 1082
Makas, E., 192, 212
Maksym, D., 1003
Malloy, G. L., 615
Marchetti, A., 620
Margolin, K. N., 621
Marion, R. L., 622
Marker, G., 623
Martin, D. C., 995
Martin, H., 624
Martin, H. P., 625, 626, 627
Martin, M., 628, 629
Martorana, G. R., 630
Mastrocola-Morris, E., 631
Masuda, S., 632, 633
Matek, O., 634

Mathus, B., 756
Matlak, M. E., 639
Matson, J. L., 635, 636, 717
Matthews, G. F., 637
Maurice, W. L., 1010
Mayer, A., 638
Mayer, T., 639
McAfee, J. K., 640
McArther, S., 641
McCaffrey, M., 642
McCarthy, L. P., 369
McCay, V., 643
McCelland, C. O., 644
McClellan, M. C., 645
McClennen, S., 646
McCombs, K., 270
McCormack, M. K., 446
McCormick, A., 139
McCown, D. E., 647
McCrone, W. P., 648
McDowell, W. A., 649
McEwen, E., 650
McFadden, E. J., 651
McFarlane, A. C., 652
McGillivray, B., 37
McGonigle, J. J., 25
McGrath, M., 147, 766
McGregor, B. M. S., 653
McHale, S. M., 449
McKay, S. E., 893
McKinlay, I. A., 301, 302
McKitric, E. J., 1093
McKown, J. M., 654
McLaren, J., 655
McLaughlin, T. F., 598
McMorrow, M. J., 340, 341, 342
McNab, W. L., 656
McPherson, C., 657, 658, 659
McQueen, W. M., 430
McQuiston, M., 522
McRae, K. N., 660
Meddin, B. J., 662
Meddock, T. D., 55
Meier, J. H., 663, 664, 665, 666, 880
Melberg, K., 667, 668, 669, 670, 671, 672
Melling, L., 673
Melton, G. B., 674
Meltzer, N. J., 556
Menninger, K., 210
Menninger, K. A., II, 429
Menolascino, F. J., 675
Ment, L. R., 676
Mercer, A., 683
Mercer, J., 683
Meredith, W. H., 1
Merson, R. M., 684
Mertz, A. W., 685
Mesibov, G. B., 686
Messeier, C., 223
Messier, C., 687

Meyer, D. J., 1047, 1048
Meyers, C. E., 79
Michael, A., 688
Michael, H., 936
Milhous, R. L., 553
Miller, T. W., 689
Miller, W. L., 690
Millor, G., 201
Mindel, E. D., 584
Mishra, K. D., 216
Mitchell, C. C., 143
Mitchell, D. R., 693
Miyoshi, T., 352, 353
Mock, P., 273
Modzeleski, W., 694
Moglia, R., 695
Monast, S., 696
Monat, R. K., 697
Monat-Haller, R. K., 698
Money, J., 699
Moore, T., 700
Morgan, R., 781
Morgan, S. R., 702
Morris, A., 703
Morris, H. L., 435
Morse, C. W., 704
Moss, S. R., 705
Motz, J. K., 743
Mowbray, C. T., 706
Mrazek, D. A., 708
Mrazek, P. B., 707, 708, 989
Mrinal, N. R., 806
Mueser, K. T., 709
Mullen, C., 710, 711
Muller, N. D., 712
Mullins, J. B., 713
Muram, D., 282, 283
Murph, J. R., 1103
Murphy, C., 363
Murphy, D. M., 714
Murphy, G. J., 715
Murphy, L., 716
Murphy, W. D., 176, 717, 718
Murray, W. J., 54
Musick, J. L., 719
Myers, J. E., 720
Myers, P. A., 762
Myre, J. G., 721

N

Naish, J., 1092
Nasjleti, M., 513
Neff, J., 726
Neistadt, M. E., 727, 728, 729
Nelson, M., 730, 915, 932, 993
Nelson, W. P., 664
Nesbit, W. C., 731

Nessel, K. L., 314
Newberger, C. M., 732
Newberger, E. H., 732
Newbern, V. B., 733
Nicholson, E. B., 736
Nigro, G., 737
Nobel, B., 738
Norelius, K. L., 555, 556
Norton, W. A., 740
Novick, B. E., 1040
Nucci, M., 741
Nuechterlein, K. H., 605
Nuehring, E., 3
Nuehring, E. M., 742, 1122
Nunno, M. A., 743

O

Oates, K., 744
O'Connor, A., 534, 745
O'Day, B., 746, 747
Ogle, P., 327, 328
Olarte, S., 365
Oliver, J. E., 119, 748, 749
O'Neill, J., 525
Orem, R. C., 448
Oreskes, M., 752
O'Sullivan, C. M., 753
Oswin, M., 754

P

Page, F., 755
Page, R. C., 756
Page, T. J., 820
Paiement, J., 757
Painsky, A., 758, 759
Paniagua, C., 760
Paradis, D. M., 761
Parish, R. A., 762
Parker, T., 4
Parmelee, A. H., 763
Parnes, P., 594
Parry, J., 736
Pasamanick, B., 765
Passer, A., 147, 766
Pate, T. C., 756
Patterson, J. B., 483
Patton, J. R., 983
Paty, D., 1010
Paty, D. W., 1009
Paul, R., 408
Payne, A. T., 767
Peacock, A., 744
Pearl, D., 66
Pelcovitz, D., 527

Pemberton, B., 604
Penfold, P. S., 768
Penny, R. E., 769
Per-Lee, M. S., 770
Perry, R. P., 1082
Persse, L., 644
Pervin-Dixon, L., 771
Petchesky, R. P., 772
Peterson, Y., 773
Pettis, K. W., 774
Phaneuf, J., 775
Phillips,. L. R., 62
Phillips, L. R., 776, 777, 778, 779, 780
Piliavin, I., 209
Pillai, V., 781
Pillemer, K., 782, 783, 784, 785
Pillemer, K. A., 1098
Pilon, J., 757
Pincus, S., 786
Pingree, C., 830
Pitceathly, A. S., 150, 787
Pitts, F. W., 423
Polloway, E. A., 983
Ponticas, Y., 820
Pope, J. G., 795
Pope, K. S., 38, 788, 789, 790, 791, 792, 793
Poteat, G. M., 795
Potter, S. J., 213
Prasad, J. K., 93
Price-Williams, D., 205
Priegert, P., 796
Pueschel, S. M., 799, 800
Purdue, C., 137
Purnick, J., 801

Q

Quackenbush, M., 932, 993
Qualey, T. L., Jr., 802
Quastel, L. N., 184
Quinn, K. M., 803
Quinsey, V. L., 415

R

Rabb, J., 804, 826
Raboch, J., 805
Radocker, M. M., 122
Ramteke, B. S., 806
Rauh, J., 147, 766
Rawicki, H., 807
Ray, C., 808, 809
Reed, J., 811
Reeves, D. J., 334
Reid, J. B., 602

Reiner, E. S., 1096
Reinhart, M. A., 813
Reiss, S., 741
Reiter, R. S., 814
Reivich, J. S., 815
Rekate, H., 644
Rempusheski, V. F., 778, 779, 780
Renvoize, J., 816
Reppucci, N. D., 457
Rhoads, F. A., 350
Ricci, L. R., 818
Richard, D., 819
Richardson, B., 510
Richardson, S. A., 563, 564
Richman, G. S., 820
Rideau, W., 821
Ridington, J., 822
Rieve, J. E., 823
Rindfleisch, N., 804, 824, 825, 826
Rinear, E. E., 827
Rioux, M., 94, 828
Risen, C. B., 587
Risin, L. I., 829
Ritvo, E. R., 830
Robertson, G., 373, 831
Robertson, G. A., 142
Robinault, I. P., 832
Robinson, D., 648
Robinson, G. A., 983
Robinson, L. D., 833
Robinson, S., 834
Roby, B. A., 149
Rockney, R. M., 835
Rogers, B., 342
Rogers, R. G., 837
Rongstaf, S., 660
Rose, E., 838
Rosen, M., 330
rosenbloom, L., 463
Ross, C. J., 81
Rotegard, L. L., 839
Rothblum, E. D., 553
Rousso, M., 840, 841
Rouyer, M., 259
Rowe, D. S., 676
Rowe, W., 842, 843
Rowitz, L., 844, 845
Rowland, C. M., 161
Rozovsky, F. A., 846, 847
Rozovsky, L. E., 846, 847
Rubenstein, G. M, 860
Rubinstein, A., 1040
Ruff, H. A., 1040
Ruff, K., 848
Runyan, D. K., 398
Rurrow, A. A., 193
Rusch, R. G., 849
Rutledge, H., 850
Ryan, B. A., 242
Rycus, J. S., 487
Ryerson, E., 852, 853, 854

S

Sahler, O. Z., 704
St. Lawrence, J., 1099
Samowitz, P., 589
Samson, J. M., 266
Sanders, G. L., 855, 856
Sandgrund, A., 406, 857
Santamour, M., 858
Sargent, L. R., 983
Sarkadi, L., 859
Saunders, S., 860
Sauzier, M., 390
Savage, S., 842, 843
Savells, J., 861
Scagnelli, B., 528
Scanlan, J. M., 114, 1001, 1002
Schachter, J., 475
Schaefer, G., 862
Scharfetter, C., 863
Schetky, D. H., 405, 864
Scheurer, S. L., 894
Schilit, J., 866
Schilling, R. F., 555, 556, 867, 868,
      869, 870, 871, 872, 873, 874, 875,
      876
Schinke, S. P., 555, 556, 867, 868, 869,
      870, 871, 872, 873, 874, 875, 876
Schirmer, B. R., 877
Schlesinger, B., 316, 878
Schmideberg, M., 879
Scholz, J. P., 880
Scholz, O. B., 332
Schopler, E., 106, 107, 686, 882
Schor, D. P., 883, 884
Schover, L. R., 885, 886
Schuler, M., 887
Schulman, V., 571
Schultz, G. L., 888
Schultz, J. B., 889
Schuster, C. S., 890, 891
Schuster, R., 364
Schwaiger, B., 1096
Schwier, K. M., 892
Scola, P. S., 800
Scott, M. L., 893
Seagull, E. A. W., 894
Sears, J. M., 413
Seemanova, E., 898
Seltzer, G. B., 39
Seltzer, M. M., 39
Selvin, H., 1083
Semmler, C. J., 899
Sengstock, W. L., 900
Senn, C. Y., 901
Sgroi, S., 906, 907, 908, 909
Shah, C. P., 910
Sha'ked, A., 335, 911
Shaman, E., 912, 913, 914, 915
Shane, J. F., 916
Shapiro, E. S., 917
Shapiro, E. T., 918

Shapland, J., 599
Shaughnessy, M. F., 919
Shaul, R., 1016
Shaw, J., 188
Sheridan, C. A., 917
Shevin, M., 920
Shore, D. A., 100, 339, 384, 519, 524,
      547, 574, 596, 634, 715, 888, 921,
      922
Shrey, D. E., 923
Shuger, N. B., 924
Sigelman, C., 96
Sigelman, C. K., 280, 281, 925, 926,
      927, 928
Silva, J. A., 929
Silver, H. K., 541
Silverman, F. N., 541
Silverman, R. A., 930
Silverton, R., 931
Simpson, K. M., 932
Sinason, V., 933, 934
Sinclair, B., 821
Singer, S., 109
Singh, T. H., 1092
Siskind, A. B., 935
Sisson, L. A., 936
Sjogren, K., 354, 937, 938
Skinner, B. F., 939
Sloan, I. J., 940
Sloan, M. P., 665, 666
Sluyter, G. V., 941
Smigielski, P., 942
Smith, J. T., 943
Smith, S., 944
Smith, S. L., 945
Smith, S. M., 946, 947
Smythe, D., 1024
Snell, M. E., 1120
Snow, W. H., 869
Snyder, R., 660
Sobsey, D., 948, 949, 950, 951, 952,
      953, 954, 955, 956
Soeffing, M., 957
Sohn, H. A., 958
Solnit, A., 959
Solomons, G., 960, 961, 962
Solz, D., 314
Somers, M. N., 963
Somerville, M. A., 964
Sorenson, K., 367
Souther, M. D., 965
Sovner, R., 493, 494, 495, 496, 497,
      966, 967, 968, 969, 970, 971, 972,
      973, 974, 975, 976, 977, 978, 979,
      980, 981, 982
Sparks, S., 983
Speake, B., 334
Spica, M. M., 984
Spicer, P. P., 124
Spinnato, J., 283
Standish, M., 524

Stark, J. A., 675
Starr, R., 986
Stavis, P., 987
Stavrakaki, C., 988
Steele, B. F., 541, 989
Steele, S., 990
Steinmann, M., 942
Sterling-Honig, A., 991
Stern, N., 421
Stiggall, L., 993
Stocking, S. H., 361, 399
Stolov, W. C., 175
Stoneman, Z., 994
Storey, K., 342
Stovall, B., 651
Stradiotti, J., 437
Streissguth, A. P., 995
Striar, S. L., 996
Strongman, K. T., 997
Stuart, C. K., 998, 999, 1000
Stuart, I. R., 718
Stuart, V. W., 999, 1000
Sullivan, G., 605
Sullivan, P., 114
Sullivan, P. M., 1001, 1002
Sumarah, J., 1003
Summers, J. A., 362, 428
Sundem, J. M., 854
Sundram, C. J., 1004, 1005
Sunjukrishnan, R., 947
Sutherland, J., 419
Swanson, C. K., 1006
Swick, K. J., 1008
Sylvester, P. E., 15
Szasz, G., 1009, 1010
Szymanski, L. S., 1011, 1012, 1013,
      1014
Szymanski, E. M., 477, 489

T

Tabachnick, B. G., 792, 793
Taitz, L. S., 1015
Talbot, Y., 1016
Tallon, R. J., 7
Tanguay, P. E., 1012, 1014
Tarantino, L., 987
Tasch, V., 1017
Taylor, M. E., 1018, 1019
Taylor, M. O., 1020
Taynard, J., 1035
Tegtmeier, W., 1021
Templin, K. H., 762
Terpstra, J., 193
Testa, W. R., 528
Thies, A. P., 1023
Thomas, A., 152, 1024
Thomas, G., 193, 1025, 1026

Thompson, V., 700
Thorn-Gray, B. E., 1027
Thornton, N. G., 238
Thurer, S. L., 1029
Ticoll, M., 94
Tilelli, J. A., 1030
Torre, D., 110
Torres, E. R., 1031
Tower, C. C., 1032
Towns, F., 1033
Traustadottir, R., 1034
Tremblay, R., 267
Trevelyn, J., 1036
Tripp, A. W., 1037
Tsai, F. Y., 289
Tucker, M., 109
Turek, D., 1030
Turk, D. C., 332
Turnbull, H. R., III, 425
Turner, J. L., 1114
Turner, T. S., 1038
Tyser, K. M., 113

U

Ufford Dickerson, M., 1039
Ultman, M. H., 1040
Underwood, N., 1041, 1042
Unkovic, C. M., 1044
Uso, T., 225

V

Vadasy, P. F., 346, 1047, 1048
Valenti, H., 709
Valentich, M., 416, 1049
Valentine, D., 141
Valkil, D. V., 910
Valles, G., 1050
Vander-Kolk, C. J., 1051
Vander Mey, B. J., 1052
VanDusen, L., 1053.
Van Hasselt, V. B., 20, 23, 24, 25
Vanier, J., 1054, 1055
van Staden, J. T., 1056
Vargo, B., 988
Varley, C. K., 1057
Varnet, T., 1058
Varnhagen, C., 953, 954, 955
Vaughan, C. E., 1059
Vaughan, J., 1059
Veltkamp, L. J., 689
Ventura, J., 30
Vergason, G. A., 900
Verkunen, M., 1060
Vernon, M., 1002

Viano, E., 930
Viossat, P., 1061
Vivian, V. L., 115, 278, 761
Vizard, E., 1062
Vockell, E., 1064
Vockell, K., 1064
Voeller, K., 407
Vogel, B., 93
Vogel, P., 1065
Vogel, P. A., 1066
von Eschenbach, A. C., 886
von Hentig, H., 1068

W

Wagner, D., 761
Wagner, G. N., 1069
Wagner, N., 560
Walbroehl, G. S., 1070
Walker, M. L., 639
Walker-Hirsch, L. W., 148
Wallace, D. H., 122
Wallander, J. L., 224
Walmsley, S., 1071
Walter, E., 1072
Wapnick, S., 273
Ward, S., 1073
Ward-McKinlay, C., 1074
Ward-McKinlay, T., 1074
Warren, R. D., 166, 167
Wasilewski, D. L., 1107
Wasserman, G. A., 1076
Watson, J. D., 1077
Watson-Russell, A., 454
Way, I. I. O., 1078
Wayment, H. A., 1079
Waynberg, J., 1080
Webster, C. D., 740
Weicker, L., 1081
Weiner, B., 1082
Weinstock, R., 929
Weisberg, S. R., 4
Welbourne, A., 1083
Wells, D., 956
West, B., 858
West, J., 808, 809
Weymar, W., 1087
Whelan, E., 334
White, R., 109, 1088
Whitmore, K., 1024
Whitson, L., 273
Whittaker, J. K., 1089
Wickens, B., 1090
Widerstrom, A. H, 1091
Wilks, C. S., 282
Williams, R., 1092
Williams, W., 67, 444
Williamson-Ige, D. K., 1093
Willmuth, M. E., 1094

Wilturner, L., 349
Winett, R. W., 1095
Winkler, R. C., 1095
Winkler, W. H., 1096
Wish, J., 270
Wolf, L., 1097
Wolf, R. S., 1098
Wolfe, D. A., 1099
Wolford, C. A., 1019
Wong, C. B., 1100
Wood, M. H., 1101
Wood, T. A., 336
Wooden, K., 1102
Woodhead, J. C., 1103
Worthington, G. M., 1104
Wortzman, G., 485
Wray, L., 305
Wright, E. C., 1105
Wright, J. M. C., 105
Wulff, L., 1088
Wynne, J. M., 474

Y

Yakovleff, A., 149
Yarmol, K., 828
Yarnold, P. R., 709
Yates, A., 1106
Yoshida, L., 1107
Yuille, J. C., 1108

Z

Zadnik, D., 1109
Zakarewski, M. S. S., 1110
Zantal-Weiner, K., 1111
Zarfas, D. E., 1097
Zeller, C., 1112
Zelman, D. B., 113
Zetlin, A. G., 1079, 1114
Ziefert, M., 651
Ziezula, F. R., 648
Ziff, S. F., 1115
Zigler, E., 81, 1116
Zigman, W. B., 514
Zimlich, N., 1117
Zimo, D. A., 475
Zirpoli, T. J., 1118, 1119, 1120
Zitzow, D., 1121
Zouhar, M. S., 395
Zuckerman, M., 3, 742, 1122
Zwarensteyn, S. B., 291
Zweier, D., 986
Zwerner, J., 1123

Subject Index

All numbers in this index refer to abstract numbers.

A

Abduction, 309, 352, 422

Abortion, 146, 324, 434, 520, 524, 1113

Abuse, 3, 11, 18, 50, 79, 91, 115, 118, 133, 153, 161, 166, 179, 193, 230, 247, 250, 251, 276, 284, 289, 300, 313, 363, 376, 398, 417, 421, 430, 558, 623, 639, 644, 665, 669, 672, 688, 689, 691, 700, 703, 704, 705, 734, 735, 742, 761, 768, 776, 777, 778, 780, 785, 801, 815, 825, 838, 848, 861, 877, 894, 939, 958, 1004, 1005, 1008, 1041, 1069, 1081, 1085, 1086, 1099, 1111, 1112, 1122

    causes, 357, 359, 360, 361, 375, 406, 407, 446, 448, 449, 465, 473, 527, 707, 749, 753, 782, 849, 861, 945

    disability as risk factor, 10, 18, 29, 61, 77, 94, 132, 135, 154, 156, 167, 189, 209, 239, 240, 245, 246, 254, 292, 336, 347, 348, 350, 351, 360, 383, 390, 398, 405, 406, 420, 458, 463, 467, 527, 559, 590, 594, 595, 601, 622, 638, 641, 647, 653, 657 664, 666, 695, 701, 702, 710, 711, 713, 723, 731, 774, 787, 796, 822, 879, 901, 916, 949, 953, 957, 960, 961, 986, 993, 1032, 1062, 1068, 1077, 1088, 1109, 1111, 1118, 1120

    effects of, 9, 15, 20, 29, 61, 85, 116, 119, 207, 274, 290, 300, 368, 410, 446, 486, 515, 521, 539, 541, 557, 602, 613, 625, 626, 627, 639, 653, 655, 676, 690, 699, 708, 748, 795, 857, 880, 884, 931, 933, 989, 1001, 1056, 1090

    financial, 11

    history of, 21, 25, 49, 147, 653, 795

    institutional, *see* Institutional abuse

    levels of, 829

    mental, 5, 11, 479, 504, 633

    organizational, 81, 868

    professionals 50, 733

    psychological 216, 410, 486, 664

    risk factors, 203, 782, 1071

    risk factors and disability, 24, 66, 292, 317, 318, 330, 348, 351, 356, 358, 379, 383, 406, 458, 552, 556, 565, 571, 662, 731, 763, 765, 871, 952, 959, 986, 1015, 1038, 1079, 1088, 1116, 1118

    secondary, 29, 58, 60, 481, 868

Acquaintance rape, *see* Rape

Acquiescence, 50, 91, 103, 203, 330, 344, 413, 425, 513, 518, 593, 610, 619, 750, 793, 871, 883, 915, 925, 926, 927, 1002, 1038, 1045, 1079, 1095, 1111

Acquired disability, 174, 561, 823, 832

Acquittals, 127, 616, 661, 670, 851

ACT (aggression control techniques), 3

Adjustment, 19, 20, 23, 59, 85, 98, 102, 175, 224, 225, 227, 252, 266, 327, 332, 346, 349, 350, 404, 488, 532, 549, 553, 566, 568, 572, 608, 683, 698, 756, 760, 773, 808, 809, 814, 832, 900, 923, 938, 986, 989, 1024, 1027, 1049, 1052, 1094, 1096, 1097, 1114

Adlerian psychology, 57

Administration, 113., 251, 272, 540, 643, 685, 752, 854, 919, 1005

Adolescence, 18, 84, 104, 155, 161, 169, 179, 193, 225, 235, 243, 276, 279, 324, 326, 344, 369, 373, 377, 382, 383, 389, 402, 404, 447, 473, 480, 535, 550, 552, 596, 607, 614, 616, 622, 637, 654, 724, 726, 766, 826, 832, 844, 853, 854, 870, 889, 895, 900, 919, 921, 927, 932, 935, 940, 959, 993, 1002, 1032, 1050, 1101, 1103, 1112, 1114

Adult protection, 5, 11, 68, 191, 235, 501, 502, 610, 659

Adult protection acts, 5, 11, 610

Adults abused as children, 246, 422, 791, 901, 1032, 1090

Adults, dependent, *see* Dependent adults

Advocacy, 33, 41, 118, 182, 232, 234, 237, 250, 251, 288, 393, 450, 464, 467, 482, 487, 515, 537, 575, 610, 659, 660, 669, 670, 723, 736, 822, 832, 848, 1005, 1023, 1029, 1078, 1081, 1122

Aesthetic aversion, 597

Affective disorders, *see* Emotional disorders

Agencies, 17, 29, 109, 121, 131, 136, 153, 157, 215, 237, 243, 250, 251, 321, 328, 363, 399, 405, 436, 437, 447, 454, 464, 528, 529, 545, 579, 658, 659, 694, 733, 736, 743, 749, 750, 751, 822, 826, 837, 868, 875, 953, 1018, 1072, 1104, 1109, 1110, 1122

AHRC training center and workshop, 1021

AIDS, 3, 55, 110, 215, 224, 249, 311, 331, 392, 528, 529, 552, 589, 617, 805, 845, 863, 900, 917, 929, 932, 972, 993, 1007, 1024, 1040, 1087

Alberta, 501, 502, 710, 711, 731, 796, 843, 859, 950, 956, 1063, 1078

Alcoholism, 104, 117, 270, 321, 355,

Alcoholism — *continued*
375, 517, 606, 653, 663, 677, 702, 707, 745, 749, 753, 995, 1022, 1060
Aleuts, 300
America, *see* United States
American Bar Association's National Resource Center of Child Advocacy and Protection and Commission on the Mentally Disabled, 736
American law, 987
American Psychiatric Association, 365
Amputation, 1096
Anal Examination, *see* Rectal examination
Anatomical dolls, 87, 88, 1108
Anatomy, 16, 40, 67, 270, 319, 323, 444, 628, 629, 698, 834, 917, 1037, 1043, 1108, 1113, 1121
Aneurism, 676, 938
   see also Stroke
Anorexia nervosa, 490, 805, 971, 1011
Antidepressant drugs, 967, 969, 971
Antilibidinal drugs, 134, 165
Antipsychotic drugs, 969
Anxiety disorder, 636
Appropriate sexual behavior, 150, 415, 609, 1049
Artificial insemination, 217, 807
Art therapy, 90
Assault, 245, 294, 379, 499, 557, 631, 992, 1084
   history of, 147, 394, 510, 745, 904
   physical, 162, 246, 285, 308, 508, 509, 510, 592, 621, 626, 641, 680, 681, 719, 746, 747, 764, 822, 827, 836, 881, 913, 998, 1063, 1078
   sexual, *see* Sexual assault
Assault Prevention Training Program, 204
Assertiveness, 116, 583, 628, 629, 746, 809, 892
   training, 102, 103, 200, 468, 1049
Assessment, 21, 22, 292, 369, 385, 415, 437, 462, 469, 485, 491, 495, 509, 584, 635, 636, 689, 718, 740, 767, 811, 823, 855, 874, 923, 931, 936, 973, 975, 977, 982, 990, 1014, 1049, 1064, 1078, 1099
   developmental, 106, 274, 290, 627, 875, 884
   sexual, 538, 416
Asexualization, *see* Sexual oppression, Sexual repression
Asthma, 768
Attachment formation, 78, 79
Attitudes, 7, 14, 29, 35, 56, 73, 92, 98, 104, 159, 169, 172, 176, 181, 184, 224, 253, 256, 264, 266, 270, 303,

329, 331, 348, 354, 371, 385, 403, 417, 419, 427, 435, 441, 442, 447, 456, 466, 487, 493, 538, 574, 578, 591, 597, 615, 645, 700, 715, 717, 729, 741, 746, 750, 768, 775, 809, 823, 834, 839, 840, 842, 843, 927, 966, 974, 998, 999, 1003, 1007, 1016, 1018, 1064, 1074, 1083, 1121
   health professionals, 5, 210, 211
   parents, 97, 150, 186, 190, 319, 391, 396, 428, 472, 603, 654, 702, 757, 766, 767, 876, 890, 900, 915, 1019, 1050, 1061, 1091, 1097
   scale, 90, 97, 1009
   society, 70, 186, 560, 667, 1100
Attribution theory, 539, 1082
Audio-visual resources, 158, 163, 173, 217, 235, 243, 261, 273, 363, 605, 703, 837, 1113
Australia, 10, 71, 77, 105, 144, 150, 276, 432, 580, 693, 712, 741, 744, 769, 834, 850, 997
Autism, 101, 107, 158, 252, 279, 382, 481, 555, 606, 686, 830, 882
Autoeroticism, 7, 54, 74, 176, 188, 211, 217, 232, 256, 270, 271, 272, 302, 328, 341, 372, 495, 520, 525, 604, 835, 842, 871, 1043, 1113
Aversive procedures 8, 186, 237, 351, 425, 447, 448, 493, 521, 651, 1002, 1099

B

Badgley Report, 36
Bailer–Cromwell Locus of Control, 102
Barbados, 387
Beck Depression Inventory 349, 1048
Behavior modification
   contingent, 188
   facial screening, 54
   management programs, 3, 21, 50, 188, 258, 282, 340, 341, 414, 425, 448, 487, 495, 562, 604, 607, 609, 610, 620, 651, 709, 789, 860, 971, 979, 1014, 1066, 1095, 1099, 1116, 1121
   negative reinforcement, 425
   overcorrection, 54, 604, 607
   positive reinforcement, 609
   time-out, 54
Beliefs, 1, 69, 190, 470, 591, 768, 793, 1074
   cognition, 2, 22, 214, 224, 235, 266, 339, 436, 464, 533, 610, 645, 713,

763, 794, 811, 884, 915, 997, 1041, 1063, 1087
Benzodiazepine, 969
Bestiality, 412
Bias, *see* Attitudes
Bibliographies, 52, 116, 123, 163, 192, 236, 260, 261, 273, 316, 320, 396, 500, 540, 614, 648, 653, 724, 730, 817, 878, 911, 916, 953
Bill of Rights, 3, 234, 237, 846
Biological factors, *see* Etiology
Birth control, 7, 65, 74, 89, 92, 145, 146, 147, 150, 199, 238, 242, 256, 264, 268, 270, 271, 272, 283, 367, 389, 433, 434, 435, 443, 520, 543, 628, 629, 766, 772, 786, 800, 834, 1113, 1123
Bisexuality, 485, 607
Blindness, *see* Visual impairment
Blood tests, *see* AIDS, Sexually transmitted diseases
   intellectual impairment, 311
Body image, 6, 140, 327, 500, 597, 654, 696, 840, 971
   see also Self-image
Boys, 9, 106, 207, 404
Boys Town, 688
Braille, 243
Brazelton scale, 995
Breaches of confidentiality, 739, 742
Breast examination, 917
Britain, *see* United Kingdom
British Columbia, 68, 437, 619, 691, 722, 750, 862
British law, *see* Law
Burnout, 143
Burns, 93, 95, 126, 410
Bus driver, 127, 128

C

Caida de Mollera, 423
Calgary, 128, 378, 379, 903, 1063, 1078
Canada, 53, 94, 254, 255, 261, 295, 388, 412, 438, 501, 632, 633, 653, 700, 740, 822, 837, 901, 953, 954, 956, 1009, 1108
Canadian Charter of Rights and Freedoms, 296, 812, 1065
Canadian Criminal Code, 36, 288
Canadian law, *see* Law
Cancer, 213, 886
Cardiovascular disorders *see* Heart conditions
Caregivers, 5, 29, 40, 41, 64, 72, 105, 112, 114, 147, 171, 176, 288, 314, 147, 171, 176, 288, 314, 351, 358, 376, 378, 428, 442, 502, 594, 610,

659, 662, 700, 779, 780, 782, 785, 804, 829, 874, 883, 885, 897, 940, 949, 960, 978, 991, 993, 1063, 1104, 1119, 1120
stress, 700, 785, 883
see also Personal care attendant
Case management, 1032
Case studies, 43, 80, 125, 201, 208, 300, 343, 415, 423, 496, 525, 596, 607, 760, 789, 856, 934, 942, 1034
CAT Scan, *see* Computer tomography
Catharsis, 860
Cause and effect, 446, 702, 857
see also Abuse
Celibacy, 554
Center for Abused Handicapped Children, 688
Cerebral palsy, 61, 78, 86, 154, 167, 240, 446, 463, 515, 555, 613, 840, 911, 960, 1024, 1115
Chapman Assertiveness Instrument, 102
Character disorder, 85, 473
Characteristics of abusive families, 18, 21, 29, 346, 351, 358, 406, 448, 537, 554, 593, 622, 749, 781, 871, 883, 1008, 1109, 1116, 1118
Characteristics of abusive parents, 18
Characteristics of offenders, 791, 1068
Characteristics of victims, 10, 117, 203, 293, 317, 336, 358, 527, 556, 663, 749, 765
Child abuse, 12, 22, 25, 43, 53, 61, 66, 75, 79, 81, 83, 85, 88, 91, 93, 95, 113, 115, 118, 132, 133, 135, 139, 153, 154, 155, 156, 157, 158, 164, 166, 167, 168, 179, 189, 193, 201, 209, 216, 230, 240, 247, 251, 260, 069, 274, 278, 289, 292, 293, 300, 306, 317, 321, 378, 350, 351, 352, 353, 356, 357, 359, 360, 363, 368, 383, 405, 406, 407, 410, 436, 446, 447, 448, 456, 458, 464, 463, 473, 474, 475, 490, 504, 515, 522, 527, 537, 540, 541, 556, 557, 558, 559, 565, 570, 571, 572, 580, 581, 590, 595, 602, 613, 622, 624, 626, 639, 642, 644, 645, 648, 651, 653, 659, 662, 663, 664, 665, 666, 676, 690, 691, 694, 699, 702, 713, 723, 725, 731, 734, 736, 748, 749, 752, 754, 761, 762, 763, 765, 781, 795, 801, 804, 813, 815, 817, 818, 824, 826, 837, 838, 857, 861, 875, 877, 880, 894, 916, 919, 931, 940, 945, 958, 959, 960, 961, 962, 986, 991, 1002, 1008, 1015, 1032, 1052, 1056, 1069, 1088, 1109, 1111,

1112, 1117, 1118
clients, 303, 570, 575, 1001, 1089
disability, 22, 66, 77, 90, 106, 135, 166, 186, 191, 209, 246, 336, 350, 449, 487, 532, 557, 559, 590, 613, 655, 659, 713, 797, 822, 867, 868, 944, 1030, 1032, 1034, 1042, 1084, 1090, 1103, 1104, 1111, 1119
elementary students, 235, 583
offenders, 2, 9, 239, 315, 390, 405, 653, 745, 791, 813, 837, 866, 883, 901, 915, 1030, 1042
preschool students, 58, 118, 167, 292, 390, 521, 762, 815
victims, 36, 77, 87, 114, 155, 168, 178, 189, 216, 218, 223, 239, 245, 247, 278, 316, 318, 355, 386, 390, 398, 405, 454, 456, 458, 490, 513, 521, 557, 571, 572, 581, 590, 594, 595, 653, 659, 666, 687, 692, 702, 733, 745, 753, 774, 791, 837, 857, 862, 866, 880, 883, 901, 915, 930, 933, 935, 940, 943, 989, 1001, 1030, 1042, 1052, 1062, 1090, 1104, 1112, 1116
witnesses, 454, 837, 940
see also Child sexual abuse; Neglect; Whiplash Shaken Infant syndrome
Child Abuse Potential Inventory (CAP), 795
Childbearing, 33
Child Behavior Checklist, 1001
Child care workers, 363, 473
Child offenders, 9, 405, 813, 1042, 1073
Child protection workers, 868
see also Advocacy
Child psychiatry, 116, 152, 404, 526, 689, 768, 1062
CHILDHELP USA / INTERNATIONAL, 663
Child sexual abuse, 12, 25, 26, 27, 36, 37, 38, 43, 58, 60, 64, 83, 85, 87, 88, 90, 113, 114, 116, 117, 163, 164, 168, 184, 185, 186, 191, 216, 218, 222, 223, 235, 236, 239, 245, 246, 254, 258, 260, 261, 272, 278, 285, 291, 293, 297, 299, 303, 306, 307, 315, 316, 317, 318, 324, 344, 348, 355, 360, 368, 369, 375, 377, 386, 388, 390, 398, 402, 405, 438, 447, 453, 456, 457, 462, 464, 468, 474, 484, 490, 504, 513, 515, 520, 522, 527, 536, 537, 539, 540, 552, 570, 571, 572, 573, 579, 580, 581, 588, 597, 618, 630, 638, 642, 643, 645, 647, 648, 653, 655, 659, 660, 666, 678, 687, 689, 692, 702, 706, 707, 708, 713, 716, 722, 725,

730, 731, 732, 733, 738, 745, 752, 753, 757, 762, 764, 774, 791, 794, 802, 810, 812, 813, 818, 822, 824, 826, 829, 837, 862, 864, 865, 871, 878, 882, 883, 892, 893, 896, 897, 898, 899, 901, 902, 906, 907, 908, 909, 910, 915, 919, 921, 924, 933, 935, 940, 943, 955, 989, 991, 1001, 1002, 1030, 1032, 1036, 1041, 1042, 1052, 1062, 1071, 1075, 1077, 1084, 1090, 1092, 1102, 1104, 1109, 1112, 1113, 1116, 1117
see also Pedophilia
Chronic disability, 832
Chronic illness, 184, 383, 413, 516, 531, 596
Circumcision, 520
Citizen's action group, 109
Civil Rights of Institutionalized Persons Act, 193, 985
Clinicians, 30, 36, 256, 436, 523, 837, 840, 885, 977, 981
Clinicolegal dilemmas, 929
Coalition of Sexuality and Disability, 1104
Co-counselors, 698
see also Therapists
Cohabitation, 476, 719
Collaboration in research, 166
Communication, 87, 145, 188, 250, 252, 271, 273, 275, 282, 285, 298, 308, 321, 326, 346, 454, 474, 514, 555, 594, 608, 655, 663, 670, 684, 697, 698, 720, 876, 877, 969, 971, 976, 977, 978, 1066, 1093
difficulties, 13, 147, 358, 883
language skills, 341, 762
nonverbal, 161, 281, 609, 1115
speech disorders, 433
Community, 7, 39, 56, 69, 71, 81, 98, 105, 115, 120, 131, 176, 201, 234, 237, 245, 250, 251, 264, 270, 278, 290, 294, 305, 311, 317, 321, 348, 360, 361, 388, 390, 393, 414, 415, 441, 448, 471, 478, 493, 505, 509, 514, 517, 528, 543, 556, 564, 569, 575, 579, 580, 592, 617, 621, 654, 673, 685, 686, 694, 706, 711, 713, 723, 731, 751, 760, 761, 781, 784, 787, 834, 837, 841, 850, 861, 871, 875, 892, 894, 916, 926, 962, 990, 1003, 1004, 1017, 1037, 1049, 1089
Compensation, 659, 678, 837
Competency, 4, 151, 328, 677, 1028
capacity, 803
children, 76, 674, 791, 803, 864, 880, 883, 940
court cases, 31, 183, 764
intellectual impairment, 210

Competency — *continued*
  witnesses, 183, 764, 803, 864
  see also Incompetency
Compliance, *see* Acquiescence
Comprehensive *Psychopathological Rating Scale*, 397
Computerized axial tomography, *see* Computerized tomography
Computerized tomography, 139, 269, 289, 644, 676
Conference, 94, 193, 261, 297, 308, 378, 465, 499, 540, 701, 749, 796, 907, 1010
Confidentiality Certificate, 706
Congenital disability, 37, 45, 65, 118, 208, 458, 832, 986
Conjoint therapy, 452
Consent, 4, 7, 146, 199, 241, 242, 295, 328, 333, 412, 415, 501, 502, 607, 616, 681, 720, 750, 810, 812, 828, 846, 901, 987, 1097
  see also Proxy
Consequences, *see* Abuse
Consumers, 14, 192, 212, 333, 385
Convictions, 307, 373, 512, 581, 710
Coping resources, 1, 345
Coronary disease, *see* Heart conditions
Cost-effectiveness, *see* Funding
Cost of services, 81, 374, 414, 653, 919
  see also Funding
Cost reimbursement, 5, 41, 610, 659, 837, 907
Counter-control, 939
Couples, 30, 64, 106, 238, 332, 346, 428, 553, 568, 773, 784, 822, 855
Court, 5, 48, 127, 141, 197, 202, 210, 295, 297, 364, 378, 459, 481, 498, 503, 585, 617, 657, 668, 679, 739, 828, 839, 851, 1022
  cases, 11, 31, 124, 126, 183, 194, 195, 196, 278, 321, 436, 592, 621, 623, 660, 670, 671, 678, 681, 682, 694, 764, 818, 837, 924, 940, 943
  children, 58, 124, 187, 278, 283, 321, 436, 454, 524, 623, 660, 672, 694, 757, 797, 837, 864, 901, 924, 940, 943
  evidence, 31, 278, 424, 599, 671, 672, 680, 681, 691, 810, 818, 837, 901, 940
  occupational therapists, 195, 924
  parents, 244, 283, 436, 454, 501, 660, 757, 924
  physicians, 436, 501, 660, 761, 818, 859, 940, 943
  procedures, 40, 41, 58, 124, 131, 146, 288, 321, 501, 812, 837, 940
  psychiatrists, 943
  psychologists, 943

  witnesses, 131, 183, 194, 195, 196, 306, 424, 454, 660, 670, 671, 678, 682, 764, 837, 864, 899, 940
Courtship, *see* Dating skills
Crime, 5, 131, 202, 251, 286, 287, 373, 378, 394, 422, 582, 583, 641, 657, 668, 670, 672, 694, 719, 739, 866, 879, 930, 998, 1068, 1069, 1113
Crime Risk Education is Essential for the Disabled (CREED), 641
Criminal cases, 195, 678, 681, 682, 803, 866, 943
Criminal complaints (charges), 719
Criminal justice process, 14
Criminal justice system, 2, 104, 196, 286, 338, 360, 451, 459, 581, 640, 694, 714, 1044
Criminal record, 497, 750
CRIPA private right of action, 739
Crisis management, 40, 41
Crisis theory, 1017
Cultural factors, 69, 105, 186, 321, 358, 384, 442, 462, 466, 520, 565, 597, 660, 832, 833, 915, 945
Curriculum, 163, 173, 179, 200, 261, 273, 323, 354, 535, 552, 598, 651, 703, 746, 747, 815, 1084
  development, 3, 16, 17, 137, 235, 236, 249, 258, 325, 327, 362, 380, 432, 470, 551, 713, 728, 853, 854, 889, 895, 896, 1058, 1113
  secondary student, 98, 99
Custody, 29, 124, 513, 767, 837, 899, 924, 964
Cystic fibrosis, 413

D

Data collection procedures, 166, 874, 979
Dating skills, 709
DAWN Canada, *see* DisAbled Women's Network
Day care, 318, 405, 573, 706, 752, 837, 1117
Day hospital, 225
De Clerambault's syndrome, 177
Deafness, 27, 56, 79, 96, 112, 114, 152, 203, 229, 275, 306, 325, 329, 337, 345, 433, 438, 451, 453, 499, 518, 540, 584, 603, 608, 643, 647, 650, 657, 673, 677, 775, 833, 911, 912, 936, 1002, 1037, 1110
  deaf-blind, 433, 936
Deaths, 9, 93, 143, 155, 178, 422, 423, 541, 557, 639, 679, 680, 694, 801, 894, 946, 1106

  see also Euthanasia, Infanticide
Decision-making, 273, 460, 528, 656, 778
Defendants, 183, 195, 197, 680, 681, 682, 764, 850, 1028
  intellectual impairment, 210, 640
Defense mechanisms, 404, 806, 974, 1031
Defense Mechanism Inventory, 806
Definitions, 135, 230, 251, 456, 457, 714, 837, 838, 940, 1095, 1113
  need for, 804
Deinstitutionalization, 311
  see also Integration; Mainstreaming; Normalization
Dentists, 357
Dependency, 330, 336, 433, 449, 479, 663, 700, 782, 785, 822, 871, 920, 1093, 1104, 1111, 1116
Dependent adults, 35, 161, 171, 798, 915, 1024, 1077
  see also Overdependency
Depo-Provera, 132, 562
Depression, 49, 117, 349, 400, 572, 655, 808, 967, 970, 971, 972, 1011, 1047, 1048
Desexualization, *see* Sexual oppression, Sexual repression
Detection, 3, 21, 61, 66, 156, 157, 171, 186, 214, 227, 235, 260, 266, 290, 318, 339, 347, 357, 379, 436, 457, 464, 487, 491, 533, 558, 570, 574, 575, 589, 598, 611, 650, 654, 723, 743, 763, 776, 778, 780, 794, 811, 817, 818, 835, 915, 934, 941, 951, 955, 960, 961, 997, 1041, 1044, 1045, 1063, 1077, 1078, 1085, 1086, 1087, 1109
  of abuse, 22, 112, 161, 360, 610, 645, 713, 768, 774, 821, 837
  of disability, 246, 713, 847
Devaluation, 69, 94, 374, 569, 715
Developmental Disabilities 3, 16, 28, 30, 34, 39, 40, 41, 71, 94, 104, 106, 118, 133, 144, 148, 150, 176, 189, 198, 201, 204, 205, 226, 232, 234, 235, 236, 237, 244, 256, 258, 272, 276, 295, 320, 327, 328, 330, 341, 350, 362, 364, 386, 391, 409, 415, 428, 429, 430, 432, 434, 445, 446, 468, 469, 487, 496, 523, 528, 542, 548, 551, 555, 556, 579, 590, 607, 664, 693, 707, 709, 712, 723, 727, 741, 742, 744, 463, 469, 830, 834, 843, 845, 850, 853, 854, 864, 868, 870, 873, 876, 881, 883, 895, 896, 897, 901, 916, 940, 851, 960, 961, 965, 981, 997, 1013, 1016, 1020, 1033, 1040, 1042, 1048, 1057, 1058, 1065, 1075, 1085, 1086, 1122

see also Intellectual impairment, Learning disabilities

Developmental psychology, 106, 1066

Dexamethasone Supression Test, 967

Diabetes, 63, 332

Diagnosis, 15, 113, 139, 155, 269, 300, 393, 394, 398, 436, 462, 474, 523, 541, 587, 588, 636, 675, 676, 748, 967, 968, 969, 970, 971, 972, 976, 978, 1010, 1085, 1086, 1105

Direct care staff, 3, 617, 620, 839
 see also Caregivers

Directory, 730, 956

Direct services, 548, 804

Disabled Persons Protection Commission, 467

DisAbled Women's Network, 254, 255, 632, 633, 822

Disavowal, 1031

Disbelief, 112, 685, 883

Disclosure, 41, 90, 306, 318, 474, 659, 691, 750, 934

Discrimination, 29, 186, 422, 767, 839, 1080, 1121
 against people with disabilities, 6, 29, 70, 73, 104, 210, 227, 767
 against women, 43, 70

Dissociative disorders, 393, 653
 see also Multiple personality disorders

District of Columbia, 132, 825

Docility, *see* Acquiescence

Documentation, 818

Domestic abuse, 275, 673

Dormitory programs, 540

Down syndrome, 283, 389

Dreams about sex, 180, 271

Drug, 50, 149, 270, 397, 490, 517, 606, 607, 663, 677, 733, 739, 749, 810, 860, 929, 1040, 1060
 antidepressant, 967, 969
 antilibidinal, 165
 antipsychotic, 969
 benzodiazepine, 965
 lithium (carbonate), 969
 neuroleptic therapy (major tranquilizers), 1057
 side-effects, 969, 1123
 therapy, 136, 165, 369, 586, 966, 967, 975, 980

Diagnostic and Statistical Manual-III (DSM-III), 397, 967, 978
 criteria, 364, 968, 971, 972, 982, 1011

Dual diagnosis, 491, 492, 494, 495, 496, 497, 523, 675, 966, 967, 968, 969, 970, 971, 972, 973, 974, 975, 976, 977, 978, 979, 980, 981, 982, 1011, 1014

Dynamics, *see* Psychodynamics

E

Early intervention, 440, 693, 882, 1048

Ecological models, 65, 69, 111, 125, 282, 283, 313, 351, 359, 361, 402, 663, 805, 986

Education, 4, 5, 6, 7, 13, 16, 17, 2, 26, 27, 33, 34, 36, 39, 41, 44, 47, 48, 50, 51, 55, 59, 67, 70, 74, 80, 86, 89, 94, 98, 99, 100, 103, 116, 123, 134, 136, 137, 142, 143, 148, 150, 163, 166, 173, 176, 182, 185, 186, 187, 189, 190, 192, 198, 199, 200, 207, 215, 217, 219, 222, 232, 235, 236, 243, 256, 257, 263, 264, 266, 267, 268, 269, 273, 279, 281, 294, 301, 302, 303, 310, 316, 320, 323, 325, 326, 327, 328, 329, 340, 342, 343, 346, 354, 356, 362, 366, 367, 369, 380, 394, 396, 401, 411, 414, 415, 426, 427, 428, 429, 431, 439, 442, 443, 444, 461, 468, 470, 480, 487, 489, 491, 495, 505, 507, 514, 519, 520, 523, 533, 535, 537, 543, 544, 545, 546, 548, 551, 552, 559, 560, 569, 576, 577, 579, 582, 583, 589, 591, 593, 598, 603, 605, 610, 622, 623, 628, 629, 635, 641, 642, 646, 651, 656, 658, 663, 671, 674, 686, 687, 691, 698, 703, 708, 709, 714, 716, 717, 718, 724, 725, 731, 735, 737, 738, 755, 769, 772, 775, 781, 787, 789, 791, 800, 815, 820, 827, 829, 834, 837, 838, 844, 845, 853, 854, 858, 863, 868, 874, 877, 883, 887, 889, 890, 891, 900, 915, 916, 917, 921, 922, 928, 932, 934, 954, 956, 983, 986, 990, 993, 996, 1002, 1003, 1007, 1010, 1014, 1018, 1019, 1020, 1021, 1024, 1035, 1037, 1039, 1047, 1050, 1057, 1058, 1059, 1062, 1064, 1071, 1072, 1079, 1083, 1084, 1091, 1093, 1095, 1100, 1101, 1104, 1113, 1118, 1120
 by parents, 871
 to parents, 895, 896, 942, 1033

Educational Plans, 489

Educators, 34, 55, 59, 82, 99, 143, 163, 173, 179, 190, 192, 232, 235, 236, 247, 249, 258, 261, 285, 316, 320, 323, 325, 326, 327, 329, 359, 360, 363, 401, 411, 454, 540, 544, 546, 558, 577, 580, 582, 593, 622, 635, 642, 645, 648, 651, 654, 659, 698, 713, 730, 747, 774, 822, 854, 875, 897, 900, 940, 942, 957, 991, 1008, 1061, 1063, 1077, 1084, 1116, 1118, 1120

Effects of abuse, 21, 61, 114, 290, 300, 483, 593, 613

Efficacy of the law, 12

Ego, 79, 162, 248, 253, 261, 270, 327, 358, 396, 404, 433, 436, 473, 502, 565, 653, 660, 697, 733, 822, 911, 959, 998, 1009, 1031, 1075

Elders, 5, 11, 62, 64, 93, 153, 221, 442, 455, 520, 554, 610, 700, 779, 782, 784, 1098

Electroejaculation, 807

Electroencephalograph, 218, 394

Emergency care (medical), 946, 1000

Emergency crisis services, 14

Emergency rooms, 398, 436, 733

Emotional disorders, 92, 276, 369, 397, 422, 511, 593, 606, 675, 733, 739, 741, 745, 767, 930, 978, 981, 989, 997, 1012, 1014, 1022, 1024, 1028, 1080, 1087, 1090, 1105

Empirical studies, 90, 102, 207, 211, 330, 485, 490, 583, 650, 709, 741, 759, 778, 804, 805, 813, 824, 1050

Employees
 applicants, 307
 screening procedures, 376, 430, 487, 750, 837, 1005

Empowerment, 13, 204, 488

England, *see* United Kingdom

English law, *see* Law, British

Epilepsy, 749, 810

Erotomanic delusion, 177

Ethics, 6, 92, 272, 715, 772, 793, 837, 918, 1092

Etiology of abuse, 10, 20, 22, 62, 330, 420, 465, 676, 699, 785, 860, 863, 945, 959, 1030, 1032, 1052, 1062, 1079, 1098
 biological factors, 284, 485, 893, 930, 1068
 institutions, 83, 473, 860, 919, 921

Eugenics, 44, 82, 506, 924

Europe, 166, 293, 947

Euthanasia, 91, 293, 863

Evaluation, 2, 3, 29, 66, 69, 71, 94, 106, 139, 155, 159, 161, 175, 189, 219, 234, 251, 273, 292, 334, 350, 353, 370, 374, 394, 415, 416, 430, 501, 533, 536, 544, 584, 598, 635, 636, 644, 686, 714, 718, 724, 727, 728, 755, 762, 767, 812, 817, 824, 875, 884, 886, 917, 923, 931, 990, 1003, 1009, 1013, 1014, 1026, 1039, 1047, 1064, 1089
 clinical, 20, 22, 284, 478, 485, 689, 740, 811, 855, 936
 forensic, 151, 210, 233, 299, 308, 659, 803
 physical, 11, 15, 114, 121, 137, 173, 196, 221, 274, 278, 290, 335, 369, 398, 437, 441, 474, 509, 538, 569,

Evaluation (physical) — *continued*
588, 651, 662, 676, 678, 683, 709,
764, 781, 856, 874, 941
psychiatric, 21, 58, 469, 491, 606,
973, 974, 975
sexual abuse, 88, 134, 394, 402,
462, 642, 715, 837, 864, 1012
"Eve" decision, 828
Evidence, 10, 31, 36, 37, 53, 60, 73,
103, 115, 130, 135, 160, 278, 284,
300, 308, 348, 383, 424, 474, 510,
599, 645, 653, 671, 672, 680, 681,
699, 743, 772, 810, 818, 822, 837,
901, 940, 995, 998, 1045, 1048,
1052, 1090
evidence kit, 751
hearsay, 248, 659
see also Courts
Evolutionary theory, 595
Exceptional children, 292, 410, 558,
622, 623, 642, 646, 815, 866, 957,
983, 1107
see also Special needs children
Exhibitionism, 271, 272, 495, 910
see also Indecent exposure
Experiment, 50, 111, 530, 604, 882,
1082
disabilities, 533, 583, 741, 837
ethics, 214
Exploitation, 39, 125, 126, 141, 153,
171, 176, 186, 200, 214, 235, 236,
272, 287, 323, 344, 362, 365, 429,
435, 468, 472, 480, 542, 551, 571,
583, 669, 685, 712, 715, 732, 772,
787, 800, 827, 837, 853, 854, 871,
879, 883, 885, 888, 895, 896, 897,
905, 906, 940, 943, 953, 955, 993,
1029, 1038, 1057, 1075, 1100,
1104, 1113, 1116
Exploitive touching, 291, 871, 661,
829, 40, 171, 235, 746
Extra-marital affairs, 211
Eysenck Personality Inventory, 397

F

Facial screening, 54
Families, abusive, 10, 18, 21, 29, 117,
203, 293, 317, 336, 351, 358, 406,
527, 556, 565, 622, 663, 702, 749,
781, 945, 1109, 1118
see also Parents, abusive
Families at risk, 10, 118

Family, 1, 16, 41, 64, 105, 190, 235,
243, 252, 268, 283, 326, 329, 349,
364, 386, 391, 400, 418, 428, 440,
464, 470, 502, 568, 593, 598, 647,
767, 773, 779, 786, 799, 816, 855,
856, 860, 869, 873, 879, 889, 890,
946, 972, 975, 978, 994, 1013,
1034, 1039, 1047, 1048, 1057,
1066, 1070, 1074, 1089, 1091
abuse, 12, 18, 24, 29, 85, 90, 133,
139, 153, 166, 167, 185, 186, 201,
251, 282, 284, 292, 313, 315, 318,
321, 355, 358, 369, 393, 399, 405,
406, 435, 447, 449, 453, 465, 490,
537, 556, 557, 558, 559, 580, 595,
624, 631, 651, 653, 663, 665, 673,
678, 700, 707, 719, 749, 753, 762,
777, 781, 785, 815, 817, 837, 871,
882, 901, 905, 906, 940, 949, 952,
959, 991, 1015, 1098, 1109, 1116
caregiving, 554
Family court, 364, 678, 940
Family Development Center
Program, 762
Family dysfunction, 292, 817
Family Environment Scale, 1048
Family-oriented treatment, 665, 762
Family strengths, 1
Fantasy, 1043
Fathers, 106, 117, 355, 749, 867, 873,
876, 1047, 1048, 1091
Federal Bureau of Investigation
(FBI), 123
Female offenders, 43, 405, 534, 572,
653, 745, 813
Feminism, 120
therapy, 214, 256, 705, 1123
Fertility, 44, 146, 147, 238, 433, 766,
807
program, 807
spinal cord, 149, 807, 887, 937,
1094, 1123
Fetal Alcohol Syndrome (FAS), 753
Figure Drawings, 689
Films, 89, 235, 362, 500, 724, 895,
896, 1113
Financial abuse, 5, 11, 1098
Financial dependency, 782
Financial hardship, 11, 246, 394, 563,
871, 1024
Fire-bombing, 286
Folk treatment (medicine), 423
Follow-up, 54, 85, 305, 340, 352, 398,
432, 465, 604, 625, 642, 704, 736,
751, 831, 875, 876, 884, 886, 919,
1003, 1015, 1046, 1047
Fondling, 291, 829
see also exploitative touching
Forensic pediatrician, 660
Foster care, 153, 223, 475, 487, 515,
651, 894
Four Preconditions Model of Sexual

Abuse, 315
French Canadian 1050
see also Quebec
French language, 185, 223, 259, 265,
267, 372, 403, 687, 721, 757, 906,
907
Funding, 81, 131, 157, 164, 214, 234,
237, 278, 414, 455, 517, 656, 837,
881, 919, 1045
Fundoscopic examinations, 155

G

Gender, 67, 219, 270, 382, 444, 587,
596, 873, 879, 1059, 1093
Genetic counseling, 37, 217, 1024
Genital self-stimulation,
see Autoeroticism
Germany, 6, 863, 1087
Glasgow Coma Scale, 639
Glossaries, 324, 730, 1078
Government, 18, 36, 136, 175, 278,
360, 412, 632, 691, 817, 837, 848,
862, 881, 947, 1025, 1045, 1046,
1081
Graduate studies, 159, 456, 588
Grandfather, 405
Greece, 12
Grief, 566, 799, 1047
*Griffith's Mental Development
Scale,* 1056
Grounded theory, 778, 780
Group homes, 97, 272, 273, 286, 619,
874, 1053
Group therapy, 464, 562, 567, 569,
570, 698, 762, 906, 907, 1006,
1013
Guardianship, 11, 234, 247, 278, 501,
659, 810, 924, 1039, 1078, 1122
Guidelines, 87, 109, 131, 142, 157,
172, 181, 210, 235, 236, 238, 250,
251, 325, 333, 416, 424, 489, 492,
517, 519, 528, 588, 621, 633, 659,
691, 716, 725, 750, 751, 778, 780,
803, 807, 817, 837, 860, 885, 887,
979, 1063, 1066, 1096
see also Protocols; Standards
Guilt, 31, 418, 521, 530, 619, 661, 678,
750, 790, 821, 862, 930, 941, 960,
1021
Gynecology, 805
disabilities, 65
health care, 65, 125

H

Hatred, 286, 327, 406, 674
Hawaii, 234, 350, 472, 764
Head injury, 9, 15, 119, 130, 155, 178, 218, 269, 289, 406, 410, 557, 586, 624, 625, 639, 644, 677, 679, 690, 951, 960, 1096
Head Start, 817
HEALTH Program, 629
Health, 12, 70, 109, 141, 274, 276, 332, 448, 458, 479, 529, 680, 763, 765, 768, 777, 783, 812, 817, 821, 846, 965, 975, 981, 1023, 1040, 1081
    care, 5, 11, 15, 29, 65, 72, 93, 100, 112 113, 118, 125, 126, 136, 145, 147, 153, 176, 186, 206, 301, 344, 348, 354, 365, 405, 434, 437, 441, 447, 452, 455, 473, 490, 502, 503, 517, 533, 555, 585, 592, 610, 623, 659, 685, 686, 696, 710, 729, 732, 733, 734, 778, 780, 835, 837, 842, 844, 847, 864, 865, 874, 885, 931, 943, 1017, 1024, 1038, 1045, 1098, 1117
    medical profession, 18
    professionals, 61, 84, 88, 169, 210, 211, 242, 256, 311, 312, 321, 329, 393, 464, 567, 576, 577, 656, 691, 790, 823, 970, 1039
    setting, 8, 71, 230
    sex, 16, 59, 134, 137, 170, 257, 282, 304, 327, 328, 355, 384, 388, 401, 416, 499, 552, 584, 591, 628, 629, 653, 655, 675, 713, 758, 771, 826, 841, 895, 896, 901, 942, 953, 983, 1018, 1019, 1064, 1075
    students, 137, 354, 401, 552, 591, 837, 895, 896, 942, 1018, 1019, 1064
    workers, 15, 18, 88, 206, 447, 452, 473, 593, 73, 778, 780, 874, 931
Health Education and Learning for the Handicapped, 629
Hearsay evidence, *see* Evidence
Heart conditions, 63, 538, 1068, 1074
Helplessness Test, 330
Hepatitis B, 311, 617
Hispanic, 133
    see also Mexican-American
History, *see* Abuse, history of
Home-based early intervention, 440
Homosexuality, 7, 56, 100, 232, 270, 271, 272, 311, 339, 386, 412, 434, 471, 485, 520, 767, 775, 842, 964, 1031, 1110
    see also Sexual preferences
Hospitalization, 14, 15, 21, 25, 77, 92, 119, 136, 156, 184, 210, 218, 225, 290, 348, 373, 383, 390, 393, 398, 417, 422, 437, 450, 476, 478, 509,

516, 533, 534, 541, 585, 592, 596, 644, 660, 685, 733, 744, 754, 755, 836, 848, 859, 863, 910, 943, 979, 1004, 1013, 1102, 1105
    procedure, 40, 41, 751, 1046
Human Sexuality for the Mentally Retarded, 1121
Hygiene, 16, 67, 282, 302, 327, 329, 434, 443, 444, 734, 983, 1113
Hyperactivity, 66, 152, 156, 458, 768, 968
Hysterical seizure, 394, 418

I

Impaired growth, 690
Impotence, 392
Impression management, 280, 281
Inappropriate sexual behavior, 415, 609, 1049
Incest, 37, 117, 147, 185, 218, 223, 239, 259, 299, 394, 412, 462, 464, 468, 513, 520, 572, 638, 645, 653, 659, 695, 707, 745, 753, 757, 791, 816, 898, 906, 1032, 1060, 1112, 1113
    brother/sister, 902
    father/daughter, 418, 647, 902
    mother/son, 43
    sibling, 405, 902
Incidence/ prevalence, 10, 15, 21, 28, 29, 36, 41, 75, 83, 93, 95, 96, 114, 117, 141, 147, 153, 157, 167, 178, 191, 214, 216, 227, 236, 239, 240, 245, 246, 286, 299, 311, 318, 347, 350, 356, 360, 364, 368, 375, 377, 397, 398, 414, 428, 436, 456, 457, 464, 475, 509, 516, 541, 579, 606, 611, 612, 633, 653, 657, 695, 714, 718, 733, 734, 742, 745, 784, 788, 790, 791, 813, 822, 826, 829, 837, 838, 845, 854, 877, 905, 924, 948, 957, 960, 972, 986, 1002, 1004, 1089, 1090, 1105, 1111
Incompetency, 210, 677
    see also Competency
Incontinence, 1024
Indecent exposure, 235, 512, 611, 745, 1075
    see also Exhibitionists
Independence, 140, 415, 696, 809, 883, 936, 940, 1013
    mental retardation, 234, 1120
    parents, 413, 854
India, 31, 216, 300, 321, 660, 678, 680, 806, 911
Indians, *see* Native American Indians

Individual therapy/counseling, 567
Infanticide, 293
Infants, 9, 10, 33, 37, 61, 66, 129, 130, 139, 153, 155, 178, 203, 269, 293, 351, 356, 400, 462, 521, 557, 644, 665, 676, 693, 702, 723, 736, 933, 959, 960, 997, 1040, 1119
    psychological problems, 763
Infectious disease policy, 617
Informed consent, 2, 48, 659, 766
Informer characteristics, 620, 824
Inquiry, 510, 752, 832, 1042, 1073
Insanity defense, 422, 1028
Institutional abuse, 81, 691, 719, 733, 804, 805, 536, 1030, 1089
Institutions, 4, 5, 6, 12, 68, 69, 70, 72, 92, 96, 100, 104, 110, 115, 143, 159, 161, 169, 179, 181, 184, 187, 193, 199, 214, 216, 270, 281, 282, 290, 309, 311, 330, 339, 342, 363, 365, 370, 376, 377, 386, 405, 410, 442, 447, 450, 467, 469, 472, 473, 503, 519, 523, 524, 544, 546, 547, 548, 574, 578, 585, 596, 610, 623, 634, 648, 654, 659, 712, 715, 733, 748, 751, 752, 754, 758, 759, 798, 810, 821, 825, 827, 834, 837, 849, 860, 874, 881, 885, 888, 901, 919, 921, 922, 926, 940, 943, 947, 962, 985, 1003, 1005, 1007, 1012, 1026, 1032, 1035, 1038, 1066, 1071, 1073, 1080, 1107, 1116, 1121
    facilities, 3, 7, 83, 93, 136, 237, 307, 384, 417, 435, 536, 579, 719, 739, 804, 1004, 1045, 1046, 1087, 1102
    long-stay hospitals, 754
    psychiatric settings, 719
    residential, 11, 81, 97, 230, 250, 251, 430, 448, 471, 504, 620, 621, 795, 826, 861, 935, 996, 1023, 1025, 1042, 1081, 1089
Instructors, *see* Educators
Intake procedures, 428, 487, 575, 491, 736
Integration, 9, 92, 186, 234, 335, 387, 579, 697, 787, 854, 978, 998, 1049, 1055
    see also Mainstreaming; Normalization
Intellectual impairment, 20, 119, 134, 144, 198, 210, 216, 156, 290, 296, 390, 404, 425, 470, 481, 547, 621, 627, 660, 664, 708, 712, 744, 834, 845, 850, 857, 858, 892, 901, 934, 957, 972, 978, 989, 992, 1003, 1015, 1035, 1062, 1079
    borderline, *see* mild or borderline
    educable, 1121
    mild or borderline, 98, 99, 129,

Intellectual impairment, (mild or borderline) — *continued*
  147, 162, 305, 306, 323, 330, 397, 496, 534, 544, 563, 564, 609, 677, 697, 709, 758, 766, 769, 831, 927, 972, 983, 990, 1006, 1028, 1057, 1079, 1099, 1114
  moderate, 147, 162, 188, 319, 323, 330, 336, 340, 367, 496, 646, 709, 766, 769, 942, 972, 981, 983
  profound, 78, 85, 525, 972
  severe, 54, 67, 78, 97, 137, 147, 161, 162, 188, 290, 301, 302, 323, 341, 397, 425, 444, 448, 496, 544, 607, 613, 623, 624, 646, 657, 666, 766, 927, 972, 1066, 1105
  see also Developmental disabilities
Intentions of offenders, 587, 776, 780
  see also Offenders
Interagency interaction, 115, 179, 590, 610, 751, 752, 817, 1006
Interdisciplinary, 282, 388, 489, 549, 596, 691, 698, 720, 837, 886, 1096
Interpreters, 145, 345, 453, 659, 668, 670, 672
Interventions, 5, 11, 49, 50, 51, 61, 64, 80, 158, 185, 188, 213, 223, 238, 291, 304, 318, 341, 393, 394, 410, 415, 440, 445, 450, 457, 461, 462, 469, 495, 499, 535, 538, 539, 561, 568, 583, 593, 596, 607, 610, 626, 645, 653, 665, 674, 675, 684, 686, 687, 693, 705, 721, 744, 762, 763, 775, 780, 789, 823, 838, 855, 861, 869, 874, 875, 876, 882, 897, 908, 909, 918, 970, 996, 998, 1001, 1010, 1027, 1032, 1047, 1066, 1074, 1075, 1082, 1089, 1099
  decision to intervene, 778
  families, 12, 21, 78, 292, 313, 360, 394, 464, 555, 627, 779, 781, 856, 860, 871, 961, 1008, 1015, 1034, 1048, 1118
  paradoxical, 497
Interviewing, 37, 45, 106, 134, 136, 160, 253, 264, 278, 280, 281, 319, 333, 416, 486, 491, 510, 522, 599, 609, 637, 651, 691, 766, 778, 780, 784, 857, 867, 926, 927, 928, 978, 981, 1018, 1034, 1074, 1078, 1110
  anatomical dolls, 87, 88, 1108
  sexual abuse, 1073
  structured, 87, 320, 509, 553, 1106
Intimacy, 38, 99, 170, 175, 224, 251, 270, 314, 339, 466, 500, 605, 729, 788, 789, 790, 791, 839
Inuit, 300, 517, 565, 575, 1072
Investigation, 11, 24, 112, 120, 122,

135, 139, 179, 186, 230, 250, 251, 278, 305, 318, 376, 402, 478, 486, 536, 581, 606, 662, 734, 736, 742, 743, 751, 752, 801, 825, 837, 859, 938, 940, 987, 997, 1005, 1042, 1069, 1073, 1122
  negligence, 801, 881
  obstacles to, 1004
Ivanovich Job Stress Scale, 143

J

Judiciary, 307, 657, 687, 798
Justice system, 2, 5, 60, 104, 131, 196, 286, 338, 360, 451, 459, 581, 640, 670, 694, 714, 1044
  see also Courts

K

Kappitz scoring technique, 518
Kidscape, 1036

L

Large print, 40, 243
Law, 2, 11, 12, 31, 53, 58, 75, 76, 88, 91, 109, 115, 116, 124, 126, 131, 153, 165, 183, 194, 195, 196, 202, 236, 241, 244, 248, 250, 251, 278, 296, 297, 298, 306, 321, 328, 357, 359, 369, 375, 376, 378, 379, 408, 412, 417, 422, 424, 426, 429, 438, 453, 462, 464, 467, 482, 498, 501, 502, 503, 505, 506, 580, 581, 585, 592, 617, 641, 642, 647, 659, 669, 670, 671, 677, 678, 679, 680, 681, 682, 694, 699, 712, 713, 736, 739, 742, 753, 764, 767, 788, 793, 794, 797, 799, 803, 812, 837, 842, 846, 847, 850, 858, 866, 912, 913, 914, 924, 929, 940, 947, 964, 985, 987, 1005, 1009, 1012, 1022, 1023, 1028, 1042, 1043, 1060, 1063, 1065, 1075, 1081, 1099, 1106, 1117, 1122
  see also Legal issues
  British, 426
  Canadian, 11, 295, 298, 412, 438, 481, 501, 632, 740, 810, 812, 837, 851, 947, 1108, 1065

Law enforcement/officer, 88, 109, 131, 250, 251, 379, 462, 694, 837, 858, 1042, 1063
Lawsuit, 498, 585
Learned helplessness, 207, 539, 700
Learning Assessment Technique Profile, 762
Learning disabilities, 30, 55, 66, 90, 135, 148, 189, 207, 235, 247, 268, 350, 366, 431, 433, 535, 555, 583, 622, 645, 699, 714, 895, 896, 911, 1036, 1101, 1106
  severe, 366, 380, 1036
Learning theory, 3, 602, 653, 700, 1066
Legal implications, 4, 720
Legal issues, 13, 91, 115, 215, 242, 360, 362, 413, 426, 462, 478, 505, 524, 557, 584, 720, 788, 803, 850, 858, 864, 901, 916, 922, 943, 988, 1038, 1065, 1097
Legal reform, 36, 53, 58, 68, 91, 104, 131, 136, 278, 286, 287, 296, 297, 298, 307, 338, 378, 408, 459, 481, 501, 502, 581, 599, 610, 612, 623, 640, 657, 659, 660, 669, 670, 671, 672, 694, 712, 714, 732, 766, 798, 821, 850, 864, 866, 882, 894, 918, 924, 947, 949, 1012, 1023, 1025, 1026, 1044, 1046, 1122
Legal representation, 858
Legal services, 5, 11, 13, 36, 234, 237, 278, 321, 328, 462, 505, 515, 537, 581, 584, 610, 674, 940, 947, 1078, 1108
Legal studies, 125, 237, 432, 791, 858, 901, 1002
Legislation, 5, 11, 68, 91, 115, 131, 153, 164, 191, 193, 242, 360, 501, 580, 581, 610, 659, 742, 766, 812, 837, 924, 940, 988
Leprosy, 433
Lesbians, 386, 964, 1110
  see also Homosexuality, Sexual preferences
Liability, 5, 11, 50, 57, 72, 106, 112, 170, 197, 204, 210, 221, 251, 306, 321, 424, 488, 573, 581, 592, 610, 621, 622, 642, 654, 656, 670, 812, 837, 943, 1044
Libraries, 158, 396, 439
Lifespan, 45, 219, 442, 569, 596, 832
Lithium, 969
  see also Drugs
Litigation, 126, 294, 503, 846
Locus of control, 102, 330, 349
London, England, 383
London, Ontario, 388
Longitudinal studies (long-term studies), 152, 400
Los Angeles, 34, 40, 41, 620

Louisiana, 31, 183, 196, 677, 739, 1028
Louisville Behavior Checklist, 390, 1001
Lung disease, 538
Luria-Nebraska, 893

M

Mainstreaming, 59, 543, 548
    see also Integration; Normalization
Male, 36, 43, 49, 70, 73, 108, 128, 138, 141, 145, 147, 177, 178, 213, 214, 226, 235, 264, 270, 299, 311, 319, 341, 344, 389, 394, 405, 424, 434, 456, 471, 490, 512, 525, 530, 534, 536, 550, 553, 563, 572, 595, 605, 609, 612, 630, 631, 653, 683, 705, 712, 719, 745, 756, 759, 764, 766, 768, 784, 792, 795, 800, 805, 806, 808, 80, 813, 820, 829, 834, 836, 841, 859, 889, 937, 943, 1031, 1037, 1052, 1057, 1068, 1098, 1101, 1106
Malpractice, 126, 882
Mania, 177, 765, 805, 968, 969, 972, 973, 982
Manuals, 102, 130, 173, 179, 236, 258, 363, 364, 397, 540, 589, 651, 746, 747, 770, 817, 1007, 1063, 1078, 1085
MAO inhibitor, 969
Marital adjustment, 252, 332, 349, 608, 756, 773
Marital counseling, 57, 64, 138, 587, 886, 887
Marlowe Crown Social Desirability Scale, 349
Marriage, 92, 98, 124, 150, 199, 253, 256, 270, 271, 272, 317, 366, 411, 428, 429, 520, 563, 786, 787, 810, 830, 855, 856, 889, 924, 988, 1050, 1091, 1097, 1113
Maslach Burnout Inventory, 143
Masturbation *see* Autoeroticism
Measurement instruments...
    Bailer–Cromwell Locus of Control, 102
    Beck Depression Inventory, 349, 1048
    Brazelton scale, 995
    Chapman Assertiveness Instrument, 102
    Child Abuse Potential Inventory (CAP), 795
    Child Behavior Checklist, 1001

    Comprehensive Psychopathological Rating Scale, 397
    Defense Mechanism Inventory, 806
    Dexamethasone Supression Test, 967
    Diagnostic and Statistical Manual-III (DSM-III), 397, 967, 978
    Eysenck Personality Inventory, 397
    Family Environment Scale, 1048
    Glasgow Coma Scale, 639
    Griffith's Mental Development Scale, 1056
    Helplessness Test, 330
    Ivanovich Job Stress Scale, 143
    Kappitz scoring technique, 518
    Learning Assessment Technique Profile, 762
    Louisville Behavior Checklist, 390, 1001
    Marlowe Crown Social Desirability Scale, 349
    Maslach Burnout Inventory, 143
    Mental status exam, 973, 974
    Modified Injury Severity Scale, 639
    Patient Abuse Questionnaire, 733
    Piers-Harris Children's Self-Concept Scale, 532
    Questionnaire on Resources and Stress, 1048
    Rorschach Test, 494
    Sexual Attitude Reassessment (SAR), 441
    Sexual Functioning Scale, 1009
    Sexual Interaction Inventory, 224
    Sexual Knowledge and Attitude Test, 224
    Sexuality Development Index, 219
    Socio-Sexual Knowledge and Attitude, 134, 270, 834
    Stress Response Scale, 518
    Tennessee Self-Concept Inventory, 224
    Thematic Apperception Test, 497, 972
    Vineland Adaptive Behavior Scales, 233
Media, 18, 21, 27, 93, 99, 162, 173, 209, 234, 247, 251, 308, 358, 361, 368, 456, 474, 490, 535, 714, 724, 727, 827, 832, 874, 1007, 1045, 1053, 1109, 1118, 1122
Medical practice, 9, 13, 14, 20, 25, 60, 74, 77, 101, 109, 138, 173, 246, 255, 260, 360, 368, 383, 394, 402,

413, 423, 433, 474, 501, 505, 553, 626, 639, 650, 736, 749, 751, 761, 763, 907, 911, 961, 975, 998, 1007, 1013, 1043, 1049, 1109
    assault, 246
    care, 5, 11, 50, 93, 100, 113, 139, 145, 146, 475, 490, 515, 516, 537, 557, 610, 623, 818, 837, 946, 960, 1063, 1093
    confidentiality, 278, 1092
    diagnosis, 139, 436, 541, 748, 1010
    interns, 793
    professionals, 5, 18, 33, 50, 115, 436, 490, 610, 837, 960, 1016
    residents, 139
    students, 837, 1016, 1093
Medicolegal issues, 947
Menstruation, 65, 217, 226, 270, 271, 272, 301, 389, 433, 434, 435, 520, 1113
Mental health, 8, 210, 242, 311, 355, 455, 458, 464, 502, 503, 567, 655, 733, 734, 763, 768, 790, 812, 846, 970, 981, 1023
    consultation, 975
    practitioner, 88
    services, 29, 71, 141, 517, 584, 593, 771, 1081
Mental illness, *see* Emotional disorders
Mental institutions, *see* Psychiatric institutions
Mental retardation, *see* Intellectual impairment
Mental status exam, 973, 974
Methodological problems, 12, 165, 838
Mexican-American, 423
Midlife (middle-age), 45, 569
Minimal brain dysfunction, 284
Minnesota Program for Victims of Sexual Assault, 1104
Misconduct, 38, 49, 344, 365, 661, 685, 719, 732, 788, 789, 790, 791, 792, 793, 885, 918
Misdiagnosis, 968
Mobility impairment, 433, 947
Models, 8, 19, 69, 89, 103, 111, 131, 223, 278, 282, 304, 313, 315, 329, 336, 343, 351, 359, 360, 361, 388, 408, 449, 453, 461, 493, 506, 519, 536, 539, 540, 550, 551, 562, 595, 605, 636, 638, 653, 654, 663, 665, 699, 707, 736, 742, 761, 778, 779, 782, 783, 789, 824, 837, 841, 850, 852, 855, 856, 883, 886, 901, 909, 921, 939, 945, 952, 1000, 1021, 1042, 1055, 1066, 1067, 1093, 1098, 1118, 1119
Models of abuse, 315, 336, 351, 449, 536, 539, 638, 653, 663, 699, 707

Models of abuse — *continued*
782, 883, 783, 909, 939, 945,
1118, 1119
Modified Injury Severity Scale, 639
Molestation, 168, 205, 306, 307, 344,
434, 468, 469, 512, 513, 520, 570,
653, 862, 893, 910, 1113
Montreal, 907
Morality, 6, 242, 271, 272, 326, 334,
438, 470, 557, 663, 712, 715, 924,
996
Mothers, 33, 46, 47, 94, 105, 106, 252,
257, 292, 305, 315, 317, 336, 406,
440, 449, 464, 486, 513, 531, 555,
556, 653, 693, 745, 749, 765, 768,
810, 812, 819, 867, 869, 873, 876,
898, 906, 995, 997, 1029, 1031,
1040, 1099
abusive, 336, 765
depression, 117, 349, 400, 572,
1047
neglect, 43, 203, 274, 348, 572,
1052
sensitivity, 203
withdrawal, 1076
Multidisciplinary teams, 12, 115,
321, 369, 436, 751, 942
Multimodal sex therapy, 322
Multiple disabilities, 822
see also Disability
Multiple family group therapy, 1013
Multiple personality disorder, 1090
Multiple placements, 473, 559
Multiple sclerosis, 202, 206, 238,
538, 856, 1009, 1010
Muscular dystrophy, 1024
Myelomeningocele, 532
Myth, 14, 403, 417, 419, 427, 442,
487, 578, 645, 654, 667, 715, 741,
746, 915, 966, 998, 999, 1007,
1091

N

Narcissism, 1031
National Legal Center for the
Medically Dependent &
Disabled, Inc, 505
National Resource Center of Child
Advocacy and Protection and
Commission on the Mentally
Disabled, 736
Native American Indians, 806
abuse, 216, 300, 321, 660, 678
children, 216, 321, 660
community, 321
disability, 31, 678, 680, 911

Natural observation, 161
Nazi, 863
Negative reinforcement, 425
see also Aversive procedures;
Punishment
Neglect, 3, 5,11,12, 20, 21, 22, 24, 25,
29, 43, 50, 53, 75, 83, 85, 88, 93,
104, 112, 115, 119, 132, 133,139,
141, 153, 157, 164, 166, 168, 179,
189, 193, 203, 216, 230, 269, 274,
278, 300, 321, 347, 348, 350, 352,
353, 356, 357, 358, 359, 361, 383,
399, 407, 410, 446, 447, 448, 452,
456, 458, 460, 462, 474, 475, 490,
498, 515, 516, 521, 522, 527, 537,
557, 558, 559, 565, 572, 580, 585,
590, 610, 623, 626, 642, 651, 655,
660, 662, 664, 665, 678, 691, 699,
702, 704, 705, 713, 720, 723, 731,
734, 735, 742, 754, 761, 762, 763,
772, 778, 779, 781, 784, 797, 801,
804, 813, 817, 818, 824, 825, 826,
836, 838, 848, 857, 861, 868, 871,
874, 875, 877, 880, 881, 884, 894,
921, 940, 959, 962, 965, 985, 991,
1005, 1015, 1025, 1032, 1044,
1045, 1046, 1052, 1056, 1069,
1081, 1082, 1085, 1086, 1088,
1098, 1122
by professionals, 50
Networks, 22, 26, 56, 120, 156, 163,
246, 254, 255, 359, 399, 414, 531,
555, 556, 633, 701, 730, 817, 822,
841, 876, 915, 932, 956, 993
Networking Project for Disabled
Women and Girls, 841
Neurological impairment, 407
Neuroscience, 206, 238
Newspaper articles, 616, 661, 796,
801, 1073
New York, 83, 405, 589, 592, 679,
681, 734, 735, 752, 764, 801, 864,
1021, 1104
New Zealand, 10, 71, 105, 144, 150,
432, 533, 693, 712, 741, 744, 769,
834, 850, 997
Nondisabled population, 28, 106, 121,
163, 245, 246, 254, 330, 331, 360,
434, 487, 520, 597, 701, 901,
1019, 1042, 1051, 1079
Nontreatment, 374
Normalization, 3, 6, 150, 187, 272,
335, 472, 712, 787, 1050, 1055,
1107
see also Integration; Mainstreaming
Northwest Territories, 859
Norway, 1066
Nova Scotia, 614
Nursing, 11, 18, 62, 97, 137, 140, 143,
206, 220, 236, 238, 263, 422, 427,

539, 553, 593, 615, 647, 654, 661,
713, 733, 751, 771, 776, 777, 778,
779, 780, 783, 802, 823, 942, 984,
990, 992, 1017, 1036
Nursing homes (auxiliary care), 97,
733, 783, 802, 992

O

Object relations, 208, 404, 1061
Observation, 11, 22, 161, 515, 609,
690, 737, 826, 839, 933, 997,
1034, 1076, 1114, 1121
see also Natural observation
Obstacles to investigation, 1004
Ocular fundi, 269
Occupational therapy, 11, 143, 184,
303, 549, 596, 727, 728, 729, 733,
755, 899, 1010
Offenders, 2, 8, 14, 36, 60, 91, 104,
109, 114, 115, 125, 151, 168, 194,
195, 196, 197, 198, 248, 288, 315,
338, 344, 378, 379, 390, 405, 410,
420, 424, 451, 459, 462, 481, 485,
527, 534, 562, 581, 582, 583, 599,
601, 602, 611, 612, 662, 669, 671,
678, 680, 681, 682, 694, 699, 705,
710, 718, 719, 739, 745, 749, 750,
822, 827, 842, 879, 883, 904, 912,
913, 914, 915, 940, 941, 943, 949,
987, 998, 1042, 1045, 1060
abusers, 15, 43, 251, 284, 318, 356,
375, 393, 438, 595, 620, 659, 687,
700, 742, 761, 776, 780, 782, 784,
829, 837, 853, 909, 935, 1002,
1030, 1052, 1098, 1116
characteristics, 10, 114, 351, 355,
356, 375, 406, 464, 612, 620, 653,
707, 745, 783, 785, 795, 822, 883,
935, 945, 1068, 1106,
intellectually impaired, 143, 210,
227, 228, 239, 286, 287, 296, 340,
414, 422, 469, 491, 495, 496, 497,
620, 640, 697, 714, 717, 733, 740,
803, 821, 851, 858, 866, 901, 924,
988, 1006, 1044
intentions, 408, 496, 776, 780
rapists, 38, 49, 63, 64, 101, 134,
143, 172, 184, 214, 303, 340, 360,
365, 484, 491, 496, 508, 533, 549,
567, 568, 596, 597, 608, 615, 653,
698, 720, 729, 733, 788, 789, 790,
791, 792, 793, 855, 885, 886, 899,
919, 924, 991, 1001
young, 209, 239, 373, 422, 490,
577, 595, 813, 837, 991, 993,
1068, 1106
Onset, 170, 174, 224, 225, 605, 704,

822, 1009, 1074, 1082

Ontario, 53, 137, 245, 388, 438, 641, 657, 701, 751, 846, 847, 851, 916

Ontario Women's Directorate, 641

Orem's Nursing Theory of Self-Care, 1017

Organizational abuse, 29, 81, 374, 919
   see also Secondary abuse

Orphanages, 1042

Orthopedics, 235, 331, 806

Ostomy, 433

Otolaryngology, 112, 114

Overcrowding, 293

Overdependency, 1116
   see also Dependency

Overmedication, 214

Over protection, 542, 614, 669, 883, 998, 1025

Overreporting, 478

P

PACER Center, 363

Pain perception, 51

Pap test, 917

Paradoxical interventions, *see* Interventions

Paranoia, 476, 1028

Paraphilia, 260, 586, 587

Paraplegia, 149, 180, 756, 807, 808, 809, 937

Paraprofessionals, 121, 897

Parent-child interaction, 10, 361, 693, 931, 1119

Parent-child relationships, 626, 665

Parent aide service, 537

Parent Education Project, 1033

Parent groups, 635

Parental adjustment, 346

Parental attitudes, 319, 766, 1050

Parental coping (strategies), 1, 61, 207, 555, 867, 870, 871

Parental perceptions, 99, 158, 321, 800, 869, 915

Parental relationships, 205

Parental rights/right to parent, 124, 674, 767, 894, 988, 1022, 1065

Parenting, 22, 89, 98, 99, 106, 120, 253, 257, 305, 321, 356, 366, 400, 626, 713, 781, 817, 830, 869, 960, 963, 964, 1017, 1033, 1097, 1099

Parents
   abusive 18, 351, 663, 749
   intellectual impairment, 53, 201,

203, 305, 336, 872, 894, 924, 1097
   maltreated child, 29, 201, 407, 1112

Parents Anonymous, 723

Parole, 422, 837, 1058

PASS, 50, 91, 128, 147, 177, 203, 330, 335, 340, 352, 384, 398, 460, 503, 513, 518, 557, 578, 588, 766, 836, 903, 907, 1038, 1064, 1070, 1079, 1095, 1111

Pathology, 8, 20, 22, 23, 80, 291, 397, 404, 406, 436, 485, 606, 636, 698, 981, 1069

Patient Abuse Questionnaire, 733

Pediatrics, 28, 37, 50, 60, 78, 84, 125, 130, 145, 147, 156, 216, 289, 290, 299, 303, 515, 539, 543, 573, 627, 639, 647, 660, 661, 732, 733, 766, 884, 899, 902, 990, 1092

Pedophilia, 239, 375, 485, 495, 638, 732, 750, 757, 893

Peer counseling, 561

Peer group, 221, 270, 342, 360, 469, 550, 561, 564, 596, 634, 709, 737, 1009, 1013, 1116

Pelvic exams, 272, 917

Penetration, 829
   see also Abuse, levels

Penile prosthesis, 886

Personal accounts, 123, 337, 832, 904, 1058, 1109

Personal care attendant, 314, 710
   see also Caregivers

Personality characteristics, 23, 29, 55, 97, 103, 152, 207, 451, 936, 1093

Phobias, 493, 974

Physical abuse, 9, 10, 15, 20, 25, 95, 130, 139, 202, 245, 246, 254, 290, 347, 369, 377, 393, 423, 460, 461, 462, 465, 479, 504, 509, 541, 563, 565, 624, 631, 632, 633, 653, 655, 660, 666, 673, 690, 744, 748, 753, 768, 784, 822, 875, 881, 893, 941, 945, 946, 1032, 1042, 1045, 1046, 1067, 1109, 1118
   etiology, 5, 11, 157, 246, 394, 563, 610, 782, 871
   secondary injury prevention, 155

Physical disabilities, 31, 42, 49, 52, 77, 93, 121, 123, 137, 171, 173, 174, 183, 194, 195, 196, 202, 208, 217, 224, 244, 248, 293, 306, 314, 347, 371, 386, 387, 398, 437, 441, 443, 448, 452, 458, 480, 484, 498, 503, 549, 561, 569, 592, 594, 615, 617, 621, 637, 654, 677, 678, 679, 680, 681, 682, 683, 687, 697, 725, 729, 736, 739, 746, 747, 764, 773, 797, 823, 852, 856, 887, 895, 896, 911, 913, 924, 932, 945, 957, 985,

998, 1019, 1022, 1027, 1028, 1031, 1068, 1088, 1111, 1119
   see also specific conditions

Physical examination for sexual assault, 368, 474, 490

Physicians, 15, 60, 88, 113, 114, 115, 139, 155, 174, 260, 368, 394, 398, 413, 423, 436, 501, 541, 588, 615, 650, 660, 676, 691, 713, 732, 733, 751, 761, 763, 786, 818, 859, 883, 918, 940, 943, 960, 961, 998, 1016, 1070, 1103

Physiotherapy, 11, 533, 733, 1024

Piers-Harris Children's Self-Concept Scale, 532

PLISSIT Model, 19, 856

Police, 40, 41, 109, 128, 251, 255, 288, 308, 380, 402, 422, 436, 454, 478, 599, 640, 659, 671, 672, 711, 719, 739, 750, 751, 764, 822, 837, 866, 1053, 1078

Policy, 4, 36, 38, 39, 94, 100, 104, 118, 131, 181, 192, 199, 215, 251, 272, 321, 325, 328, 339, 362, 380, 455, 472, 478, 499, 517, 536, 540, 581, 589, 617, 621, 642, 691, 700, 717, 719, 736, 750, 772, 815, 817, 825, 837, 842, 845, 919, 957, 996, 1029, 1089

Political factors, 44, 776

Pornography, 36, 271, 520, 837

Post-marital counseling, 138

Post-traumatic stress disorder, 344

Poverty, 141, 203, 321, 867, 959, 963

Power, 13, 204, 221, 244, 308, 314, 399, 420, 421, 469, 488, 501, 539, 610, 631, 719, 791, 812, 824, 828, 909, 939, 943, 1004, 1025, 1038, 1042, 1107

Prediction, 10, 595, 600

Predisposing factors, 930

Pregnancy, 6, 89, 140, 238, 434, 435, 524, 621, 772, 807, 810, 834, 844, 889, 959, 995, 1037, 1045, 1113

Prejudice, 6, 43, 422, 427, 659

Premature birth, 178, 347, 348, 642, 702, 765, 919, 960

Preschool, 58, 118, 167, 292, 390, 521, 762, 815

Preteen, 324, 927

Prevalence, *see* Incidence/prevalence

Prevention, 3, 10, 13, 14, 15, 26, 27, 36, 41, 60, 61, 66, 72, 112, 125, 131, 153, 155, 157, 163, 168, 171, 185, 193, 204, 230, 258, 261, 316, 318, 321, 348, 352, 353, 356, 360, 362, 363, 379, 393, 398, 414, 426, 446, 447, 457, 462, 499, 517, 522, 542, 552, 558, 559, 571, 573, 574, 583, 589, 641, 643, 645, 648, 651, 669, 674, 676, 687, 692, 699, 725,

Prevention — *continued*
730, 734, 735, 742, 746, 791, 792, 793, 815, 817, 825, 827, 837, 852, 853, 861, 865, 867, 871, 874, 877, 882, 883, 885, 892, 901, 906, 912, 913, 914, 915, 920, 922, 932, 935, 941, 948, 953, 955, 956, 958, 962, 991, 993, 1000, 1004, 1012, 1030, 1032, 1036, 1071, 1084, 1100

Prince Edward Island, 5, 812

Prison, 8, 104, 227, 311, 422, 425, 512, 592, 612, 618, 671, 705, 767, 798, 821, 858, 925, 1068

Prisoners, 311, 422, 425, 705

Privacy, 328, 339, 362, 621, 646, 698, 715, 750, 751, 839

Private right of action, 739

Procreation, 44, 124, 149, 371, 887, 924

Professional liability, 5

Profound disabilities, *see* Intellectual impairment

Program development, 17, 517, 642, 825

Program evaluation, 335, 353

Projection, 404, 600, 806

Prosecution, 109, 318, 422, 424, 426, 498, 640, 659, 670, 671, 672, 694, 827, 837, 987, 998, 1005

Prostitution, 36, 653, 1046
sex for drugs, 739

Protection, 12, 75, 115, 131, 234, 237, 268, 296, 297, 323, 378, 402, 429, 462, 467, 551, 598, 648, 658, 669, 703, 721, 736, 742, 780, 853, 854, 881, 1081, 1122
adults, 5, 11, 191, 235, 502, 610, 659
children, 88, 91, 179, 186, 191, 223, 235, 236, 247, 283, 358, 363, 376, 434, 468, 482, 516, 542, 614, 623, 644, 659, 674, 743, 825, 826, 837, 868, 872, 882, 894, 924, 940, 983, 1023, 1025, 1112

Protection and Advocacy for Mentally Ill Individuals Act, 1081

Protective services, 11, 29, 141, 462, 662, 674, 736, 761, 797

Protocols, 3, 40, 41, 58, 79, 91, 124, 131, 134, 146, 151, 166, 173, 226, 251, 288, 299, 318, 321, 341, 343, 352, 353, 398, 408, 415, 425, 428, 434, 491, 501, 502, 505, 528, 540, 558, 575, 581, 609, 643, 651, 659, 691, 716, 735, 736, 742, 751, 761, 766, 791, 812, 817, 820, 825, 837, 860, 917, 924, 940, 941, 973, 1005, 1046, 1063, 1078, 1117
see also Guidelines; Standards

Proxy, 48

see also Advocacy; Consent

Psychiatric impairment, *see* Emotional disorders

Psychiatric institutions, 25, 92, 104, 309, 417, 450, 476, 585, 859, 863, 985, 1087

Psychiatrists, 49, 73, 116, 469, 473, 803, 857, 859, 918, 943, 1057, 1062, 1092

Psychiatry, 2, 10, 49, 58, 73, 76, 117, 119, 149, 152, 203, 229, 241, 253, 347, 348, 366, 369, 373, 390, 393, 404, 406, 412, 417, 418, 424, 476, 478, 508, 509, 510, 517, 526, 534, 604, 630, 652, 689, 740, 745, 749, 768, 785, 803, 918, 929, 964, 972, 982, 1004, 1057, 1076, 1088, 1105, 1106

Psychoanalysis, 370, 933, 1031

Psychodynamics, 62, 114, 166, 236, 313, 318, 321, 420, 440, 496, 497, 651, 663, 665, 705, 760, 779, 837, 994

Psychoemotional response, 1103

Psychological dwarfism, 699, 931

Psychologists, 38, 69, 73, 111, 143, 263, 462, 513, 591, 599, 619, 635, 733, 792, 793, 857, 943, 950, 1066, 1081

Psychology, 20, 23, 48, 50, 57, 106, 151, 160, 207, 210, 233, 253, 345, 366, 506, 531, 543, 583, 599, 635, 653, 789, 795, 806, 936, 950, 956, 1008, 1061, 1066, 1076, 1082, 1094

Psychopathology, 20, 22, 23, 404, 606, 636, 981

Psychosexuality, 150, 169, 184, 451, 833, 1049

Psychosis, 101, 162, 291, 356, 494, 513, 606, 630, 636, 967, 968, 969, 976, 979, 981, 1028, 1057, 1105

Psychosocial, 42, 59, 108, 213, 394, 553, 593, 687, 699, 760, 931, 975, 1074, 1094, 1116, 1123
development, 21, 66, 414, 475, 763, 978, 1049
needs, 414, 475, 771

Psychotropic, 50, 397, 966, 969, 980

Puberty, 6, 101, 174, 225, 324, 382, 1074, 1121

Public awareness, 5, 123, 185, 256, 551, 610, 837, 852, 1100

Public education, 5, 34, 36, 123, 136, 142, 163, 185, 187, 256, 266, 269, 369, 396, 411, 495, 505, 579, 610, 737, 772, 827, 837, 845, 871, 915, 932, 993, 1041, 1072, 1100

Public opinion, 372, 396, 1080, 1107

Punishment, 8, 186, 237, 447, 448, 521, 651

see also Aversive procedures

Puppetry, 26, 27, 755, 1036

Q

Quadruplegia, 180, 507, 756

Qualitative research, 1003, 1018, 1034, 1057
see also Grounded theory

Quality of care, 734, 779, 987

Quality-of-life-argument, 374

Quantitative, 875, 893, 1120

Quebec, 223, 266, 848, 1050, 1112

Questionnaire on Resources and Stress, 1048

R

Rape, 12, 14, 28, 38, 40, 41, 49, 63, 64, 85, 101, 109, 116, 131, 134, 143, 162, 172, 183, 184, 194, 214, 235, 236, 256, 258, 295, 303, 309, 323, 340, 360, 365, 368, 373, 412, 418, 420, 447, 462, 468, 469, 484, 491, 492, 496, 506, 508, 519, 533, 549, 551, 561, 567, 568, 585, 596, 597, 608, 615, 649, 653, 679, 697, 698, 720, 722, 729, 733, 746, 751, 755, 757, 762, 764, 788, 789, 790, 791, 792, 793, 794, 810, 812, 822, 827, 852, 854, 855, 882, 885, 886, 895, 896, 897, 899, 905, 912, 913, 914, 915, 919, 924, 934, 991, 996, 998, 999, 1001, 1045, 1046, 1075, 1084, 1113
acquaintance, 822

Reading disability, 40

Rectal examination, 308, 474

Recovery, 171, 186, 630, 884, 886, 998, 999, 1000

Referral, 11, 141, 186, 189, 402, 474, 487, 537, 575, 593, 696, 723, 781, 817, 975, 1027, 1085, 1086

Registers, 303, 533, 733, 742, 837, 941, 1092

Rehabilitation, 14, 21, 35, 52, 102, 108, 138, 174, 186, 211, 212, 227, 277, 303, 331, 335, 338, 354, 371, 452, 464, 499, 500, 507, 538, 549, 553, 569, 597, 601, 605, 621, 637, 641, 656, 683, 684, 696, 733, 737, 759, 771, 858, 874, 923, 937, 1003, 1007, 1010, 1029, 1037,

1063, 1070, 1094, 1123
counselor, 19, 367, 394, 483, 489, 808, 1051
personnel, 385
practitioners, 140, 173, 1027, 1043, 1096
teams, 33, 489
Relationship, 6, 35, 135, 140, 205, 224, 263, 292, 323, 324, 329, 332, 349, 389, 410, 418, 436, 462, 480, 492, 564, 626, 653, 712, 761, 791, 855, 856, 898, 900, 994, 1013, 1054, 1061, 1106
personal, 737, 834, 1007
sexual, 39, 42, 231, 257, 264, 314, 387, 416, 427, 500, 507, 737, 756, 800
social, 99, 302, 888
Relationship of disability to abuse, *see* Abuse
Relaxation therapy, 593, 709, 741, 990
Religion, 396, 447, 538, 565, 597
Religious beliefs, 1, 414, 436, 613, 837, 1042, 1043, 1055
Remands, 202, 680
Reporting, 3, 15, 18, 28, 31, 38, 43, 65, 109, 121, 128, 132, 133, 135, 138, 141, 152, 161, 167, 169, 174, 177, 183, 194, 195, 196, 202, 214, 227, 244, 245, 246, 248, 250, 251, 252, 254, 255, 278, 285, 307, 318, 331, 332, 336, 349, 350, 357, 365, 373, 377, 389, 398, 410, 422, 424, 447, 456, 458, 478, 486, 490, 503, 504, 509, 510, 529, 570, 572, 594, 618, 633, 642, 645, 647, 653, 662, 664, 677, 678, 679, 680, 681, 682, 695, 701, 710, 711, 720, 730, 733, 734, 752, 756, 761, 764, 776, 784, 785, 795, 797, 801, 807, 810, 811, 813, 832, 857, 862, 867, 885, 901, 907, 918, 941, 949, 953, 957, 972, 976, 985, 1004, 1022, 1028, 1030, 1042, 1045, 1073, 1076, 1077, 1086
barrier, 72, 147
education, 5, 36, 166, 185, 186, 189, 192, 219, 303, 323, 514, 537, 582, 610, 622, 716, 772, 791, 837, 853, 883, 895, 896, 954, 1050, 1079, 1095, 1113
fear, 72, 542, 657, 812, 822, 1002, 1111
immunity, 115, 164, 498, 592, 940
informer, 620
legislation, 5, 68, 115, 131, 164, 191, 360, 501, 580, 610, 659, 742, 766, 812, 837, 940
mandatory, 5, 11, 306, 580, 610, 617, 659, 713

practice, 166, 508, 699, 719, 837
private right of action, 739
procedure, 41, 131, 166, 341, 425, 501, 558, 716, 736, 742, 750, 766, 791, 812, 825, 837, 940, 1005, 1046, 1063
protection, 5, 11, 75, 88, 115, 131, 186, 191, 234, 235, 323, 378, 516, 542, 610, 659, 736, 742, 743, 825, 826, 837, 853, 881, 940, 1025
reportable, 824, 940
retribution, 72, 1005
willingness, 345, 824
Research, 36, 38, 55, 57, 66, 104, 120, 132, 146, 153, 157, 176, 177, 192, 214, 263, 278, 284, 308, 315, 333, 336, 338, 358, 371, 379, 380, 385, 437, 450, 499, 502, 527, 538, 563, 564, 663, 675, 684, 723, 742, 753, 778, 788, 793, 795, 796, 800, 811, 820, 824, 832, 844, 916, 917, 921, 938, 948, 988, 995, 1063, 1079, 1091, 1093, 1116
barrier, 122, 365, 706, 901
normative, 88
reviews, 20, 22, 24, 76, 103, 135, 165, 199, 293, 452, 466, 635, 700, 731, 775, 782, 783, 808, 837, 838, 870, 872, 873, 877, 880, 936, 952, 953, 957, 958, 986, 994, 997, 1026, 1052, 1088, 1094, 1111
role of, 602, 837, 945, 1025
studies, 103, 135, 165, 188, 209, 224, 246, 318, 332, 343, 365, 370, 404, 456, 465, 486, 501, 615, 662, 706, 733, 749, 759, 783, 785, 789, 837, 838, 872, 880, 901, 925, 949, 952, 953, 954, 957, 986, 994, 997, 1001, 1034, 1047, 1111, 1117, 1123
Resignations, 719, 801, 809, 859, 1002
Resilience, 22
Resources (materials), 1, 6, 41, 52, 86, 88, 89, 120, 124, 132, 142, 157, 163, 217, 235, 243, 256, 258, 261, 272, 273, 307, 321, 324, 325, 326, 349, 358, 360, 362, 363, 380, 396, 415, 431, 468, 487, 505, 511, 522, 538, 540, 555, 614, 641, 642, 648, 686, 722, 723, 724, 725, 746, 752, 793, 799, 832, 833, 837, 865, 900, 912, 913, 914, 915, 924, 932, 942, 993, 994, 1000, 1033, 1043, 1048, 1067, 1072, 1113
Respite care, 144, 167, 487, 877
Responsibility, *see* Liability
Retarded ejaculation, 322
Retina, 139, 155
Reviews, *see* Research
Rheumatoid disorder, 63
Rights, 3, 31, 196, 241, 294, 296, 482,

592, 670, 680, 742, 776, 846, 846, 1028
civil, 11, 19, 812, 839, 985, 987
human, 6, 97, 136, 186, 234, 328, 416, 496, 671, 1038
institution, 6, 11, 97, 100, 136, 193, 214, 237, 250, 376, 447, 450, 503, 524, 621, 623, 962, 985, 1007, 1023, 1026, 1038, 1089
liberty, 186, 237
parent, 53, 97, 124, 150, 186, 193, 362, 391, 501, 674, 767, 871, 894, 924, 942, 964, 988, 1022, 1034, 1065, 1078
personal, 11, 97, 171, 186, 237, 496, 698, 1007, 1026
reproduction, 6, 328
safety, 871
sexual, 6, 11, 33, 94, 97, 100, 150, 171, 186, 214, 221, 266, 362, 391, 416, 450, 501, 524, 542, 576, 617, 621, 671, 698, 767, 871, 942, 964, 987, 1007, 1078
Risk factors, 22, 24, 114, 292, 315, 317, 318, 358, 360, 383, 458, 502, 653, 662, 731, 743, 882, 901, 954, 959, 1071, 1088, 1089
Role model, 519, 550, 841, 921, 1093
Role playing, 58, 381, 533, 605, 895, 896, 1036
Rorschach Test, 494
Ruling, 248, 295, 498, 617, 797, 828

S

Safety, 13, 27, 112, 182, 204, 323, 414, 464, 577, 641, 746, 750, 871, 912, 913, 914, 1036
Schizophrenia, 66, 476, 605, 606, 618, 630, 805, 968, 976, 1028, 1057, 1105
Schizophreniform psychosis, 630, 1057
Schools, 17, 18, 27, 54, 59, 85, 89, 112, 173, 185, 188, 189, 215, 236, 250, 311, 350, 355, 359, 369, 380, 404, 432, 438, 447, 472, 479, 483, 493, 535, 540, 544, 546, 551, 552, 558, 560, 571, 579, 580, 591, 593, 604, 635, 642, 655, 656, 688, 713, 731, 851, 853, 854, 862, 875, 881, 883, 889, 942, 957, 1002, 1017, 1043, 1084, 1100, 1106, 1109
day care, 837, 1053
elementary, 235, 583
junior high, 598
preschool, 58, 118, 167, 261, 292, 390, 521, 762, 815
secondary, 98, 431, 598, 724

Screening, 54, 66, 110, 251, 307, 311, 376, 402, 405, 428, 430, 475, 487, 575, 626, 643, 659, 710, 750, 837, 903, 1005, 1085, 1086, 1117
  costs, 750
Seattle Rape Relief, 28, 235, 236, 323, 468, 551, 852, 854, 912, 913, 914, 915, 1075
Secondary abuse, 58, 60, 214
Seductive patients, 885
Segregation of sexes, 242, 339, 547, 715
Seizure, 78, 139, 155, 162, 218, 284, 394, 418, 647, 677
Self-abuse, 152
Self-defense, 13, 235, 236, 323, 468, 551, 598, 658, 703, 780, 827, 853, 854, 983, 1036
Self-determination, 5, 11, 100, 542, 656, 990
Self-esteem, 49, 140, 272, 322, 353, 406, 808, 932, 945, 1007
  abusive parents, 406, 945, 960
Self-fulfilling prophecies, 10
Self-image, 35, 90, 108, 160, 190, 208, 217, 224, 404, 413, 435, 469, 480, 500, 532, 537, 645, 657, 834, 839, 844, 879, 960, 971, 1049, 1054, 1093
Self-injurious behavior, 152, 404, 936, 970
Self-monitoring, 305, 342, 635
Self-perception, 35, 160, 971
Self-referral, 781
Sensory impairment, 59, 118, 158, 273, 603, 635, 932, 993
Sentencing, 5, 248, 287, 403, 422, 512, 581, 612, 618, 821, 837, 862
Sequelae, 2, 20, 61, 119, 181, 216, 274, 287, 332, 340, 410, 472, 535, 553, 572, 626, 638, 644, 645, 657, 664, 694, 720, 731, 788, 790, 804, 854, 863, 916, 938, 941, 986, 995, 1082
Service reform, need of, 18, 28, 29, 36, 81, 82, 96, 105, 112, 132, 138, 153, 187, 192, 201, 205, 212, 214, 227, 228, 229, 275, 278, 321, 331, 374, 376, 379, 477, 483, 487, 509, 510, 511, 515, 517, 526, 533, 548, 575, 590, 591, 615, 620, 632, 633, 673, 698, 705, 719, 727, 743, 752, 754, 767, 768, 770, 771, 784, 821, 822, 833, 837, 849, 861, 868, 874, 889, 905, 919, 941, 943, 947, 949, 950, 953, 954, 990, 1001, 1002, 1004, 1012, 1026, 1029, 1042, 1045, 1046, 1071, 1073, 1089, 1095, 1102, 1104, 1110, 1122
Services, 6, 11, 14, 34, 40, 66, 79, 104,

121, 136, 141, 143, 166, 183, 191, 209, 215, 220, 223, 255, 258, 261, 263, 274, 307, 318, 324, 328, 335, 338, 362, 363, 382, 385, 398, 422, 439, 447, 454, 455, 460, 462, 479, 499, 511, 529, 537, 540, 555, 566, 574, 584, 589, 593, 614, 636, 641, 642, 645, 651, 662, 665, 678, 691, 710, 734, 736, 747, 749, 772, 796, 797, 825, 826, 877, 901, 903, 904, 915, 956, 965, 966, 993, 1005, 1009, 1022, 1024, 1030, 1033, 1034, 1039, 1057, 1067, 1075, 1078, 1081, 1086, 1099, 1108, 1111, 1117, 1121
  community, 71, 81, 105, 131, 201, 234, 237, 245, 275, 278, 321, 393, 414, 448, 471, 505, 509, 517, 528, 564, 575, 579, 580, 673, 694, 706, 751, 761, 784, 837, 861, 894, 990, 1004, 1089
  special, 5, 13, 18, 28, 36, 41, 82, 94, 96, 109, 112, 113, 133, 138, 153, 179, 187, 190, 192, 227, 229, 234, 237, 243, 245, 278, 323, 329, 393, 396, 414, 437, 477, 579, 581, 610, 653, 659, 673, 674, 675, 694, 705, 716, 743, 801, 821, 837, 870, 905, 919, 940, 954, 1001, 1002, 1063, 1089, 1095, 1104
Severe disabilities, 67, 78, 97, 107, 137, 161, 175, 208, 253, 273, 323, 425, 443, 444, 448, 666, 703, 756, 773, 920, 923, 956, 994, 1119
  see also specific conditions
Severe learning disability, 366, 380, 1036
  see also Learning disability
Sex, 2, 46, 54, 73, 122, 146, 160, 172, 182, 202, 206, 259, 265, 267, 273, 283, 342, 370, 372, 403, 420, 431, 433, 437, 478, 524, 525, 547, 550, 576, 578, 584, 586, 614, 636, 646, 668, 675, 721, 786, 802, 823, 841, 911, 1006, 1009, 1034, 1055, 1074, 1110, 1121
Sex education, 4, 16, 17, 34, 39, 47, 67, 74, 80, 98, 99, 100, 116, 123, 142, 150, 176, 185, 187, 190, 192, 198, 199, 200, 217, 219, 222, 243, 263, 268, 279, 301, 302, 310, 319, 320, 325, 326, 327, 328, 329, 362, 366, 367, 380, 396, 401, 411, 427, 429, 439, 441, 442, 443, 444, 470, 471, 480, 507, 514, 520, 523, 525, 537, 543, 544, 545, 546, 548, 560, 591, 603, 605, 614, 628, 629, 635, 646, 656, 686, 698, 717, 718, 724, 737, 738, 755, 769, 772, 775, 787, 800, 834, 844, 858, 883, 889, 890, 891, 900, 915, 917, 921, 922, 932, 942,

983, 996, 1018, 1019, 1021, 1024, 1035, 1037, 1057, 1058, 1059, 1064, 1072, 1083, 1093, 1100, 1113, 1121
Sexual abstinence, 547, 554, 888
Sexual abuse, 25, 26, 27, 28, 30, 43, 58, 60, 68, 72, 83, 85, 87, 88, 94, 113, 114, 116, 123, 125, 147, 163, 164, 171, 191, 200, 214, 222, 223, 236, 239, 245, 254, 258, 260, 261, 278, 282, 285, 291, 297, 298, 299, 307, 309, 312, 315, 316, 318, 324, 344, 365, 377, 378, 388, 390, 402, 405, 426, 427, 435, 438, 456, 457, 468, 474, 481, 490, 499, 504, 509, 513, 522, 537, 540, 570, 572, 573, 577, 579, 580, 581, 588, 618, 633, 638, 653, 660, 685, 687, 697, 698, 706, 719, 722, 732, 733, 746, 747, 757, 774, 791, 794, 813, 818, 864, 865, 878, 881, 883, 888, 892, 902, 905, 907, 908, 909, 910, 921, 934, 935, 943, 948, 949, 950, 953, 954, 955, 956, 987, 993, 1002, 1012, 1030, 1032, 1036, 1042, 1052, 1053, 1071, 1073, 1075, 1077, 1080, 1084, 1092, 1104, 1117
  by medical professionals, 344, 661, 685, 732, 733, 793, 885, 918, 943
  by therapists, 38, 49, 344, 365, 500, 788, 789, 790, 791, 792, 793, 885, 859, 918
  of adolescents, 38, 58, 101, 147, 235, 260, 261, 324, 344, 369, 386, 388, 390, 394, 403, 418, 435, 464, 480, 499, 519, 572, 574, 577, 596, 616, 621, 630, 645, 715, 733, 750, 802, 844, 883, 888, 922, 933, 940, 990, 996, 1057, 1113
  of boys, 43, 299, 316, 319, 344, 405, 474, 490, 572, 630, 645, 687, 794, 813, 829, 933, 943, 1002, 1042, 1052, 1073
  of children, *see* Child sexual abuse
  of males 36, 235, 344, 536, 943
  of psychiatric patients, 653, 719, 848
Sexual adjustment, 19, 59, 160, 175, 224, 549, 572, 698, 814, 923, 1027, 1049, 1094, 1096
Sexual aids, 249, 311, 392, 552, 589, 617, 886, 900, 917, 932, 993, 1007, 1024
Sexual alternatives, 63, 549, 842, 937, 1007, 1123
Sexual assault, 14, 40, 41, 72, 94, 127, 147, 162, 191, 235, 245, 246, 255, 285, 288, 297, 307, 308, 337, 378, 394, 419, 481, 499, 508, 510, 512,

585, 600, 601, 621, 630, 641, 657, 659, 673, 681, 692, 695, 710, 711, 719, 746, 747, 751, 794, 796, 822, 827, 842, 881, 893, 904, 912, 913, 914, 915, 922, 950, 953, 956, 998, 999, 1000, 1057, 1063, 1078, 1104

Sexual Attitude Reassessment (SAR), 441

Sexual behavior, 7, 16, 54, 63, 80, 92, 100, 148, 150, 211, 219, 224, 232, 262, 311, 335, 339, 415, 427, 429, 469, 589, 607, 609, 646, 656, 717, 758, 759, 805, 831, 833, 834, 842, 858, 871, 944, 1049, 1050, 1064, 1066, 1077, 1094, 1113

Sexual companions, 181, 520

Sexual counseling, 63, 84, 175, 180, 331, 354, 385, 469, 520, 533, 615, 729, 887, 984, 996, 1094

Sexual development, 17, 150, 169, 184, 212, 224, 232, 253, 282, 303, 319, 326, 362, 451, 466, 519, 634, 715, 726, 805, 833, 834, 996, 1049, 1103, 1114

Sexual devices, 392, 1113

Sexual drugs, 270, 607, 739, 810, 929, 969

Sexual dysfunction, 30, 32, 42, 49, 175, 238, 322, 413, 605, 805, 887, 937, 1010, 1027, 1043

Sexual exploitation, 39, 125, 126, 171, 186, 214, 235, 236, 272, 323, 344, 362, 365, 429, 435, 551, 685, 712, 732, 772, 853, 854, 883, 885, 888, 895, 896, 897, 905, 906, 940, 943, 1029, 1057, 1075, 1104

Sexual expression, 4, 101, 137, 150, 159, 176, 181, 211, 221, 232, 266, 293, 324, 371, 384, 391, 429, 445, 466, 709, 729, 921, 996, 1012, 1061, 1101

Sexual Functioning Scale, 1009

Sexual habilitation, 184, 303, 304

Sexual identity, 219, 327, 587, 596, 654, 726, 758, 775, 790, 1007, 1114

Sexual Interaction Inventory, 224

Sexual intercourse, 7, 147, 279, 389, 551, 810, 938, 1113

Sexual intimacy, 38, 99, 170, 175, 224, 270, 314, 339, 466, 500, 605, 729, 788, 789, 790, 791, 839

Sexual Knowledge and Attitude Test, 224

Sexual misconduct, 38, 49, 128, 344, 365, 540, 661, 685, 719, 732, 788, 789, 790, 791, 792, 793, 885, 918, 943

Sexual neglect, 921

Sexual oppression, 386, 450, 542, 548, 524, 715, 888, 922, 1080

Sexual permissiveness, 756

Sexual preferences, 415, 607

Sexual positions, 549, 1123

Sexual rehabilitation, 549, 684, 771, 1007, 1070

Sexual relations, 39, 42, 217, 231, 257, 264, 314, 381, 387, 389, 416, 427, 500, 507, 737, 756, 764, 792, 800, 887, 918, 964, 1019

Sexual repression, 4, 74, 159, 176, 339, 411, 427, 445, 996, 1012

Sexual therapy, 11, 19, 49, 73, 80, 85, 90, 123, 172, 184, 214, 256, 291, 303, 322, 369, 381, 442, 452, 453, 462, 533, 538, 549, 561, 562, 570, 584, 586, 587, 605, 630, 636, 684, 698, 727, 728, 755, 788, 789, 814, 831, 855, 856, 886, 887, 906, 907, 933, 1001, 1006, 1010, 1013, 1014, 1024, 1057, 1066, 1074, 1096, 1101, 1121, 1123

Sexual variations, 937

Sexuality Development Index, 219

Sexually inappropriate behavior, 27, 415, 609, 655

Sexually transmitted diseases, 3, 55, 110, 215, 249, 260, 270, 311, 324, 392, 435, 520, 529, 552, 589, 617, 628, 629, 659, 834, 845, 900, 917, 929, 932, 993, 1007, 1024, 1040, 1046, 1087, 1113

Shelters, 97, 131, 214, 290, 409, 486, 546, 632, 633, 822

see also Transition houses

Short-term intervention, 5, 1075

Side-effects, 969, 1123

SIECUS, 169, 439, 695, 853

Signs, *see* Symptoms

Sign language, 56, 161, 306, 345, 747

Single parents, 440, 869, 959, 963, 964 mothers, 556, 869

Social attitudes, 768

Social anxiety, 327, 381

Social exchange theory, 779

Social identity, 327, 381

Social Learning of Independence through Functional Experience (LIFE), 415

Social networks, 22, 359, 399, 531, 555, 556, 876

Social support, 359, 399, 555, 556, 867, 869, 870, 871, 875, 1047, 1048

Social work, 15, 18, 32, 73, 104, 141, 143, 205, 213, 221, 263, 322, 402, 416, 436, 452, 472, 473, 521, 523, 566, 567, 568, 575, 593, 596, 672, 683, 700, 720, 733, 739, 751, 778, 780, 801, 875, 921, 931, 996, 1015, 1073

Socialization, 35, 39, 67, 99, 169, 190, 224, 262, 271, 272, 302, 329, 340, 362, 381, 414, 415, 444, 521, 523, 534, 538, 561, 562, 564, 700, 709, 718, 745, 840, 883, 888, 936, 983, 1049, 1116

Society, 2, 6, 15, 22, 43, 70, 94, 111, 186, 204, 216, 262, 330, 358, 359, 361, 387, 410, 427, 438, 467, 481, 523, 560, 562, 576, 584, 599, 656, 667, 702, 706, 732, 816, 832, 883, 962, 963, 1006, 1009, 1012, 1026, 1041, 1100, 1102

Socio-Sexual Knowledge and Attitude Test 134, 270, 834

Sodomists

Sodomy, 478, 813

South Africa, 1056

Special education, 22, 51, 82, 86, 99, 142, 189, 190, 236, 257, 323, 327, 346, 380, 535, 579, 582, 598, 622, 628, 629, 714, 854, 895, 896, 942, 954, 986, 1047, 1084, 1095, 1118, 1120

Special needs children, 1, 18, 51, 57, 113, 187, 292, 348, 358, 359, 360, 410, 531, 558, 622, 623, 642, 646, 674, 694, 716, 725, 815, 866, 870, 957, 983, 1001, 1021, 1039, 1064, 1089, 1091, 1107, 1119

see also Exceptional children

Specialization of services, 28

Speech and communication therapy, 11, 281, 433, 684, 698, 973, 1024, 1093, 1115

Spina bifida, 84, 253, 257, 1024

Spinal cord, 63, 149, 160, 263, 413, 538, 553, 644, 756, 771, 807, 808, 809, 887, 911, 937, 984, 1074, 1094, 1096, 1123

Spousal abuse, 673, 795

Spouses, 1, 15, 30, 64, 106, 238, 332, 346, 412, 428, 440, 450, 452, 461, 476, 534, 553, 556, 568, 576, 653, 773, 784, 822, 855, 869, 964, 994

Staff, 3, 5, 7, 11, 75, 83, 92, 97, 100, 121, 128, 131, 136, 143, 150, 153, 176, 181, 199, 221, 251, 263, 334, 339, 376, 380, 389, 405, 411, 430, 448, 471, 472, 476, 487, 504, 514, 533, 570, 574, 585, 603, 620, 642, 643, 651, 659, 685, 719, 739, 742, 750, 751, 752, 783, 802, 817, 824, 837, 839, 843, 849, 860, 861, 874, 888, 915, 919, 922, 941, 943, 979, 985, 992, 1001, 1003, 1005, 1007, 1026, 1045, 1046, 1066, 1078, 1084, 1089, 1102, 1117, 1121, 1122

attitude, 5, 7, 92, 97, 150, 176, 181, 472, 487, 574, 603, 719, 843,

Staff (attitude) — *continued*
 1003, 1007, 1121
 levels, 5, 251, 861
 safety, 136, 585, 617
 screening, 251, 307, 376, 430, 659, 710, 750, 837, 903, 1005, 1017
 stress, 83, 143, 620
 training, 3, 7, 97, 121, 131, 199, 251, 334, 339, 376, 487, 514, 533, 570, 574, 642, 651, 719, 742, 750, 817, 837, 843, 849, 860, 874, 915, 922, 1003, 1005, 1007, 1084, 1089, 1121
Status, 20, 66, 108, 176, 203, 228, 246, 387, 518, 625, 867, 875, 973, 974, 975, 1038, 1040, 1044, 1120
Stereotypes, 105, 318, 683, 741, 840, 883, 1093
Sterilization, 124, 146, 199, 241, 242, 271, 272, 283, 295, 408, 429, 434, 501, 502, 506, 547, 717, 766, 772, 810, 812, 819, 902, 924, 1097, 1113
Stress, 21, 22, 60, 62, 85, 104, 107, 113, 115, 130, 140, 144, 182, 252, 279, 284, 285, 292, 313, 321, 336, 344, 348, 368, 375, 382, 383, 390, 406, 449, 459, 465, 518, 527, 531, 532, 549, 553, 555, 571, 573, 649, 651, 652, 653, 663, 686, 698, 700, 707, 713, 720, 729, 740, 741, 773, 785, 817, 850, 853, 867, 869, 870, 871, 876, 883, 885, 915, 942, 945, 952, 961, 981, 986, 994, 1047, 1048, 1051, 1078, 1079, 1097
 fathers, 867, 869, 873, 876, 1047, 1048
 mothers, 252, 336, 348, 406, 449, 531, 555, 653, 867, 869, 876, 1047
 parents, 21, 22, 83, 85, 113, 182, 285, 313, 321, 348, 465, 527, 531, 571, 573, 651, 663, 686, 713, 720, 817, 867, 869, 870, 871, 876, 915, 942, 945, 1047, 1048, 1078, 1097
Stress reduction, 21
Stress Response Scale, 518
Stroke, 676, 938
Students, 7, 67, 89, 98, 99, 137, 142, 159, 163, 185, 189, 190, 219, 235, 236, 268, 306, 323, 325, 345, 352, 354, 401, 431, 443, 444, 456, 461, 518, 540, 551, 552, 582, 583, 591, 598, 603, 646, 683, 703, 724, 728, 746, 747, 755, 829, 837, 854, 889, 895, 896, 900, 912, 913, 914, 920, 942, 1016, 1018, 1019, 1035, 1036, 1051, 1064, 1084, 1093, 1095, 1100, 1101, 1113
 elementary, 58, 235, 329, 583, 895
 junior high, 598

preschool, 58, 118, 167, 274, 292, 390, 521, 762, 815
 primary, 58
 secondary, 98, 99, 431, 598, 724
Suicide, 71, 373, 394, 418, 499, 526, 593, 677, 749, 790, 970
Support persons, *see* Caregivers
Supporting Extended Family Members Program (SEFAM) Fathers' Program, 1048
Surveys, 7, 29, 38, 39, 77, 78, 88, 96, 119, 122, 132, 136, 139, 167, 176, 184, 191, 192, 211, 224, 227, 228, 236, 245, 246, 256, 263, 266, 283, 303, 317, 319, 320, 330, 331, 349, 373, 380, 389, 415, 430, 456, 489, 511, 533, 537, 541, 553, 615, 633, 641, 701, 717, 733, 784, 793, 822, 825, 826, 833, 854, 868, 875, 877, 940, 953, 990, 1003, 1037, 1045, 1048, 1050, 1097, 1101, 1110, 1121, 1122
Symbolic interactionism, 779
Symbolic sexual vocabulary, 27, 746, 1115
Symptoms of abuse, 25, 37, 41, 114, 139, 155, 156, 238, 330, 332, 344, 369, 490, 541, 573, 675, 690, 691, 716, 747, 761, 790, 835, 855, 901, 944, 957, 971, 972, 974, 979, 981, 1011, 1040, 1075, 1077, 1105
Systems theory, 204, 453, 313, 1017

T

Tardive dyskinesia, 969
Teachers, *see* Educators
Tennessee, 195
Tennessee Self-Concept Inventory, 224
Terminal illness, 386
Thematic Apperception Test (TAT), 497, 972
Theory, 3, 6, 57, 79, 129, 260, 343, 527, 535, 539, 595, 602, 653, 700, 763, 778, 779, 780, 783, 912, 913, 914, 959, 984, 994, 997, 1010, 1017, 1066, 1082, 1088
Therapeutic alliance, 491, 492
Therapists, 19, 38, 49, 63, 64, 70, 101, 121, 125, 134, 143, 150, 172, 184, 190, 192, 214, 236, 303, 306, 340, 345, 360, 365, 367, 394, 454, 470, 483, 484, 489, 491, 496, 508, 533, 549, 567, 568, 577, 596, 597, 608,

615, 698, 720, 729, 733, 787, 788, 789, 790, 791, 792, 793, 808, 851, 855, 885, 886, 899, 919, 991, 1001, 1051
 characteristics, 1001
 characteristics of sexual offenders, 49, 791
Therapy, 11, 13, 19, 29, 37, 41, 42, 49, 57, 63, 64, 65, 73, 80, 84, 85, 90, 108, 123, 136, 138, 141, 165, 172, 173, 175, 180, 184, 188, 190, 192, 199, 208, 214, 217, 219, 251, 253, 255, 256, 257, 277, 282, 291, 305, 322, 331, 338, 345, 354, 356, 367, 369, 381, 385, 386, 394, 413, 418, 442, 452, 453, 462, 464, 469, 470, 471, 477, 483, 484, 488, 489, 491, 492, 520, 523, 533, 538, 549, 553, 561, 562, 566, 567, 569, 570, 575, 584, 586, 587, 593, 598, 600, 602, 604, 605, 608, 615, 630, 636, 649, 652, 654, 683, 684, 696, 698, 705, 720, 723, 727, 728, 729, 754, 755, 762, 775, 787, 788, 789, 790, 809, 814, 831, 840, 843, 855, 856, 876, 879, 882, 886, 887, 899, 903, 906, 907, 923, 933, 941, 966, 967, 972, 975, 980, 984, 996, 1001, 1006, 1010, 1013, 1014, 1021, 1024, 1051, 1057, 1066, 1074, 1094, 1096, 1099, 1101, 1121, 1123
Tomograph, *see* Computer tomography
Toronto, 245, 246, 254, 255, 408, 438, 618, 641, 657, 658, 910, 955, 1033
Tort liability, 621
 see also Law
Touch, 40, 89, 171, 221, 235, 466, 551, 561, 598, 646, 746, 871, 890, 1101
Trainers, *see* Educators
Training, *see* Education
Transition houses, 632, 633
 see also Shelters
Treatment
 intervention, 5, 11, 21, 50, 64, 213, 223, 304, 360, 410, 415, 450, 457, 462, 495, 499, 535, 607, 610, 674, 675, 686, 687, 855, 856, 860, 871, 874, 882, 908, 996, 1001, 1010, 1027, 1074
 services, 5, 11, 13, 29, 113, 136, 141, 153, 223, 228, 237, 278, 321, 398, 414, 422, 447, 448, 462, 499, 505, 537, 574, 581, 584, 610, 636, 659, 674, 675, 694, 736, 749, 751, 826, 837, 874, 901, 919, 940, 947, 956, 965, 1001, 1039, 1057, 1111
Trials, 5, 31, 151, 210, 306, 424, 459, 619, 677, 680, 681, 940, 1028

U

Underreporting, 18, 36, 41, 28, 43, 377, 410, 509
Unethical experimentation, 214
United Kingdom (UK), 44, 166, 170, 199, 249, 373, 412, 501, 613, 690, 740, 1005, 1030
United Nations, 6, 186
United States, 4, 9, 17, 18, 25, 38, 39, 49, 53, 56, 58, 69, 76, 79, 85, 96, 111, 112, 114, 115, 117, 129, 136, 143, 151, 153, 157, 164, 166, 187, 196, 197, 203, 210, 233, 234, 237, 243, 248, 252, 270, 278, 280, 281, 286, 287, 303, 305, 307, 321, 330, 336, 342, 347, 351, 365, 369, 376, 400, 402, 404, 406, 412, 417, 418, 423, 435, 439, 449, 455, 462, 487, 501, 505, 510, 516, 517, 518, 527, 537, 540, 565, 582, 590, 592, 603, 612, 617, 620, 630, 639, 643, 704, 706, 727, 728, 736, 737, 739, 740, 742, 761, 775, 785, 786, 788, 792, 793, 798, 803, 825, 839, 843, 849, 857, 864, 877, 907, 927, 940, 941, 947, 948, 951, 952, 956, 987, 988, 1002, 1005, 1011, 1019, 1025, 1034, 1057, 1081, 1088, 1097, 1102, 1107, 1114, 1117

V

Vancouver, 27, 68, 437, 822
Victims
    characteristics, children in institutions, 448, 1116
        consequences of abuse, 287, 572, 645, 657, 854
    typology, 930
    victim-offender relationship, 154, 601, 631, 653, 666, 753, 791, 853, 857, 883, 1068, 1120
Victimization, 104, 213, 227, 239, 316, 481, 490, 571, 582, 630, 641, 697, 733, 746, 747, 774, 796, 802, 827, 829, 879, 883, 904, 939, 950, 1039, 1052, 1104
Victimology, 275, 699, 930
Video, 156, 158, 173, 258, 278, 281, 306, 500, 589, 691, 837
Vineland Adaptive Behavior Scales, 233
Virginia, 31, 1120, 1086, 1085
Visual impairment, 17, 45, 78, 89, 155, 215, 243, 277, 291, 322, 433, 550, 555, 560, 567, 603, 652, 657, 726, 746, 747, 794, 890, 891, 911, 914, 936, 942, 1059, 1083, 1109
Vocabulary, 27, 86, 551, 740, 746, 1115
Voyeurism, 272
Vulnerability, 9, 10, 39, 55, 112, 117, 118, 119, 130, 136, 162, 179, 207, 218, 276, 287, 344, 353, 362, 379, 390, 405, 427, 435, 527, 565, 571, 582, 601, 657, 659, 692, 715, 716, 719, 741, 750, 772, 791, 827, 837, 871, 877, 882, 883, 888, 892, 901, 905, 909, 949, 959, 960, 1012, 1014, 1015, 1038, 1057, 1062, 1068, 1071, 1077, 1079, 1104

W

Wales, 412, 580
Whiplash Shaken Infant syndrome, 129, 130, 139, 155, 178, 269, 423, 644, 951
Wife abuse, *see* Spousal abuse
Winnipeg, 214, 701
Witnesses, 131, 183, 194, 195, 196, 298, 306, 424, 454, 482, 660, 670, 671, 678, 682, 764, 770, 803, 817, 837, 864, 865, 899, 940, 941, 1053, 1108
    see also Courts
Workshops, 28, 97, 150, 193, 199, 273, 308, 320, 409, 441, 546, 641, 817, 843, 1000, 1021, 1084

Y

York Behaviour Management Services Treatment Program, 414
Young offenders, 653, 750, 813, 1106